MW01148157

From Breviary to Liturgy of the Hours

Stanislaus Campbell, F.S.C.

From Breviary
to Liturgy of the Hours

The Structural Reform
of the Roman Office 1964–1971

A PUEBLO BOOK

The Liturgical Press, Collegeville, Minnesota

Design by Frank Kacmarcik.

A Pueblo Book published by The Liturgical Press.

© 1995 by The Order of St. Benedict, Inc., Collegeville, Minnesota. All rights reserved. No part of this book may be reproduced in any form or by any means, electronic or mechanical, including photocopying, recording, taping, or any retrieval system, without the written permission of The Liturgical Press, Collegeville, Minnesota 56321. Printed in the United States of America.

Library of Congress Cataloging-in-Publication Data

Campbell, Stanislaus, 1935-
    From breviary to Liturgy of the hours : the structural reform of
the Roman Office, 1964-1971 / Stanislaus Campbell.
        p.   cm.
    ''A Pueblo book.''
    Includes bibliographical references.
    ISBN 0-8146-6133-5
    1. Divine office—History. 2. Catholic Church—Liturgy—History.
I. Title.
BX2000.C26   1995
264'.0201—dc20   95-4794
                                                                      CIP

In memory of
Leo Joseph Campbell
and
Mary Topping Campbell

Contents

List of Tables

Preface

Twenty years have elapsed since the publication of *Liturgia Horarum*, the revision of the Roman Divine Office decreed by The Constitution on the Sacred Liturgy, yet interest in implementing this reformed ritual seems to wane as the years pass and new issues absorb the interest of liturgiologists and pastoral practitioners of the Church's liturgy. In parishes and religious communities, however, the need for viable forms of communal prayer continues to make itself felt—a need seldom fulfilled, it seems, by recourse to the Liturgy of the Hours. "Prayer around the Cross," for example, while not, strictly speaking, Liturgy of the Hours even though derived from the Taizé Community's practice and, ultimately, more ancient models, seems to be well received almost everywhere it is introduced. Some religious communities that have prayed the reformed Liturgy of the Hours for almost two decades have performed it so routinely that weariness with its current form compels them to seek other models of communal prayer without attempting a searching look at the possibilities available for a satisfying celebration of the Hours. Still others who rightly lament the profusion of exclusive language in the officially approved versions of the Hours or who find little if any relevance in the archaic language of the psalms turn to more appealing prayer services that seem to meet their tastes and needs. In light of this ennui regarding "the official prayer of the Church," it may seem pointless to publish a study of the reform of the Roman Divine Office. Aside from those who have a special interest in the history of the postconciliar reform of the Liturgy, who really cares what happened to the Breviary between 1964 and 1971?

The picture, however, is perhaps not as bleak as just described. The only publisher of the American edition of the four-volume *Liturgy of the Hours* and the major publisher of *Christian Prayer*, the one-volume edition, is experiencing increased sales of both editions, which have been continually published since 1975 and 1976 respectively.[1] Even discounting discarded and unused copies from an apparently large quantity of these books in print, one must conclude that a great number of people are using at least some portion of the Hours for prayer, either privately or in common. Many parishes and religious communities use adapted forms of the Hours. Furthermore, the International Committee on English in the Liturgy has begun the initial phase of a projected revision of the Hours that will embrace not only new translations of psalms, readings, and prayers but possible additions intended to enhance communal celebration.[2] There is in planning as well a catechesis to enable a proper understanding and appreciation of the Hours.

If, then, there is renewed interest in and concern for the celebration of the Liturgy of the Hours and if communal prayer rooted in tradition is critical to the life of the Church on every level, it would seem that some attention to former practice and to the recent reform of that practice is warranted for sound progress. The Constitution on the Sacred Liturgy states that "care must be taken that any new forms adopted should in some way grow organically from forms already existing" (23). New forms of communal prayer will be cut off from nourishing roots if the framers of those new forms are ignorant not only of the great riches embedded in the centuries-old tradition of daily communal prayer in the Roman Rite contextualized in the Church's universal practice but also of the lengthy, painstaking, and careful (even if flawed) work of the postconciliar reformers of the Roman Office. It is with an eye to such framers and to all who pray the Liturgy of the Hours that the present study looks. An understanding of the strengths and weaknesses of the current structure of the Liturgy of the Hours would seem to be an indispensable condition for further productive reform or renewal of communal prayer, and it would also seem that those who wish to pray the Liturgy of the Hours well cannot but benefit from a thorough consideration of the process that transformed the shape of the Roman Office.

The reform of the Roman Office decreed by the Second Vatican Council was only one among many in the sacramental life of the Church. This reform adhered closely to the norms stated in articles 22 through 46 and 89 through 101 in chapters 1 and 4 of

Sacrosanctum Concilium (the Constitution on the Sacred Liturgy, henceforth SC). Adherence to these norms as interpreted by the majority of the members of the postconciliar Consilium for the Implementation of the Constitution on the Liturgy and its successor within the Sacred Congregation for Divine Worship, the Special Commission for the Completion of the Liturgical Renewal, has resulted in an evolution, to some degree, of the structure of the Roman Office in the new *Liturgia Horarum,* or Liturgy of the Hours. Both the structure of the individual Hours and the structure of the Hours taken as a whole have undergone change.

The interpretation of the norms of the constitution, however, seems to have been influenced by the presuppositions and views of the reformers regarding the nature and purpose of the Office as well as by their views on contemporary possibilities for its use. These differing presuppositions and views allowed for more than one interpretation of a number of the norms or, at least, a greater emphasis being placed on some rather than others. In fact, records of the process of the reform indicate that members and consultors of the Consilium/Special Commission argued for one or another structural reform of the Office based on differing interpretations of the norms—interpretations deriving from differing understandings of the nature, purpose, and possible use of the Office.

This study will be concerned with the structural evolution of the Roman Office in the process undertaken by its reformers between 1964 and the publication and promulgation of *Liturgia Horarum* (henceforth LH) in 1971 and 1972. More specifically this study attempts (1) to delineate the process of the structural reform of the Office, (2) to determine as far as possible the options available to the reformers for structuring the revised Office both as a whole and in its individual Hours, (3) to determine as far as possible why certain options were ultimately selected over others, and (4) to offer a critical evaluation of what occurred in the process of structural reform, what options were available, and the choices that were made for the finalized structure of LH itself. Not of concern here will be the selection, composition, or content of the various elements of the Hours (hymns, psalms, readings, prayers, etc.) considered by themselves but only insofar as that selection, composition, or content affects the structure of the Office as a whole or of a particular Hour.

During the years from 1965 to 1971 a number of those directly involved in the work of the Consilium gave summary accounts of the reform of the Office as it was in progress. These appeared under the title "Labores a Coetuum a Studiis" and in the reports of the plenary sessions of the Consilium in the publication *Notitiae*.[3] These reports do little more than indicate proposals and decisions made and the tentative forms and texts of the revised Office. There is no presentation of the discussion in the meetings either of the *coetus* (study groups of consultors) or of the Consilium. Thus little or nothing can be discerned of the process involving the differing views and arguments out of which the structure of the Office evolved.

More comprehensive studies of the reform of the Office appeared at the time of the publication of LH or shortly thereafter. While many of these studies provide a general description and evaluation of the definitive shape and content of the Office in LH, and some are even concerned with the history of the liturgical reform, none deals specifically and in detail with the evolution of the structure of the Office in the postconciliar process of reform.

Msgr. Pierre Jounel, a consultor for the Consilium and one closely associated with the reform of the Office, discussed in a two-part article the development of LH from three points of view: (1) how the Office was inserted in a progressive way into the whole renewal of the Western Liturgy, (2) how the Office came to be one of the more notable expressions of this renewal, and (3) how the reformed Office furnishes "choice food" *(un aliment de choix)* in the renewal of the Liturgy. While Monsignor Jounel provides some information about certain aspects of the process of reform, he does not specifically discuss the evolution of the structure of the Office within that process.[4]

The late Prof. Emil Lengeling, also a consultor for the reform of the Office, has sketched the preliminaries to the postconciliar reform as well as the work of the Consilium in his brief study of the characteristics of LH and the options available in its use. He gives no consideration, however, to the actual process in which the evolution of the structure of the Office occurred.[5]

Canon Aimé Georges Martimort, who presided over the postconciliar reform of the Office, in a commentary on the *Institutio generalis* (General Instruction on the Liturgy of the Hours, henceforth IGLH or General Instruction) devoted a section of his study to tradition and progress in the structure of the Hours. Here he indicates some of the principles adhered to in the evolution of the structure, but he does not go beyond a mere statement of what that structure is in the definitive LH.[6] In a more recent study of the Liturgy of the Hours he considers the Office in a number of the Church's traditions including the Roman. In his discussion of the recent Roman reform, however, little indication is given of how the revised structure of the Office was arrived at or what other possibilities were considered by the reformers.[7]

Fr. Vincenzo Raffa, still another of the consultors for the Consilium, contributed a relatively lengthy study of the history of Breviary reform from Cardinal Quignonez to Paul VI in Ferdinando dell Oro's anthology on LH. His consideration of the structure of the Hours, however, is brief and, like Canon Martimort's, confined to statements of what in fact the structure of the revised Office is and what a few of the reasons were for the adoption of some of the structural elements.[8]

Although he was not a member of the postconciliar groups that revised the Office, Fr. J. D. Crichton offers a valuable commentary on LH with some attention given to the structure of the new Office. He makes no use, however, of the schemata issued by the Consilium and the Sacred Congregation for Divine Worship and so does not get beyond a statement of what the structure is and what some of the reasons for this structure are as they can be discerned in the General Instruction and in easily accessible published material regarding the reform of the Office.[9]

A critical assessment of the structure of LH occurs in Prof. W. Jardine Grisbrooke's consideration of the Office as a contemporary liturgical problem. While his critique of the structure of the Office (forthcoming at the time he wrote) is pointed, Professor Grisbrooke does not consider the process itself of the reform, and so he provides no description of the actual evolution of the structure of LH or evaluation of that evolution.[10]

Two somewhat recent doctoral dissertations explore some aspects of the reform of the Roman Office following the Second Vatican Council. Dr. Thaddeus Schnitker concerns himself with Lauds and Vespers as common public prayer in the twentieth century. In one segment of the dissertation he describes some aspects of the process of the postconciliar reform of the Office, but because his focus is Lauds and Vespers, he ignores the evolution of the structure of the Office as a whole and relies principally on accessible published materials for his description and evaluation of the reform of these Hours.[11] Daniel de Reynal's dissertation seeks to expose the theology underlying the euchological texts of LH. No attempt is made to trace the history of the reform that produced the texts or to discern and evaluate the evolution of the structure of the Hours.[12]

In *The Reform of the Liturgy 1948–1975,* a comprehensive account of the postconciliar reform of the Liturgy, the former secretary of the Consilium, the late Archbishop Annibale Bugnini, does consider the history of the structural reform of the Office. Even though Archbishop Bugnini presents a wealth of first-hand information on the liturgical reform, some of which has been utilized in this study, and delineates what occurred in the various phases of reform of the Office, he does not describe in a chronologically detailed way the process of its structural reform.[13]

Fr. Robert Taft devotes a few pages of his comprehensive study of the Liturgy of the Hours in East and West to the recent reform of the Roman Office. He outlines the structure of revised Lauds and Vespers and offers an evaluation of the reform based on Archbishop Bugnini's account. There is no attempt to present chronologically the history of the reform in any of its aspects.[14]

Thus with the exception of Archbishop Bugnini's work, none of the studies considered here deals specifically or in any detail with the process of the reform of the Office. Even the archbishop's account lacks a detailed description of the evolution of the structure of the Hours within the process of the liturgical reform. It is with the latter and with a critique of it that this study is primarily concerned.

In order to contextualize the postconciliar reform of the structure of the Office, this study will first investigate the structure of the Roman Office as it has existed from pre-Gregorian times (sixth century and earlier) until the reforms of Pope Pius X at the beginning of this century (ch. 1). The aim here will be to present as succinctly as possible the basic structure of the Office as a whole and of its Hours as well as the modifications these structures underwent in the course of time together with the reasons for the modifications.

Next, the reform of the structure of the Office under Pope Pius X, the work of the papal commission on reform of the liturgy and other projects for reform of the Office (1945–60), the revision of the rubrics in 1960, the work of the Pontifical Preparatory Commission on the Liturgy for the Second Vatican Council (1960–62), and the debate of the council members on the portions of the schema for SC that pertain to structural reform of the Office will be examined (ch. 2). Here the aim will once again be to provide the context in which the actual reform of the Office must be situated.

The major part of this study will consist of an investigation of the process of the postconciliar reform of the structure of the Office, that is, the arrangement and relationship of the Hours among themselves and the arrangement and mutual relationship of the elements constituting each Hour. First the process of the postconciliar reform will be examined chronologically (ch. 3), then the structural reform of the Office as a whole (ch. 4), finally, the structural reform of the individual Hours (ch. 5). Throughout the presentation of this history the views of the principal protagonists of the reform, the process itself of reform, the principal options considered for structural reform, the arguments for these options, the decisions made, their bases, and the final structural form assumed by LH will be investigated insofar as available evidence allows. The principal evidence to be utilized in this investigation will be the schemata *De Breviario*, issued under the auspices of the Consilium or SCDW throughout the years of reform, and the testimony, either written or oral, of those members or consultors of the Consilium who had first-hand knowledge of the structural reform of the Office and who were willing to provide such testimony.

An evaluation both of the options presented in the reform process and of the choices made for the definitive structure of LH will conclude the work (ch. 6). This evaluation will be based on an interpretation of the norms established in SC for the reform of the Roman Liturgy in general and for the Office in particular consonant with a reading of the Church's tradition of the Office, which sees it as fundamentally and principally the common prayer of the entire Church, actually to be prayed in common as far as possible by all the faithful. This reading of the Church's tradition is discerned from recent and contemporary research on the origin and development of the Office, particularly that which distinguishes the cathedral and monastic traditions and clarifies their distinctive natures. The evaluation will also take into account the expressed needs—before, during, and after the council—of those who pray the Liturgy of the Hours daily.

Throughout this study the Vulgate numbering of the psalms is used, since that sequence is traditional for the Latin Psalter utilized exclusively in the first edition of the reformed Liturgy of the Hours. All translations into English are those of the author unless indicated otherwise.

Many have contributed to the completion of this study. William G. Storey, professor emeritus of the University of Notre Dame, directed the dissertation that is the basis of this work. Fr. John A. Rotelle, O.S.A., and the late Prof. Niels Rasmussen, O.P., provided advice, encouragement, and essential documents. The late Prof. Emil Lengeling, Canon Aimé Georges Martimort, Fr. Juan Mateos, S.J., and Fr. Vincenzo Raffa, F.D.P., answered questions and shared with me in interviews their personal experience of the reform of the Office. To Canon Martimort, especially, my thanks goes for documents not elsewhere obtainable, and to Fr. Joseph Gelineau, S.J., I am grateful for written responses to my requests. Interpreters, providers, mediators, and guides are also in my debt: Fr. John Melloh, S.M., Prof. Ellen Weaver, Dr. Thaddaeus A. Schnitker, Br. Manuel Vega, F.S.C., Fr. Paul La Chance, O.F.M., Dennis McManus, Fr. Edward Beutner, Betty Cassayre, Rosewitha Vitrac, Fr. Pascal Pierini, O.C.D., and the late Br. Henry De Groote, F.S.C. Edmund Yates and the late Dr. Thomas O'Brien of the International Commission on English in the Liturgy rendered invaluable assistance in providing needed documentation. To Fr. Robert Taft, S.J., I owe special thanks for invaluable assistance in the publication of this work. Without his intervention, whatever of value inheres in it would not be as widely available as it now is. Finally, without the permission and encouragement of provincial superiors over the years, Brs. Raphael Willeke, F.S.C., Norman Cook, F.S.C., and Mark Murphy, F.S.C., the research for and production of this study could not have been completed. The contributions of these many have enriched this work; its deficiencies are those of the author alone.

Abbreviations

AAS   *Acta Apostolicae Sedis* (Vatican City, 1909–)

ADCOVA   *Acta et documenta Concilio Oecumenico Vaticani II apparando,* series 1: 4 vols., series 2: 3 vols. (Vatican City, 1960–69)

ASSCOV   *Acta Synodalia Sacrosancti Concilii Oecumenici Vaticani II,* 4 vols. and appendix (Vatican City, 1970–83)

CCD   Congregatio pro Culto Divino (Congregation for Divine Worship)

CNPL   *Centre national de pastorale liturgique de France*

de Vogüé, RB   A. de Vogüé, *La Règle de saint Benoît,* Sources chrétiénnes 185 (Paris, 1972)

DOL   International Commission on English in the Liturgy, *Documents on the Liturgy, 1963–1979: Conciliar, Papal, and Curial Texts* (Collegeville, 1982)

DSOD   Consilium ad Exsequendam Constitutionem de Sacra Liturgia, *Descriptio et specimena Officii Divini iuxta Concilii Vaticani II decreta instaurati* (Vatican City, 1969)

EP   A. G. Martimort, ed., *L'Église en prière,* 3rd ed., (Tournai, 1965)

ICEL   International Commission on English in the Liturgy

IGLH   *Institutio generalis de Liturgia Horarum* (Vatican City, 1971). *The General Instruction on the Liturgy of the Hours* (Washington, 1973)

LDO	F. dell'Oro, ed., *Liturgia delle ore: Documenti ufficiali e studi*. Quaderni de Rivista Liturgica 14 (Torino-Leumann, 1972)
LMD	*La Maison-Dieu: Revue de pastorale liturgique*
LOH	*The Liturgy of the Hours*, 4 vols. (New York, 1975)
LH¹	*Liturgia Horarum iuxta Ritum Romanum*, 4 vols. (Vatican City, 1971–72)
LH²	*Liturgia Horarum iuxta Ritum Romanum: Editio typica altera*, 4 vols. (Vatican City, 1985–87)
MRL	Sacra Rituum Congregatio, Sectio Historica, *Memoria sulla Riforma liturgica*, 1 vol., 4 supplements (Vatican City, 1948–1957)
ODMA	P. Salmon, *L'Office divin au moyen âge: Histoire de la formation du breviaire du IX au XVI siècle* (Paris, 1967)
RB	Rule of St. Benedict
RG	A. G. Martimort, "Rapport général sur l'Office divin" (Toulouse, 1966)
RM	Rule of the Master
RL	A. Bugnini, *The Reform of the Liturgy (1948–1975)* (Collegeville, 1990)
SC	"Sacrosanctum Concilium" ("Constitutio de Sacra Liturgia"), AAS 56 (1964) 97–138; ASSCOV 2.6:409–39. *The Constitution on the Sacred Liturgy.* (Collegeville, 1963)
SCCD	Sacra Congregatio pro Cultu Divino (Sacred Congregation for Divine Worship)
SCDO	Consilium ad Exsequendam Constitutionem de Sacra Liturgia, "Schema completum Divini Officii persolvendi a die 9 ad 15 aprilis 1967" (Vatican City, 1967)
Schema	Consilium ad Exsequendam Constitutionem de Sacra Liturgia, "Schemata" (Vatican City, 1964–1970)

SCR	Sacra Congregatio Rituum (Sacred Congregation for Rites)
SDO	Consilium ad Exsequendam Constitutionem de Sacra Liturgia, "Specimen Divini Officii pro diebus a 12 ad 25 novembris 1967" (Vatican City, 1967)
SRG	A. G. Martimort, "Supplément à la relation général sur le bréviaire" (Toulouse, 1966)

Chapter 1

The Structure of the Roman Office from the Sixth to the Twentieth Century

To understand and to evaluate properly the scope of the structural reform of the Roman Office after the Second Vatican Council it is necessary to sketch at least the broad lines of the historical development of the structure of this Office. The major phase of this development, from the sixth century to the early twentieth century, is considered here under the following headings: (1) The structure of Roman Offices in the sixth century; (2) the Roman structure in the Carolingian era (eighth to tenth century); (3) the Roman structure in the Middle Ages (eleventh to fifteenth century; (4) later reforms of the Roman Office (sixteenth to twentieth century).

THE STRUCTURE OF ROMAN OFFICES IN THE SIXTH CENTURY

Obscure as the origins of the Roman Office are, it is nonetheless clear from the evidence available that one must speak of various Offices in Rome before and during the sixth century rather than of a single, uniform Office. In the *tituli*, the presbyteral churches of Rome, only the two Hours of Lauds and Vespers were probably celebrated daily in the cathedral tradition. The series of prayers for morning and evening in a section of the *libelli* constituting the so-called Verona Sacramentary (represented by Codex Vat. Reg. lat. 316) and in the seventh-century Gelasian Sacramentary bear witness to the probable existence of this Office, but nothing can be said of its structure from this or any other direct evidence.[1] Something of its structure possibly left its mark on the Office of the basilicas served by various monastic communities in Rome. This monastic Office, which itself was undoubtedly pluriform, consisting of the full complement of the Hours (Vigils, Matins [Lauds], Prime, Terce, Sext, None, Vespers, Compline), perhaps overlaid and drastically modified a primitive daily Office of Morning and Evening Prayer and a weekly Vigil—all in the cathedral tradition.[2]

In this basilican Office at least some of the elements of the weekly Vigil and daily Lauds and Vespers from the cathedral tradition can probably be discerned. The *Regula magistri* (*Rule of the Master* [RM]) and *Regula monasteriorum* (*Rule of St. Benedict* [RB]) are witnesses, at least in part, to this basilican Office; perhaps each Rule to a somewhat different form of it. The third nocturn of Sunday Vigils in RB appears to be based on the ancient weekly cathedral Vigil, as it includes three canticles with "alleluia" refrain and a proclamation of a resurrection account from the Gospel. The psalmody for Lauds in RB, especially that for Sunday, would seem to represent that of Roman Lauds in the cathedral tradition: Psalms 50, 62, 66, 148-50. The intercessions (*Rogus Dei* in RM, *litania* in RB) at Lauds and Vespers would seem also to derive from the cathedral tradition. The gospel canticle in RB, and quite possibly in RM, (*Benedictus* at Lauds, *Magnificat* at Vespers) as well as the hymn in RB at Lauds and Vespers, while perhaps not reflecting Roman cathedral practice, may ultimately derive from such practice elsewhere. Finally, the responsory and verse at Lauds and Vespers in RM and RB may well be the remnants of responsorial psalmody at those Hours in the cathedral tradition.[3]

The monastic elements of the basilican Office are also reflected in RM and RB. The well-known major characteristics of the monastic tradition of the Office are continuous recitation of the integral Psalter and the reading of Scripture. The principle evident in RM and RB of the continuous recitation of the entire Psalter and, in RB, of recitation within the course of a week, was certainly that of the basilican Office. In the latter, Psalms 1-108 were probably used entirely and consecutively at Vigils; Psalms 109-50, at Vespers. The invariable psalmody at the other Hours repeated psalms already present in the continuous series or *cursus* of Vigils and Vespers. The principle of the recitation of the integral Psalter at Lauds and Vespers throughout each week had probably been modified before Benedict by removing from those Hours psalms that were used at the other Hours. For example, Psalms 148-50 were removed from Vespers because they were already used at

Lauds. Thus all psalms were recited within the course of a week, but distribution was extended throughout the Hours. A semi-continuous arrangement of Psalms 1–108 was maintained at Vigils and of Psalms 109–47 at Vespers. This modification was perhaps due to the need of the urban monks serving the basilicas to combine better the elements of both traditions, monastic and cathedral, of which they were heirs. The probable distribution of psalms in this modified basilican Office is given in table 1 below. Both the Master (author of RM) and Benedict provided for further modification of this arrangement to suit their respective monastic communities, which, unlike the Roman basilican monasteries, were not bound to a liturgical ministry for the basilicas. These modifications are not of major concern here, since it is primarily the Roman basilican Office from which derives later practice in the Roman tradition.[4]

Although RM and RB indicate scriptural readings at all the Hours, they do not indicate the length of these readings or how they were distributed throughout the year. With respect, at least, to the readings at Vigils (Nocturns), other witnesses to the Roman basilican Office are more helpful. Principal among these is Michel Andrieu's *Ordo XIV*, which gives the order of readings used at St. Peter's Basilica perhaps from the time of Pope Gregory the Great (590–604). In the oldest redaction of this *Ordo* it is stated that "all of Scripture . . . is read from the beginning of the year to the end," and, as needed, the "treatises of Jerome, Ambrose, and the other Fathers are read." Later redactions add that the "passions of the martyrs and lives of the catholic fathers are read." *Ordo XIIIB*, from the eighth century, indicates that the scriptural readings in the Office at Rome (perhaps the Lateran Basilica) were rather lengthy.[5] Thus the use of the integral Psalter, probably each week, and the reading of the whole of Scripture and selections of the Fathers in a yearly cycle were two major characteristics of the Roman basilican Office.

Other aspects of the structural development of the basilican Office are more or less conjectural: reduction of the number of psalms at Vespers from six to five; introduction of an Old Testament canticle into Lauds; absence of the later introduction *Deus in adiutorium* (except, if Fr. Adalbert de Vogüé is correct, at Prime and the minor Hours) and absence of *capitulum* (little chapter); and

TABLE 1

PROBABLE DISTRIBUTION OF PSALMS
IN THE WEEKLY PSALTER
OF THE ROMAN OFFICE
IN THE SIXTH CENTURY

	Sun.	Mon.	Tues.	Wed.	Thurs.	Fri.	Sat.
Vigils	1 11 19	26 32	38 45	52 59	68 74	80 86	97 103
	2 12 20	27 33	39 46	54 60	69 75	81 87	98 104
	3 13 21	28 34	40 47	55 61	70 76	82 88	99 105
	6 14 22	29 35	41 48	56 63	71 77	83 93	100 106
	7 15 23	30 36	43 49	57 65	72 78	84 95	101 107
	8 16 24	31 37	44 51	58 67	73 79	85 96	102 108
	9 17 25						
	10 18						
Matins	50 (92)	50	50	50	50	50	50
	117 (99)	5	42	64	89	142	91
	62 + 66	62 + 66	62 + 66	62 + 66	62 + 66	62 + 66	62 + 66
Prime	53	53	53	53	53	53	53
	118	118	118	118	118	118	118
	(1–4)*	(1–4)	(1–4)	(1–4)	(1–4)	(1–4)	(1–4)
Terce	118	118	118	118	118	118	118
	(5–10)	(5–10)	(5–10)	(5–10)	(5–10)	(5–10)	(5–10)
Sext	118	118	118	118	118	118	118
	(11–16)	(11–16)	(11–16)	(11–16)	(11–16)	(11–16)	(11–16)
None	118	118	118	118	118	118	118
	(17–22)	(17–22)	(17–22)	(17–22)	(17–22)	(17–22)	(17–22)
Vespers	109–113	114–116	121–125	126–130	131–132	137–141	143–147
		119–120			134–136		
Compline	4	4	4	4	4	4	4
	90	90	90	90	90	90	90
	133	133	133	133	133	133	133

SOURCE: A. de Vogüé, *La règle de saint Benoît* 1:102.

*Numbers in parentheses refer to sections (octanaries) of Psalm 118.

hymn. Hagiographical readings did enter into the basic basilican structure of the Roman Office, as noted above, but apparently not without resistance. Such readings were clearly part of Vigil services—occasional Offices—at the tombs of martyrs or in churches where their relics lay. If *Ordo XII* is correct, they were first introduced into the basilican Office at St. Peter's during the pontificate of Hadrian I (772–95) and were to become in many later medieval Offices the major or only readings. The *Pater* appears as a concluding prayer for Lauds and Vespers in RB and may have functioned in the same capacity for those Hours in the basilican Office.[6]

THE ROMAN STRUCTURE IN THE CAROLINGIAN ERA (EIGHTH TO TENTH CENTURY)

Benedict's reform of the classic Roman Office for his monks (RB 8–20) did not supplant the older basilican Office, which was spread and adapted throughout the Latin West. While the Benedictine Office had some influence on later Roman-Gallican practice, as will be indicated below, it was minor. With the strenuous efforts of Pepin the Short (714–68) and Chrodegang, bishop of Metz (d. 766), to substitute Roman liturgical usage for Gallican, the Roman basilican Office became with some modification firmly established in the churches of western Europe. Charlemagne (ca. 742–814) furthered the cause of Roman practice through legislation and pressure on bishops and synods. The *Institutio canonicorum* of the Council of Aix-la-Chapelle (816) imposed on all clerics the obligation to participate daily in the complete Office of their Church.[7]

Amalarius of Metz (ca. 780–850) in his *Liber officialis* 4.1–2, and *Liber de ordine antiphonarii* 1–7 is the first witness to the structure of the Roman Office as received and modified on Frankish soil. Abbot (later Bishop) Pierre Salmon observed that while Amalarius' description is probably the result of a combination of sources and his own adaptations, it is a reliable enough witness along with Andrieu's *Ordo XII*, a contemporary Roman document, to the structure of the Romano-Frankish Office of the ninth century.[8]

The structure of the Roman Office as gleaned from Amalarius and *Ordo XII* can be represented as follows:

Nocturns/Vigils

Sundays	Feasts	Weekdays
	INVITATORY	
	Domine, labia	
	Gloria Patri	
	Psalm 94 (with antiphon)	
	FIRST NOCTURN	
12 psalms without antiphons; 3 groups of 4 psalms with *Gloria Patri* after each group	3 psalms	12 psalms 6 antiphons repeated alternately by choirs between vv. of psalms
	Versicle	
	Silence (later: *Pater* silently)	
	Capitulum (= *oratio;* later, absolution)	
	3 readings (Each preceded by a blessing and followed by *Tu autem* and responsory with *Gloria Patri* after last one)	

SECOND NOCTURN

    3 psalms with antiphons

    Versicle

    Silence

    Oratio (Absolution)

    3 readings (as at first nocturn)

THIRD NOCTURN

    3 psalms with alleluia (Sunday) or antiphon (feast)

    Versicle

    Silence

    Oratio (absolution)

Sundays	Feasts	Weekdays
	3 readings (as at first nocturn with last responsory replaced by *Te Deum*	

Matins/Lauds

Sundays		Weekdays
4 psalms with antiphons		Ps 50 + 3 psalms with antiphons
Daniel 3:57-88		O.T. canticle (variable)
	Laudes (Pss 148–50) with alleluia	
	Capitulum	
	Versicle	
	Benedictus with antiphon	
		Preces
	Collect	
	Benedicamus Domino	

Day Hours

PRIME		TERCE, SEXT, NONE
	Deus in adiutorium	
Ps 53		
2 sections of Ps 118 without antiphon		3 sections of Ps 118 without antiphon
		Short reading
		Short responsory with *Gloria Patri*
	Versicle	
	Kyrie	
	Pater	
Apostles' Creed		*Preces*
	Psalm 50	
Versicle		
	Collect	
		Benedicamus Domino

Vespers

Deus in adiutorium

5 psalms with antiphons

Short reading *(capitulum)*

Short responsory

Versicle (Ps 140:2 with incense offering)

Magnificat with antiphon

Preces (on ferial days only for Amalarius)

Collect

Compline

Deus in adiutorium

4 psalms (invariable, without antiphons)

Versicle

Nunc dimittis[9]

Some features of this scheme are noteworthy. Hymns are lacking at all Hours, as are readings at Prime and Compline, the *Pater* at Matins (= Lauds) and Vespers, the *Deus in adiutorium* at Matins (= Lauds), and elements from the *Officium capituli,* which later appeared in Prime. The presence of the versicle from Psalm 140 in Vespers may be the remnant of that entire psalm prayed universally at cathedral Vespers. Canon Aimé Georges Martimort, in his recent summary of the development of the Liturgy of the Hours, acknowledges this but is surprised at the lack in Roman Vespers of other elements from the cathedral Office. Father Juan Mateos, however, as will be noted later, made known to those reforming the Roman Office after Vatican II the existence of a unit in Roman Vespers that contained at least rudimentarily and sequentially the elements expected in cathedral Vespers:

Hymn

Versicle (Ps 140:2)

Offering of incense *(Magnificat)*

Preces (intercessions)

If Amalarius' witness to the offering of incense at the versicle is a witness to an ancient Roman tradition, then perhaps there is further substantiation for claiming that this unit points to the existence of cathedral Vespers at one time in Rome. The hymn, of course, appears with certainty in the Roman structure only in the twelfth century, but it was already in Benedictine Vespers at this point, and the Benedictine Office is itself, at least partly, a witness to a more ancient, Roman, basilican, monasticized Office. When the hymn is eventually introduced into Roman Vespers, it is placed at the very spot where it has occurred since the sixth century in Benedict's scheme.[10]

Another feature of the structure of the Roman Office at this period is worth noting in view of the much later post–Vatican II reformers' attempt to provide for organic union of two Hours of the Office. *Ordo XII* provides a way to combine the minor Hours in case of necessity or in case given Hours cannot be said at their appropriate times. Under one *Deus in adiutorium* could be said the psalms of the Hours, one responsory, one versicle, and the prayer concluding None.[11]

THE ROMAN STRUCTURE IN THE MIDDLE AGES (ELEVENTH TO FIFTEENTH CENTURY)

Neither the birth and gradual increase of the Breviary (understood initially as a kind of *Ordo*) from the eleventh century nor the widespread adoption of the curtailed Office of the Roman Curia from the thirteenth century radically changed the structure of the Roman Office. Some heretofore missing elements in the structure of the Hours, however, begin to appear more consistently.

Throughout the early part of the era no single uniform Roman Office prevailed despite the Carolingian effort to impose one. Although there were numerous variations, the structure reported by Amalarius can be seen generally as the framework for the Romano-Frankish Office of this period.

Vigils (Nocturns) tended to open with *Domine, labia mea aperies* followed by *Deus in adiutorium*, invitatory, and hymn. The remainder of the structure appears to be generally that given by Amalarius. Absolutions and blessings were not universal, and there was great variety in the number, kind, and extent of the readings. Generally, throughout the era, as the cult of the saints increased the hagiographic readings tended to increase in length and even to abridge and to dislodge the patristic and scriptural readings. As Breviaries became more than Ordos and the attempt was made to include in them the readings of the Lectionary for the Office, the scriptural readings themselves were greatly reduced, so that in some books only the incipits (first words) appeared while in others they disappeared altogether.[12]

Lauds and Vespers in this era show the addition of a short response after the *capitulum*. Hymns were apparently more frequent at both Lauds and Vespers in the positions they had occupied in the Benedictine Office since the sixth century, namely, after the responsories. It would seem that Benedictine practice was influential in this development. There appeared a diminishing use of the *preces* on weekdays and an increase in the number of suffrages following the prayer at the conclusion of these Hours.[13]

Prime became more extensive in this epoch. To it were added elements from the monastic *Officium capituli*, particularly the reading of the Martyrology and the *preces*. The Athanasian Creed appears to have been more widely used than the Apostles' Creed, especially in the Sunday Office. In some instances there was an expansion of the psalmody at this Hour on Sundays from three to nine psalms.[14]

Little change affected the minor Hours and Compline. The major structural modifications in the minor Hours were the addition of antiphons to the psalmody and the inclusion of a hymn after the introduction. Compline remained essentially unchanged. It would appear that, as at the other Hours, a hymn came to be more widely used in its customary Benedictine position, which at Compline was after the psalmody and before the brief reading.[15]

Numerous accretions to the traditional structure of the Office, however, were gradually made in this era, first to the monastic Offices, then to the Roman Office. Among the principal additions were the Office of the Dead, the Office of the Blessed Virgin, the gradual psalms (Pss 119–33), the penitential psalms (Pss 6, 31, 37, 50, 101, 129, 142), the Athanasian Creed, litany of the saints, suffrages, and lengthened *preces*.[16]

The thirteenth-century Office of the Roman Curia provided to some extent an antidote to the burden of celebrating the traditional Roman Office. The structure of this curial Office, especially in the codification made under Pope Innocent III (1198–1216), maintained essentially that of the earlier Romano-Frankish Office, and some more recent modifications in various forms of that Office seem simply to have been accepted into the curial Breviary. For example, the number of psalms at Nocturns (Matins) on Sunday was maintained at eighteen, but some of the psalms removed from its sixth-century sequence are found added to Prime of the same day. Abbreviated scriptural readings, already widespread, were not noticeably longer in the curial Breviary. In fact, hagiographic and patristic readings could entirely replace the scriptural lessons on occasion. The Office of the Blessed Virgin (added almost daily), the Office of the Dead (said on ferial days), the penitential psalms added to Prime (during Lent), *preces* at the minor Hours, *Pater* (in low voice) at the beginning and end of the entire Office, antiphon to the Blessed Virgin after Compline, were not absent from the curial Office.

One of the advantages of this curial Office over the Roman as celebrated elsewhere, however, was its elimination or curtailment of some other recent accretions to the basic structure. Major modifications, due largely to the spread and multiplication of major festal Offices (or doubles), included reduction of the suffrages at Lauds and Vespers and recitation of the gradual psalms before the Office in Advent and Lent only. Perhaps the most significant modification was not structural but procedural in that the Office was chanted, as in the new mendicant orders, more quickly than was the monastic custom.[17]

LATER REFORMS OF THE ROMAN OFFICE
(SIXTEENTH TO TWENTIETH CENTURY)

The curial Office was adopted by the Franciscans and through them spread throughout western Europe. Although widespread it by no means displaced the Romano-Frankish Office described above. Both the curial Office and the traditional Romano-Frankish Office were burdensome to their participants not only because of the additions, noted above, to the basic structure of the Office but also because of the legendary character of many of the hagiographical readings in Nocturns. The more satisfying long scriptural and patristic readings were abbreviated because of the encroachment of the hagiographical readings. This development, the overload of other elements, and the limitations imposed by the attempt to include all elements of the Office in a Breviary made little or no sense. Thus was subverted a major structural principle of the Roman Office, namely, the reading of the whole of Scripture and a portion of the Fathers of the Church in the course of a year. Also subverted was the other major structural principle of the Roman Office, the weekly recitation of the integral Psalter. In order to avoid the accretions to the Office that had become obligatory on ferial days, excessive use was made of the sanctoral cycle with its fewer, select psalms and lack of additional elements.[18]

Furthermore, by the sixteenth century, due to the decline of common life among the clergy, the increase in varied apostolic or pastoral endeavors often exercised by individuals alone, and the development of more individualistic spiritualities to support clergy in these ministries, the Office had become for many, by obligation or personal desire, a privately recited compendium of prayers and readings to edify and to provide some spiritual nourishment. The advent of printing and the inclusion of all elements of the Office in one volume—the Breviary—directly served the new needs of this "pastoral clergy."[19]

It was no wonder, then, that after some feeble and abortive attempts to reform the Roman Office, the drastically modified form prepared by Francisco Cardinal Quignonez (1485–1540) and his associates at the direction of Pope Clement VII (1478–1534) won speedy and widespread acceptance when its first recension was published with the approval of Pope Paul III (1468–1549) in 1535. The structure of this Office was a modification of that of the Roman with a view to private recitation and spiritual edification. Thus those elements that were strictly choral found, at least initially, no place in Cardinal Quignonez's Office.[20]

Perhaps the most prominent features of this innovative Office were a reduction in the amount of psalmody for each Hour and an increase in the readings from Scripture. For each Hour there were only three psalms, and the whole Psalter was newly distributed so that it would be recited in its entirety each week. This arrangement was invariable. There were no proper psalms for feasts as in the then-current Roman Office. The sequential use of psalms was abandoned and an attempt made to assign them according to their suitability for a given Hour. The triadic structure of the psalmody was not without precedent, for such an arrangement could be found in the Roman Office for Matins (Nocturns) of Easter and Pentecost and in diocesan Breviaries for the whole paschal season. A *lectio continua* (continuous reading) of scriptural passages was reestablished for Matins so that most of the Bible would be read in the course of a year. There were three readings at Matins, and except on saints' feasts when the third reading was the legend of the saint, all three were from the Scriptures—the first from the Old Testament and the second and third from the New Testament. The legends of the saints were purified somewhat of outlandish elements. Thus Cardinal Quignonez restored two major principles of the traditional Roman Office—the distribution of the integral Psalter on a weekly basis and the reading of almost the whole of Scripture in a year.[21]

Some prominent features of the first recension of this Office included hymns at the beginning of the Hours, omission of *capitula* (little chapters), patristic homilies, gradual psalms, and the relegation to special times of the Office of the Blessed Virgin, Office of the Dead, penitential psalms, and litany. A second recension, however, in 1536, restored limited use of antiphons and an excerpt from a patristic homily as the ordinary third reading at Matins.[22]

Despite its popularity (over one hundred printings between 1536 and 1568) and service as model for reform of local Offices (Breviaries of Orleans [1542], Arles [1549], etc.), the second recension had vocal and influential critics, the principal of whom was Spanish theologian Juan de Arze.[23] Perhaps the most notable criticism directed at the Quignonez Office was that it hit at the essential ecclesial and doxological dimensions of the prayer of the Hours by being conceived on the notion that the Office could be, normatively, both a private recitation (thus the elimination or reduction of choral elements) and a means of edification or instruction (thus the attention to an almost invariable *lectio continua* of Scripture).[24]

While Cardinal Quignonez's Office was short lived and never officially replaced the old choral Office, its popularity was undoubtedly due to its answering the needs of many before and during the Council of Trent—needs apparently similar to those expressed just before, during, and after the Second Vatican Council. The post–Vatican II structure of the Roman Office is, in fact, remarkably similar to that of the Quignonez Office, although there was apparently no conscious effort on the part of the postconciliar reformers to imitate it.[25]

Bishops of the Council of Trent (1545–63) read Juan de Arze's protracted critique of Cardinal Quignonez's Office and, although it is not clear to what extent they were influenced by his arguments, decreed the establishment of a commission to "correct" the old Roman Office but not, as the cardinal had attempted, by altering its structure. That commission, formed by Pope Pius IV (1559–65), produced a "correction" of the Roman Office that attempted to eliminate or modify some of the more recently added features (additional elements and Offices, numerous saints' feasts, overly complex calendar, and legendary elements in the hagiographical readings). The psalmic structure remained the same as that in the traditional Office. Scriptural reading was more regularly assured in Matins, although it remained abbreviated, largely nonsequential, and still on a number of days nonexistent. The purging of the hagiographic readings was less than successful, as was the attempt to upgrade the quality of the patristic readings.[26]

In the bull *Quod a nobis* (1568) by which Pope Pius V (1566–72) promulgated the "corrected" Office and imposed it (with few exceptions) on the entire Western Church, further use of Cardinal Quignonez's Office was explicitly forbidden. The structure of the Roman Office apparent from the ninth century but still carrying many of the accretions and deletions from the ensuing centuries thus became the standard form in the West, notwithstanding various further attempts at Breviary reform, until the major revision of Pope Pius X in 1911.[27]

Some of the more notable attempts at Breviary reform before that of Pius X occurred in France in the seventeenth and eighteenth centuries. Dioceses undertook their own reforms of the Office, resulting in the neo-Gallican Breviaries in which the structure of the Hours, while remaining essentially the same as that in the Roman Office, was shaped according to some of the principles followed by Cardinal Quignonez. Thus there was greater utilization of Scripture, redistribution of the psalms to allow for more equal length at most Hours, abbreviation of Nocturns (Matins), reduction of the *laudes* (Pss 148–50) to one psalm of praise at Lauds each day, and use of ferial psalms on all but major feasts to encourage recitation of the whole Psalter weekly. While intended for choral as well as private use, these Breviaries were regarded primarily as sources of instruction, edification, and spiritual nourishment of the clergy.[28]

Private recitation by clergy in France and elsewhere in Europe, however, did not replace the public choral celebration of the Office. Throughout the sixteenth and seventeenth centuries and up to the French Revolution of 1789, celebration of the Office survived in cathedrals and parishes. Laity were encouraged to attend at least Vespers on Sundays and major feasts, and they did so even though the celebration in Latin was not widely understood. Still, the choral Office was in decline, and the abolition of chapter foundations after the French Revolution brought it quickly to an end, at least temporarily, and struck it a blow from which a recovery has been almost impossible. Outside of monasteries and priories, the Office became almost exclusively the private concern of the major clergy for their personal spiritual growth and edification.[29]

It was principally to the Office as privately recited by secular clergy that subsequent projected or desired reforms in the eighteenth and nineteenth centuries were directed. Answering to and somewhat influenced by the neo-Gallican reforms of the Office, the project of Pope Benedict XIV (1740–58) for reform of the Roman Office, though extensive, was never promulgated. It was really a projected reform of the calendar and, to a lesser extent, the content of the Office, of which the structure was to remain intact. Attempts apparently made under Pope Pius IX (1846–78) to revive the project of Benedict XIV were to no avail. Some voices at the First Vatican Council (1869–70) called for redistribution of the Psalter, shortening of the Office on days when the clergy had extensive pastoral responsibilities, and provision for sound, historically accurate readings, but the council took no action on these matters.[30]

Thus the basic structure of the Roman Office as witnessed by Amalarius in the ninth century was still that of the Roman Church in the nineteenth century. The first significant structural reform was to be achieved at the beginning of the twentieth century, to be followed a half century later by the major revision of the postconciliar reform. It is to these achievements we now turn.

Chapter 2

Developments in the Twentieth Century

Five major events affecting the development of the structure of the Roman Office occurred in the twentieth century: (1) the reform of Pope Pius X (1911), (2) the work of the Pian Commission and other projects for reform (1945–60), (3) the publication of the new Code of Rubrics in 1960, (4) the work of the preparatory liturgical commission of the Second Vatican Council (1960–62), and (5) the action of the council itself in preparing and promulgating the Constitution on the Sacred Liturgy (1962–63). Each one of these events bears some consideration because each had its influence on the postconciliar reform of the Roman Office.

THE REFORM OF POPE PIUS X (1911)

Unrealized projects for the reform of the Roman Office by Pope Benedict XIV (1740–58) at the beginning of his pontificate, by Pope Pius IX (1846–78) in 1854, and by the First Vatican Council (1869–70) attest to the recurring need and desire to refashion the Hours in some way to serve more adequately those who were obliged to pray them.[1] Furthermore, the scholarly work in the nineteenth century of Augustus Roskovany, Prosper Gueranger, Pierre Batiffol, and Suitbert Baumer had shed new light on the history of the Roman Office. The stage was set for the major reform of Pius X.[2]

Forestalling the publication of a new *editio typica* of the *Breviarium Romanum* by the Congregation of Rites, the Pope established a commission to study the requests for Breviary reform submitted to the Holy See and to draw up a scheme of reform. This scheme, once approved by the Congregation of Rites, was elaborated by the commission with the result that the distribution of the psalms was revised and new rubrics giving precedence to the *temporale* over the sanctoral cycle were drawn up. The whole was approved by Pope Pius X and promulgated by the bull *Divino afflatu* on

November 1, 1911.[3] Both in *Divino afflatu* and in Pius' *motu proprio Abhinc duos annos* (1913) the Pope indicated that the new distribution of psalms and the revised rubrics were but the first steps in a comprehensive reform of the Office.[4]

The purpose of this first stage of reform was to restore the Psalter to weekly recitation, to restore the primacy of the temporal cycle in the Office without detracting from the cult of the saints, and to reduce the burden of the Office for the clergy at those times when pastoral duties were heaviest. To achieve the restoration of the weekly Psalter, supplementary Offices (those of the Blessed Virgin and of the Dead, the penitential psalms, gradual psalms, and votive Offices) were suppressed entirely as daily obligations. Accessory prayers (suffrages and *Quicumque*) were restricted, and *De profundis* and *Miserere* were eliminated from the intercessions at Lauds and Vespers. Most importantly, a reduction in the amount of psalmody for each day was achieved, so that Matins on *any* day henceforth had but nine psalms; Lauds, four psalms and Old Testament canticle; Vespers, its customary five psalms; the other Hours, three psalms each. Longer psalms were divided so that distribution could occur throughout *all* the Hours over a week. Entailed in this redistribution and division was the loss of the *laudes*, Psalms 148–50, as a daily component of Lauds—a rupture with a centuries-old, universal tradition. Table 2 below illustrates this redistribution of the Psalter.[5]

The third purpose of the reform, restoration of the primacy of the temporal cycle without unduly curtailing attention to the cult of the saints, required some forthright but delicate maneuvering. One of the problems endemic to the Roman Office since the reform of Pope Pius V was the ever-increasing predominance of the sanctoral Office over that of the temporal cycle of the liturgical year. This state of affairs was due to multiplication of saints' feasts but, more particularly, to the increased ranking of these feasts as doubles, semidoubles, and lesser doubles, giving their *shorter* Offices precedence, according to the rubrics, over the *longer* ferial and ordinary Sunday Offices. In order both to safeguard the primacy of the temporal Office and to respect the cult of the saints, the Pope's reform provided for the mixing of ferial and sanctoral Offices in such a way that the readings and psalmody were of the day and certain proper elements were of the saints' feasts. Such a mixture, however, entailed rendering uniform the number of psalms in festal and ferial Offices and thus of redistributing and dividing the psalms. This redistribution and division of the psalms served, then, this third purpose of the first step of the Pian reform and was its most significant aspect. Additionally the restoration of the primacy of the temporal Office was aided by detailed rubrics regarding precedence and transference. These along with the equalizing, at least, of the length of the temporal Office with that of the sanctoral Office and the confinement of use of propers and commons in their entirety to doubles of the first and second class effectively subordinated the sanctoral Office to the temporal.[6]

One problem left untouched by the reform was that of the readings at Matins. The scriptural readings were left in their abbreviated form, often only incipits of books, and there remained little sense of the continuous or semicontinuous reading of the Scriptures. The hagiographic readings of the second nocturn with all of their exaggerations and unhistorical assertions were left unrevised. Pius X in *Abhinc duos annos* had promised an eventual reform of the readings, especially the hagiographic, but this was to occur neither in his lifetime nor at any time before the Second Vatican Council.[7]

THE WORK OF THE PIAN COMMISSION
AND OTHER PROJECTS FOR REFORM (1945–1960)

The devastation of two world wars certainly hindered the progress of the further reform anticipated by Pius X but did not obliterate either the desire for it or work toward it. In 1930 Pope Pius XI (1922–39) created the historical section of the Congregation of Sacred Rites (founded by Pope Sixtus V in 1588 and reshaped by Pope Pius X in 1908), also known as the Sacred Congregation of Rites (SCR). One of the purposes of this historical section was to insure better that the decisions of the congregation would be based on a proper understanding of the history of rites and not simply on their current shape. This historical section, under Pope Pius XII (1939–58), became instrumental in the establishment, discussed below, of a pontifical commission for the reform of the liturgy. A major concern of the commission was reform of the Office.[8] In 1941 Pius XII entrusted to the Jesuits of the Pontifical

TABLE 2

DISTRIBUTION OF THE PSALMS IN THE WEEKLY PSALTER OF THE ROMAN OFFICE

	Sun.	Mon.	Tues.	Wed.	Thurs.	Fri.	Sat.
Matins	1 9b 2 9c 3 9d 8 10 9a	13 17c 14 19 16 20 17a 29 17b	34a 36a 34b 37a 34c 37b 36a 38 36b	44a 49a 44b 49b 45 (50) 47 48	61 67c 65a 68a 65b 68b 67a 68c 67b	77a 77f 77b 78 77c 80 77d 82 77e	104a 105c 104b 106a 104c 106b 105a 106c 105b
Lauds	92/50 99/117 62 Cant.* 148	46/50 5 28 Cant. 116	95/50 42 66 Cant. 134	96/50 64 100 Cant. 145	97/50 89 35 Cant. 146	98/50 142 84 Cant. 147	149/50 91 63 Cant. 150
Prime	117/92 99 118a 118b	23 18a 18b	24a 24b 24c	25 51 52	22 71a 71b	21a 21b 21c	93a 93b 107
Terce	118c 118d 118e	26a 26b 27	39a 39b 39c	53 54a 54b	72a 72b 72c	79a 79b 81	101a 101b 101c
Sext	118f 118g 118h	30a 30b 30c	40 41a 41b	55 56 57	73a 73b 73c	83a 83b 86	103a 103b 103c
None	118i 118j 118k	31 32a 32b	43a 43b 43c	58a 58b 59	74 75a 75b	88a 88b 88c	106a 106b 106c
Vespers	109 112 110 113 111	114 120 115 121 119	122 125 123 126 124	127 130 128 131 129	132 136 135a 137 135b	138a 140 138b 141 139	143a 144b 143b 144c 144a
Compline	4 90 133	6 7a 7b	11 12 15	33a 33b 60	69 70a 70b	76a 76b 85	87 102a 102b

SOURCE: A. Rose, "La répartition des psaumes dans le cycle liturgique," LMD 105 (1971) 99.

*Two sets of canticles, one set for each scheme of Lauds, were given as follows: Sun., Dan. 3:52-88, 56/Dan. 3:52-57; Mon., 1 Chr. 29:10-13/Is. 12:1-6; Tues., Tob. 13:1-10/Is. 38:10-22; Wed., Jdt. 16:15-21/1 Kgs. 2:1-10; Thurs., Jer. 31:10-14/Ex. 15:1-18; Fri., Is. 45:15-26/Hab. 3:2-19; Sat., Sir. 36:1-16/Deut. 32:1-43. See, e.g., *Roman Breviary in English, Winter* New York: Benziger Brothers, Inc., 1950) 40–247.

Biblical Institute the preparation of a new Latin translation of the Psalter, to be made from the Hebrew. This translation, published in 1945, complemented the reform initiated by Pius X and quickened interest in further reform of the Office.[9]

Shortly after publication of the new Psalter, proposals by a number of scholars for reform of the Breviary began to appear. While most of these proposals seem to have been concerned with reform of texts (scriptural readings, hagiographical material, etc.), some called for structural change in the Office, notably an abbreviation in view of increased pastoral demands on priests. Fr. P. M. Gy, in summarizing these structural changes, noted that they would include the total or partial suppression of the *preces*, suffrages, *Quicumque*, and *Pater* before and after each Hour. A more radical reform might adopt the Milanese principle of a two-week Psalter and allow the reduction of the number of psalms at Matins or the abandonment of Prime.[10] He was quick to add, however, that "It must be said that the history of the Divine Office is currently a field left almost entirely untilled by historians. Much work and especially some good workers are needed before the structure of the Breviary can be reasonably touched."[11] In an appendix to his article, Gy briefly notes one of the new and more striking proposals, that of Dr. Balthasar Fischer, lately brought to his attention, regarding structural reform of the Office. Dr. Fischer would extend the paschal order at Matins (three psalms and three readings) to all Sundays of the year and to the whole of paschal time. This reordering, said Father Gy, would demand a new distribution of the Psalter.[12]

Projects for reform of the Office, however, were not confined to studies and reports of scholars in the 1940s and 1950s. Two movements especially were significant. One, at a grass-roots level, produced adaptations or abbreviations of the Roman Office for those not bound to that Office; the other, under papal auspices, laid the groundwork for the reforms decreed by the Second Vatican Council. Both movements affected the postconciliar reform of the Office.

Abbreviations of the Roman Office
Most modern abbreviations of the Roman Office in the form of "short Breviaries" or books of Hours appeared after the publica-

tion of Pius XII's *Mediator Dei* with its endorsement of the Office as "the prayer of the Mystical Body of Jesus Christ" (142), a prayer incumbent on clergy and religious and in which the laity should participate at Sunday Vespers (150). The monks of St. John's Abbey in Collegeville, Minnesota, however, had already published in 1941 *A Short Breviary for Religious and Laity* as a prelude to the anticipated celebration in 1943 of the fourteenth centenary of the death of St. Benedict. A very popular short Office for some three decades, it consisted of all the Hours, each having the basic structure of those in the Roman Office, and it utilized 104 psalms of the Psalter, some 90 of them each week. There were fewer psalms at all the Hours than in the complete Roman Office. Matins had one nocturn with three psalms and provision for long scriptural reading. In early editions this reading was for Sunday Matins only, but in later editions such a reading was provided for each day of the week at Matins or any other Hour. In the later editions, also, there was provision for a four-week cycle of psalmody at Matins so that one could utilize all 150 psalms within a month if so desired.[13]

Of the short Offices that followed the publication of *Mediator Dei*, the Dutch *Klein Brevier* (1950), edited by T. Stallaert, preserved much of the structure and content of the full Roman Office. The psalms were reduced to 110 per week, and hymns and readings were abbreviated. Throughout the 1950s French, English, Italian, Spanish, German, and Portugese editions of this Breviary appeared. In 1950 there also appeared the *Officium Divinum Parvum*, edited by H. Fleischmann, O.S.B., in both Latin-German and German-only editions. A new edition of *Officii Divini Parvi Secoviensis*, which had been first published in 1933, this short Breviary had 128 psalms distributed over two weeks throughout all the canonical Hours. Matins, Lauds, and Vespers each had three psalms; the other Hours each had one. The one reading at Matins was either scriptural or patristic. French and Italian editions of this short Breviary appeared in following years. In 1954 *Breviario Romano dei Fedeli*, edited by A. Mistrorigo in Latin and Italian, was published. While this short Breviary contained all the psalms, not all of them were used in the Psalter. The complete Roman Office was given for major feasts and for Holy Week. For other feasts and ordinary times the Office for a day consisted of Matins (one nocturn with three psalms and three readings), Lauds with Prime, and Vespers with Compline. The minor Hours were preserved for Sundays and feasts, and the complete text of the Roman Office for Vespers and Compline was given for Sundays, feasts, and ferial days. The *Livre d'Heures latin-francais*, published by the Abbaye d'En-Calcat in 1952, maintained the integral Psalter but distributed the psalms over four weeks and provided scriptural canticles outside the Psalter for a fifth week when needed. Psalms were assigned according to their appropriateness for a day or an Hour. Matins was suppressed altogether; Lauds and Vespers each had three psalms; the minor Hours, one psalm. A separate Lectionary contained scriptural readings and patristic commentaries for the entire year to be used at Prime or Compline. *Bréviaire des fidèles* (1951), edited by A. M. Henry, O.P., differed from the other short Breviaries considered here in that it was a collection of psalms, biblical readings, patristic homilies, and hagiographical readings, to be selected and organized by those availing themselves of its contents according to their abilities and circumstances. Different schemes of one, two, three, or seven Hours for a day were suggested.[14]

With respect to overall structure of the Roman Office, then, the short Breviaries tended to reduce or combine Hours, shorten the psalmody of the individual Hours, reduce the total number of psalms utilized, sometimes distribute them over a period of time longer than a week, and provide for extended scriptural reading. These popular vernacular Offices were not without influence, particularly regarding psalmody, on the structural reform of the Roman Office, as will be considered in chapter 4.[15]

The Pian Commission

The other movement, under papal auspices, that more directly prepared for the reforms decreed by the council began, it seems, as a result of the new Latin translation of the psalms. Pius XII was encouraged by the publication of the new Psalter to pursue the general reform of the Liturgy. He first requested that the SCR study the problem of the general reform of the Liturgy (May 1946); then he called for a special commission to consider the reform and to make specific recommendations (July 1946).[16]

The historical section of the SCR prepared, over a period of two years, a project for liturgical reform to be considered by the special commission, and in 1948 the commission itself was born. The project prepared for this commission began to be published *sub secreto* that year by the Vatican Press as *Memoria sulla riforma Liturgica* (MRL). While reform of the entire Roman liturgy was considered in MRL, two interrelated areas were given special attention—the liturgical year and the Divine Office.[17]

With respect to the Office, 136 pages of MRL were devoted to a comprehensive consideration of *Il Breviario Romano*. Considered first were the nature of the Roman Office and its constitutive elements—psalmody and antiphons; biblical, patristic, and historical readings; *capitula* and short readings; responsories and versicles; absolutions and blessings; hymns; the *preces*; suffrages; and the introductory and concluding elements at the beginning and end of each Hour, including the *Pater, Ave,* and *Credo* at the beginning and *Dominus vobiscum, Benedicamus,* and *Fidelium animae* at the conclusion. An appendix to this material considered two propositions: (1) the suppression of all traditionally monastic or collective elements in the Roman Office and (2) the introduction of two kinds of obligation to recite the Office—one, for the "contemplative Church" ("clergy without the care of souls" [sic]; the other, for the "active Church" ("clergy with the care of souls" [sic]). A final section examined very briefly parts of the Roman Breviary itself—the ordinary, the Psalter, the proper of time, the proper of the saints. The common of saints was given extensive consideration as being the most problematical.[18]

The only considerations of MRL directly germane to the structure of the Roman Office are those in the first section regarding the elements of the Office and the suppression of those termed "monastic" or "collective." It will suffice here to note the principal questions posed by MRL to the papal commission regarding these elements in order to ascertain what structural reforms were deemed appropriate and/or necessary for consideration by the commission.

Regarding the psalmody as it pertains to the structure of the Office, the following questions were posed: (1) Should the principle of nine psalms or sections of psalms be maintained for festive, Sunday, and ferial Matins as was established by Pius X? (2) Should the traditional number of five psalmic pieces (psalms or sections of psalms) be maintained in Lauds and Vespers? (3)

Should the traditional number of three psalmic pieces be maintained in the minor Hours? (4) In the ferial arrangement of the psalms, should the objective "continuous recitation" maintained by the Church "from the beginning" (sic) or a subjective, systematic arrangement based on a fundamental theme for a day or even for an Hour be used? (5) In the festive psalmic *cursus*, should the ancient, traditional principle of a specific, progressive selection be maintained or should the modern but subjective principle of a fundamental theme or preestablished concept occurring throughout the psalmody be adopted? (6) Should a study be made, case by case, of the possibility for eventual reduction of the length of the psalmody with appropriate division of a very long psalm in the festive *cursus*? (7) Should there be a change from the current distribution of the Psalter over a week to a new biweekly distribution with the intent, above all, to safeguard, on the one hand, the traditional structure of the Psalter and, on the other hand, to foster effectively reduction of the daily measure of psalmody in the Office?[19]

Regarding other major elements of the Office, MRL raised few structural questions. The existence itself of antiphons was not questioned, only their content and the manner in which they were performed. The system of long readings for Matins was acknowledged as deficient, and new possibilities, including a biennial cycle and the inclusion of a gospel pericope in the third nocturn, were broached. The only other points with respect to the readings touching the structure of the Office had to do with their number and length. Regarding the number of readings for Matins, the expressed desire to safeguard the biblical readings was considered and two questions were posed: (1) Should the second and third current biblical readings be united or (2) should the three biblical readings with proper responsories be maintained separately, with the historical or patristic reading added as a fourth lesson? Regarding the length of the readings, the question was, Should each reading have a medium length not to surpass 100 to 120 words? While there were some questions about the content of *capitula* in the Office, there seems to have been no question about their retention. However, the retention of long and short responsories was questioned, and the fate of absolutions and blessings was left open.[20]

Several other elements of the current Office came under scrutiny. A reordering of "penitential elements," namely, *Miserere* and *preces*, in a way that would reduce their occurrence was suggested, and the elimination or reform of the suffrages was proposed. Suppression or reduction of elements at the beginning and at the end of each Hour was suggested. This proposal involved restoration of solemn recitation of the *Pater* at Matins, Prime, and Compline and the elimination of the silent recitation of the *Pater* at the beginning of those Hours, with the possible exception of Matins. The proposal also involved the elimination of the *Pater* and *Credo* (introduced into the Roman Office in 1568 from thirteenth-century monastic use) at the end of Compline and the retention of the silent recitation of the *Ave* (introduced into particular Breviaries in the sixteenth century and into the Roman Office by Pope Pius V in 1568) only after the last Hour of a day. The so-called *elementi facoltativi* (the prayer *Sacrosanctae*, the versicle *Beata viscera*, and a silent *Pater* and *Ave*—perhaps introduced in the thirteenth century, indulgenced by Pope Leo X [1513–21], and inserted definitively into the Roman Office by Pope Clement X [1670–76]) would be eliminated if this proposal were adopted.[21]

A perusal of the questions and proposals of MRL regarding structural reform of the Office indicates that the major concern was with the later accretions to the Office. With the exception of the proposals regarding the psalms and readings, particularly those for a biweekly distribution of the psalms and for a biennial cycle of readings, few of the recommendations could be considered radical. Most of them concerned minor elements, which, by reason of their accumulation, had rendered the Office unnecessarily complex.

In its attempt to wrestle with and resolve all the questions and proposals, the papal commission sought the advice of three scholars—Frs. Josef Jungmann, Bernard Capelle, and Mario Righetti—who were asked to comment on each numbered section of MRL.[22] Armed with their advice, the commission was able by 1955 to be instrumental in the taking of a first step since the reform of Pius X in revision of the Roman Office. This small but significant step was the publication on March 23, 1955, by SCR with the approval of Pius XII of a general decree and directives for modifying rubrics entitled *De rubricis ad simpliciorem formam redigendis.* This simplification of the rubrics affected the structure of the Office but slightly. Eliminated from the beginning and end of the Hours were the obligatory *Pater, Ave,* and *Credo* as well as the optional elements, *Aperi Domini* (at the beginning of the Office) and *Sacrosanctae, Beata viscera,* and silent *Pater* and *Ave* (at the conclusion of all the Hours). Each Hour now concluded with *Fidelium animae* ("May the souls of the faithful departed . . .") without the heretofore additional *Pater* and *Dominus det nobis.* The ferial *preces* were limited to Vespers and Lauds of the ferial Offices on Wednesdays and Fridays of Advent, Lent, and Passiontide as well as to the ember days outside of the octave of Pentecost. Suppressed altogether were the suffrage of the saints and commemoration of the Cross at Lauds and Vespers. The Athanasian Creed *(Quicumque)* at Prime was limited to the feast of the Most Holy Trinity.[23]

Thus a number of the proposals in MRL for reform of the Office were effected. It is clear, however, that this reform was considered provisional. The *Decretum generale* says explicitly that the papal commission, after studying the whole matter of reform of the liturgy, decided to simplify the rubrics in such a way as not to require new liturgical books "until some other provision is made" *(donec aliter provisum fuerit).*[24]

Eight months following the promulgation of the simplified rubrics (November 25, 1955) the papal commission initiated the idea of a consultation of the entire episcopate regarding reform of the Office. The Pope authorized the consultation on January 31, 1956, and a letter *(sub secreto)* dated May 17, 1956, by Cardinal Cicognani, prefect of the SCR, was sent to all metropolitans requesting within six months their personal opinions and those of their suffragans and possibly even of "more outstanding priests" *(praestantioribus sacerdotibus)* on reform of the Office. By November no responses had been received, so another attempt was made to solicit opinion. This time the response was overwhelming. To the 400 letters of request came 341 responses. Forty-seven different topics regarding reform of the Office were distinguished in the compilation of results.[25]

Sixteen of these topics could be said to relate directly to the structure of the Office. Although there were often differences in what was advocated for each of the topics, the most frequently urged recommendations were for (1) reduction of Matins to one nocturn (45.7 percent); (2) reduction of the amount of Office each day (40.8 percent); and (3) creation of a double Office, one for "active clergy," the other for those pursuing community life (21.4 percent). Some recommendations, although proposed by a minority of respondents, are indicative of desires that became reality in whole or in part through the reform after the Second Vatican Council: (1) distribution of the Psalter over two or four weeks (7.6 percent); (2) reduction of the Office to three hours— Morning Prayer, Midday Prayer, Evening Prayer (6 percent); and (3) reduction of the number of psalms in Vespers to three (2 percent).[26]

The letter soliciting the bishops' opinions had been distributed in mid-May 1956. Four months later what might be considered as a notable convergence of the movements thus far described as these affected the Office, namely, the scholarly, pastoral-popular, and papal, occurred in the First International Congress of Pastoral Liturgy at Assisi and Rome from September 18 to 22, 1956. The meeting, organized by institutes and centers of pastoral liturgy in Italy, France, Germany, and Switzerland, culminated a series of meetings in 1951 regarding liturgy begun by scholars, mostly from Germany, France, and Belgium, at the abbey of Maria Laach, near Koblenz, Germany, followed by a larger gathering in 1952 of scholars at Ste. Odile, near Strasbourg, France, and a year later by a more pastorally oriented congress at Lugano, Switzerland. The Lugano Congress, like that at Assisi, brought together not only scholars and those concerned with pastoral liturgy but also members of the hierarchy, including officials of the SCR. Before both the Lugano and Assisi Congresses, scholars met separately. Some thirty of them meeting before the Assisi Congress devoted three days (September 14-17) to a consideration of historical questions regarding the Office.[27]

At the Assisi Congress itself, Giacomo Cardinal Lercaro (Bologna) delivered a major address on the simplification of the rubrics and reform of the Breviary in general. With due acknowledgment of the positive contribution the simplification of the rubrics had made to reform of the Office, he raised a number of questions that seemed to him to call for serious deliberation of and resolution by the papal commission for reform of the liturgy.

The first major question was, Can the Office of the secular clergy and of the people continue to be modeled on the lines of the monastic Office? Citing the difficulties the secular clergy experience in "reciting the Office," and noting that "the people" used to participate in Lauds and Vespers, Lercaro suggested that he personally would find preferable not only a distinction between clerical and monastic Offices but between clerical and lay Offices where those Hours (Lauds and Vespers) in which lay people customarily participated are concerned.[28]

The cardinal's second major question pertained exclusively to the subject of clerical spirituality. Concerned that the modern cleric is confronted with two often divergent modes of fostering his spiritual life, one through practices of personal piety (prescribed by the Code of Canon Law), the other through liturgy, particularly the Office, Lercaro proposed that "the unity of the spiritual life has everything to gain from a liaison that would simplify and reduce the burdens while it would revitalize the ascetical activity of the priest."[29] While Cardinal Lercaro did not advocate the insertion of personal practices of piety into the structure of certain Hours of the Office, he voiced a desire, which both the Second Vatican Council and the postconciliar reformers briefly entertained, of fulfilling by a more radical revision of Matins and the minor Hours, into which would be incorporated or to which might conveniently be added certain "spiritual exercises."[30]

Of reforms more particular in nature, Lercaro considered several. He advocated confining certain imprecatory psalms to the realm of readings; expanding the distribution of the Psalter to a longer period of time—even four weeks; finding a better choice, number, distribution, and length of the readings and allowing them to form the lectio divina that nourishes the prayer of the priest and, in the case of Lauds and Vespers (or Vespers, at least) of the people as well; shortening the minor Hours (hymn, short psalm, Pater, prayer); eliminating some choral elements in private recitation; and perhaps reducing the number of psalms in Vespers with the people.[31]

THE *CODEX RUBRICARUM* OF 1960

Despite Cardinal Lercaro's detailed suggestions, recommendations made in the 1940s and 1950s (as summarized in Pere Gy's article cited above), and twelve years of labor by the Pontifical Commission for Reform of the Sacred Liturgy, in 1960 the SCR could produce only some relatively minor structural reforms in the Office through the papally decreed "Rubricae generales Breviarii Romani," part of a new *Codex rubricarum* for Breviary and Missal.[32] The major modifications included the following: (1) Matins was reduced to one nocturn of nine psalms and three readings on all Sundays of the year (except on Easter and Pentecost and on their octaves, for which Matins had only three psalms). This reduction to one nocturn applied also to all ferial days (except those of the sacred triduum in Holy Week), all vigils, all feasts of the third class, and the days within the octave of Christmas. (2) The readings for the one nocturn were rearranged. On Sundays the first two readings were from the occurring Scripture (the first being the one given as first in the traditional arrangement followed by the first responsory, the second being a combination of the old second and third readings followed by the old third responsory). The third reading was the first part of the homily of the old third nocturn. (3) Matins for ordinary feasts also consisted of one nocturn having two scriptural readings, ordinarily those assigned to the day, and a third reading from the proper of the feast or, if the feast lacked proper readings, from the common. (4) On ferial days, too, Matins had but a single nocturn with three readings drawn from the occurring Scripture or from the occurring homily on the gospel of the day. Other minor structural changes introduced by the new rubrics included the substitution of *Domine, exaudi orationem meam* for *Dominus vobiscum* in private recitation and use of the whole antiphon before and after a psalm or canticle whatever the rank of a feast.[33]

The new Code of Rubrics was hardly the answer to the widespread desire for major reform of the Office. Certainly the structural reform of Matins for certain days corresponded somewhat favorably to the one request for structural revision of the Office most often voiced in the survey of the episcopate in 1957 and represented almost universally in the short Breviaries, namely, reduction of Matins to one nocturn. But lack of provision for other desired and major reforms was due to the expectation and, indeed, explicit desire of Pope John XXIII (1958–63) that the ecumenical council, announced first by this Pope on January 25, 1959, would enunciate the basic principles or, as Pope John termed them, the *altiora principia* (fundamental principles) for all future liturgical reform.[34]

THE WORK OF THE PREPARATORY LITURGICAL COMMISSION FOR THE SECOND VATICAN COUNCIL (1960–1962)

On June 5, 1960, preparatory to Vatican Council II, Pope John instituted the Pontifical Preparatory Commission on the Liturgy. The story of the work of this commission has been well told elsewhere.[35] Its purpose and procedures, however, need to be stated briefly here in order to describe adequately its proposals regarding the Office. The commission of sixty-three members and consultors (augmented later by thirty more consultors, called *consiliarii*) undertook for itself four tasks: (1) to select the topics or questions to be examined and to assign them to subcommissions, (2) to coordinate the work of the subcommissions through the general commission, (3) to redact through its secretary a schema for a "Constitution on the Liturgy," (4) to approve the schema of the constitution in full session. One of the thirteen topics finally selected by the general commission for consideration and assigned to a subcommission was *De officio divino*. The members of this subcommission were Joseph Pascher (Germany), *relator,* or chairperson; Herman Schmidt, S.J., (Holland), secretary; Joseph Walsh (Ireland); Mario Righetti (Italy); John O'Connell (Great Britain); Johannes Wagner (Germany); and Peter Siffrin, O.S.B. (Germany).[36] This subcommission and the others worked from November 15, 1960, until April 12, 1961, at which date the general commission began to examine their accomplishments. After ten days of meetings in Rome, the general commission entrusted to its secretary, Fr. Annibale Bugnini, C.M., the drafting of the schema for a constitution on the Liturgy. This work was completed in August 1961. After fifteen hundred opinions were received a second draft was prepared and submitted to the full commission in November 1961. With further suggestions incorporated, a third draft was examined by the full commission, meeting again in Rome (January 11–14, 1962).[37]

The text discussed by the full commission, now entitled "De Sacra Liturgia," contained eight chapters, of which the fourth was "De Officio Divino." In this chapter as in the others, the *altiora principia* (or fundamental principles) presented in chapter 1 of the schema were supposed to have served as guidelines. These principles, substantively the same as those found in the first chapter of the definitive conciliar text, are as follows: (1) The liturgy is central to the life of the Church whether that be considered as its external activity, the spiritual life of its individual members, or its pious exercises. (2) Liturgical education, especially of the clergy, and active participation of all in the liturgy are requisite. (3) The liturgy is to be restored according to *(a)* general norms, which include reform of the liturgical books, provision for directives for the faithful, and revision in which tradition is preserved but a legitimate progress is admitted; *(b)* norms drawn from principles of adaptation to the culture and traditions of various peoples; *(c)* norms drawn from the didactic and pastoral nature of Liturgy; *(d)* norms drawn from the communitarian and hierarchic nature of Liturgy.[38]

Chapter 4, as well as the other chapters, contained not only provisions for enactment by the council but, after some of the articles, a section entitled "Declaratio," which gave the rationale for certain provisions and in some instances enumerated more minute modifications, which might be made after the council but were considered inappropriate for the council's document, which should confine itself to the fundamental principles.[39] The text of the chapter began, as does the definitive conciliar text itself, with an introduction that associated the Office with the prayer of Christ himself. In order that this prayer become better in practice what it is by nature, a number of proposals for revision were offered. Among them were several pertaining to the structural revision of the Office. The first would restore the traditional sequence of the Hours so that they might be prayed at the same time of day to which they were related. Lauds and Vespers were called the "double hinge" *(duplex cardo)* of the daily Office and designated the chief Hours for celebration. Compline should be a prayer to end the day. Matins, retaining its character as nocturnal praise, should become a prayer for any Hour of the day. The minor Hours should be revised in such a way that they could be prayed at the appropriate times.[40]

A *declaratio* following the stipulations regarding the sequence of the Hours affirmed the traditional communitarian character of the

Office and thus rejected the move for a double Breviary—one communitarian, the other private. It was recommended to a postconciliar commission that Matins generally be reduced to one nocturn and that the minor Hours neither be totally abolished nor kept as they were but that their performance be rendered more easily possible and desirable.[41]

A second proposal affecting the structure of the Office called for the distribution of the psalms over a period of time longer than one week. The stated purpose of this revision was to allow the sequence of the Hours actually to be celebrated at the appropriate times.[42]

Also proposed but scarcely characterized as fundamental principles were the use of morning and evening collects found in ancient Sacramentaries for Lauds and Vespers, intercessions (preces) daily at Vespers, and the Lord's Prayer in place of the prayer of the day at the close of each of the minor Hours. A declaratio here stated that the morning and evening collects would substitute for the current repeated use of the Sunday collect at Lauds and Vespers and introduce a variety favorable to fostering piety. The intercessions, or preces, incorrectly termed penitential, would serve better at Vespers than at Lauds because such prayers, also to be restored to the Mass, would normally be duplicated in the morning if found in Lauds, and Vespers would, more likely than Lauds, become a popular Hour. The declaratio also indicated that conclusion of the minor Hours with the Lord's Prayer would be a return to a traditional use.[43]

The response of the full commission to the draft is reflected in the report (relatio) given to the central preparatory commission at the meeting of this body on March 30, 1962, by Cardinal Arcadio Larraona, who in February 1962 became the prefect of SCR and new president of the preparatory liturgical commission after the death of Cardinal Cicognani. The cardinal's remarks reveal, first of all, what is evident in the draft and in all the discussions of it—that reform of the Office was conceived of primarily from the point of view of the diocesan priest with pastoral care.[44] Regarding the structure of the Office, several considerations were made. First, the retention in the draft of the seven-hour cursus for the Office was not well received by the liturgical commission. Some noted that contemporary clergy, regular or secular, given their pastoral ministry, can hardly pray the Office seven times a day. Obligatory prayer in the morning, at noon, and in the evening only was considered feasible, but the arrangement for this would best be left to a postconciliar commission.[45] Second, Cardinal Larraona indicated that members of the liturgical commission saw a need to modify what the draft presented regarding *one* Breviary for the whole Latin Church ("De Sacra Liturgia" 70). In the one Breviary there could be two schemes, one brief and obligatory as a minimum, the other longer and optional but especially recommended for religious or monks dedicated to the contemplative life. Third, the vague reference in the draft to the distribution of the Psalter over a longer period of time was specified more precisely as two weeks. Fourth, the omission or rare recital of some psalms "lacking the spirit of evangelical charity" was urged. Finally, the prescriptions of article 74 of the draft (restoration of morning and evening collects at Lauds and Vespers respectively, insertion of intercessions at Vespers, and restoration of the Lord's Prayer at the end of each minor Hour) were deemed inopportune.[46]

Some major recommendations, in many cases similar to those raised in the liturgical commission, emerged in the discussion and voting by the central commission. Those that elicited the support of several members of the commission were as follows: (1) The council should give only fundamental principles (*altiora principia*) for reform of the Office, leaving the practical implementation to a postconciliar commission (Cardinals Alfrink of Utrecht, Jullien, Ferretto, and Bea of the Curia; Archbishops Felici [Curia] and Perrin [Carthage]) or to the Holy See (Cardinals McGuigan [Toronto] and Gilroy [Sydney]). (2) One form of the Office for the whole Latin Church poses difficulties, and some kind of provision must be made to meet the needs of the diverse groups who pray the Hours (Cardinals Leger [Montreal], Copello [Curia], Gracias [Bombay]; Archbishop Perrin). (3) Omission or rare use of imprecatory psalms and psalm verses would benefit praying the Psalter (Cardinals Ruffini [Palermo], Valeri [Curia], Montini [Milan]; Archbishop Bazin [Rangoon]).[47]

Although some paragraphs were repositioned, the text of chapter 4 of "De Sacra Liturgia" was not, finally, modified when it was discussed by the members of the council itself.[48] Before its presentation to the council, however, modification of the text of chapter 4 and of other parts of the schema was made by a special subcommission for amendments, which received proposed modifications from the central commission of the preparatory commission. Cardinal Larraona, additionally, appointed a "secret" or special committee to revise the draft of the constitution to reflect his conservative tendencies. Thus the text initially distributed to the members of the council prior to their first assembling was the modified text drafted by the subcommission for amendments but altered by Cardinal Larraona's special committee and approved by the Pope on July 13, 1962.[49]

THE WORK OF THE COUNCIL IN PREPARING AND PROMULGATING *SACROSANCTUM CONCILIUM* (1962-1963)

The Second Vatican Council was solemnly opened on October 11, 1962. As part of its initial organizing, the bishops elected (on October 20) sixteen of their peers to the Conciliar Commission on the Liturgy under the presidency of Cardinal Larraona, thus bypassing curial plans for electing commission members who had already served on the preparatory commission and, by that fact, had been curially approved. Pope John XXIII appointed nine others. Twenty-five *periti* (experts) were appointed to assist the bishops who were members.[50]

At its fourth general congregation (October 22, 1962) the council began debate on the first of its documents, the "Schema Constitutionis de Sacra Liturgia." The text initially distributed, in which the modifications did not represent the majority view of the preparatory commission on the Liturgy, had already been withdrawn from the council floor; and the original text, as presented to the central preparatory commission, had been substituted with repositioned paragraphing but without the *declarationes*, which were sections in the document giving the rationale for certain proposed modifications. This substitution had been urged through the alert action of former members of the preparatory liturgical commission, who had the original text of the schema in hand. None of the modifications in the altered text pertained to proposals for revision of the structure of the Office, but the elimination both in the modified text and in the restored original text of the *declarationes* by which practical effects of some proposals or reasons for them could be understood by council members jeopardized the acceptability of many of these proposals, including those pertaining to structural modifications.[51]

After spending two weeks in discussion of the preface and first two chapters of the schema, council members spent less than three days on both chapter 3 (on the sacraments and sacramentals) and on chapter 4 (on the Divine Office). Two days, November 9 and 10, 1962, were devoted to consideration of chapter 4.[52] Thirty-eight council members spoke regarding the provisions of the chapter, and these almost without exception viewed the Divine Office as that official prayer of the Church recited primarily by priests, other clerics, and monks. Only three speakers—Cardinal Bea of the Curia, Bishop Guano of Leghorn (Livorno, Italy), and Fr. Van Hees, superior general of the Congregation of Holy Cross— seriously considered the Office as the public prayer of the whole Church, which should involve lay participation and not just the representational participation of clerics, canons, monks, and some other religious.[53] Private recitation by the secular clergy was certainly seen as the norm in most interventions from bishops and others on the floor of the council. Thus the major concerns were with those articles of the schema related to the questions of whether Latin or the vernacular should be the language for recitation of the Office and whether the obligation to recitation of *all* the Hours should remain binding on secular clergy.[54]

Structural matters of the Office, however, got a fair share of the attention. These matters can be reduced to five principal issues: (1) Whether it is realistic to expect from most people reciting the Office that they do so at the hours of the day and night corresponding to the Hours of the Office *(veritas horarum)*; (2) whether there should be a reduction of the Office as a whole and in each of its Hours; (3) whether two or three forms of the Office are needed; (4) whether the council should confine itself to the enunciation of general principles *(altiora principia)*, leaving to the Holy See or a postconciliar commission the implementation of the particulars of a structural reform; and (5) whether elements from the New Testament and compositions of the Church should replace some elements drawn from the Old Testament. It is in order that we consider each of these issues briefly.

While several speakers, namely, Cardinals Goncalves Cerejeira (Lisbon), Doepfner (Munich), and Landazuri Ricketts (Lima), ad-

dressed the need to adapt the Office to the conditions of contemporary life, meaning specifically, to the life of the active priest
engaged in pastoral ministry, some others favoring that adaptation, namely, Archbishop Meyer (Chicago), Bishop Flores Martin
(Barbastro, Spain), and Fr. Van Hees, spoke particularly against
the provision in the schema for respecting the *veritas horarum*
(praying the Hours at the times of the day to which they correspond). It is too difficult to insist on this, they said, for clergy
absorbed in the active ministry. As an antidote to activism prayer
is essential to the pastoral clergy, so the praying of the Office at
whatever time that is possible is more important than the need to
restore *veritas horarum*. Proponents of this view also included
Cardinals Wyszynski (Warsaw) and Godfrey (Westminster) and
Bishop Franic (Split, Yugoslavia).[55]

Reduction of the length of the Office as a whole and modification of the length of each Hour in some way were assumed necessary by most speakers. Cardinals Wyszynski and Godfrey and
Bishop Carli (Segni, Italy) were notable exceptions in maintaining
that the Office should remain unchanged.[56] Opinions, however,
varied on how to accomplish this reduction. The schema (art. 68;
originally art. 70) set forth general principles for modification involving some reduction.[57] Several speakers proposed specifics.
Archbishop Weber (Strasbourg, France) and Bishop Corboy
(Monze, Northern Rhodesia) advocated reform on the model of
the ancient and briefer Roman Office for Easter Week. While supporting the article of the schema (art. 69; originally art. 71) that
called for distribution of the psalms over a period of time longer
than one week, several speakers in addition to Archbishop Weber
and Bishop Corboy specifically recommended reduction of
psalmody within certain Hours. Matins could have, at least on
Sundays, one nocturn of three psalms (Cardinal Santos [Manila],
Bishops Franic and Flores Martin); the minor Hours, one psalm
(Bishops Franic, Vielmo [apostolic vicar, Aysen, Chile], and
Pierard [Chalons, France]). A reduction to three psalms in Lauds
and Vespers, at least in some instances, had the support of Bishop
Vielmo and Father Fernandez, master general of the Dominicans.[58]
One speaker, Cardinal Landazuri Ricketts, opposed the addition of
preces to Lauds and Vespers as recommended in the schema (art. 72;
originally art. 74) on the grounds it would lengthen or complicate

an Office the burden of which needed to be reduced. Prime should either be united somehow to Lauds (Cardinal Doepfner) or suppressed (Bishops Flores Martin, Vielmo, Pierard).[59]

Although a *declaratio* in the original schema for article 70 (later, art. 68) had rejected a double form of the Roman Breviary on the grounds that the Office is communal prayer and that a form solely for private recitation would exclude the necessary communitarian dimension of the Office, several speakers advocated differing forms of the Office to meet the needs of various groups obligated to it. The wide-ranging proposals included advocacy of three different forms (monastic, common, and pastoral) of the Roman Office (Bishop Vielmo); provision for a Breviary for private recitation (Bishop Reh [Charleston, United States]); provision for an Office for clergy with pastoral care consisting of two Hours (chorally structured) and spiritual reading (Bishop Aguirre [San Isidro, Argentina]), and reduction of the obligation to recite the whole Office to an obligation to two Hours and spiritual reading for clergy with pastoral care (Bishops Reuss [auxiliary bishop, Mainz, West Germany] and Pierard) or three Hours (Lauds, Midday, Vespers) and some kind of Hour principally for reading (Archbishop Garrone [Toulouse]).[60]

The argument that the council should refrain from decreeing particular revisions in the Office and confine itself to enunciation of general principles for reform was first expressed by Cardinal Bacci (Curia) but undoubtedly uttered most forcefully by Cardinal Bea. He reviewed the recent history of attempts to adapt the Roman Office to the changing conditions of time and concluded that abundant information regarding desired particulars was already at hand to enable a postconciliar commission to implement general conciliar norms. Although the cardinal's proposal was apparently well received judging from the applause following it, Bishop Guano, alone of the twenty-seven remaining speakers, explicitly supported such a procedure and offered suggestions for the formulation of these norms.[61]

Structural reformation of the Office ought to include the addition of more elements from the New Testament and from compositions of Christian authors as replacements for inappropriate Old Testament selections. This position was maintained by Archbishop Melendro (Anking, China), Bishop Garcia Martinez (retired bishop, Calahora, Spain), and perhaps most forcefully, by Bishop Vielmo. The latter viewed the Office as a collection of the best in the Scriptures and in ecclesiastical compositions—a *flos florum*. Thus in this view there would be no compelling reason to maintain the integral Psalter or other scriptural passages deemed relatively less productive of spiritual nourishment for a Christian. While such a selection would pertain principally to the content of the Office it could affect its structure as well, particularly the distribution of psalms and the number of them in a given Hour.[62]

After debate on the entire schema concluded at the nineteenth general congregation (November 14, 1962) and the council members overwhelmingly accepted it as a basis for further deliberation, the Conciliar Commission on the Liturgy began, through thirteen subcommissions, its arduous task of composing revisions and emendations based on the 625 interventions by council members.[63] The emendations for chapter 4 were not considered by the council until the fifty-second general congregation on October 21, 1963. There thirteen emendations were proposed for chapter 4. A *relatio* (report) presented to the council by Bishop Joseph Albert Martin (Nicolet, Canada) on behalf of the Conciliar Commission on the Liturgy served to explain the reasons for the proposed emendations.[64]

The first of these proposals (*Emendatio* 4) concerned the reform of Matins mentioned in article 68 (formerly art. 70, now revised to art. 88). The emendation stipulated that Matins, able to be recited at any Hour of the day but retaining its nocturnal character in choir, would consist of fewer psalms and longer readings. Bishop Martin explained that the commission tried to reconcile by this emendation several points of view expressed by council members: (1) the desire to retain Matins in briefer form as a nocturnal Hour of prayer, (2) the desire to have, especially for active clergy, an Hour of *lectio divina* or spiritual reading able to be used at any time of the day, (3) the desire to retain the character of public prayer in this Hour even if it would consist in lengthier reading. Although the emendation does not propose how the nocturnal character of Matins could be maintained while it is at the same time suitable for use at any Hour, Bishop Martin suggested that the nocturnal hymns could be collected in an appendix for those who would pray Matins as a night Hour. The proposed lengthier readings for Matins should provide for the desired spiritual reading, but the retention of psalmody (although briefer to satisfy the desire for reduction in the length of the Hour) should insure its prayerful character.[65]

The schema had said nothing explicitly about Prime. The second emendation (*Emendatio 5*) affecting the structure of the Office proposed (as part of a new art. 89) the abolition of this Hour. Bishop Martin noted that several council members had spoken in favor of this because it uselessly duplicated Lauds and that the Pian Commission in 1957 had come to the same conclusion after consultation with the bishops.[66]

A most troublesome emendation (*Emendatio 6*), a compromise arrived at after "long and mature discussion" in the conciliar commission, according to Bishop Martin, was that concerning the minor Hours. Proposed as part of article 89 (originally art. 70; later art. 68) was the retention of Terce, Sext, and None in choir and the optional selection of one of these Hours, in keeping with the time of day, outside choir. This proposal, said Bishop Martin, was an attempt to satisfy those who sought one "Midday Hour" especially for clergy with pastoral care, those who wanted retention of all the minor Hours as an incentive to unceasing prayer, and those who desired simplification of the minor Hours so that they could be said from memory. The difficulty such a proposal would create with respect to maintaining the integral Psalter and distribution of the psalms throughout the whole course of the Hours was noted but no solution suggested. Such a solution, apparently, would be the task of a postconciliar commission.[67]

The final proposal (*Emendatio 9*) was the omission of article 72 (formerly art. 74) of the schema. This article had mandated the inclusion in Lauds and Vespers of morning and evening collects, respectively, from Sacramentaries and of *preces* for various needs. It also asked that the Lord's Prayer be included in the minor Hours after the prayer of the day. The commission, according to Bishop Martin, concluded from observations of council members that it had to steer a middle course between stating *altiora principia* on the one hand and decreeing particular changes in the Office on the other. The commission held that the council should address particular questions about the psalms, readings, hymns, and communitarian character of the Office but that the matters mentioned in article 72, being very specific, were best left to a postconciliar commission to consider. To this postconciliar commission, he said, would be given all the recommendations of council members for reform of specific elements of the Office.[68]

Bishop Martin's *relatio* also situated the structural reform of the Office as detailed in the schema within general principles accepted by the conciliar commission. First, the Roman Office as a whole is to be reformed because, while it is the traditional public prayer of the Church, a venerable and age-old treasury, it is also to be the personal prayer of each priest *(sic)*. Thus, while tradition is to be respected, the contemporary conditions of clergy called to pastoral care must be considered in reshaping the Office as prayer both possible and nourishing to them today. Second, the *veritas horarum* is to be maintained, against the wishes of some council members, because prayer at certain times throughout the day and night is of the nature of the Office. If the *veritas horarum* is not maintained a certain formalism and even falsity is admitted into the prayer. The Pian Commission had come to the same conclusion in 1957. Third, the Office is to be abbreviated, not only because Pope John XXIII in publishing the new Code of Rubrics said that the council would undertake a more profound reformation of it, but also because the majority of council members seemed to desire this, even though ways of easing the burden of many obliged to the Office could be found that would not entail abbreviation. Such ways would include removing the obligation to certain Hours or rendering it *sub levi* (a light obligation) or *laudabiliter* (praiseworthy) rather than *sub gravi* (a serious obligation). Finally, the manner in which the Office is reformed must take into account the various groups of people who pray it. Reforms undertaken for clergy engaged in pastoral ministry ought not be imposed on monks, nor should primarily monastic forms of the Office be imposed on active clergy. Nevertheless, the conciliar reform is undertaken with a view especially to those engaged in apostolic works.[69]

All four of the emendations affecting the structure of the Office were accepted overwhelmingly by the council at the fifty-third and fifty-fourth general congregations (respectively October 22 and 23, 1963). *Emendationes* 5 (abolition of Prime) and 6 (faculty of choosing one minor Hour), however, received the greatest number of negative votes (509 and 371 respectively) of any of the thirteen emendations.[70] The whole of chapter 4 of the schema was accepted at the fifty-fifth general congregation on October 24, 1963, with 1,636 votes *placet;* 43, *non placet;* 552, *placet iuxta modum.*[71] The *modi* (suggested modifications of the text) were considered by the conciliar liturgical commission, and only three—merely formal changes— were made in the text. No substantive revision was deemed necessary. The many *modi* recommending very specific modifications for articles 88 and 89 regarding the *cursus horarum* (sequence of the Hours) were simply gathered for consideration by the future post-conciliar commission.[72] At the seventy-third general congregation on November 22, 1963, the final draft of chapter 4 was approved with 2,131 votes *placet;* 50, *non placet.* The entire schema was accepted that same day with 2,158 votes *placet;* 19, *non placet.*[73] At *Sessio Publica III* of the second session of the council, December 4, 1963, *Sacrosanctum concilium* (Constitution on the Sacred Liturgy), as the schema now became, was formally accepted (2,147 votes *placet;* 4, *non placet*) and was promulgated by Pope Paul VI (1963–78).[74] The stage was set for the establishment of a post-conciliar commission, presupposed by articles 21–25 of the constitution, and the immense labor of detailed ritual reform. It is that matter, as it affects the structural reform of the Roman Office, to which we now turn.

Chapter 3

The Consilium, *Coetus IX,*
and Their *Modus Operandi*

Even before the promulgation of SC in December 1963 planning
for the implementation of its directives had begun. While some of
these directives could be implemented immediately, most would
require the prolonged work of a body of experts—a postconciliar
commission. Once established this commission would have to
determine how it was to function in fulfilling its mandate. The
massive task of reforming every major component of the Roman
liturgy called for the enlistment of numerous experts to work in
small groups, each given to an aspect of the reform. Such an
undertaking was a complex one to organize and a difficult one to
maintain with some equilibrium. Because of the complexity and
difficulty of this process, the description of the way in which the
postconciliar commission, that is, the *Consilium ad Exsequendam
Constitutionem de Sacra Liturgia* (hereafter referred to as the Consilium), carried out its role in the reformation of the liturgy in conjunction with the group of consultors responsible for revision of
the structure of the Office, that is, *Coetus IX* (hereafter referred to
as Group 9), is best told chronologically. A generally adequate
history of this process has been given by the late Archbishop
Annibale Bugnini (d. 1982), former secretary of the Consilium, in
his *Reform of the Liturgy, 1948–1975.* His account forms the basis of
the description given here.[1] This description of the development of
the organization of both the Consilium and Group 9 and the
manner of their operation both independently and in conjunction
with each other will be given in three phases: (1) first phase
(1963–66); (2) second phase (1966–67), and (3) third phase (1968–71).

FIRST PHASE (1963–1966)

Archbishop Bugnini, who had been, as a Vincentian priest, the secretary of the Pian Commission and of the preparatory liturgical commission for the Second Vatican Council before he became the secretary of the Consilium, has described in some detail, though not without his personal judgments, the organization and initial work of the postconciliar commission.[2] Here it suffices to note some salient lines of that organizing effort, particularly as they affected the beginning of the work to reform the Office. Characteristic of this first phase was the formulation of plans followed by reconsideration or reformulation of them in the light of experience or criticism.

In October 1963, during the second session of the Second Vatican Council and before the promulgation of SC, Pope Paul VI asked Cardinal Giacomo Lercaro, archbishop of Bologna, to prepare a provisional order for reform of the liturgy.[3] The Pope wished to have the order ready by the end of the second session so that some provisions of SC could be effected immediately. Cardinal Lercaro asked Father Bugnini to find experts to assist in the formulation of this order. The group consisted of liturgical experts Canon Aimé Georges Martimort, Msgrs. Johannes Wagner and Emmanuel Bonet and Frs. Cipriano Vagaggini, O.S.B., Josef Jungmann, S.J., Herman Schmidt, S.J., and Frederick McManus. Father Bugnini acted as secretary. Although the document was drafted quickly, revised, and completed by the end of October, it was not published in time for the close of the second session. The publication was, in fact, delayed until the end of January 1964 by further revisions, first, of a juridical nature by the SCR and the secretariat of the council, then by members of the incipient Consilium (discussed below), who, while accepting some of the juridical revisions, reincorporated material from the October draft. The document eventually became the papal *motu proprio Sacram Liturgiam*, and all the members of the group that created its original draft became consultors to the Consilium. The struggle over revisions to the document between this group and the members of the incipient Consilium on the one hand and the SCR on the other began the tension that characterized the relationship between SCR and the Consilium throughout the existence of the latter.[4]

Meanwhile, in December 1963 the Pope asked both the secretary of the conciliar liturgical commission, Fr. Ferdinando Antonelli, O.F.M., and Cardinal Lercaro each to prepare separately a project for the organization of a postconciliar commission to put SC into effect. Cardinal Lercaro gave Father Bugnini the task of drafting his project, and it was his rather than Father Antonelli's that the Pope accepted in January 1964. The project called for the establishment of an international commission consisting of a cardinal president, twenty to thirty bishops, a "supercommission" of cardinals, and a secretary assisted by a group of experts. The basic work would be distributed by the full commission to the experts in two series of study groups. The first series would be organized according to the liturgical books of the Roman Rite; the second, according to the doctrinal, biblical, theological, ascetical, and pastoral dimensions of the reform. The groups in the second series would review the work done by the groups in the first series. When the work to be done by the study groups was completed, the full commission of bishops would examine it. If approved, it would go next to the "supercommission" of cardinals for examination and approval, then to the national or regional episcopal conferences, and finally to the Pope for definitive approval. Five years were projected for the duration of the reform.[5]

Through his secretary of state, Amleto Cardinal Cicognani, Pope Paul VI on January 13, 1964, named the "constituent assembly," or initial core of the commission, and designated its official title. The constituent assembly consisted of Cardinal Lercaro; Cardinal Larraona, president of the conciliar liturgical commission; and Father Bugnini, secretary. This group met for the first time on January 15, 1964. The draft of the projected *Sacram Liturgiam*, already revised several times, was examined, and as noted above, the project was submitted to further revision. A first sketch of the work projected for the Consilium was considered. Two phases of work were foreseen. In the first phase reform of the Breviary, Missal, Pontifical, Ritual, and Martyrology (calendar) would be undertaken. In the second phase the ceremonial of bishops and the liturgical code would be revised. Priority would be given in the first phase to reform of the Breviary and the Missal.[6]

The Pope finally issued *Sacram Liturgiam* on January 25, 1964. In it was the first public announcement of the formation of a special commission (the Consilium) for the reform of the Liturgy. In fact, according to *Inter oecumenici*, the first instruction on the proper implementation of SC (September 26, 1964), it was by this *motu proprio* that the Consilium was officially established. Among the concessions granted in the *motu proprio* for immediate implementation of SC were two regarding the Office: (1) Outside of choir Prime may be omitted, and (2) also outside of choir only one minor Hour corresponding to the hour of the day need be said.[7]

At the second meeting of the constituent assembly on February 15, 1964, the three members examined and approved a list of potential members of the Consilium. The Pope in turn approved it, and the names were published in *L'Osservatore Romano* on March 5, 1964. The forty-two members included cardinals, archbishops, bishops, the abbot primate of the Benedictines, and three priests. At this meeting the three members also set the following March 11 as the date for the first plenary meeting of the Consilium.[8]

Between the meeting of February 15 and the publication of the names of the members of the Consilium, the cardinal secretary of state in a letter dated February 29 to Cardinal Lercaro indicated what the Pope expected of the Consilium: (1) to suggest the names of people who would form the study groups for the revision of the rites; (2) to follow and coordinate the work of these study groups; (3) to prepare an instruction that would elucidate practically the *motu proprio Sacram Liturgiam* and define clearly the work of the territorial bodies of bishops mentioned in SC 22.2; and (4) to apply literally and in the spirit of the council the provisions of SC, responding to the proposals of the episcopal conferences of bishops for its proper application. The letter also indicated that recourse against the decisions of the Consilium and solution to particularly delicate and serious questions or questions beyond its competence should be referred to the Pope.

In effect the letter made the Consilium, as Archbishop Bugnini has observed, a *qualified* study group with temporary administrative responsibilities directly dependent on the Pope. Both the strength and weakness of the Consilium inhered in this arrangement. Its direct dependence on the Pope outside the juridical framework within which the permanent congregations of the Roman Curia had to function gave it security and a certain freedom in its deliberations and actions; but its uniqueness, temporary nature, and lack of clear, juridical norms within which to function rendered it open to misinterpretation and abuse by some among the curial congregations, particularly by the SCR, which had juridical competence in the regulation of the Roman liturgy. The letter of February 29, in fact, failed to establish the relationship that should exist between the Consilium and SCR. This deficiency was somewhat rectified only in January 1965 in another letter of the cardinal secretary of state by which the Consilium was given competence to oversee and regulate experiments with rites in the process of reform, and the SCR was to approve their definitive form for publication.[9]

As stipulated at the meeting of February 15 the Consilium met in plenary session for the first time on March 11, 1964. Twenty-four of the forty-four members were present. At this meeting Cardinal Lercaro set forth the purposes of the commission as outlined by the secretary of state in his letter of February 29. Father Bugnini reported on the plan for the internal organization of the Consilium. He indicated that the remainder of the year would be devoted primarily to this internal organization. Among other tasks requiring immediate attention was that of preparing an instruction to implement both SC and *Sacram Liturgiam*. The members approved unanimously the method of work for the Consilium as accepted in the meetings of the constituent assembly and as presented by Father Bugnini.

Although the Consilium was not a curial congregation and thus not bound juridically to follow its procedures, it nevertheless agreed at this first plenary meeting to follow the curial practice of holding two types of meetings, ordinary and plenary. Ordinary meetings were to consist of members present in Rome along with seventeen consultors drawn from the SCR, the Congregation for the Propagation of the Faith, and the Consilium. These meetings would be held twice a month and attend to ordinary administrative concerns, fix the agenda of the plenary meetings, prepare material to be presented for approval at them, resolve questions about the interpretation of SC, and confirm the acts of the episcopal conferences. Decisions of the plenary meetings, unlike those of the curial congregations, which had legislative power, were subordinate to the approval of the Pope. These meetings, then, would simply recommend action to him.

At plenary meetings of a curial congregation only cardinals and bishops could participate. At plenary meetings of the Consilium, however, all members as well as consultors from the study groups could be present. All would have voice, the members by right, the consultors if invited. Only members would vote. Members would thus have at their immediate disposal the experts who could answer their questions. Because of the great number of consultors and the limitations of space at a general meeting, only those consultors who chaired the study groups, that is, the *relatores*, and those consultors whose advice was deemed desirable because of the nature of the material at hand could be present.[10]

Consultors were not present at the first meeting of the Consilium. The task of securing them, of assigning them according to their competencies to the two series of study groups, and of enabling them to function according to an established procedure was a lengthy one and was left largely in Father Bugnini's hands. He had begun to assemble the corps of consultors in January 1964 with the assistance of scholars he knew personally. In the general plan for the reform of the liturgy presented to the Pope on March 16, 1964, following the first meeting of the Consilium, was included the list of the twenty-nine *coetus*, or study groups, in the first series (compositional section) and the ten groups in the second series (revisory section).

Nine groups, the largest number for any one liturgical book, were established among those in the first series for the reform of the Roman Office, or "Breviary," as it was designated. These groups, numbered as designated in the general plan, were Group 1, the calendar; Group 2, revision of the Psalter; Group 3, distribution of the psalms; Group 4, biblical readings of the Office; Group 5, patristic readings; Group 6, hagiographic readings; Group 7, hymns; Group 8, chants of the Office; Group 9, general structure of the Divine Office. Each group was to consist of five to seven consultors chosen according to specialization, diversity of nationality, and possibility of meeting and working together. For particular problems either permanent or temporary advisors, *consiliarii*, could be named. These were to submit written opinions and might, in certain instances authorized by the president of the Consilium, participate in the meetings of the study group to which they were assigned. *Consultores*, consultors strictly speaking, were to be approved by the Pope; *consiliarii*, by the president of the Consilium.[11]

Submitted also as part of the general plan was the procedure to be followed by the study groups and the full Consilium in bringing the reform to completion. The study groups in the compositional section, which corresponded to sections of the various Roman liturgical books, would work simultaneously, each developing a scheme of the material for which it was responsible. The criteria to be used were the text of SC, material gathered in the preparatory liturgical commission for the Second Vatican Council, the desires of bishops and clergy, and the results of liturgical studies. When ready, a scheme would be forwarded to all consultors and a fitting number of advisors. Advice received from them in a determined period of time would be used to prepare a second scheme, which would be handled in the same way as the first. When final formulations from all the groups concerned with a given liturgical book were ready, the group responsible for the general structure of all the rites in the book would prepare a general scheme for the whole book.

Before schemata prepared by study groups in the compositional section were presented to members of the Consilium they were to be submitted to the study groups making up the revisory section for examination and revision according to the various competencies (e.g., theological, biblical, juridical, pastoral, stylistic) of these groups. In the course of the work, however, only the groups in the compositional section functioned. The other section was seen as unnecessary, since in most of the groups of the compositional section there were experts competent to deal with those matters originally foreseen as the provenance of groups in the revisory section. Besides, there developed the practice of the chairpersons (*relatores*) of the study groups meeting together before each plenary session of the Consilium to examine and to revise, if necessary, the schemata proposed for consideration at the plenary session. So in practice, the Consilium deliberated on material presented to it by the *coetus relatorum,* or Group of Relators, and if the schemes presented were in relatively definitive form and approved by a majority of the members of the Consilium, they would be presented to the Pope for his examination and approval. If the schemes were not acceptable, they would be returned to the study groups for further revision. Submission of schemes to a supercommission of cardinals and to episcopal conferences was apparently abandoned in the early planning. In practice, too, some study groups, including Group 9, often requested and received direction from the members of the Consilium in plenary session. At times, too, schemes approved by the membership of the Consilium were returned to it by the Pope or a curial congregation with observations necessitating further consideration. Where the elements of a given liturgical book were numerous, as in the Breviary or Missal, each homogeneous part (e.g., biblical readings, patristic readings) would be presented to the Consilium separately before submission of the general scheme.[12]

Very soon after he was appointed secretary of the Consilium, Father Bugnini asked Canon Martimort, who was professor of liturgy for the Faculty of Theology in Toulouse and at the Institut Supérieur de Liturgie of Paris, to assist him in forming the study groups. Canon Martimort was also the editor of *L'Église en prière* and had been the director of Centre de Pastorale Liturgique. The initial effort in the formation of the study groups, apparently, was to find one or two key people for each group and let them, in turn, choose the remaining membership of their respective groups. Father Bugnini and Canon Martimort had served on both the preparatory liturgical commission for the council, the conciliar liturgical commission, and the committee Pope Paul VI had constituted late in 1963 to draft *Sacram Liturgiam*. It was to the consultors, especially, of the two commissions that they turned to find the expertise needed to fulfill the task of the Consilium. Each of the study groups was to have a *relator*, that is, a chairperson (hereafter, relator), and a secretary.

To Group 1 (the calendar), Father Bugnini succeeded in drawing Fr. Ansgar Dirks, a Dutch Dominican, director of the Dominican Liturgical Institute in Rome. Father Dirks became secretary and Father Bugnini himself, initially, relator of the group. Eventually, in 1967, Msgr. Pierre Jounel, professor at the Institut Supérieur de Liturgie in Paris, assumed the position of relator.

Named as relator of Group 2 (revision of the Psalter) was Fr. Pietro Duncker, another Dutch Dominican, but from the Angelicum in Rome. Fr. Jean Gribomont, a French Benedictine and patristic scholar, assumed the role of secretary for this group.

Msgr. Joseph Pascher, specialist in the liturgical Psalter from the University of Munich, became relator of Group 3 (distribution of the Psalter). Chosen as secretary for the group was Canon André Rose, biblical scholar and liturgiologist from Belgium.

Canon Martimort at first reserved for himself the role of relator for Group 4 (biblical readings) and had the assistance of Prof. Emil Lengeling of the University of Münster as secretary. Canon Martimort, however, was designated *relator generalis* (general expositor or coordinator) of the entire section of study groups for the Office. The work entailed in this responsibility was so great that in 1967 he withdrew from Group 4 altogether. Professor Lengeling became relator and Canon Rose, secretary.

The leadership of Group 5 (patristic readings) had during the course of its existence the greatest turnover of any of the study groups for the Office. Msgr. Michele Pellegrino, a patrologist from the University of Turin, was selected as the first relator of Group 5 and Fr. Ignacio Onatibia, professor in a diocesan seminary in Vitoria, Spain, as its secretary. Monsignor Pellegrino became archbishop of Turin, member of the Consilium, and later cardinal. His replacement as relator of Group 5 was Fr. Umberto Neri, a patrologist from Bologna. Father Neri went off to Greece shortly for some apostolic work, and Father Onatibia assumed the role of relator. But he resigned after a brief period, perhaps because of some personal difficulty with Father Bugnini. Fr. Franz Nikolasch, secretary of the group after Father Onatibia became relator, then assumed charge. Other responsibilities, however, necessitated his withdrawal from the group, so Fr. John Rotelle, Augustinian patrologist from the United States, became the relator who saw the work of this group through to completion. This he did in collaboration with the Benedictine Henry Ashworth of Quarr Abbey, Isle of Wight, and the Trappist Bernard Backaert of Orval Monastery in Belgium.

The relator of Group 6 (historical or hagiographic readings) was originally designated as Fr. Beauduin De Gaiffier, Jesuit director of the Bollandist Society from Brussels. The secretary was the Franciscan Church historian, Fr. Agostino Amore, from the Ateneo Antonianum in Rome. Father Amore succeeded Father De Gaiffier as relator; and the Roman Msgr. Benedetto Cignitti, editor of *Bibliotheca sanctorum*, became secretary.

For Group 7 (hymns) Father Bugnini nominated the Benedictine Anselmo Lentini of Monte Cassino, an expert in Latin hymnology, as relator. The secretary's post was assumed by another Italian Benedictine, Ildefonso Tassi, a specialist in music and liturgy from the Lateran University.

Father Bugnini secured still another Italian Benedictine, from the area of Padua, Fr. Pelagio Visentin, to head Group 8 (chants of the Office). Msgr. Igino Rogger, seminary professor in Trent, became secretary of the group.

Group 9 (general structure of the Divine Office), the coordinating, directive center for all the other groups working on reform of the Office, was chaired from its beginning to its demise by Canon Martimort. He wanted as his secretary Ansgario Mundo, Benedictine monk of the Abbey of Montserrat, but the latter could not assume this role, apparently because of ill health. Father Bugnini suggested the Italian Vincenzo Raffa, member of congregation of Sons of Divine Providence and professor of liturgy at his congregation's theological scholasticate, Don Orione, in Tortona. Group 9 was to differ from the other study groups for the Office in that its membership was to be drawn primarily from the relators and secretaries of Groups 1 through 8. Added to this group was the Italian rubricist Msgr. Salvatore Famoso from Catania. Relators and secretaries of several other groups whose work had some bearing on the Office could and did attend the meetings of Group 9.[13]

Before the second plenary meeting of the Consilium, April 17–20, 1964, there were two ordinary meetings (March 20 and April 13) of that body. One matter considered at the second of these meetings pertained to the Office, namely, the extension to those obliged to choral recitation of the Office of the faculty granted in *Sacram Liturgiam* to omit Prime and to recite only one of the three minor Hours. Lack of unanimity in a decision on this question postponed it to another time. Inability to deal decisively with this and most other matters in these two ordinary meetings contributed to their abandonment. None were held after the second meeting. Factors other than an inability to decide, however, contributed to the demise of the ordinary meetings. Once the study groups were organized, their work became so intense that they scarcely had time to submit material to the members of the Consilium for the plenary meetings. Once, too, that the Consilium had established criteria for confirmation of the acts of episcopal conferences, it seemed more efficient to have the presidency of the Consilium confirm them than to have an ordinary meeting do so. Furthermore, since so much considered in the ordinary meetings was referred to the plenary meetings, the former appeared superfluous. The need remained, however, especially when the Consilium began to meet in plenary session only twice each year, for a small executive body within the commission to expedite some matters that could not wait for a plenary session or that might assist the plenary session to function smoothly. Such a body, the Council of the Presidency, was formed in 1966.[14]

By the time of the second plenary session of the Consilium (April 17–20, 1964), the relators were able to meet together (April 14–16) to prepare for the session. Canon Martimort presented first to the relators, then in revised form to the Consilium a first *relatio* (report) regarding reform of the Office. In it he suggested that four principles should direct the work: (1) a certain fidelity to the practice of the past but most especially a sensitivity to the current conditions of pastoral clergy *(sic)*; (2) an ability of texts of the reformed Office to nourish spiritually those using it; (3) provision for the faithful to participate in fruitful, common celebration of the Office; (4) arrangement for the Hours of the Office to be celebrated at the corresponding true and fitting hours of the day.

Canon Martimort also listed thirty-three questions deemed necessary for the study groups to ask about the structure of the Office, the cycle of the psalms, the biblical and patristic readings, the calendar, the sanctoral cycle, the chants, hymns, and other elements of the Office. Both the proposed principles and the questions were based on the provisions of SC, chapter 4, and the two *relationes* read to the council by Bishop J. Albert Martin on behalf of the conciliar liturgical commission. The members of the Consilium gave their approval to the plan as presented by Canon Martimort.

Soon after this plenary session the Pope, through the cardinal secretary of state, stated (May 19, 1964) that in the promulgation of decrees regarding liturgy as these derived from Vatican II, the Consilium should be associated with SCR. Preparation of such decrees would be the work of both bodies in consultation with each other, and publication would be by SCR with the signatures of the president of the Consilium and of both the prefect and the secretary of SCR appended.[15]

As the number of people involved in the work of the Consilium increased and the work of the study groups got underway, the secretariat developed various publications to keep members, experts, and those outside the Consilium informed. Schemata, numbered consecutively as a whole (in one sequence) and within each section of study groups according to the liturgical books (in another sequence), were mimeographed sheets reporting the discussions and actions of the study groups, that which was to be proposed for consideration at the plenary sessions, and some of the proceedings of the meetings of the *coetus relatorum* (hereafter referred to as the Group of Relators) and of the plenary sessions of the Consilium. *Questiones tractandae* presented to the Consilium for its discussion the problems arising outside the study groups. *Relationes*, sent only to members and relators, contained especially the material to be considered at the plenary sessions. *Res secretariae* were general communications from the secretariat in which were contained the reports of the secretary to the plenary sessions. More general information on the reform was provided in *Notitiae*, originally duplicated sheets distributed not only to those involved in the work of the Consilium but also to presidents of liturgical commissions and others involved in the liturgical renewal. In 1965 this publication became an even more widely distributed, printed periodical.[16]

The study groups for the reform of the Office began their work in earnest by late spring of 1964. The third meeting of the Consilium (June 18–20, 1964), involving only the members, did not include any report on the Office from Canon Martimort. By the time of the fourth plenary session (September–November 1964), the canon had compiled a report giving the results of his query put to the experts concerned with reform of the Office. The relators had examined this report during their meetings from September 19 to October 1. They requested the Consilium to vote on the principal questions raised in Canon Martimort's report, but the members of the Consilium felt unprepared to decide, since so much was of a technical nature. Besides, some members had reservations about the large number of votes foreseen if this procedure were to continue. Father Bugnini, as secretary, declared that the voting was orientational when it was a matter of planning the work. That decision facilitated the voting for some, leaving open the possibility of changing their votes at a later date when better solutions or new evidence dictated renewed consideration. Others, however, did not view their voting on one occasion as reversible on another. It was a gray area, admitted the secretary, an example of the members and consultors of the Consilium being summoned to function more out of good will than according to procedures juridically prescribed.[17]

During this fourth plenary session, extended over two months because meetings were interspersed with those of the third session of the council, members and relators considered reform of the Office at three meetings, held respectively on September 28 and 29 and October 1. Group 9 itself held three meetings (September 26 and 27) immediately before these meetings of the Consilium and one meeting (October 2) following the last one of the Consilium concerned with the Office. During the session the Consilium gave an orientational vote on twenty-one propositions for reform of the Office. The specifics discussed and voted regarding the structure of the Office are considered below in chapters 4 and 5. Here it need only be noted what Archbishop Bugnini has described as a double tendency in the discussion. The majority of the members and consultors was preoccupied with *shortening* the Office for the sake of clergy engaged in pastoral care. A minority was primarily concerned with a simplified structure for communal celebration by religious and faithful. Warnings by this minority that more attention was being given to private recitation than to public communal celebration of the Office were met by retorts that public celebration was in the realm of the ideal, incapable of achievement in any broad way. Yet the minority's views were heard, and both in this and in future sessions of the Consilium voting favored to some extent that which would foster communal celebration without excluding provision for private recitation. Thus compromise characterized many of the decisions of the Consilium regarding the structure of the Office. To Canon Martimort himself, this compromise, represented in the final form of the Liturgy of the Hours, is one of its greatest strengths.[18]

Between the fourth and fifth plenary sessions some noteworthy developments occurred. To ease continuing tension between SCR and the Consilium, the secretary of state informed the prefect of SCR (January 7, 1965) that there were three phases to the liturgical reform: (1) preparation of the liturgical books and examination of questions, (2) experimentation, and (3) promulgation of definitive reformed rites. The first two phases were in the competency of the Consilium; the third, in the competency of SCR. While this information may have clarified matters it did not reduce the tension between the two entities.

Meanwhile, to prepare for the fifth plenary assembly of the Consilium (April 26-30, 1965) Group 9 consulted, coordinated, and met in Rome on March 1 and 2. At the April plenary session it presented to the Consilium another series of proposals regarding most elements of the Office (psalmody, biblical and patristic readings, hymns, and chants). The Consilium gave a favorable response to most of the proposals and deferred response to a few to a later time. Relators of Groups 1 (calendar), 3 (distribution of the psalms), 4 (biblical readings), 5 (patristic readings), 7 (hymns), and 8 (chants of the Office) reported on the work of their respective study groups. But there was obviously some uneasiness among members of the Consilium in responding to the presentations of the consultors. Meeting on April 30 without the consultors, the members examined the role of the experts in the process of the reform. Some members felt uncomfortable with the sometimes technical disquisitions of the consultors and wanted them only to clarify problems the members had with proposals under consideration. Undoubtedly part of this reaction was attributable to the abundance of proposals and reports regarding reform of the Office.

Reaction was not confined to the members of the Consilium. Shortly after completion of the fifth plenary session some consultors, in addition to some members, submitted to the secretariat of the Consilium their serious doubts about the adequacy of the proposed revision of the Office. The appearance in the first printed volume of *Notitiae* (1965) of the reports given to the fifth session by the study groups for reform of the Office provoked further protest from many who were in no way involved with the work of the Consilium and whose first glimpse of the projected reform came through the pages of this periodical.[19]

The outcry of protest was not confined to a single theme. Some complained to the secretariat that the proposed Office by its abbreviation of the current Office would contribute to a decline of prayer. Others maintained, on the contrary, that the proposed lines of reform would produce an Office little less monasticized than the current one, highly unsuitable for contemporary pastoral clergy. A few protested that an Office developed as proposed would not be very accessible to laity. With these objections the Consilium had to deal in its sixth plenary session (October 18–26, November 22–26, December 1, 1965). In a meeting of members only, on October 19, Father Bugnini synthesized the proposals the secretariat had received in reaction to the proposed lines of reform of the Office and asked that the members judge whether to continue along the lines proposed or to give new directives to Group 9 and the other study groups concerned with the Office. He reminded the members that the work of these study groups was already in an advanced stage, and in order that these groups might not work in vain, further consideration of their proposals would be excluded from the agenda of the sixth session until the more fundamental decision as to the direction of the reform of the Office had been made.[20]

Father Bugnini's synthesis of proposals given to the members at their closed meeting on October 19 comprised five items: (1) Let the fundamental moments of daily prayer, at least for the diocesan clergy and those regular clergy engaged in pastoral activity, be morning, midday, and evening. (2) Let the character of nocturnal prayer be provided for in Matins of great feasts, of Sundays, and of other particular days only, so that on other days Matins would have the character of a prolonged, obligatory *lectio divina*. (3) Let the number of psalms in each Hour be reduced so that a calm, meditative celebration could ensue with fitting pauses for silence. (4) If the previous principle be accepted, let the Psalter be distributed over a monthly cycle from which are removed the imprecatory and historical psalms. The imprecatory psalms would be placed at a fitting time in the liturgical cycle and the historical psalms used as readings. (5) Let the minor Hours be structured in such a way that those who celebrate only one of these Hours do not omit any psalms in the ordinary cycle.[21]

Discussion by the members on Father Bugnini's presentation was animated. Some objected it was dangerous to reverse decisions already made because everything could then be subjected to repeated discussion. Others, led by Bishop René Boudon of

Mende, emphasized that priests *(sic)* do not find their true prayer in the Breviary, since the structure of the Office does not meet the expectations of the majority of them. Added seemingly as an afterthought to this contention was that maintaining the proposed lines of reform would result in the exclusion of the people from participation in the Office. The president, Cardinal Lercaro, finally concluded that more time was necessary to reflect before coming to a decision. He postponed further discussion until a later meeting at which the consultors would also be present. Meanwhile, he sent to Canon Martimort an account of the difficulties.[22]

On December 1 members and consultors met to consider again the fundamental issues regarding the Office. Canon Martimort read a two-page report attempting to specify the issues as he understood them, to express his own opinion on each of these, and to offer his observations on what could and should be done to resolve the dilemma the Consilium found itself in. He saw three major issues: (1) the quantity of psalmody proposed for the various Hours, particularly the five psalms for Lauds and Vespers and the three for the minor Hours; (2) the desire of some to remove, at least from the ordinary cycle, the imprecatory psalms; and (3) the difficulty with the structure of Lauds and Vespers, particularly for popular participation and involvement of secular clergy. With regard to the last point, he noted that requests had been made that traditions of the Office in the East and in the Anglican and other Protestant Churches be utilized in the Roman reform.

In Canon Martimort's own opinion the quantity of psalmody, already approved by the Consilium, was appropriate, and various aids were to be provided to render it more accessible as Christian prayer. With regard to proposals to remove imprecatory psalms from the ordinary *cursus*, he simply stated that SC, a *sacra lex* (sacred law) for the reform, had left a broad field open for considering different solutions to problems and had really only prescribed the number of Hours of the Office and the general character of the reform. As to the structure of Lauds and Vespers, he noted that provision had been made, approved by the Consilium, for reduction of psalmody and introduction of a long reading at Vespers when laity were present; that popular participation in Lauds would be exceedingly unlikely; that Anglican and other

Protestant Offices might not be very helpful in the Roman reform, since only Morning and Evening Prayer exist in them, whereas SC had prescribed the complete Office for the Roman Rite; that although the East possesses all the Hours of the Office, there is often only the obligation to the public celebration of Lauds. Canon Martimort then indicated what he thought could and should be done. The Consilium, he said, was certainly free to reconsider what it had previously voted on since the previous voting was provisory, and the consultors would probably favor a reconsideration following the directives of the members. He asked only that after oral discussion the members submit their written opinions for consideration by the study groups. Finally, he requested that the Consilium not decree anything regarding the Office until the objections and propositions had been examined by the study groups for the Office and, if needed, a *relatio* had been prepared and submitted to the members.[23]

In his summary of the discussion that followed Canon Martimort's report, Archbishop Bugnini notes that little was added to what had already been considered in previous discussions. On the one hand were those who maintained that the Consilium's role was simply to put SC into effect, not to search out new paths. Some kind of harmony had to be found between implementing the prescriptions of SC and current exigencies. On the other hand were those who argued that some vital form of Office was needed for clergy and faithful, particularly the secular clergy for whom the Office should be a fount of personal prayer. Cardinal Lercaro brought the discussion to a close by noting that (1) the Office must retain the traditional structure of hourly prayer; (2) the entire Psalter must be used, but the distribution of it is not determined; (3) Matins must be adapted for use at any hour of the day and lend itself to meditation; (3) outside choir one can choose one of the minor Hours, but the psalmody should be arranged so that a person making this choice does not have to omit any psalms of the *cursus*.[24]

According to Archbishop Bugnini, Msgr. Emmanuel Bonet, Spanish canonist and consultor, proposed that a questionnaire on the disputed points concerning reform of the Office be sent to all the members of the Consilium. After consulting with other bishops and priests, he suggested, the members could give their written responses to the questionnaire. Father Bugnini drew up the questionnaire, which was distributed from the secretariat on December 16, 1965, not only to the members but also to some consultors and advisors. The various parts of the questionnaire concerned with the structure of the Office are discussed below in chapters 4 and 5. To be noted here is that the document contained nineteen questions coordinated with five topics: (1) participation in the Office, (2) adaptation of the structure of the Office to the necessities of contemporary life, (3) length and number of the psalms in the different Hours, (4) the integrity of the Psalter in the ordinary cycle and the question of the imprecatory psalms, (5) The question of the minor Hours.[25]

On March 18, 1966, while the questionnaire was in circulation, Cardinal Lercaro met with the Pope and informed him of the difficulties in the Consilium regarding the Office. In a letter to Canon Martimort dated April 5, 1966, Cardinal Lercaro communicated the papal views on some of the debated issues. These views of the Pope are considered below (in chs. 4 and 5) as they correspond to the parts of the structure of the Office discussed. Generally speaking, one can say that the Pope's views favored to some extent those seeking a radical revision of the Office. He advocated, for instance, the abandonment of two of the minor Hours, keeping only one at midday. At the conclusion of his letter, Cardinal Lercaro told Canon Martimort that he would be pleased to present the work of Group 9 to the Pope at the next audience he had with him, on June 16. At this point it should be noted that the Pope gave his personal opinion and did not mandate anything regarding reform of the Office. The Pope's views, however, were received differently by at least Canon Martimort and Father Bugnini. The canon did not hesitate to counter the Pope's suggestions, as will be made clear below, where he thought the Pope mistaken or ill advised. The secretary, however, gave evidence of his displeasure at such boldness on Canon Martimort's part. Even if only opinion, the Pope's views, he would say, should simply be implemented. Furthermore, it is less clear in this first papal intervention into the working of the Consilium and its study groups than it is in later interventions whether Pope Paul VI offered his opinion spontaneously or was asked in some way to intervene.[26]

The results of the questionnaire were known to Canon Martimort by early May 1966. Of the forty-seven members of the Consilium at that time, only twenty-four responded. Twenty-three
experts gave their opinions. Roughly two-thirds of those who did
respond favored a type of reform that would conserve the traditional structure of the Office. Canon Martimort was not sure,
however, how to utilize the disappointing response as a guide to
the reform. At the time he received the results he was engaged in
his own personal reexamination of the major issues as well as
study of the Anglican and other Protestant Offices. The secretary
of Group 9, Don Vincenzo Raffa, had, on May 13, requested of the
consultors of Group 9 their opinions on the issues. Each consultor
in the group received a copy of Schema 167 containing the results
of the December questionnaire. Responses were to be submitted to
Canon Martimort by July. So based on the results of the questionnaire, his own personal study, and the notes received from members of Group 9, members of the Consilium, and other consultors,
he sent, at the end of July, a thirty-four page mimeographed report ("Rapport général sur l'Office divin") to those making up
Group 9 so that they could understand the state of the questions
that the group would have to consider at its meeting the following
September in order to submit to the Consilium a report giving the
group's recommendations for the general lines to be followed in
reform of the Office. Canon Martimort's report was followed on
August 5 by a supplement ("Supplément a la relation générale sur
le bréviaire") treating further questions.

Together, the report and its supplement dealt with six questions:
(1) Is it necessary to conserve in the Office the entire Psalter? (2)
How resolve the problem of the minor Hours? (3) What should be
the general structure of Vespers and of Lauds? (4) Is it necessary
to change completely the decision on the whole of Vespers and of
Lauds and even on the whole of the Office? (5) Should there be
one or several Breviaries? (6) Should one be for or against the elements from the choral tradition in the Office?[27]

SECOND PHASE (1966-1967)
The second phase of work in the Consilium and in Group 9 was
marked by (1) new agreement on the lines of reform for the Office,
(2) experiments with its proposed structure and texts, (3) changes

in the internal structure of the Consilium, (4) review by the Synod of Bishops of some principles of the reform, and (5) further interventions of the Pope. While it can be said that none of these events had the magnitude of impact on reform of the Office as did the questioning and searching of the sixth plenary session and of the period following it, each contributed in a major way to the development of the reformed structure of the Office. Thus each will be considered at some length in what follows.

After a period of reflection on the results of the questionnaire and on Canon Martimort's special report, Group 9 met in Genoa from September 6 to 8, 1966. From the lengthy discussion at that meeting on the issues raised in the questionnaire and in the report emerged Schema 185, a twenty-five page report intended for the next plenary session of the Consilium but considered and expanded somewhat by the Group of Relators in their meeting from September 19 to October 1. The details of what Group 9 proposed and the Consilium's response to them are left to chapters 4 and 5. While concessions were made to some requests for more radical reform (e.g., provision for both obligatory and optional psalmody in the minor Hours so that those using one Hour would not permanently lose some psalms of the *cursus*), more compromising solutions were proposed for others (e.g., one structure for Lauds and Vespers suitable for both common celebration and private recitation) and still others were resisted (e.g., reduction of the minor Hours to one). Canon Martimort himself has said that Schema 185 (and its revised form, Schema 194) were directed as much to the Pope as to the members of the Consilium, both to comply with some requests of both the Pope and the members and to resist others in a way that explained why, according to Canon Martimort and the other members of Group 9, these requests should not be granted. It was especially against requests for a more radical reform of the Office, particularly of the minor Hours, that Canon Martimort, in Schema 185, presented several reasons. Fulfillment of such requests, he noted, were certainly possible, but fulfillment would weaken the estimation of many people for the seriousness and foresight of the bishops of the council, since derogation from some articles of SC would have to occur. It would appear, too, he said, useless to establish norms as the council had done if they could be overturned so soon. Furthermore, he noted, those who impugn the liturgical reform could say that "hodie liturgistas hoc petere, cras vero aliud velle" ("today liturgists ask for this, tomorrow they want something else").[28]

When the Consilium met for its seventh plenary session from October 6 to 14, 1966, it endorsed the proposals of Group 9 and of the Group of Relators. Work on the reform of the Office could then continue again on the basis of the newly adopted principles. The Consilium, however, had internal problems, which occupied the members in a meeting on October 8 closed to the consultors. There the members decided that consultors would have a renewable term of three years in order to allow the insertion of a new element in their midst. It was proposed that a statute be drafted to regulate the functioning of the study groups, the assignments and functioning of plenary assemblies, the presidency, and the secretariat. The members of the Consilium also decided to establish a group within the Consilium to be known as Council of the Presidency. This group, composed of the president and vice president of the Consilium and seven members elected by the plenary assembly, would meet periodically to resolve the most serious problems occurring between one plenary session and another. It would also inform the Consilium of developments affecting their work (e.g., the actions of the congregations of the Roman Curia and the approval of documents).

The presidential council was approved by the Pope, and it met twice between the seventh and eighth plenary sessions of the Consilium. At its meeting of January 12–13, 1967, the council engaged in a lengthy discussion on the request of some monastic communities in missionary countries to adapt the Office to their needs. The request had been submitted also to the Congregation for the Propagation of the Faith and the Congregation of Religious. The former body was favorable to granting the request; the latter, reluctant. The council ultimately was favorable provided that the fundamental elements of the Office decreed in SC were respected. This decision marked the beginning of an experimentation with the Office and an adaptation of it before reform of its structure was complete.[29]

A report of the work completed in the seventh plenary session had been made to the Pope on November 10, 1966. Canon Martimort summed up the situation regarding the Office thus:

"The basic problem which we face today and which the present report attempts to deal with and resolve is this: How is the Divine Office, while continuing to be the prayer chiefly of the clergy and religious, to be also accessible to the faithful so that they may find in it, not something that is, as it were, a concession to them, but rather the exercise of a function that truly belongs to them as members of the praying ecclesial community?"[30]

This statement is revealing on several counts. While it still seems to suggest that reform of the Office should have clergy and religious especially as beneficiaries, there is implicit acknowledgment that reform to date has regarded lay participation in the Office as a concession. This will be clearly evident in the consideration below (chs. 4 and 5) of the early stages of proposed reforms for Lauds and Vespers. Furthermore, although there is now determination, born of criticism and minority opinions, to pursue reform in such a way that the Office will be the *rightful* prayer of *all* in the Church, the path to be followed is a compromised one: reform the Office for all, but let the arrangement and measure of it be dictated primarily by the special needs of clergy and religious.

The remainder of Canon Martimort's report outlined the principles, agreed to by the Consilium, that governed to a great extent the final phase of structural reform of the Office. These are considered in chapters 4 and 5. Canon Martimort also indicated to the Pope that Group 9 and the other study groups for the Office would prepare a sample of the proposed reformed Office for use at the next plenary session of the Consilium. On the basis of this experience, then, the members and consultors of the Consilium could make further observations that might prepare the way for further experimentation with the proposed Office among suitably prepared groups of people.[31]

Group 9 met again in Genoa from February 6–8, 1967. Every part of the structure of the Office was considered in view of the preparation of a specimen for use during the upcoming plenary session. In preparing the specimen the group adhered to the principles adopted at the seventh plenary session. Where the content of a given part of the Office was not yet in a usable form, that of the current Roman Office was utilized. Between February and April a mimeographed booklet of 250 pages, "Schema completum Divini

Officii persolvendi a die 9 ad 15 aprilis 1967," was produced. It contained not only the entire Office for use during the week the Consilium was to meet but also the Psalter for the remaining three weeks of the four-week cycle. By March 15, Canon Martimort had a *relatio* (report) prepared to introduce the specimen to the members and consultors. Concluding the document were sixteen questions to be put to the members after they had heard the reports of the study groups for the Office and had experienced, both publicly and privately, the proposed structure and forms in the specimen.[32]

During the eighth plenary session of the Consilium (April 10–19, 1967) the consultors and members used the specimen both communally and in private. In communal use, under the leadership of either Canon Martimort or Dom Pelagio Visentin (relator of Group 8: the chants of the Office), the psalms were even chanted. The response, given on April 17 to this experimental Office, was largely favorable. Details of the response are discussed below in chapters 4 and 5.

The Consilium, however, was preoccupied at this eighth session with matters other than the Office. Besides dealing with reports from the various study groups, it heard from the secretary of problems with unauthorized experimentation in liturgy, of requests for indults for experimentation, of virulent opposition to liturgical reform sometimes issuing in libel against persons of the Consilium. Cardinal Lercaro himself had been deprecatingly called a *Luther redivivus*. Besides, in response to the Pope's request material and questions on the proposed reform of both Mass and Office had to be prepared for presentation to the forthcoming Synod of Bishops, and the general statute prepared by the Council of the Presidency to govern the functioning of the Consilium had to be discussed and put to vote. The statute was approved on April 15, but when submitted to the Pope, it was rejected.

Archbishop Bugnini tells the sinister story of a letter (source unnamed) received by the Pope shortly before the proposed statute was presented for his approval. The letter warned him not to approve the statute, which would give the Consilium unprecedented power, make the SCR the only curial congregation subject to an authority other than the Pope, and even undermine papal authority. Despite all protestations and evidence that the allegations in the letter were baseless, Paul VI, for reasons he never explained, not only refused approval but told Father Bugnini in audience that the matter of the statute must not be discussed. The Consilium thus had to continue to function according to a few rather informal directives and the good will of its members and consultors.[33]

In light of the response made to the proposals for the Office at the eighth plenary session, Group 9 undertook the task of preparing yet another specimen of the Office for use at the ninth plenary session. Meeting in Munich from July 20 to 23, 1967, Group 9 was first informed by Canon Martimort that the secretariat of the Consilium was trying to have published the proposed hymns for the new Office for wider circulation and criticism. The secretariat wished to do the same for the biblical, patristic, and hagiographic readings as well as for the four-week cycle of psalms with their antiphons and titles. Twenty-four questions regarding both structure and content of the new Office were then discussed and put to a vote. These were to be presented to the Group of Relators at their next meeting and then to the members of the Consilium at their ninth plenary session. Group 9 does not seem to have been concerned with formulating a presentation on the Office for the synod. This the secretariat of the Consilium did in submitting a set of four *relationes* to prospective synodal participants. The four reports explained the principles adopted for restoration of the liturgical year and calendar, the order of the Mass, the Lectionary of the Missal, and the Breviary *(sic).*[34]

Before the ninth plenary session met, the Synod of Bishops, meeting in Rome from September 29 to October 29, 1967, considered the *relationes* on various aspects of the liturgical reform and among the seven questions put to a vote, replied with a two-thirds majority responding favorably to three of the four questions on the Office. The question having only a simple majority in favor was one asking whether all the psalms, including imprecatory and historical, should be retained in the ordinary *cursus* of the four-week psalter. This question and the others submitted to the synod are discussed below in chapters 4 and 5, but it is important to note that it is the question on the psalms that became the burning one for this and the final phases of structural renewal of the Office.[35]

Preceding the ninth plenary session, the Group of Relators met from November 14 to 20, 1967. On November 15 a special Group of Relators met under the presidency of Bishop Spulbeck (Meissen, East Germany) to consider how to manage the *modi* (proposals or suggestions for modification) regarding liturgical reform presented by the synod for consideration by the Consilium. Four criteria were adopted: (1) Individual *modi* will be considered, with reasons for and against them, so that a proposed solution may be offered; (2) *modi* requesting anything against SC or documents implementing it are not to be considered; (3) *modi* repeating in words the same as or similar to those in a given proposition will be counted as positive votes. *Modi* absolutely against the proposition in question will be counted as negative votes; and (4) individual *modi* need not be discussed in a plenary session of the Consilium but only those of great importance or to which a number of bishops have subscribed. These would be such as to provoke reconsideration of some of the reform plans already approved by the Consilium.[36]

Members and consultors gathered in Rome for the ninth plenary session from November 21 to 28, 1967. Among items in the secretary's report were mention of the establishment of a new study group, Group 12*bis*, for formation of the *preces* or intercessions that were to be included in Lauds and Vespers and the preparation of the volume containing the proposed hymns for the Office. A major part of the report, however, was devoted to the response of the Synod of Bishops to the questions on liturgical reform. Father Bugnini indicated that the response was somewhat unfavorable. He blamed the lack of experts present at the synod, an incomplete vision of the problems, confusion between arbitrary experiments and those controlled by the Consilium, and various defamatory campaigns in the press for negatively influencing the synod. He suggested it would be necessary to examine seriously and attentively the *modi* and various proposals submitted by the bishops. It is not altogether clear why Father Bugnini's report characterized the bishops' response as unfavorable when the results of the voting were largely supportive of the reform as approved by the Consilium. Father Bugnini's pastoral sense may have inclined him to view even the positions of the Consilium on some matters as favoring preservation of certain traditional elements in the liturgy—elements the preservation of which would not meet contemporary pastoral needs. Thus the synod would be supporting a somewhat narrow, traditionalistic reform. Evidence of this mentality in Father Bugnini will be adduced below.[37]

The ninth plenary session devoted the greater part of its meetings to examination of the synod's *modi* on the Mass and the Office. Among other items considered, two new matters regarding the Office were reviewed, namely, the work of Group 12*bis* on the *preces* for Lauds and Vespers and the problem of uniting organically an Hour of the Office with Mass. The Council of the Presidency, meeting on November 23, tried to resolve the emerging problem of the size and number of books foreseen for the Office. It appeared that because of the voluminous amount of material it would not be possible to publish the Office in two volumes as some had hoped. Four hefty volumes, it seemed, would scarcely contain the text of the revised Office. That prospect, contended some, would be discouraging to the clergy *(sic)* who were already abandoning the Office and impelling bishops to insist on the need to hasten the reform. Some proposed a revision of the work already done on the Office to reduce its quantity, but a decision was postponed.[38]

During both the meeting of the consultors and that of the plenary assembly, the second specimen of the revised Office provided by its use a further basis on which to judge the adequacy of the proposed reforms. Entitled "Specimen Divini Officii pro diebus a 12 ad 25 novembris 1967," it was arranged according to the scheme of the revised calendar approved by the Consilium, contained elements borrowed from the current Breviary where revisions were not yet ready, and, like the previous specimen, presented in brackets those psalm verses considered imprecatory. Use of this specimen, however, did not entirely precede consideration of questions on the Office as did use of the previous specimen in the spring, for discussion and voting on the various proposals for the continuing work on the Office took place on November 22 and 23, whereas use of the specimen continued through November 25.[39]

Two developments, which were to come to term only in 1968–69 but which in progress following the ninth plenary session, had significant impact, the one on the liturgical reform generally, the other on the structure of the Office. The first was the reform of the Curia, which Paul VI began to consider in 1966 and which he decreed in the apostolic constitution *Regimini Ecclesiae* of August 15, 1967. Submitting in 1966 at papal request a project for its own reform, SCR described the Consilium as a technical organ for reform of the liturgical books but left to the cardinals of the congregation the great decisions concerning the reform. Even in the galley proofs for *Regimini Ecclesiae* the *members* of the Consilium were said to be *periti* or expert consultants for SCR. The definitive text, however, did state accurately what the relationship would be of the Consilium to the reformed SCR (henceforth to be simply Congregation of Rites). Revision of the liturgical books and execution of the liturgical reform were to continue to be the responsibility of the Consilium. Its final decisions, however, were to be submitted to a plenary session of the worship section of the congregation. *Consultants* of the Consilium would be *periti* of the congregation. This reform, however, was to be but the first step in a more radical restructuring of both the Consilium and the congregation that proceeded through 1968 into 1969 and that will be considered below among developments in the third and final phase of the reform.

The second development following the ninth plenary session, more directly affecting reform of the Office, began with the submission to the Pope on December 10, 1967, of a *relatio* concerning the action of the ninth session. According to Archbishop Bugnini, the "presidency" of the Consilium sent a note along with the *relatio* concerning the issue of the imprecatory and historical psalms in the Office. The note explained that although the Consilium had decided that all the psalms should be kept in the ordinary cycle, it should be evident that the number of those desiring only a selection of psalms and the reservation of the imprecatory and historical psalms to certain times of the year had increased over the last few years. Various arguments were presented for the removal altogether from the *cursus* of imprecatory psalms and verses as well as of historical psalms. Then, curiously, it was said that "the secretariat" desired the Pope to give his thought on the matter. It is not clear whether one should understand this seemingly unwarranted intervention as coming from the presidential council, Cardinal Lercaro himself, the cardinal and Father Bugnini, or the secretary himself. But the fact that the Pope is told in the letter that the "secretariat" desired his response and the fact that Father Bugnini advocated "pastoral positions" as opposed to "traditional positions" throughout the reform leads one to believe that he was the principal behind this move. The Pope's response and subsequent developments belong to the story of the third phase.[40]

THIRD PHASE (1968–1971)

The final phase of the work of the Consilium and Group 9 on revision of the Office saw (1) the restructuring of the Consilium itself, (2) the struggle over inclusion of the integral Psalter in the revised Office intensified and concluded, (3) the preparation and promulgation of the General Instruction on the Liturgy of the Hours, (4) a worldwide consultation of bishops on the reformed Office, (5) various regional experiments with the revised Office, and (6) the publication of the definitive *Liturgia Horarum*. Each of these developments can perhaps best be understood in the context of the chronology of this phase.

The curial reform, already alluded to, was to have been effected on January 1, 1968. In December 1967 however, the Pope postponed the effective date to March 1, 1968. On January 9 of that year, perhaps anticipating the later restructuring of SCR and the Consilium, Paul VI accepted the resignation of Cardinal Lercaro as president of the Consilium on the grounds of ill health and asked Cardinal Larraona to resign as prefect of SCR. On the same day he appointed Cardinal Benno Gut, former abbot primate of the Benedictines and member of the Consilium, as president of that body and as prefect of SCR. This move, according to Archbishop Bugnini, helped ease the tension and promote collaboration between the two entities.[41]

A few days earlier the Pope had responded to the request of the "secretariat" of the Consilium that he open his mind on the matter of retaining the whole Psalter in the Ordinary cycle of the Office. In an autograph note given to Father Bugnini on January 3 he said:

"In my view it is preferable that a selection be made of psalms better suited to Christian prayer and that the imprecatory and historical psalms be omitted (though these last may be suitably used in certain circumstances)."[42]

On January 30 the presidential council met with the new president and decided to deliver to Canon Martimort through Bishop Boudon a photocopy of the Pope's note to Father Bugnini together with a letter from Cardinal Gut. In his letter the cardinal said in part:

"At its meeting of January 30 the presidential council gratefully acknowledged that the Holy Father had deigned *to decide* a question so long debated, and it asked His Excellency Msgr. René Boudon to bring this letter to you.

"The Holy Father's *decision* will discomfit the group that has done such fine work on the distribution of the psalms, but I am sure that it will make the needed revisions with its customary generosity, even if also with no little sacrifice."[43]

Group 9 met in Genoa from February 27 to March 1, 1968, to prepare for the tenth plenary session of the Consilium. Among the numerous items considered for reform of the Office at that meeting was again the question of retaining the imprecatory and historical psalms in the ordinary cycle. Canon Martimort, in a report dated February 20, 1968, disclosed the Pope's very words to Father Bugnini on the matter, reviewed the whole history of the debate on it, and respectfully indicated the perils involved in agreeing to the Pope's suggestion. While Group 9 was willing to acquiesce in the Pope's preference, it is evident that the papal note was not considered as having *decided* the issue, as Cardinal Gut maintained in his letter to Canon Martimort. A solution, discussed below in chapter 4, in keeping with the Pope's opinion was agreed to if it became necessary to accept his suggestion, but the group proposed reexamination of the whole question by the Consilium. At this meeting, also, Canon Martimort outlined for the first time a scheme for the *Institutio generalis* (General Instruction) to preface the revised Office. He asked for contributions to its composition from all those responsible for the various aspects of the new Office.[44]

The Group of Relators meeting in Rome from April 14 to 22, 1968, heard Canon Martimort read three typewritten pages (Schema 288, addendum) defending the position already adopted regarding the imprecatory and historical psalms but outlining a proposal for complying with the Pope's suggestion should that be necessary. After discussion of the matter, the relators voted in favor of presenting to the Pope the previously accepted solution to the problem of the imprecatory and historical psalms because, it was said, he might not have been presented with a full explanation of that solution. If it was still not agreeable to him, then the alternate solution proposed by Group 9 could be presented. When this matter came to the tenth plenary session (April 23–30, 1968) the members by a large majority supported the positions of Group 9 and of the Group of Relators. The *relatio* of May 10, 1968, however, in which Father Bugnini reported to the Pope the action taken in the tenth plenary session, contained, remarkably, Father Bugnini's personal observations on the arguments for and against retention of all psalms in the ordinary cycle. He took and advocated a position, contrary to that adopted by the Consilium, that would exclude three so-called imprecatory psalms, imprecatory verses of other psalms, and the so-called historical psalms from the ordinary cycle. The position advocated by Father Bugnini was accepted by the Pope in an audience granted to the secretary on May 18, 1968. Cardinal Gut conveyed the Pope's desire to Canon Martimort in a letter dated June 7, 1968:

"He [the Pope] desires that there be omitted from the ordinary cycle of the psalter in their entirety the 'imprecatory' psalms, namely, psalms 57, 82, and 108 and those parts [of psalms] which had been proposed as optional and therefore were to be included in parentheses. The psalms, however, which are called 'historical' may be kept for certain special times."[45]

Father Bugnini's seemingly bold and unwarranted interventions against the majority opinion of the Consilium might be attributed to his belief that he knew the mind of the Pope on the matter and that the Pope's every wish should be assented to by members and consultors of the Consilium. When one adds to these the secretary's personal inclination toward pastoral solutions, his ready access (as secretary of the Consilium) to the Pope, his understanding of his secretarial role, the dependence of the Consilium directly on the Pope, and the lack of a juridical framework within which the Consilium might operate, one can at least begin to understand both how Father Bugnini could have intervened as he did in good faith and how his interventions could pass without formal protest from the Consilium.

But clearly Father Bugnini's forcefulness and at least some of his wishes irked Canon Martimort. The latter has said that it was not clear whether the wishes fostered by the secretary came from him or from the Pope. In Canon Martimort's opinion many of them were unsound from the perspective of liturgical tradition. What Group 9 strove to do, he said, was to assist the Pope to understand as clearly as possibie the reasons for what the group was proposing. This the consultors tried to do circumspectly, since, not having direct access to the Pope, they did not know for certain the origin of his suggestions.[46]

Besides the major question on the psalms, the tenth plenary session also discussed the matters of the obligation of the Office and the organic union of Mass and Office. Other minor questions (various elements and aspects of the Office of Readings, the *preces* [intercessions] at Lauds and Vespers, and the relationship of the Lord's Prayer to the *preces*) were remanded to a special committee of members and consultors. The scheme for the General Instruction was presented and approved.[47]

Group 9 met in Verona from July 16 to 19, 1968. There Canon Martimort informed the consultors of the Pope's decision regarding the psalms, and work proceeded on the General Instruction. Canon Martimort had complained to his colleagues in Group 9 that he was not receiving quickly enough from them the material they had promised for the General Instruction, but by the time of the meeting in Verona he had ready a forty-page typewritten draft of the instruction for the group to discuss. The questions of the name to be given the revised Office and of the structure of Compline as well as a host of details regarding elements in the various Hours were also considered at this meeting.[48]

Preceding the eleventh plenary session of the Consilium, Canon Martimort prepared another draft of the General Instruction (July–August 1968) with the assistance of the consultors for the Office. The plenary session, preceded by the meeting of the Group of Relators (October 1–7, 1968), was held from October 8 to 17. Since the major structural elements of the Office had now been agreed to, discussion of proposals on the Office focused on the General Instruction (and within it particularly on the obligation to the Office) and the possibility of allowing episcopal conferences to use the new distribution of the Psalter on an experimental basis before publication of the revised Office.[49]

A period of wider consultation on and experimentation with the revised Office was ushered in by the request of the French episcopate, meeting at Lourdes from November 2 to 9, 1968, to use the texts of the Office prepared by the Consilium before publication of the *editio typica.* The Consilium, apparently through the presidential council, on January 3, 1969, submitted its opinion on the request to the secretary of state: The printing in French of the four-week Psalter as approved by the Consilium could be permitted provided the experiment with it was the responsibility of the French bishops and conducted only until the publication of the typical Latin edition. Since many of the texts for the new Office were not yet ready, the missing parts would have to be taken from the current Office. The secretary of state, in a letter to Cardinal Gut (January 22, 1969), left the matter to the prudent judgment of SCR and the Consilium. On January 31, in an audience with Father Bugnini, the Pope allowed that the concession could be given to all French-speaking episcopal conferences. Within the next two days Cardinal Gut approved norms for the experiment and signed a letter granting the concession. The Centre National de Pastorale Liturgique de France (CNPL) prepared the text for the experiment and on May 26, 1969, sent it to the Consilium for approval.

At this time the Consilium was just undergoing insertion as a special commission into the new *Congregatio pro Cultu Divino* (Congregation for Divine Worship). This fact may account for the delay in approval (July 19, 1969) of the French experiment. On July 4, 1970, *Prière du temps présent: Le nouvel Office Divin* was published in Paris, and the 50,000 copies then produced needed by October of that year to be augmented by 100,000 more. A questionnaire requesting laity, religious, and priests to give their impressions of the Office was printed at the end of the volume. The response to it, according to CNPL, was overwhelmingly favorable. The success of the French experiment encouraged other episcopal conferences to attempt the same. Within a few months of the start of the French project Holland, Spain, Germany, England, and Brazil each had an experimental edition in the language of the respective country.[50]

Meanwhile, Paul VI had decided (December 1968) to send to all the bishops of the world and to all superiors general of religious congregations a sample of the new Office with the request that they examine the norms and the Office itself—the bishops with their presbyteral councils, other priests, and qualified lay people; the religious superiors with members of their congregations. Observations were to be sent to the Consilium. The Pope approved the sample, entitled "Descriptio et specimina Officii Divini," on January 17, 1969, and the small printed volume was issued on the following January 29. It contained a description of the new Office and its complete text for February 1 (then the memorial of St. Ignatius of Antioch) and February 3 *(Feria II hebdomadae IV "per annum")*. The Consilium received 873 responses regarding the sample, most of which indicated satisfaction. The Pope received a compilation of the responses on January 2, 1970. These responses, in the hands of the consultors of Group 9, induced some changes in the draft of the General Instruction, particularly about the obligation to the Office and about the names and conclusions of the Hours.[51]

Another of the Pope's initiatives during this phase of reform, although it had a profound effect on the constituency and operation of the Consilium, did not substantially affect the remainder of the process by which the structure of the reformed Office took shape. On April 5, 1969, Paul VI received from an unnamed source a request that the two sections of SCR be separated into two distinct congregations within the Curia, one congregation for worship, the other for causes of the saints. Cardinal Lercaro had expressed a similar desire in 1965. In a consistory held on the following April 28, the Pope announced the creation of the *Congregatio pro Culto Divino* (CCD) distinct from a separate congregation for causes of the saints. The Consilium was to be absorbed into the CCD as *Commissio specialis ad instaurationem liturgicam absolvendam*. The Pope gave as his reason for the change the central importance of liturgy in the life of the Church, which demanded one central organism uniquely dedicated to promoting the prayer of the Church. Thus through the apostolic constitution *Sacra Rituum Congregatio* of May 8, 1969, the new congregation, headed by Cardinal Gut, was established effective immediately. The Consilium, however, did not cease to function in its accustomed way until April 1970 because the apostolic constitution had specified that for the purpose of completing the liturgical reform the CCD "may for the present make use of the members and *periti* of the Consilium."

The document further specified that the diocesan bishops (usually *appointed* to a curial congregation) who were to be members of CCD would, at the start of this new congregation, be *elected* by and from the membership of the Consilium. The election called for a plenary session, the next one of which would normally occur in the autumn of 1969. Thus it was that the Group of Relators met from November 4 to 8, 1969, and the twelfth plenary session gathered, one year since the last plenary session, from November 10 to 14. No meeting had been held the preceeding spring because of the amount of work both the study groups and the secretariat had to accomplish as most of the reformed rites entered the final stage of preparation. Group 9 had met three times since the eleventh plenary session, primarily to perfect the draft of the General Instruction. Several questions, most on relatively minor aspects of the Office as these were stated in the draft of the instruction, were asked of the assembly. Perhaps the major question concerned the title to be given to the revised Office. Group 9 proposed *Liturgia Horarum* as one that would foster an understanding of the Office as a true liturgical action and clearly indicate the action as related to times of day and night. But other titles were considered: *Liber Officii Divini, Liber precum, Liber precum sacerdotalium, Officium Divinum,* and *Liber Liturgiae Horarum.* Those containing the word *Officium* were dropped because the term seemed too generic. There was general agreement that the "hourly" character of the prayer should be indicated, but the use of *Liber* in the title seemed, according to Archbishop Bugnini's account, a throwback to medieval terminology. Thus *Liturgia Horarum* prevailed.

The session also confirmed the two-year cycle of biblical readings and the one-year cycle of patristic readings for the Office. It then elected seven of its episcopal members to serve in the new congregation, as had been stipulated in *Sacra Rituum Congregatio.* The full membership of the abolished Consilium, however, met for a thirteenth and final plenary session from April 9 to 10, 1970. Now known officially as *Commissio specialis ad instaurationem liturgicam absolvendam,* yet meeting in fact as the Consilium, it took final action on the General Instruction and sent it on for scrutiny and approval to the Congregations for the Doctrine of the Faith, for Clergy, for Catholic Education, for Religious, and for the Evangelization of Peoples. It also recommended the publication of the revised Office in *two* volumes. When the first plenary congregation of the new CCD met from November 10 to 13, 1970, the difference between its *modus operandi*, governed by the rules for curial congregations, and that of the Consilium was evident particularly in the reduced number of members meeting by themselves without the presence of the consultors. But by this time the questions on the structure of the Office, even to most of its details, had been settled.[52]

After its passage through the various curial congregations, the General Instruction reached the Pope on March 3, 1970. The Pope examined it carefully over a period of several months, conferring with Father Bugnini on a number of points in it. By September 1970 the Pope had approved all parts of the document. On November 1, 1970, Paul VI promulgated the new *Liturgia Horarum* by the apostolic constitution *Laudis canticum*. The work of producing the volumes of LH, however, was attended with numerous problems, and so the publication of both *Laudis canticum* and the General Instruction was delayed until February 2, 1971. According to Archbishop Bugnini, it was he who persuaded the Pope to Issue the General Instruction before the first volume of LH was ready for publication so that all in the Church might be prepared for the reformed Office when it eventually became available.[53]

The final process by which the four volumes of LH were produced was slower than anticipated. Group 9 prepared the text for printing, and even in that process found that some material or provisions had been overlooked, so last-minute, on-the-spot decisions had to be made. Canon Martimort has related that he, Fr. Joseph Pascher, Prof. Emil Lengeling, and others met in the archbishop's palace in Turin and there assembled the texts for the Office on an immense table. At times they discovered something was missing (e.g., a form of *Sunday* Compline for Saturday night after *Sunday* Evening Prayer I had been used on Saturday evening) and had to supply it then and there. The recommendation of the Consilium (April 1970) for publication of the Office in two volumes had to be abandoned because, according to Archbishop Bugnini, one volume would contain the readings, the second volume, the other parts of the Office. Thinking again primarily of "private recitation," priests, and those obliged to the Office, he noted that such an arrangement requiring the use of both volumes at every use would simply be discouraging and impractical. The CCD then proposed publication in four volumes. The secretary of state approved this arrangement on August 22, 1970.

Father Bugnini, in a memo (March 27, 1971) to Canon Martimort, various Latinists, and correctors of proofs, indicated the desire to have all volumes published within 1971. But the Vatican printing office encountered problems, and in June 1971 it informed Father Bugnini that it was impossible to print as desired the two-year cycle of biblical readings within the compass of the projected four volumes. Apparently, among at least Father Bugnini, Canon Martimort, and Professor Lengeling (relator of Group 4, biblical readings), a decision was made to select texts randomly from the two-year cycle to construct a one-year cycle of biblical readings. These would be printed in the Office of Readings in their appropriate places throughout the four volumes. The texts of the two-year cycle would be relegated to a supplementary volume to be produced sometime later. The choice was made hurriedly and to no one's satisfaction, but the final printing and binding of LH then proceeded. Volume 1 *(Tempus adventus–Tempus nativitatis)* appeared in July 1971; Volume 2 *(Tempus quadragesimae–Tempus paschale)*, in December 1971; Volume 3 *(Tempus per annum–Hebdomadae I–XVII)*, in April 1972; Volume 4 *(Tempus per annum–Hebdomadae XVIII–XXXIV)*, in July 1972. Each volume followed the same order: proper of time, ordinary, Psalter in four weeks, Compline of one week, complementary psalmody for the minor Hours, proper of saints, commons, and an appendix giving various introductory formulae for the Lord's Prayer and short formulae for the *preces* at Lauds and Vespers. Volume 1 contained, additionally, the apostolic constitution *Laudis canticum* and the General Instruction.[54]

The processes by which the Consilium and Group 9 were constituted and by which they interacted in the reform of the structure of the Office were thus uneven, not to say at times tumultuous or unnerving ones. A full critique of these processes will be given in chapter 6. A closer consideration will now be given to the restructuring of the Office as a whole.

Chapter 4

The Structure of the Hours as a Whole

Fundamental principles for the structural reform of the entire Office are given in SC 88, 89, 91, and 94. Group 9, after briefly entertaining a proposal for a very radical revision of the Office, adhered rigorously to these principles in its revision of the structure of the Office.[1] After a brief reference to these principles consideration will be given here to those questions that were major in the process of revising the structure of the Office as a whole: (1) the proposals for radical revision of the Office, (2) the relationship of the Hours to one another, (3) the essential elements of the Hours, (4) the distribution and division of the psalms, (5) the structuring of an Hour of the Office when it is joined to another liturgical action, (6) the position of the hymn in all the Hours. For each of these issues there will be presented, insofar as they are known, (1) the principal options proposed, (2) the major arguments for or against them, and (3) the final decisions and their bases.

The basic principles for structural reform provided in SC included the suppression of Prime and the distribution of the psalms throughout a longer period of time than one week.[2] Another basic principle in SC, namely, that the Hours be prayed, if possible, at times most closely corresponding to their true canonical time (the principle of *veritas horarum*) played, as will be seen, a subtle role in some questions regarding the structure of the Hours as a whole.[3] These fundamental principles of SC for structural reform were seriously questioned early (1964–66) in the process of reform by proposals for a more radical reform of the Office than that envisioned by the framers of SC.[4]

THE PROPOSALS FOR RADICAL REVISION OF THE OFFICE

Two proposals for radical reform of the Office were considered by Group 9. The first proposal came from Fr. Juan Mateos, S.J., professor at the Pontifical Oriental Institute in Rome and consultor to the Consilium, though not a member of any of the study groups charged with reform of the Office.[5] The second proposal, which stemmed, like the first, from the suggestions for revision or modification (the *emendationes* and the *modi*) submitted on the drafts of SC, called for the creation of a double Office—one choral for contemplatives, the other presumably private for those living an active life.[6] Both proposals were considered by Group 9 in 1964. Father Mateos' proposal was rejected relatively soon in the discussion of structural reform on the grounds that it deviated from what SC had decreed concerning the reform of the Office.[7] The second proposal in its various forms was debated until the end of 1966, when it was dropped in favor of restoring one form of the Roman Office adaptable to the needs of various and diverse groups within the Church.[8] It is useful to examine in some detail both of these proposals because, although both were eventually rejected, certain aspects of them were incorporated into the definitive structure of the Hours. These aspects might not have been so incorporated had the proposals not been made as forcefully as they were.[9]

The first proposal to be considered, that of Father Mateos, called for the restoration of the so-called cathedral or ecclesiastical Office, that is, the Office of lay people and their clergy in parochial churches of the Mediterranean world in the fourth and later centuries. Father Mateos, a specialist in Eastern liturgies, first presented his recommendation in response to a series of thirty-three questions proposed to the Consilium in Schema 6 on April 18, 1964, by Canon Martimort. The second of these questions posed to all members of the Consilium seems to be the one that provoked Father Mateos' proposal: "*Question:* Is it necessary to adapt Lauds and Vespers (*Const.* art. 89a), especially when they are celebrated with the people or in a parish church? (art. 100). If so, how?"[10]

Father Mateos' suggestions were preceded by some ten typewritten pages of information on the origins of Lauds and Vespers—the whole submitted as "Adnotationes ad schema 31, De Breviario 10."[11] The Latin text of this unpublished document bears the date November 22, 1964. This is just over two months after the dissemination of Schema 31 (September 14, 1964), in which the results of the work in various study groups responding to the questions in

Schema 6 (April 17, 1964) were reported to the Consilium. The late submission by Father Mateos suggests that he is responding not only to the questions posed in April but also to the report in Schema 31 of the discussions of the consultors on the reform of the Office, especially the reform of Lauds and Vespers. In that report the results of a discussion on the question of how Lauds should be adapted for celebration with the people is summarized as follows:

"To this question the experts gave a negative reply. For indeed, Lauds is less popular and will remain less popular than Vespers, especially because it is celebrated in the morning. Those who are present for Lauds are few, and they are the flower of the faithful who are able to sing five psalms devoutly. In fact, as one of us has testified, they are content with the current structure of Lauds. So it would be useless to draw up a special scheme for Lauds."[12]

Thus most of the consultors (apparently of Group 9) were opposed to a special scheme for Lauds rendering it more accessible to laity generally.[13]

The summary of the discussion on a similar question regarding Vespers indicated there was a desire among some consultors to draw up a double scheme for that Hour. This scheme was outlined as follows:

Vespers without the People	Vespers Celebrated with the People
five psalms	three of five psalms
short reading	longer reading
	homily
other parts (hymn, canticle, intercessions)	other parts[14]

Consultors speaking of the special scheme for Vespers when "the people" would be present acknowledged certain difficulties with their proposal, especially that it would introduce a "separation . . . between the prayer of the people and the prayer of the clergy." It would, they added, depart from the monastic structure of Vespers and return

"to a structure which is called 'cathedral' and which is kept in 'Great Vespers' of the Byzantine Rite or in Vigils of the Ambrosian Rite where, clearly, more readings and less psalmody are present."[15]

Undoubtedly sensing confusion in the minds of some of the consultors regarding both the former popular character of Lauds and the nature of cathedral Vespers, Father Mateos makes it clear in his submission that both the morning and evening Offices in antiquity were celebrated by people with clergy, that both of these Offices were distinct from a monastic Office, and that not only were there no long readings in cathedral Vespers, but there were seldom readings at all.[16] Father Mateos put the heart of his proposal thus:

"In the liturgical restoration, which has a pastoral emphasis, it seems that the ecclesiastical Offices destined for the laity ought to be highlighted by clearly distinguishing them from the monastic Offices. They ought to have a structure suitable for celebration with the laity and fit for nourishing Christian life among them.

". . . The *cursus* or Breviary consisting of two daily Offices, one in the morning and one in the evening, is universal and ordinary practice in the Church. The *cursus* of seven or eight Hours is exceptional, neither universal nor ordinary. It is a *cursus* for those who live an ascetical or contemplative life.

"So our second conclusion is that the two cathedral Offices ought to be proper not only for the Christian laity but also for the secular clergy. If the rest of the monastic Hours are not celebrated in the parish churches, the secular clergy ought not to be obliged to celebrate these Hours. An exception might be made for that spiritual reading drawn from the former night Office.

"For this usage to flourish there is need that Lauds and Vespers not merely be recited but truly be celebrated with some participation of the faithful. For if the celebration of each Office with the people would become the rule, the clergy would easily and fittingly utilize the time needed for daily liturgical prayer by celebrating these Hours with the people and, from another point of view, they would be using the Divine Office in a pastoral way.

"It might also be allowed that some readings from Sacred Scripture, drawn from the Office of Readings (former Nocturns), could be read publicly in Offices with the laity, but this could be done at the choice of those celebrating and as time allowed."[17]

This proposal for a restoration of a cathedral Office—basically a Morning Prayer and an Evening Prayer for people and the diocesan clergy—went counter to the prescriptions of SC, chapter 4, which anticipated a retention and reform of all the Hours of the current Roman Office with the exception of Prime.[18]

When asked by this author if he understood that the implementation of his proposal would require papal intervention, since it went beyond the prescriptions of SC, Father Mateos replied affirmatively. He was quick to add, however, that in his opinion a very traditionalist mentality was operative among most of the consultors charged with preparing the reform of the Office. They were primarily concerned with the Breviary as "priestly prayer—priestly, private prayer. . . . They were worried about the spirituality of priests."[19]

Father Mateos attempted to enlighten the minds of the consultors by uncovering the origins of the Office as prayer of all Christians. He deemed an awareness of liturgical practice and developments in the East essential for an authentic pastoral reform of the Roman liturgy, an awareness he judged lacking in the consultors of the study groups reworking the Roman Office, whose concern often seemed to be with details of rites traceable in Western liturgical sources only to the earliest of these texts in the seventh or eighth century. What was needed, he maintained, was not the preservation of liturgical details as these appear in the sources of one portion of the Church but the capturing of a spirit evident in the ancient common tradition of the liturgies of the Churches in both East and West and an attempt to revive that spirit in rites appropriate to the needs of people today.[20]

When Group 9 met on March 1 and 2, 1965, to discuss the work to date on the Office done by the various study groups, Father Mateos' proposal was considered in connection with Msgr. Joseph Pascher's report on the distribution of the psalms for the Hours. No indication is given in the schema reporting the action of this meeting as to what extent Father Mateos' proposal was discussed. It is simply noted:

"The members did not accept the proposition of Father Mateos regarding the reduction of the Office for diocesan clergy to Lauds and Vespers because the task of the commission is to apply the liturgical constitution, which has established the *cursus* of the

Hours, not to change it. A certain member said that the constitution has already satisfied exigencies springing from the ancient cathedral Morning and Evening Prayers by declaring these Hours the hinge of the entire Office."[21]

Thus, what must be called a strict interpretation by Group 9 of SC prevented further consideration of Father Mateos' proposal. Elements implicit in his proposal, however, survived. Some consideration will be given below and in chapter 5 to these (e.g., Ps 62 [63] as the morning psalm in Morning Prayer, Sunday, Week I; Ps 140 [141] as the evening psalm par excellence at the beginning of Sunday Evening Prayer I, Week I; greater provision for popular participation at Lauds and Vespers, and intercessions at those Hours).[22]

The rejection of his proposal did not, however, deter Father Mateos from offering another piece of advice. Issued as an appendix to Schema 68 was a five-page summary of the history of the cathedral Vigil of the Resurrection with a recommendation for its revival in the Roman Office. These "Adnotationes circa Officium Dominicae seu de Vigilia Cathedrali" (April 5, 1965) were offered as a suggestion for fulfilling SC, chapter 5, articles 102 and 106. Father Mateos states his purpose thus:

"According to the conciliar Constitution on the Sacred Liturgy (chapter 5, nos. 102, 106), Sunday ought to stand out among the days of the week as the day consecrated to the remembrance of the paschal mystery, as the weekly Pasch.

"It will be useful, therefore, to consider what the ancient Church did to highlight the special character of this day."[23]

After briefly recounting the origin and diffusion of this Office as witnessed in Egeria's diary, the Chaldean, Armenian, Byzantine, and Ambrosian Rites, and in the Benedictine tradition, Father Mateos offers his recommendation:

"It is not to be denied that the cathedral Vigil was an Office of great pastoral value due to its simple and profound signification. It preserves, besides, the paschal character of Sunday even though, as is appropriate, the formula of Mass follows the temporal cycle. Its brevity and variety of elements also commend it. It would easily be possible to construct at least four different formulas consisting of a selection of canticles and paschal psalms related to the four gospel pericopes that narrate the resurrection appearance to the women.

"The restoration of the cathedral Vigil would not be the introduction of some novelty in the Roman Office, but a true restoration of an ancient Office still in existence by giving it again the scope that it formerly had.

"The celebration of this Office could be recommended on Sunday mornings before Lauds but without considering it obligatory either in public celebration or private recitation."[24]

While there is no indication in the schemata of any discussion in Group 9 of Father Mateos' suggestion, Canon Martimort proposed in September 1966 an expansion of the Office of Readings for the Vigils of Sundays along the lines of the ancient cathedral Vigil. The details of this will be discussed below in the consideration of the structure of the Office of Readings.[25] To what extent Father Mateos' proposal was utilized in Canon Martimort's recommendation is unclear, but the structure and content of the ancient Vigil, as outlined by Father Mateos, are well represented in Canon Martimort's proposal.[26] Whereas Father Mateos proposed the restoration of the Vigil as a *popular* Hour of the Office, however, Canon Martimort proposed his version of a Vigil for the use primarily of contemplatives and those who have the leisure on Sunday for a more protracted celebration of Vigils.[27]

Thus, Father Mateos' second proposal, namely, to restore the Sunday Vigil of the Resurrection as a popular Office, like his first proposal regarding Lauds and Vespers, died an early death in Group 9. An evaluation of Father Mateos' contribution is reserved to chapter 6. Here it must be noted that his suggestions regarding Lauds and Vespers were not without connection to a second major proposal, to be considered now, regarding radical reform of the Office—a proposal that occupied Group 9 and the Consilium for some two years.

This second major proposal called for two forms of the Office. One would be choral, intended primarily for monastic or semi-monastic groups; the other, for those in the "active life"—diocesan clergy, laity, and so on. The proposal sprang from a question put to the Consilium by Canon Martimort at the beginning of the work on reform (April 1964):

"Question: Should the reform of the Office be extended to the choral Office, that for monks, or should a double Office be established, one choral for contemplatives and the other for those who lead an active life?"[28]

The sources of this question were the explanations of the *emendationes* to article 89 of chapter 4 in SC proposed by the conciliar commission on the liturgy and presented to the council members in the *relatio* of Bishop J. Albert Martin on October 21, 1963, and the responses of the commission to the *modi* of the council members pertaining to article 89 presented to the council by Bishop Martin on November 22, 1963.[29] When Group 9 met on September 14, 1964, the focus of the answer to this question was on Lauds and Vespers. As noted above, the group rejected the formulation of a special scheme for Lauds.[30] A lengthy discussion ensued, then, on whether or not to provide two schemes for Vespers. A more detailed consideration of this discussion will be given below in this chapter regarding the structural reform of Vespers in relation to the other Hours, but it is important to note here that while the original question was not really being addressed in this discussion, the evident tendency to create *two forms* for Vespers, one for clergy and one for use when laity were present, had bearing on the need to provide for different groups praying the Office, as did the proposal to have two forms of the Office as a whole.[31]

There followed, as explained in chapter 3, the publication in *Notitiae* in 1965 of reports on the work of various study groups, the outcry by a number of scholars and members of the Consilium against the direction this work was taking, and the ensuing questionnaire of December 1965 for members and consultors of the Consilium to assist in determining the direction the work should take.[32] The first three questions of that inquiry dealt with the problem of whether there should be one or several forms of the Office. Fr. Annibale Bugnini, compiler of the questionnaire, prefaced the inquiries with some important comments on the implications of SC 90:

"Article 90 of the Constitution foresaw that 'in the revision of the Roman Office its age-old treasure be so adapted that all those to whom it is handed on may more extensively and more easily enjoy it.' According to the Constitution itself, participation in the public prayer of the Church includes, besides clerics in holy orders and religious bound to it by their constitutions, all religious (art. 98) and lay people themselves (art. 100)."[33]

Father Bugnini thus recalled to members and consultors of the Consilium crucial articles of SC that should direct the reform of the Office so that it benefits *all* in the Church. He then posed the three questions in the light of best fulfilling article 90 as he had just interpreted it:

"1. Does it seem sufficient to prepare a normative Breviary for the whole Church and afterwards adapt it in various ways to different groups and circumstances?

   or rather

"2. Does it seem better to prepare different forms of the Divine Office, namely, one for choral recitation, one for the clergy having pastoral care, and one for lay people?

"3. Does it seem appropriate that even other forms should be provided, for example, 'little Offices' for parish communities to be used by clergy and people praying together?"[34]

In May 1966 when tabulation of the responses to the questionnaire had been completed, the results of voting on these questions were as follows (I.M. = *iuxta modum*, or yes with reservations):

	Yes	No	I.M.
Question 1 (Normative Breviary)			
Members	10	11	2
Consultors	8	5	9
Question 2 (Diverse Offices)			
Members	10	11	1
Consultors	6	11	6

Question 3
(Parochial Offices)

	Yes	No	I.M.
Members	7	16	-
Consultors	12	13	-

The consultors showed themselves slightly more favorable to the preparation of one Office adaptable to various groups (Question 1) than to various forms of the Office for differing needs (Question 2). They were almost equally divided on the question of providing short Offices or Breviaries for use in parishes by clergy and people together (Question 3). The members, however, were slightly more inclined to provide a variety of Offices to meet the needs of different groups. The small number of respondents and the inconclusive nature of the voting led Canon Martimort to ask if this opinion could really serve as a guide for the reform.[35]

After some months of personal study and reflection (as described in ch. 3), Canon Martimort communicated his views (in RG and SRG) on the issues to his colleagues in Group 9.[36] In giving his personal answer to the question of whether there should be one or several Breviaries, he noted, first of all, that the three questions on the December questionnaire seemed to represent an oversimplification of a problem dealt with by both the preconciliar preparatory liturgical Commission and the conciliar liturgical commission itself. He then attempted to formulate the difficulty as he saw it: (1) There exist in the Church different Offices acording to rites (Byzantine, Chaldean, Syrian, Maronite, etc.). In the West there are the Ambrosian, Mozarabic, monastic and Roman Breviaries. A number of communities "living a full monastic life" (specified as Carmelites, Augustinians, Dominicans, etc.) use the Roman Office or a variant of it. (2) There exist other forms of communal prayer (Rosary, Office of the Blessed Virgin Mary, etc.) utilized by religious congregations, especially those founded since the seventeenth century. Furthermore, for the last thirty years there have existed short Offices (or short Breviaries) modeled on the Roman Office but briefer and celebrated in the vernacular. (3) The traditional Office itself can be executed in three very different ways: chorally with solemnity, communally with simple recitation, or privately. (4) The rubrics of the Roman Office indicate that the group celebrating the Office is not an assembly of the faithful over whom preside the hierarchy but a "couvent," a group of clerics or monks whose president is an officiant *(hebdomadarius)*, a "first among equals" *(primus inter pares)*.[37]

An attempt is then made to describe what should be done: First, acknowledging that Question 3 is somewhat equivocal in that it could be interpreted as asking for a judgment either on the short Offices in themselves or on the appropriatenes of clergy and laity utilizing such Offices when praying together, Canon Martimort notes that those who responded negatively to this question follow a general theme: A concession to the use of the short Offices constitutes a form of clericalism in depriving the laity of access to the full Office, which is theirs by right. Such clericalism relegating laity to "Christians of the second rank" is entirely opposed to the teaching of the Second Vatican Council. A reprobation, however, of these Offices would, he says, go directly against SC 98, which allows that such Offices are public prayer of the Church. Canon Martimort acknowledges that he spoke against such a recognition of short Offices from the time of the preparatory liturgical commission through that of the council itself, but since the council gave these Offices such status and allowed the liberty of their use, the Consilium would do well to say nothing about them.[38]

Second, Canon Martimort argues against the so-called normative Breviary about which Question 1 was concerned. Pointing out that in the preparatory liturgical commission some experts proposed there be one Roman Office and that he frequently opposed this notion as having neither historical nor doctrinal foundation, he explains that a normative Breviary would not respect the very different situations and categories of persons obliged to the Roman Breviary. He notes that the wording of Question 1 has been interpreted in two different ways: (1) preparation of an essential structure of the Office allowing for necessary adaptations by different groups using the Office; (2) preparation of a uniform Office to be used by all, at least for Lauds and Vespers. The latter understanding is unacceptable, he says, for it does not respect the great principles of SC 38 calling for variations and adaptations for different groups, regions, and peoples.[39]

Finally, Canon Martimort proposes the necessity to safeguard all the traditional possibilities in the Roman Office, especially for the sake of contemplatives obliged to this Office. The preoccupation with disengaging active clergy and religious from a cadre of prayer more suitable to monks and contemplatives should not dictate a uniform structure of the Roman Office that would deprive monks, contemplatives, and others with the desire and leisure to prolong prayer of the possibility of doing so within the provisions of the Roman Office.[40]

Thus the relator concludes:

"It is possible, then, to agree on the following points:

(a) to propose to the Consilium that it leave outside its study the Little Offices lest, on this matter, the liberty given by the conciliar Constitution to religious communities be restricted.

(b) to affirm clearly the necessity of providing in the framework of the Roman Office all the traditional possibilities for contemplative prayer while at the same time of disengaging the office for clergy from monastic elements.

(c) to try to organize Lauds and Vespers so that they can be used by the faithful and communities not bound to the Office according to the arrangement I have already outlined previously, and let us speak no longer of a 'normative Office.'

(d) that these points would suffice temporarily, but it would be well to reaffirm the principles of the Constitution to counteract any tendency toward uniformity that would contradict these principles solemnly willed by the Council."[41]

Evaluation of the canon's position is reserved to chapter 6, but it is necessary to note here that at least some whose positions differed from his were, in fact, aware of the diversity for which some provision had to be made in the reformed Office. The difference would seem to be primarily modal: *How* to provide for diverse groups and situations. Father Mateos, for example, who advocated a position that seemed to be, at least with respect to Lauds and Vespers, a call for a "normative Office," which Canon Martimort opposed, did so seemingly without seeking to impose a uniform arrangement in whole or in part on all. Father Mateos has said:

"We were proposing—I wrote the proposal for the Office—to create, so to say, an ecclesiastical Office, a popular Office with two hours only—morning and evening prayer . . . *and then let the religious orders make their own Offices,* especially the monks, because for secular priests that would be enough: to celebrate or to recite these two hours. . . . The Church must do something that is valuable for the whole Church and not for special groups inside. That was our idea—so the Divine Office could come back to be a real Christian prayer and not monastic prayer or priestly prayer."[42]

Others, like Bishop J. Albert Martin, the relator for the conciliar liturgical commission, also respected the need for diversity. Bishop Martin, however, took a firm stance in support of a double form of the Roman Office. He said, as part of his response to the questionnaire of December 1965: "Let there be two Offices, one for those who are not monastic (for clergy, religious men and women, laity) and another for those who live the monastic life. The latter form should retain a monastic structure; the other should not."[43] Bishop Martin's view, however, was not as open to variety in the Office as Canon Martimort's and Father Mateos' views were, for he said in speaking against the use of short Breviaries:

"Why adopt a pattern in widely distributing little Offices by which the laity (nonclerical religious, religious, and lay people) would still be deprived of the great, official prayer of the Church, or why artificially restrict the psalmody as someone has proposed for Vespers? An excessive timidity in the reform of the Breviary would have as a consequence a falling into the same errors as in the past, namely, a proliferation of little Offices that have kept a great number of laity (religious or simple lay people) from the great prayer of the Church."[44]

His view, of course, suggests that there should be a clearly discernible Roman Office, an official prayer of the Church (with two forms, according to his latter proposal), which all are called to celebrate.

After his long period of study and reflection following the objections raised to the lines the reform of the Office was taking, Canon Martimort and the other members of Group 9, meeting at Genoa, September 6–8, 1966, had a lengthy discussion about the matters raised in the questionnaire, including the matter of whether or not there should be one or several Breviaries. No details of this discussion are given in Schema 185, which reports on this meeting, but it is apparent from the schema that Group 9 adopted Canon Martimort's positions found in RG.[45]

The same matters were discussed in the meeting of the Group of Relators, September 26–27, 1966. According to the report, the relators, after long discussion on all the matters raised in the questionnaire, also agreed with Group 9 and Canon Martimort.[46] The position adopted with regard to one or several Breviaries was, Let the principles of SC 38 remain intact. That article called for preservation of the substantial unity of the Roman Rite with allowance for adaptation to diverse groups, regions, peoples. Thus the decision was against a double form of the Office and for a single structure with some kind of adaptation to be allowed to various groups.[47]

At its seventh plenary session (October 6–14, 1966) the Consilium was not asked any question pertaining specifically to the proposed double Office. Instead, questions and statements focusing on the hinge Hours of Lauds and Vespers, the minor Hours, and Vigils and calling for one form of these Hours adaptable to various situations were posed. The Consilium, in responding to these questions or tacitly accepting proposals, indicated its preference for one form of the Office adaptable to various situations:

"General Question: Is it acceptable that the structure of specific Hours, those that are like the hinge of the Office, that is, Lauds and Vespers, be so conceived that these Hours can be celebrated both by an ecclesial community gathered together and by a single individual? [*yes,* 33; *no,* 0; *yes with reservations,* 1].''[48]
"Question 7: Is it agreeable to construct the obligatory Hour in the day so that it consists of a psalm or psalms from the current Psalter that are said together with a hymn (and perhaps a prayer) suited to the Hour of the day (namely, Terce or Sext or None)? [yes, all].''[49]

With regard to Vigils (Matins or Nocturns) Group 9 and the Group of Relators proposed two forms of the Office—one for celebration during the night, the other for celebration at any time of the day. The difference, however, between the two forms would not be structural but formulaic.[50] Reasons behind these questions and statements will, of course, be considered in chapter 5. Here it is simply to be noted that the Consilium by affirming them put an end, in effect, to the proposal for a double Office.

THE RELATIONSHIP OF THE HOURS TO ONE ANOTHER

Article 89 of SC specified the norms to be observed in revision of the Office. These norms concerned each of the Hours of the Roman Office current at the time of the acceptance of SC by the council. Lauds and Vespers were specified as the *duplex cardo* of the daily Office, to be considered and celebrated as such. Compline was to be a suitable prayer to end the day. Matins was to take a double form, one for celebration as nocturnal praise, the other for recitation at any Hour. Fewer psalms and longer readings were to characterize it. Prime was to be suppressed. The minor Hours (Terce, Sext, and None) were to be kept in choir, but outside of choir only one of these Hours need be prayed—the one closest to the respective time of day at which it would be used.[51]

The stipulations of SC 89 posed two structural questions for the postconciliar reformers: (1) How should Lauds and Vespers be structured so that they appear as major Hours in relation to the other Hours? (2) What should be done with the invitatory at Matins if Matins is to become for some an Office of Readings and not necessarily the first Hour of prayer in the day? A third concern was the reduction of the three minor Hours to one outside choir, but this concern really posed no structural questions for these Hours in their relationship to the other Hours. The primary question here was with content, particularly the psalmody, and this question will be considered below in the discussion of the distribution of the psalms.[52]

A major structural question, however, did arise in the course of the reform with respect to the minor Hours and their place in the Roman Office. With the explicit support of Pope Paul VI a strong effort was made to reduce the three minor Hours to one, not only for those praying the Office outside choir but for *all* who prayed the Office in choir or outside of it. How these issues, then, pertaining to the relationship of the Hours to one another were dealt with by the reformers is the subject of the following considerations.

In the meeting of Group 9 in Rome (June 20–21, 1964) at which the responses to Canon Martimort's questions of April 17 (presented April 18 to the Consilium) were examined, Fr. Joseph Pascher and Canon André Rose, relator and secretary, respectively, of Group 3 (the distribution of the psalms), reported on the recommendations of their group for the distribution of the psalms in the revised Office. They proposed that for Lauds there be a one-week cycle having a structure of psalmody consisting of one morning psalm, an Old Testament canticle, and the *laudes* (Ps 148–50).[53] The length of the psalmody for Lauds thus stood in some contrast to that proposed for all the other Hours, including Vespers. In these Hours only three psalms would be utilized. Father Pascher justified the diminution of psalmody thus:

"It is evident from a comparison of articles 89 and 91 [of SC] that the Council seemed to have had in mind a reduction of the psalmody beyond that for Matins. For since article 91 of the Constitution decreed that the psalms are to be distributed 'through some longer period of time,' it expressly regarded the whole of article 89, not just 89c. Therefore, the Psalter should be distributed over a longer time not only for Matins but for the whole course of the Hours. However, an extension necessarily entails a diminution of the number of sections from the psalms. So it does not follow from article 89c that outside of Matins no diminution of psalmody is possible."[54]

Lauds would retain its five psalmic pieces partly because Psalms 148–50 did not (despite practice since Pope Pius X's time) readily lend themselves to division in view of the long-standing tradition of praying them together. None of the members of Group 9 seem to have disagreed with this proposal initially, but discussion provoked some difficulties.[55] These were nothing, however, compared to the difficulties seen in giving a ternary structure to the psalmody at Vespers. Canon Martimort summed up the discussion thus:

"All agreed that five psalms would be excessive in a popular celebration that would include a longer reading and a homily.

"Several said that three psalms would scarcely suffice in a celebration without laity present, one in which the reading would be shorter and a homily omitted. *Vespers would lose its character of a major Hour,* and it would be difficult to preserve the collection of antiphons for great feasts."[56]

A similar reason against the ternary structure of the psalmody at Vespers was given in the consideration of the arguments against a double scheme for Vespers: If Vespers were reduced to three psalms even in private recitation *its character as a major Hour would be lost.*[57]

Canon Martimort reported that ten consultors were favorable to a quintuple structure of psalmody for Vespers without the people present and three were against such. Father Pascher and Canon Rose managed, however, to secure the agreement of Group 9 for a presentation by Group 3 to the Consilium of their Schema II for the distribution of the psalms in which the psalmody of Vespers and of all the other hours with the exception of Lauds would have a ternary structure.[58] Father Pascher's defense of this proposal was a pastoral one:

"The possibility of observing the course of the Hours stated in article 89 and explained in article 91 is to be understood as a spiritual possibility not a physical one. For the question is whether a cleric who has pastoral responsibilities in our times is able to keep the course of the Hours and derive from it spiritual nourishment. It was because of this question that the Council seems to have decreed in article 89c the abbreviation of the psalmody at Matins and to have made this possible by article 91.

"Psalmody in the Roman Breviary is quite extensive. The quantity comes from the monastic tradition and seems to befit monastic conditions. For even in our times those who are experts in monastic life—although not all of them—assert that psalmody, indeed lengthy psalmody, is necessary for nourishing monastic spirituality.

"The conditions of the modern clergy who have pastoral care, however, differ exceedingly from monastic conditions. No one questions this. As far as psalmody is concerned, it would be very useful if it fit the conditions of the clergy. So it should not be lengthy. There are some, however, who think that lengthy psalmody is necessary for the clergy so that it may foster peace and a kind of ongoing colloquy with God. But, alas, this rather attractive theory is rendered ridiculous by the very difficult circumstances of life. Indeed, if we persist in insisting on impossibilities, spiritual harm may well result."[59]

The insistence by the majority of Group 9 on retaining for Vespers a quintuple structure of psalmody as that which constituted it a major Hour met with resistence not only by Father Pascher and the rest of Group 3 but also in the comments of at least one other consultor, Fr. Frederick R. McManus, canon lawyer at The Catholic University of America, who responded to the questions and commentary presented to the Consilium in Schema 31.[60] To the argument that reduction of the number of psalms in Vespers to three would weaken its character as a major Hour he responded:

"Concerning the rest [of the matter], the following argument is not intelligible: 'If Vespers is reduced to three psalms even in private recitation, its character as a major Hour would be lost.' The quantity of words or of psalms does not determine the importance of Vespers."[61]

To the question as to whether or not to adapt Lauds for celebration with the people and to the report that Group 9 was opposed to such adaptation he responded:

"This solution is very displeasing. Today Lauds and Vespers are not popular, and they require a radical restoration.

"Unless I am mistaken, the desire of the Preparatory Commission was that it be possible for these special Hours to be recited by the Church: by priests, by men and women religious, by lay people, by a parish in which religious brothers and sisters are joined by at least a few of the lay faithful. It is the glory of the Anglicans that priests daily recite Lauds and Vespers (Morning Prayer and Evensong) in their churches with the faithful even if they are very few.

"It seems to me that this report smacks of excessive clericalism and archeologism. The importance of Lauds will not be shown by the length or number of psalms but only by the simplicity of the Hour, its authenticity as a Morning Prayer able to be recited by all even if that happens rarely."[62]

Thus, Group 9 received at least one strong statement to the effect that the quantity of psalmody did not make an Hour major but that its suitability to the time at which it is prayed and to the participation of all rendered it such.

When the Consilium met for its fourth plenary session (September 28 to October 9 and November 16, 1964), Father Pascher and Canon Rose presented the arguments for both five and three psalms in Vespers:

"1. Everyone agrees that if Vespers is celebrated with the people, it should have only three psalms.

2. But there is disagreement about the recitation of Vespers by a cleric without the people present. One opinion opts for five psalms. The reasons:

(a) Nothing prevents omitting some psalms in a celebration with the people and drawing up two types of Vespers: the first, a complete scheme for the clergy; the other, a form adapted for the people.

(b) An important reason would be the tradition of five psalms, which has flourished in the Roman liturgy for many centuries.

(c) It seems a parallelism ought to be kept between the fivefold schema for Lauds and that for Vespers. Besides, it seems that the character of major Hour is better preserved in having five psalms.

"A second opinion opts for three psalms even if Vespers is celebrated by a cleric alone. The reasons:

(a) No distinction should be made between the Office for a cleric united with the people and the Office for a cleric alone, especially for that Hour which, beyond all others, ought to be celebrated 'communally in church' according to article 100 of the Constitution.

(b) A reduction in the number of psalms does not result in abbreviation, for other elements would take the place of the psalms omitted, e.g., longer reading, homily, prayer of the faithful.

(c) The tradition of five psalms is not altogether universal, and the number 'five' is not sacred."[63]

So, a principal reason for maintaining five psalms for the clergy privately reciting Vespers was that such has been the practice for ages, whereas a principal reason for reducing the number to three psalms even for clergy engaged in private recitation was that no distinction should be introduced between the Office for clergy and that for people. This question, then, was put to the Consilium:

"Is it acceptable to keep one scheme having five psalms for
Vespers whether Vespers is celebrated by a cleric without people
present or together with the people, the option being given by the
rubrics for the latter case of omitting two psalms and adding a
longer reading, a homily, and perhaps a prayer of the faithful?"[64]

The response of the Consilium was unanimously in favor. Thus
the majority position of Group 9 in favor of five psalms for private
recitation of Vespers by the clergy and three psalms with longer
reading, homily, and perhaps intercessions for Vespers with the
people was upheld.

The question, however, of how the major character of Lauds
and Vespers should be manifested vis-à-vis the other Hours
shifted from a focus on their structure (greater number of psalms
and greater length of these Hours) to pastoral foci, namely, their
suitability for active clergy and for celebration by the whole
Church. This shift occurred in the controversy surrounding the
work of the reformers as this became known through publication
of reports on it. These reports, as already noted, appeared in the
volumes of *Notitiae* during 1965. The shift can be detected in
Canon Martimort's summation for the Consilium of the negative
response received to these reports and discussed at the sixth plenary session of the Consilium (October 19–26, November 22–26,
December 1, 1965). Regarding the structure of Lauds and Vespers
he said:

"A third difficulty presents itself with respect to Lauds and
Vespers. Is the celebration of the Morning and Evening Offices in
the Eastern Rites or among the Anglicans or Protestants to serve
as a model so that both of these Hours can be celebrated daily
with the people or at least some part of the Christian community?
The Roman Office, even if shortened according to the norm of the
Constitution and with your agreement, remains, they say, something monastic and thus unsuitable for the secular clergy."[65]

According to the relator of Group 9, then, the objection the critics
were bringing to the proposed reform of Lauds and Vespers was
that they remained "something monastic," unsuitable for celebration by the secular clergy with the people. For rendering these
Hours suitable for such celebration, according to the critics, the

Oriental, Anglican, and other Protestant Offices should be used as models for the Roman reform. Canon Martimort was not without a ready response to this objection:

"Wisely, we have provided with your approval for the celebration of Vespers with the people on certain days. At such celebrations, you will recall, the psalms are reduced to three and a longer reading replaces the short reading or *capitulum*. The presider may give a homily on this reading and the universal prayer or prayer of the faithful may be used.

"Frequent and daily popular participation in Lauds and Vespers, however, is very doubtful. For the present, these Hours in the daily Office should be drawn up in such a way that a priest, who must recite the Hour of Readings according to the norm of article 89, will not be wearied. Let me point out emphatically that neither the Anglicans nor the Protestants have kept a complete Office such as the Vatican Constitution prescribes for us, but only the Morning and Evening Hours. In the East, certainly, all the Hours are found in the books, but there is an obligation often only for the public celebration of Lauds."[66]

Canon Martimort thus considers that sufficient provision has been made for popular participation in Lauds and Vespers—something, he thinks, that will probably not occur often. He is obviously concerned about the welfare of priests and sees very limited value in utilizing Protestant Offices, which bear so little resemblance to the Roman Office.

Partly because of the critics' insistence, alluded to in the foregoing remarks, that Lauds and especially Vespers be structured both for popular celebration and profitable recitation by secular clergy, perhaps on the model of Protestant or Eastern Offices, Father Bugnini posed the following in the questionnaire of December 1965, sent to all members and consultors of the Consilium:

"4. Does it seem acceptable what the Consilium has already decided, namely, that in celebrations of Lauds and Vespers with the people there be a common scheme for certain times and feasts, that the psalms be reduced to three, and that a longer Scriptural reading with a homily be added in place of the short reading?

"12bis. Is it acceptable for Lauds and Vespers to have five psalms with the option of reducing them to three if Vespers is celebrated with the people?"[67]

The meager response from members was, *yes*, 16; *no*, 4; *yes with reservations*, 3. The consultors were more divided on the question: *yes*, 12; *no*, 10. Of the consultors casting negative votes, seven opted for a fewer number or for three psalms; one wanted a special structure for the people, and two would have five psalms always at Vespers. For Question 12bis, ten members answered affirmatively but eight had reservations: three would reduce the number of psalms for clergy and laity to three; one would reduce the number to two psalms; one opted for a new structure for clergy with pastoral care; one wanted five psalms in choral recitation and the matter for clergy and laity subject to further investigation. Two others were unwilling to fix any number. Of the consultors, ten also were favorable, but four wanted three psalms always at Lauds and Vespers; five wanted a maximum of fifteen psalm verses at Lauds and Vespers, and four wished to have four psalms at Lauds and Vespers to show that these Hours were more important than the minor Hours.[68]

Two months after the publication of the results of the questionnaire and after his several months of personal study, Canon Martimort devoted twelve of the thirty-three pages in his "Rapport général sur l'Office divin" to the question of the structure of Lauds and Vespers. Among the many aspects of the problem of restructuring these Hours, he subtly treated the aspect of what constitutes Lauds and Vespers as major.

First, there is in his report a summary of opinion expressed in answer to the inquiry of December that psalms ought not be divided in a given Hour to maintain a theoretical, traditional number for that Hour.[69] Second, the reasons for maintaining five psalms at Vespers no longer include that of marking them as major in contrast to the other Hours where fewer psalms would be used. The reason that might give pause to a move to reduce the number would be the desire to preserve the antiphons of Sundays and feasts. But the admission is made that reduction is a real possibility:

"Group 3 has proposed that there be only three psalms for Vespers. The proper Offices with their antiphons for Sundays and feasts have led the Consilium to retain five psalms for Vespers. Our colleague, Father Dirks, recalls this reason in his *votum:* It is necessary to take into account the technical problem of conserving ancient elements when a radical transformation of the structures of the Office occurs. But he says that there is no reason why Groups 3 and 9 should not examine the possibility of reducing the number of psalms (even though for Lauds this reduction was not seriously envisaged in 1964), and it should not be difficult to do this.''[70]

Turning, then, to the points made by several bishops responding to the questionnaire that a profound restructuring of Lauds and Vespers is called for so that these Hours always enable participation by all and that it is the quality of Lauds and Vespers that render them major in comparison with the others, Canon Martimort reports some of the opinions offered. Cited, for example, is the opinion of Bishop Isnard of Nova Friburgo, Brazil:

"The future Breviary ought to be the official book of prayer for the people of God, not in all its parts but at least in the fundamental Hours, Lauds and Vespers. This Breviary ought to be the book of prayer serving laity and clergy at least in certain of its parts.''[71]

Given at length with a remark that his considerations are based on historical arguments are the remarks of Bishop Joseph Albert Martin of Nicolet (Canada). Bishop Martin says in part:

"The true sense of the conciliar Constitution is to recover that which it calls 'the venerable tradition of the universal Church.' The studies of A. Baumstark have definitively established the existence of what is called the cathedral Office: a daily celebration of the morning and of the evening, universally attested from the third to the fourth century in the nonmonastic Churches, in the presence of the bishop or of his representative. . . . Let's make a radical distinction between the monastic Office and the Office of the universal Church. On this condition only will it be possible to realize fully the wish of the Council and to know that all can participate either communally or privately in the Divine Office of the Church. The great current of liturgical prayer, which must be renewed, will then be vitally established in the unity of the universal prayer for clergy, religious, and laity. . . . An excessive timidity in the reform of the Breviary will lead to the same errors as those of the past, which produced a proliferation of little Offices depriving a large number of Christians of participation in the great prayer of the Church."[72]

Bishop Martin suggested as a structure for Lauds and Vespers the following:

Introductory verses
Three psalms
Biblical reading (short or long)
Hymn
Benedictus or *Magnificat*
Litany
Presidential prayer
Concluding verses[73]

Canon Martimort, quite skeptical of these views, devotes several pages to a response. He finds that the arguments of the bishops are based on the opinion only of several experts, especially those who in published articles have criticized the projected reform of the Office as too monastic or too clerical and have advocated a structure for Lauds and Vespers based either on celebrations of the Word (e.g., the ecumenical service at St. Paul's Outside the Walls held on December 4, 1965) or on the Anglican Office.[74] He claims that efforts to distinguish between the spirituality of the priest engaged in active ministry from that of one who is a monk and to provide forms of the Office suitable to both are laudable. While the council rightly emphasized the place of the laity in the liturgy, even in the Office, and insisted on communitarian celebration of rites, it is not necessary to conclude that the prayer of priests ought not be more insistent than that of laity. If the structure of Lauds and Vespers were conceived on the lines of a communal celebration of the Word and were imposed on all, what would happen to the life of prayer of priests, 95 percent of whom are not able (according to a remark of Fr. Herman Schmidt) to pray the Office except privately?[75] Then, in a remarkable manifestation of his personal views on the real possibility of popular restoration of Vespers and Lauds, of use and abuse of historical research on liturgy, and on the irreversible evolution of doctrine, spirituality, and liturgical practice, Canon Martimort writes:

"It is true that the Council invites the faithful to participate in the Office, especially in Lauds and Vespers on Sundays and feasts. This invitation is based on a legislative tradition that goes back to the Middle Ages and that is found in the documents issued immediately prior to the council: the encyclical *Mediator Dei* and the instruction of September 3, 1958. But we must be prudent. How many laws in the past have remained a dead letter! Far from promoting a renewal of Vespers, the documents cited above of 1947 and 1958 are contemporaneous with its complete disappearance. Does anyone really believe it is possible to restore the daily celebration or even the Sunday celebration of Vespers, to say nothing of Lauds?

"Frequently, liturgists refer to the results of historical study and base their projects and desires on these studies. This is legitimate. Pius XII himself mentioned the progress of the historical study of liturgy as one of the reasons for its renewal in our epoch, but Pius XII could not foresee that this renewal would end in the Second Vatican Council and in the Constitution on the Liturgy. History is one of the great criteria that governs the authenticity of the work of our Consilium.

"It must be admitted, however, that historical science risks being utilized in an inexact way as a criterion of reform. That which was good for one epoch is not necessarily good for another. Some developments are irreversible even from a doctrinal point of view. So too, the results of historical study have sometimes been spread abroad in an imperfect or inexact way through popular reviews, meetings, etc. Certain requests, then, are based on these erroneous historical data. It is just such data regarding Vespers and Lauds in recent articles by Fr. Louis Bouyer and by Pedro Farnes, already cited, of which one needs to beware. It is not exactly true that in ancient times the assemblies, where they were held daily, always included readings. Readings were rather reserved for the more important stations and for solemnities such as 'vigils' of feasts (of which there remains, among others, the Great Vespers of the Byzantine and Ambrosian Rites) or Lent. Furthermore, the lives of different Churches, when examined closely, do not lend themselves well to rather confident historical generalizations. These daily assemblies took a long time to develop; their golden age was rather brief—from the end of the fourth to the middle of the fifth century. One of their more popular elements, the *lucernarium*, could be restored today only with difficulty. On the other hand, at the moment when these assemblies were flourishing, Mass was celebrated daily only, possibly, in Africa, and this point deserves emphasis because it is necessary henceforth to take into account daily Mass, which achieved a place of honor in medieval and especially in modern spirituality; daily Communion, to which Pius X has summoned Christians, and the continuous reading of the Bible and of the Gospel, which is currently being arranged."[76]

Having stated his predilection for providing for active clergy and monks, his caution in utilizing the results of historical research, his accurate view of the lack of readings in the cathedral Office, his profound skepticism regarding the irreversibility of praxis in the Church, Canon Martimort asks if what some bishops propose, namely, that the structural reform of Lauds and Vespers be based on the Morning and Evening Prayer of the Protestant Offices, especially that of the Anglican Church, is feasible for the Roman Rite. Reviewing in some detail the structure of Morning Prayer and Evening Prayer in the *Book of Common Prayer* (1928), the Morning and Evening Prayers in several Lutheran bodies, that of the Swiss Calvinists in *L'Office divin de chaque jour,* edited by R. Paquier and A. Bardet, and that of the community of Taizé, he notes that these Offices are largely closed systems. They make little, if any, provision for Hours other than Lauds or Vespers, and they do not provide for the daily celebration of the Eucharist. Both provisions, he says, must be considered in the Roman reform.[77]

The canon's conclusion from these many considerations on Lauds and Vespers is, then, that

"the Office of Lauds and of Vespers can be revised in such a way as to be practical for the priest, for a lay person, for a small group (religious, retreatants, students, etc.), for an assembly, for a conventual choir. But it is clear that these different types of celebration presuppose carefully planned revisions of the rite. We need to see if this can be done."[78]

To be noted here in his conclusion is the openness to a reconsideration of the already partially agreed upon structure of Lauds and Vespers as a result of the criticisms made of the proposed revision and also the lack of insistence on a number of psalms or length of these Hours as characteristics of their major position vis-à-vis the other Hours.

When Group 9 met next at Genoa from September 6 to 8, 1966, the structure of Lauds and Vespers was reexamined in the light of the responses to the questionnaire of December 1965. The opinions expressed by Canon Martimort in his report to the members of Group 9 in the previous July were endorsed and the following conclusion reached:

"Therefore, so that a plan of action may be developed based on the desires of many and answering the difficulties currently being expressed, we must find a structure that favors the participation of the people as well as individual recitation. Furthermore, it is possible that all of this might be connected somehow with the Office of Readings or with the continuous reading of daily Mass. Perhaps this will be better evident when the individual elements of Lauds and Vespers are considered."[79]

A compromise was thus to be sought between the views favoring reform of Lauds and Vespers primarily for the good of clergy and monks and those favoring reform that would allow greater participation of the laity in the Office.

Reporting the action taken on the question of the number of psalms at Lauds and Vespers, Canon Martimort first reviews the history of the discussion heretofore and the decision of the Consilium made in 1964 for five psalms in Lauds and in Vespers. He notes that a sizeable minority of those responding to the questionnaire wanted a reduction in the psalmody and were opposed to a double structure of Lauds and Vespers, one for popular celebration, the other for private recitation, on the grounds that the structure itself of these major Hours ought to manifest a communitarian and popular character. He then cites a number of additional reasons that persuaded the majority of Group 9 to reverse the previous decision: (1) Group 3 had from the beginning proposed three psalms for Vespers; (2) experience (with short Breviaries) has shown that in the vernacular the psalms could be recited more slowly; (3) other elements are to be proposed as additions to Lauds and Vespers, which would be unreasonably lengthy hours if the five psalms were retained; and (4) a solution to the problem of preserving the best of the "treasury of antiphons" could probably be found. By a vote of eleven to one Group 9 finally agreed to reduce the number of psalms at Lauds and Vespers to three.[80] The group then posed this question for the Consilium: "Is it acceptable that in Lauds and Vespers, whether with or without the people present, there be only three psalms?"[81]

The other elements considered by Group 9 for Lauds and Vespers, namely, longer reading in place of *capitulum*, *preces* or intercessions in Lauds, and universal prayer in Vespers were viewed as possibly rendering these Hours more suitable for popular communal celebration and thus contributing to their major character.[82] Since these elements were not of as major concern as the psalmody in the debate over the major character of Lauds and Vespers, a consideration of the proposals and decisions regarding these elements will be reserved for the discussion of the structure of Lauds and Vespers in the next chapter.[83]

In the report of the September meeting of Group 9, Canon Martimort also notes that the question of whether Lauds and Vespers are fittingly celebrated in a uniform way by all in the Church could not be discussed for lack of time. Acknowledging the importance of the question, he comments that proponents of uniform celebration fall into two camps: (1) those arguing from a practical point of view who want all to be able to participate in these Hours, wherever they may be; and (2) those arguing from a theoretical point of view, who note that these Hours pertain to the cathedral Office.[84]

When the Group of Relators met (September 26–27, 1966) previous to the seventh plenary session of the Consilium (October 6–14) the matter of the structure of Lauds and Vespers was discussed again. The relators interjected a new note into the discussion. Instead of beginning with a consideration of the structure of the Hours they spoke of the spirit, importance, and end of Lauds and Vespers. Starting again with article 89a of SC, which names Lauds and Vespers as *duplex cardo*, the two hinges of the daily Office, the discussion of the relators turned on several points: First, Lauds and Vespers were, by witness of many historical documents, daily celebrated for several centuries by clergy and people, though not everywhere with the same intensity nor in the same manner. Second, the structure of Lauds and Vespers contributed to the spirit of sanctifying the beginning and the end of the day respectively. Third, Group 3, especially with the aid of Fr. Jorge Pinell, Spanish Benedictine member of that group and professor at the Pontifical International Institute of Sant Anselmo in Rome, had painstakingly selected psalms and canticles based on the spirit of each of these Hours.[85] Fourth, a number of the members of the Consilium had opted for a structure of these Hours

"so that they may clearly appear as the prayer of the entire Christian community and not only as that of the clergy and of monks. The participation of the faithful at these Hours should not be seen as some kind of concession but as a right belonging to them."[86]

While it was admitted that all of the aforesaid points needed to be attended to, other factors also should play their parts in the final determination of the structure: First, the priest and monk need "more frequent and richer prayer" *(frequentior et ditior oratio)* that can be combined harmoniously with popular liturgy. So Lauds and Vespers must have a structure and content harmonious with the whole corpus of the Hours and with the daily celebration of Mass. Second, the Offices of the Protestant Churches, though admirable in themselves, are not suitable bases for the Roman Office, since they are complete systems usually not related to daily celebration of the Eucharist or to a system of *lectio continua* as in Matins (Office of Readings). Finally, cases where priests have to recite Lauds and Vespers without the people must be attended to, since, it is said, "the greatest number of priests will recite Lauds and Vespers by themselves or at least without the people present."[87]

The relators then proposed a new question for the Consilium:

"Do you agree that the structure of the special Hours, which are, as it were, the hinge of the Divine Office, that is, Lauds and Vespers, should be so conceived as to allow both for celebration by an ecclesial community meeting together and for private recitation?"[88]

When proposed to the Consilium at its seventh plenary session, this question was answered affirmatively by thirty-three of the bishops. None were opposed and only one voted "with reservations."[89]

With regard to the principal structural element in Lauds and Vespers, namely, the psalms, both the Group of Relators and the Consilium agreed to three psalms in these Hours. It was maintained, however, by Canon Martimort that the number three should not be taken in a mathematical sense. One lengthy psalm might be used rather than two short psalms. Also, the Old Testament canticle in Lauds and the New Testament canticle (if introduced) in Vespers would be counted in the ternary structure. The vote in the Consilium on the question posed by Group 9 regarding reduction of the psalmody was, 32, yes; 2, no; 1, yes with reservations.[90] These decisions effectively ended the long discussion on the principles underlying the structure of Lauds and Vespers vis-à-vis the other Hours of the Office.

The obvious compromise represented in the first agreement deserves some comment here. Compromise was to characterize many of the major decisions on the reform of the Office. This fact will be evident in the consideration of other structural questions (e.g., the structuring of the intercessions at Lauds and at Vespers). When asked by this author if he thought compromise had weakened the acceptability of the reformed Office in its definitive form, Canon Martimort replied negatively. He maintained that every good decision is the result of compromise. The results are more solid, more durable. If an uncompromising route had been followed, he said, the result (*Liturgia Horarum*) would not have been so well accepted as it has been.[91]

The Invitatory as Prelude to the First Hour

Because article 89c of SC mandated the adaptation of Matins so that this Office could be celebrated at any hour of the day, Group 9 in its earliest sessions (April and June 1964) discussed the difficulty of retaining the invitatory at the beginning of Matins (Office of Readings) when this was not the first Hour of prayer in a day. After some discussion, the content of which is not reported, Group 9 unanimously agreed that the invitatory should be retained and that it should precede the Office of Readings or Lauds, whichever came first.[92]

Several questions pertaining to the invitatory were presented to the fourth plenary session of the Consilium (September 28–October 9 and November 16, 1964). One of these questions was, "If the

Office of Readings is not recited as the first Hour, should the invitatory be made obligatory before the first Hour, that is, Lauds?" Of the twenty-four members present, nineteen voted yes; four, no; and one vote was null.[93] This decision remained unquestioned through the storm of protest against the direction reform of the Office was taking as this erupted in the sixth plenary session (November–December, 1965).[94]

In February 1967 Group 9 again discussed the invitatory and agreed that in addition to Psalm 94, an antiphon for the psalm should be retained.[95] The first specimen of the Office, "Schema completum Divini Officii persolvendi a die 9 ad 15 aprilis 1967" (SCDO), was then prepared for the eighth plenary session of the Consilium (April 10–19, 1967). In SCDO the invitatory was termed "Introduction to the Office" and appeared before the Office of Readings.[96] In his explanation to the Consilium of some of the decisions underlying the shape of SCDO, Canon Martimort revealed that a reason for maintaining the invitatory before Lauds when it did not precede the Office of Readings was an ecumenical one: The use of an invitatory before Morning Prayer was found in the Anglican Church and in many Protestant communities.[97]

Some members and consultors of the Consilium, however, after experiment with SCDO, were not pleased with the retention of the invitatory. For example, Bishops Hervas (Ciudad Real, Spain) and Young (Hobart, Australia) thought the invitatory weighed down the Hour and begot mechanical recitation. Consultor Jacques Cellier (director of the Centre National de Pastorale Liturgique, Paris) felt that the invitatory would render Lauds exceedingly ponderous if said with that Hour. In view of the criticism, Canon Martimort suggested that the invitatory remain experimentally as part of the Office. He noted that several possibilities of abbreviation and of substitution existed.[98]

When Group 9 met in Munich from July 20 to 23 the group considered at length several questions regarding the invitatory. To assist their deliberation Canon Martimort had prepared a summary of opinions he had received from members and consultors on the subject.[99] Most of these opinions were concerned with whether to retain the whole of Psalm 94 and whether to provide alternate psalms for the invitatory—matters that will be considered in the next chapter.[100] The questions of concern here are those of the retention and placement of the invitatory. Group 9 was aware, through Canon Martimort's summary, that Father Bugnini was skeptical of the value of the invitatory and that the Italian consultor, Msgr. Salvatore Famoso, believed that the proposed mobility would lead to its becoming an accessory part of the Office. He proposed it be attached always to Lauds.[101]

Group 9 considered the difficulties attending the mobility of the invitatory and its making ponderous, perhaps, the Hour to which it was attached. Four solutions were envisaged and discussed: (1) Retain the invitatory only on major solemnities or in choral celebration; (2) retain Psalm 94 or others daily; (3) suppress the invitatory altogether; (4) retain the invitatory as an option. To the question finally posed—Is the invitatory psalm to be kept before the first Hour of the Office and to be made obligatory daily?—eleven members voted yes and three no.[102]

In a report to the Consilium before its ninth plenary session (November 14–20, 1967), Canon Martimort acknowledged that the discussion in Group 9 "in such a great storm of opinions" was long. He then proposed to the Consilium that it consider the same question, given above, which Group 9 had answered affirmatively.[103] Since, as discussed in chapter 3, major questions regarding the Office proposed to the Synod of Bishops meeting at approximately the same time as the Consilium in November 1967 occupied most attention, no record has been found of a vote by the Consilium on this question. The Consilium used, at its ninth session, the specimen "Specimen Divini Officii pro diebus a 12 ad 25 novembris 1967" (SDO), in which the invitatory or "Introductio Officii" was printed at the beginning of the booklet with the directive "always to be put before the first part of the Office of the day."[104] If asked at all, the question undoubtedly received an affirmative answer because the existence and placement of the invitatory is not later questioned, and it appears in the first widely distributed printed specimen of the revised Office, *Descriptio et specimena Officii Divini iuxta Concilii Vaticani II decreta instaurati* (DSOD) in 1969 with the explanation that "the invitatory is done before the first Hour (whether the Office of Readings or Lauds) in which the divine praise begins."[105] Early drafts of the "The General Instruction of the Liturgy of the Hours" (IGLH) proposed a similar explanation of the place of the invitatory:

"The invitatory has its place at the beginning of the whole course of daily prayer; that is, it is placed either before Lauds or before the Office of Readings depending on which liturgical action begins the day."[106]

When responses of the world's bishops to DSOD were examined, however, Group 9 found sufficient reason to propose "that it may be allowed, when necessary, to omit the invitatory at the beginning of Lauds."[107] Thus the definitive text of IGLH reads:

"The invitatory is placed at the beginning of the whole sequence of the day's prayer, that is, it precedes either Morning Prayer or the Office of Readings, whichever of these liturgical actions begins the day. The psalm with its antiphon may, however, be omitted when it should precede Morning Prayer."[108]

The invitatory (the term *invitatorium* was finally kept), then, came to be a separable part of the entire Office attached either obligatorily to the beginning of the Office of Readings or optionally to that of Lauds.

The Reduction of the Minor Hours to a "Middle Hour"

SC 89e had specified the maintenance of the minor Hours of Terce, Sext, and None for those bound to choral celebration of the Office but allowed those not so bound to select any one of these according to the respective time of day. Group 9 in its earlier sessions occupied itself with finding a way to preserve the recitation of the integral Psalter and yet allow for the omission of two Hours by those who could and did choose to do so.[109] There was, however, a significant attempt by Father Bugnini, in the meeting of Group 9 on June 20, 1964, to raise among the consultors the question of whether it would be possible to reduce the number of Hours in the Office for all—those bound to choral celebration and those not so bound—by eliminating altogether two of the minor Hours. The response of Group 9 to Father Bugnini's question was that: "so intricate a problem has already been solved by the council."[110] When Father Bugnini questioned the retention of the names of the three minor Hours when only one might be appropriate, he was reminded that the council had made a wise decision and ". . . what the Constitution says must stand lest detractors say, today liturgists want this; tomorrow, something else."[111]

Father Bugnini's question was put to rest only temporarily. In December 1965, following the objections made to the lines being pursued on reform of the Office, the questionnaire posed to the Consilium contained three queries regarding the minor Hours. Preceding the questions was a statement of the problems foreseen by some in the retention of all the minor Hours. These were basically two: (1) If SC 89e were implemented the danger *(periculum)* would exist that part of the Psalter would be habitually omitted by those who chose only one of the Hours and this the same one every day; (2) the "truth of the Hours" *(veritas temporis)* would probably not be kept by those bound to choral celebration because of the difficulty in assembling three times during the day for these Hours. It was noted that if the minor Hours were reduced to one for all who would pray them, the express approbation of the Pope would be needed, since such a provision went beyond the stipulations of SC 89c.[112] So one of the three questions—the one of concern here—was

"Does it seem fitting, in keeping with contemporary conditions and pastoral necessity, to abolish the distinction pertaining to the minor Hours between choral recitation of the Divine Office and private recitation by establishing only one Hour between Lauds and Vespers to be recited, perhaps, around midday?"[113]

Of the members responding to this question, thirteen voted affirmatively and four negatively. Four others would keep three Hours for monks and one for nonmonastic clergy. One member thought there should be no discussion of the question until the Pope gave permission for such a reduction. Of the consultors, ten voted affirmatively and five negatively. Five others wanted the three minor Hours kept for monks and one Hour for others. One consultor suggested that Sext and Compline be prayed by clerics living together.[114]

As was discussed in chapter 3, the inconclusive results of the questionnaire prompted a meeting (on March 18, 1966) of Cardinal Lercaro, president of the Consilium, with Pope Paul VI. The Pope, in his written response (April 5, 1966) to questions raised at the meeting, endorsed with respect to the minor Hours the view that there should be only one Hour between Lauds and Vespers for both those bound to the choral Office and those not bound to it. The papal response was communicated to Canon Martimort by Cardinal Lercaro.[115]

Following the publication of the results of the questionnaire and the study he engaged in for several months, Canon Martimort revealed in RG his position on the minor Hours to the other members of Group 9. He began by recounting the origin of the minor Hours, acknowledging their monastic institution but emphasizing that the times at which they were prayed had been proposed as times for prayer to *all* Christians in antiquity. He indicated some of the commonly used sources for this view.[116] Acknowledging, also, that the minor Hours have been observed with difficulty, particularly regarding the "truth of the Hours" (*veritas temporis*), from medieval times to the present, he noted that both the Code of Rubrics of 1960 and SC 84 and 88 stress the importance of the "truth of the hours" in praying the Office. Those bound to choral celebration of the Office ought to maintain the ideal of praying all the Hours at their proper times—an ideal for those who cannot ordinarily interrupt the course of their work for common prayer and a public service for the rest of the Church. The council, he said, in providing for the reduction of the minor Hours to one, had solely in view the needs of clerics not bound to the choral Office. Since the council, however, members of the Consilium as well as communities bound to the choral Office have objected to maintaining the three minor Hours. Canon Martimort acknowledged that under the designation of communities bound to the choral Office are diverse groups: secular canons, monks living the contemplative life, mendicants, canons regular, and clerics living in monasteries but leading an active life. Thus there have been numerous requests for interpretations, indults, and the like allowing reduction of the minor Hours for some of these groups.

Another difficulty since the council's decision on the minor Hours is how to preserve the recitation of the integral Psalter for those who legitimately pray only one of the Hours. Recalling that the proposition of several bishops at the council for the replacement of the three minor Hours by one Midday Hour (*Hora meridiana*) was rejected by the conciliar liturgical commission and that an overwhelming number of bishops approved the decision in SC

89e, he noted that the radical solution of abandoning altogether two Hours of the Office not only would be damaging to the authority of the council, since it would be a derogation from SC, but also, even if juridically possible (as it seemed to be), it should be the solution of last resort, since the ideal might be maintained with allowance for particular needs by a less radical solution.[117]

If the radical solution were attempted, he reported, Prof. Emil Lengeling, Fr. Vincenzo Raffa, and others had expressed their opinion that it would be necessary to submit a proposal for this solution to a general consultation of bishops or to an episcopal synod, since it is a matter of exceptional importance surpassing the competence of the Consilium. Canon Martimort claimed there were less radical solutions. One solution would be to maintain the three Hours with one psalm each. A person praying only one Hour would use all three psalms of the Hours with hymn and prayer of the Hour corresponding to the time of its recitation, thus assuring the "truth of the hours" as well as the integrity of the Psalter. This solution had been considered by the preparatory conciliar commission but rejected by the conciliar commission itself.[118]

A second solution would allow the choice of psalms from any minor Hour when only one Hour is prayed. Group 3 had proposed that a person who recited only one of the minor Hours could take the psalms from any one of these Hours but would not be obliged to do so. A question (no. 18) to this effect had appeared in the questionnaire of December 16, 1965, and a large majority responded affirmatively (17 to 5 of the members and 18 to 3 of the consultors).

Canon Martimort himself proposed a third solution: For each day have one variable psalmody obligatory for all bound to the Office. This psalmody would be used at any of the Hours along with the hymn and prayers proper to each Hour. If one must pray or wishes to pray the other Hours, that person would use supplementary psalmody, either the gradual psalms or octaves of Psalm 118 such as in the ancient Roman Office or in the Office of Taizé.

As for the problem of maintaining all three Hours by communities bound to choral celebration, Canon Martimort proposed that each congregation or order ought to resolve the problem for itself.

He stated his belief that SC provided for that in article 95 by the reference to the choral obligation as "by law or constitutions" *(ex iure vel constitutionibus)* for regulars and "by general or particular law" *(ex iure communi vei particulari)* for chapters. He quoted Msgr. Emmanuel Bonet, a consultor, canonist, and auditor of the Sacred Roman Rota: "The conciliar Constitution does not oblige these things unless proper law dictates them."[119] Besides, he concluded, the revision of the choral obligation by each order or group separately would be more in the spirit of the conciliar Decree on the Up-to-Date Renewal of Religious Life *(Perfectae caritatis)*, which invites a distinguishing of the different vocations.

When Group 9 met in Genoa, September 6–8, 1966, to discuss, among other questions, that of the reduction of the minor Hours, Canon Martimort's positions were accepted unanimously. The summary of the discussion in Schema 185 repeats, generally, the relator's positions in RG. There is no indication of differing points of view.[120] The solution proposed to the Consilium was formulated in two questions:

"*Question 17:* Is it agreeable to so constitute the obligatory Hour during the day that it consist of a psalm or psalms from the current Psalter to be said with a hymn (and perhaps a prayer) fit for the Hour of the day (namely, Terce or Sext or None)?
"*Question 18:* Is it agreeable that the optional minor Hours consist of invariable psalms already used in the ordinary cycle, either gradual psalms or others?"[121]

Note was made that the solution proposed in these questions was unanimously accepted by Group 9, is consonant with SC, and maintains both the integral Psalter for all and the "truth of the Hours." Canon Martimort, the author of Schema 185, noted also:

"Moreover, the priest, when having a certain amount of leisure or making time for spiritual exercises, will be able to enjoy all the traditional Hours. The perfect form of prayer toward which the Church aims will be shown in the book."[122]

As to the choral obligation, Group 9 was reported to be in agreement with their relator's view that each group is so bound by particular law that it can modify the obligation on its own.[123]

At the meeting of the Group of Relators (September 26–27, 1966) in preparation for the seventh plenary session of the Consilium (October 6–14), twenty-five of the twenty-eight relators approved the proposals of Group 9. The two questions were submitted to the Consilium and were accepted unanimously.[124]

This major decision did not end all battles over the structure of the minor Hours. Canon Martimort has maintained that Father Bugnini was the primary proponent of one middle Hour for all, and that even after this decision he continued to argue for such and for a structure different from that agreed to by the Consilium. That, however, is a matter for consideration in chapter 5.[125]

The minor Hours, with one psalmody provided for all of them, appeared in both SCDO and SDO in 1967.[126] The Synod of Bishops in that same year endorsed the work of Group 9 and of the Consilium regarding the minor Hours by an overwhelming majority.[127] The specimen of the Office sent to the bishops of the world in 1969 (DSOD) as well as the definitive edition of LH with its General Instruction (IGLH) in 1971 indicate for the minor Hours the essential structure agreed to by the Consilium in October 1966.[128]

Some major structural reforms, then, were eventually achieved (1) in rendering both Lauds and Vespers briefer and perhaps somewhat better suited to celebration by all and (2) in making the invitatory a part of the Office distinct from the Office of Readings and something to be used before whatever Hour of the Office was prayed first in a given day. However, with the proposal regarding reduction of the minor Hours to one Midday Hour rejected, primarily in the name of fidelity to SC, what might have been the greatest structural change in the Office as a whole and an innovation welcome to individuals and communities alike did not come to pass.

In addition to considering major structural changes discussed above that would affect the Hours as a whole, Group 9 and the Consilium deliberated the retention or rejection of those structural elements of each Hour of the Office not already decreed by SC. These are the object of consideration next.

THE ESSENTIAL ELEMENTS
OF EVERY HOUR OF THE OFFICE

Chapter 4 of SC stated that a reformed Office would include psalmody, readings, and hymns.[129] Once Group 9 had agreed definitively that the postconciliar reform must adhere rigorously to the prescriptions set forth in SC, there was little appetite for even considering proposals that countered explicit prescriptions of the council document.[130] So at least those elements prescribed in SC, chapter 4, namely, psalmody, readings, and hymns, were considered as essential elements in the structure of the reformed Office.

Such was not necessarily the case, however, with antiphons, responsories, versicles, absolutions, blessings, prayers, and the commemoration of the faithful departed—all elements of the former Office. Decisions were reached regarding these latter sometimes only after prolonged discussion. It is best to take up each of them separately or in related groups.

Antiphons

Although there were no stipulations regarding antiphons in either The Schema for the Constitution on the Liturgy or in SC itself. Bishop J. Albert Martin, in conveying the thought of the conciliar commission drafting the text of SC, implicitly recommended that the postconciliar commission for reform of the Liturgy consider retaining both antiphons and responsories, not only as expressions of the essentially communitarian character of the Office but also as elements most supportive of prayer and contemplation.[131]

During the early stages of the work of reform, then, Group 8, which was responsible for the work on antiphons, versicles, responsories, absolutions, and blessings, through Fr. Pelagio Visentin, its relator, presented to Group 9 at its meeting of March 1–2, 1965, two major questions regarding antiphons in the structure of the revised Office. The first was whether antiphons should be part of the Office at all when this is recited privately; the second was, if antiphons are to be retained, where are they to be placed: before or after each Hour? with individual psalms or divisions of psalms?[132]

Regarding the question of the retention of antiphons, the consultors of Group 8 were evidently divided. Some argued against their inclusion in the Office at all for two reasons. First, antiphons are choral elements and thus unsuitable for inclusion in a Breviary that would be used for the most part in private by clergy in pastoral care. Second, proposed titles for the psalms could well serve the purpose of antiphons.

The majority, who favored retention of antiphons, gave six reasons for doing so. First, SC 26 and 27 emphasized the communal and ecclesial nature of all liturgical action. Antiphons as choral elements help to preserve and recall the communal character of the Office. Private recitation may need to be provided for, but communal celebration is the norm to be considered. Second, antiphons give needed variety and relief. They are beautiful poetic elements in the Office. Third, and most importantly, antiphons foster prayer and contemplation in the Office. They bring a more specific sense to the generic and indeterminate sense of psalms. Fourth, the proposed titles for the psalms cannot fulfill the function of antiphons. Titles relate to the psalms in themselves, whereas antiphons highlight the significance psalms have for various feasts and liturgical times. Fifth, and closely related to the foregoing reason, psalms in themselves may appear "uprooted" (deracines). Antiphons help relate them to some theme, hour of the day, or spirit of a feast. Finally, antiphons have been one of the chief means by which Christians from the first centuries have turned psalms into Christian prayer. Cardinal Quignonez himself learned by experience the need for them and included them in the second recension of his Breviary.[133]

Group 9 found the reasons for retention of antiphons persuasive. It was noted also in the report of this group that while antiphons have come to have a musical function in providing the tone for chanting the psalms to which they are related, their primary function is to foster prayer and contemplation, to give a typological sense to a psalm, to illuminate a certain idea contained in a psalm, to interpret a psalm, or to apply a psalm to the theme of a feast. Group 9 was unanimous in its recommendation that antiphons be retained in the new Office.[134] This recommendation of Group 9 accompanied a question on the retention of antiphons submitted to the fifth plenary session of the Consilium on April 28, 1965. The question was, "Is the general principle acceptable that in the new Breviary psalms with suitable antiphons are sung or recited even by those who recite the Office privately?"[135] The Consilium assented unanimously and thus accepted a traditional structural element for the reformed Office that could emphasize its public and communal nature even when recited privately.[136]

The question of whether antiphons should be retained in the reformed Office settled, Group 9 turned its attention next to the placement of antiphons in the structure of the Office. At the meeting of the group on September 25–26, 1965, Father Visentin presented the various opinions in Group 8 on the number and placement of antiphons. Some in the group desired one antiphon for each psalm even in the minor Hours and even if the psalm was divided into two or more parts. Others preferred an antiphon for each division of a psalm. There was no agreement on placement of an antiphon with a psalm, some preferring it be said or sung before and after the psalm, others preferring some other arrangement not specified.[137]

Opinions in Group 9 were varied as well. Those who preferred one antiphon for each psalm were confronted with the difficulty that if some psalms were divided and the parts distributed over several Hours or even several days, these sections would have no antiphons. Msgr. Joseph Pascher proposed that each division of a psalm have a proper antiphon except in those cases where a psalm has one sense throughout. In these cases one antiphon could be repeated for each division of the psalm. Fr. Balthasar Fischer and Canon Martimort foresaw difficulties in this solution for Psalms 118 and 77—psalms that have one sense throughout but would undoubtedly be divided into several parts over a number of days. In any case, each division of a psalm would have an antiphon. A vote on the proposal revealed that the majority (fourteen consultors) favored this principle, that each division of a psalm have its proper antiphon.[138]

But the very existence of antiphons in the reformed Office was called into question by the protests against the direction of the reform as this work became more widely known, especially through the first issue of *Notitiae*. As Canon Martimort made clear to the sixth plenary session of the Consilium on December 1, 1965, some questions previously decided could be reopened, since nothing was definitive yet.[139] Among the questions sent by Father Bugnini to the members and consultors of the Consilium in the December questionnaire reexamining the reform of the Office to date were two regarding the choral elements that included antiphons:

"9. Does it seem fitting that certain more strictly speaking choral elements be omitted in private recitation or, at least, be optional?

"10. If choral elements of this kind are retained even for private recitation, should they be drawn up so that they inspire or direct personal prayer?"[140]

A majority of those responding to the questionnaire replied affirmatively to these two questions.[141] But Canon Martimort did not rely, as already noted, on the meager affirmative response to the questionnaire to support the retention of antiphons.[142] After his several months of study, during which time he examined the vernacular Offices of various Protestant Churches and the short Offices used among Catholics, he recalled to the Consilium that antiphons are used in all the vernacular Offices, Protestant and Catholic. They aid, he noted, in identifying the literary genre of a psalm, in enabling a psalm to be prayed personally, in giving a typological or festal interpretation to a psalm, and in lending special color to it.[143]

Both Group 9, meeting in Genoa (September 6–8, 1966), and the Group of Relators, meeting in Rome (September 26–27) in preparation for the seventh plenary session of the Consilium (October 6–14), agreed to the retention of antiphons and to the resubmission of the question to the Consilium in these words: "Should antiphons, drawn up according to the aforesaid notes, exist in the Office?"[144] The Consilium apparently responded favorably, because Group 9 at its next meeting (February 6–8, 1967) proceeded with considerations regarding the *texts* of antiphons.[145]

One further point regarding antiphons insofar as they affect the structure of the Office was also made at the February meeting of Group 9. Antiphons, it was suggested, should be brief so that they may be used, if desired, after each strophe of a psalm. This principle, among others, was to govern the selection and creation of antiphons for the specimen of the Office (SCDO) to be readied for use by the Consilium at its upcoming eighth plenary session (April 10–19, 1967).[146]

When SCDO appeared at the April session, it did include antiphons for each Hour of the Office during Week I of the Easter season. According to traditonal practice for the Easter season, only a triple "alleluia" served as the antiphon before and after each setting of the psalms (and canticle) in Lauds, the minor Hours, and Compline.[147] But Canon Martimort explained to the Consilium that this arrangement was due only to the lack of selection of a proper antiphon for each of the psalms in those Hours.[148] For Vespers, however, the revisers had assigned a newly selected antiphon to be said before and after each psalm. Each of these antiphons consisted of a short scriptural verse concluding with "alleluia." This arrangement contrasted with the triple "alleluia" enclosing the set of five psalms in the preconciliar Roman Office.[149] No objection was raised by the Consilium to the placement of antiphons as used in the specimen, and there was general approval of the principles governing selection and placement of them as reviewed for the members by Canon Martimort.[150]

Compilation of the corpus of antiphons and determination of sources for them proceeded throughout the remainder of 1967 and early 1968.[151] During its ninth plenary session (November 14–20, 1967) the Consilium utilized SDO, the mimeographed booklet containing all the Hours for two weeks (November 12–25) in the form of the revised Office to date. As explained in the *praenotanda* of that volume, elements not yet selected or revised for the Office were taken from the then-current Roman Office. Most notable in this regard were the three psalms for the "middle Hour" still grouped under one antiphon.[152]

By March 1968 a corpus of antiphons, assembled by Group 8, for the Psalter of the revised Office was complete with the exception of those for Terce, Sext, and None. These were not compiled, apparently, because a structural question regarding antiphons in these Hours remained unresolved. In the meeting of Group 9 from February 27 to March 1, 1968, the question—whether one antiphon for the entire setting of the psalms in each Hour is sufficient or whether each psalm should have its own antiphon—was answered in favor of an antiphon for each psalm except in some cases to be left to the judgment of Group 8. Although traditionally one antiphon sufficed for the entire setting of psalms in these Hours, the principles previously agreed upon regarding the function of antiphons in the Office prevailed in this decision of Group 9.[153]

One other structural question regarding antiphons was also resolved on the same basis as the previous one at this meeting: Should each division of a psalm have a proper antiphon when the sense of the division differs from that of the previous division? Group 9 gave an affirmative answer to this question, which had been asked and favorably responded to by the same group in September 1965. The answer given then was apparently understood to have been called into question with other decisions regarding the Office at the sixth plenary session of the Consilium in December of that year, so a reconsideration seemed necessary.[154]

Further consideration was given at this meeting of February–March to the text of antiphons for special seasons and times—matter generally not bearing on the structure of the Hours. One consideration regarding text, however, does relate to the use of some antiphons and to their placement in the structure of a given Hour. Father Visentin expressed his reluctance to drop the then currently used "beautiful antiphons" for Lauds of the Nativity, Circumcision, and Epiphany, even though some were rather lengthy.[155] Retention of these antiphons would almost certainly preclude their use responsorially after each strophe of a psalm, as was envisioned at an early stage of the reform process. As will be discussed later, Father Visentin's reluctance did lead to the retention of many of these lengthy antiphons, thus rendering their responsorial use difficult if not impossible.[156]

To the tenth session of the Consilium (April 23–30, 1968) and on the basis of the discussion in the February–March meeting of Group 9, Canon Martimort posed the following question regarding antiphons: "Is it agreeable to provide antiphons for each of the psalms in the minor Hours and for individual sections of psalms having their own meaning except in special cases?"[157] Either this question was withdrawn before presentation to the Consilium or the results of the voting by the Consilium were omitted from Fr. Vincenzo Raffa's report on the tenth plenary session, for there is no mention of the question or results of voting on it.[158]

In the printed specimen of the Office published by the Consilium and sent to the bishops of the Church in 1969, there is clear indication that each psalm or division of a psalm will have an antiphon: "(f) Each one of the psalms or each division of a psalm has its own antiphon, which was selected to suggest the meaning of the psalm and, in popular celebration, to be repeated, possibly, after each of the strophes."[159] In the two samples of the Office given in this specimen, however, one for the memorial of St. Ignatius of Antioch on February 1 and the other for the ferial Office of February 3 (Feria II hebdomadae IV "per annum"), the three psalms at the middle Hour are grouped under one antiphon.[160] Apparently Group 8 had not completed its selection of antiphons even then.

Only with the appearance in 1971 of the first volumes of the definitive edition of LH did every psalm and every division of a psalm (with the exception of those at Terce, Sext, and None on solemnities or in special seasons) have their own antiphons.[161] This arrangement was not exactly in keeping with the decision of Group 9 at its meeting of February–March 1968. There it had been agreed that each division of a psalm would have its own antiphon only if the sense of that division differed from that of the previous division.[162] In the first draft (June 1968) of IGLH this understanding is expressed thus: "When a psalm because of its length is divided into several parts within one and the same canonical Hour, only one antiphon is said unless the parts are so different that they have entirely different meanings."[163]

In the second draft (August 1968), however, issued after the meeting of Group 9 from July 16 to 19, 1968, the pertinent text has been modified to read almost exactly as it appeared in the definitive text of IGLH: "When, because of its length, a psalm is divided into several parts within one and the same canonical Hour, a proper antiphon is placed with each part to lend variety, especially in sung celebration, and to illuminate better the riches of the psalm. Those who wish to use the whole psalm without interruption, however, may use only the first antiphon."[164]

From the initial draft of IGLH to its definitive text, it is clear that there would be exceptions to this principle of placing an antiphon with each psalm or division of a psalm in the minor Hours. The IGLH provides, as do its drafts, that psalms or parts of psalms are used in these Hours with their antiphons.[165]

In preparation, however, for the twelfth plenary session of the Consilium (November 4–8, 1969), Canon Martimort informed the members that Group 9 was proposing a further modification of the principle of one antiphon for each psalm or division of a psalm. This modification affected the complementary psalmody to be used at two of the minor Hours. When these Hours are celebrated on solemnities "in each Hour one proper antiphon is said with three psalms selected from the complementary psalmody unless special psalms are provided."[166] The arrangement proposed was adopted but with some modification in the text of the proposal on which the Consilium voted. The principle, however, remained the same.[167]

Thus every psalm and every division of a psalm with the exception sometimes of those in the minor Hours were to have an antiphon. The option was given, however, of using only the first antiphon given for the several parts of a divided psalm if one preferred to pray the entire psalm without interruption. No *relatio* of the proceedings of the meeting of Group 9 in July 1968 seems to have been sent to the Consilium, so the reasons for the change in the provision of antiphons for parts of psalms are no clearer than can be deduced from a reading of the definitive text of the IGLH.

One further outcome of the work on antiphons was the retention in the definitive text of LH of some of the traditional but usually longer antiphons, especially those for Christmas, its octave day, and Epiphany. Their retention, as noted above, was anticipated by Father Visentin in 1968 and rendered difficult, if not virtually impossible, their use as refrains after strophes of the psalms or canticles with which they were associated, even though such a procedure was envisioned for all antiphons in IGLH 114.[168] It must be noted regarding this procedure that the question of placement of antiphons in the definitive edition of LH seems not to have arisen in the final meetings of Group 9. In the definitive text the antiphon assigned a psalm or canticle appears, as in former editions of the Roman Office, both before and after the psalm or canticle. IGLH, however, in the section on antiphons says nothing about beginning a psalm or canticle with its antiphon or repeating the antiphon at the end of a psalm or canticle. It does, however, speak of using the antiphon as a refrain after each strophe of psalm or canticle. Only in the section "Methods of Singing the Psalms" does IGLH refer to obligatory use of the antiphon at the beginning of a psalm and optional use at its conclusion. In this same section, though, there is again reference to use of the antiphon as a refrain after each strophe of a psalm.[169]

Responsories

The exclusion of responsories from the Office had been demanded by some bishops at Vatican Council II, since, it was claimed, responsories pertain to communal celebration of the Office, and such celebration was not the norm in contemporary use of the Office.[170] The definitive text of SC, while omitting all reference to responsories, laid emphasis in articles 26 and 27 on all liturgical action being preferably and, indeed, normatively communal in character. As noted above with respect to antiphons, Bishop J. Albert Martin, on behalf of the conciliar commission, had implicitly recommended retention of antiphons and responsories to emphasize even in private recitation the communal and prayerful nature of the Office.[171]

With little difficulty the consultors constituting Group 9 agreed early in the process of reform to retain long responsories at the Office of Readings whether celebrated communally or recited privately. At the group's meeting of March 1 and 2, 1965, reasons stated for retaining responsories were that they (1) foster devotion, (2) turn the reading into prayer, and (3) in the case of responsories with a historical cast, serve to put the accent on a certain idea or an important moment in the history of salvation.[172] The only question of major concern for the group was, Is it necessary to respect the repetitious character of the responsory? Some members of Group 9 believed that the repetitive element *(repetenda)* was essential to the nature of a responsory and thus no effort should be made to delete repetition of the whole versicle even if repetition of part of the versicle (repetition *a latere)* were discarded on the grounds of meaninglessness.[173]

In a meeting previous to that of Group 9, Group 8 had argued the retention or deletion of responsories. Those opposed to their retention found the "whole meaning and value" *(totus sensus et valor)* of responsories in their sung or choral execution. Since execution of this kind was practically never the case in recent times, they said, responsories should be dropped or some skillful attempt made to simplify the melodies so that they could at least be sung in choir by some groups. Most consultors in Group 8 defended retention of responsories for reasons similar to those for retaining antiphons: They can recall the communal nature of the Office to those reciting it alone; their variety removes a sense of monotony; and, most importantly, they provide a transition from reading to prayer or meditation. The last reason calls for a careful attention, they said, to connecting the responsories with the readings that precede them.[174]

As with Group 9, however, the major problem regarding responsories in the first discussion of Group 8 revolved around the *repetenda*. It was noted, however, that a number of the conciliar bishops, the greater number who responded to the consultation on the Office in 1956-57, and the majority of the consultors in Group 8 favored retention of the *repetenda* because (1) without it the structure of the responsory would be destroyed and (2) it is proper to prayer and contemplation to dwell lovingly on the same object even with the same words used over and over.[175] Group 8, having agreed at least in principle on the retention of responsories, formulated a question to present to the Consilium: "Is it agreeable to the Fathers as a general principle that some kind of responsory occur after the reading in the Office even if it is recited privately?"[176] In its fifth plenary session (April 26-30, 1965), the Consilium responded affirmatively to the question.[177]

In the questionnaire resulting both from objections to the lines the reform was taking and from discussion in the sixth plenary session of the Consilium there were no questions specifically concerning the responsory.[178] Group 9, however, at its meeting of September 6-8, 1966, summarized again the reasons for retaining responsories and reformulated the question already submitted to and answered affirmatively by the Consilium at its fifth session. To this was added a new question, which the members of Group 9 had discussed and answered affirmatively by a vote of nine to one: "Should responsories of this kind be obligatory even in private recitation?" The one negative vote in Group 9 on this question was against obligation, at least in the vernacular.[179]

The first question received a unanimously favorable vote from the Consilium. With respect to the second question, twenty-two favored the obligatory nature of responsories and eleven preferred that they be optional (*ad libitum*).[180] With the decision firm regarding the existence of responsories, Groups 8 and 9 turned their attention to the selection and composition of responsories for the two specimens of the Office (SCDO and SDO) used respectively at sessions eight and nine of the Consilium in 1967. Generally, the consultors and members at the eighth session of the Consilium (April 10-19, 1967) were pleased with the responsories in the specimen, but some found too great an artificiality in them and expressed the desire for provision for a freer response.[181] In principle, however, by April 1967 the responsory as an element in the structure of the reformed Office was assured a place. Considerable discussion ensued regarding a short responsory in Lauds and Vespers, but that will be considered in the next chapter.[182]

Versicles, Blessings, and Absolutions

At the meeting of Group 9 from March 1 to 2, 1965, Fr. Pelagio Visentin reported that Group 8 did not see the question of whether to retain versicles, blessings, and absolutions as a question of great importance. The other members of Group 9 at that same meeting agreed and said they were prepared to see the suppression of these elements in the Office.[183] No action, however, was taken to do that.

To the general question regarding the advisability of omitting certain choral elements (including versicles, blessings, and absolutions) put to the Consilium in the questionnaire of December 1965, twenty-one of the twenty-four respondents replied in the affirmative, although there were widely varying opinions as to which of these elements (including antiphons and responsories) should or should not be retained.[184]

Canon Martimort, in his lengthy commentary on the elements of the Office in the light of the response to the questionnaire, advocated retention of the choral elements in general because these elements (1) recall to those praying the Hours privately their essentially communal character, (2) do fulfill a profitable function where the Office is prayed in common, (3) constitute a treasure trove of piety and assist the understanding of the psalms, and (4) bring an element of joy and variety to the Office.[185]

Group 9 at its meeting of July 20–23, 1967, came to a final decision about some of the choral elements, namely, the versicles, absolutions, and blessings in Matins. Father Visentin suggested that the versicle and response in Matins between the psalmody and the readings of the first nocturn be retained in the new Office of Readings to function as a transition from psalmody to reading. A number of consultors, however, requested an explanation of the "end, nature, and character" (*finis, natura, et indoles*) of this element before making a decision. Canon Martimort suggested that such an investigation should only precede the attempt to explain the purpose of the versicle, if retained, when the instruction that would precede the new Office is composed. Some others saw the versicles, if well chosen, as elements giving "a proper festive cast" (proprium colorem festivum) to special Offices. When used outside of feasts, they were seen to serve as introductions to the readings.[186] Fourteen of the fifteen consultors present at this meeting responded favorably to a question that proposed, for the reasons mentioned above, retention of the versicle between the psalmody and readings in the proposed Office of Readings.[187]

The versicle appeared in all the specimens of the Office in 1967 and 1969 and, of course, in LH. The introduction to DSOD (1969) said of it: "A verse drawn from the Bible only precedes the readings. It was selected to prepare minds for hearing the word of God."[188] The IGLH, making more explicit Father Visentin's view of the function of the versicle as providing a transition from psalmody to reading, says: "Between the psalmody and the readings there is customarily a verse by which prayer makes a transition from psalmody to hearing the readings."[189]

While the members of Group 9 found reason to preserve the versicle in the Office of Readings, they were almost unanimous in their opinion that absolutions and blessings be suppressed. Noting that Cardinal Gut at the eighth plenary session of the Consilium (April 10–17, 1967) had expressed the wish that at least one absolution be retained in the Office of Readings, Group 9 objected to retention of any absolutions on the grounds that contemporary celebrants of the Office do not seem to find elements of this kind agreeable, and such elements do not seem necessary to the structure of the Office.[190] The reason given for removing the blessings before the readings was that in the Mass of the Roman Rite, with the exception of the gospel, a blessing is never given before a reading. No reason was evident, then, for a blessing to occur before a reading in the Office.[191]

In the relatio prepared by Canon Martimort for the ninth plenary session of the Consilium (November 14–20, 1967) Group 9 is said to favor the suppression of the blessing not only in private recitation, as had already been permitted by Pope Paul VI in Tres abhinc annos (May 4, 1967), but also in choral and public celebration because the reason for its existence is not clear. Some, it is said, viewed the absolution as an embolism of the Lord's Prayer at the conclusion of each nocturn of Matins, but Group 9 unanimously agreed to the suppression of the Lord's Prayer at the conclusion of each nocturn because it is not a place of sufficient dignity for that prayer.[192]

The same reason as given in the July meeting of Group 9 for the suppression of the blessings was presented to the ninth session of the Consilium for the suppression of absolutions. The members were asked: "Shall the absolution and blessings in the Office of Readings for the Roman Rite be suppressed?"[193] The Consilium apparently responded affirmatively and without difficulty to the question.[194] In the specimens of the Office (SCDO and SDO) used at the eighth and ninth plenary sessions, and in the DSOD, distributed to the bishops of the world in 1969, no absolutions or blessings occur in the Office of Readings (Officium lectionis); and, of course, they do not appear in the definitive text of LH.[195]

Prayers

Another category, which included the structural elements of intercessions, orations, and Lord's Prayer, was termed simply "Prayers." Discussion in the various study groups and in the sessions of the Consilium involving one of these elements often affected the others, and their position at the close of an Hour as well as their intercessory character usually allowed them to be discussed together. They will be considered here in the following order: (1) intercessions, (2) orations, (3) Lord's Prayer.

As early as 1964 a number of consultors—following the recommendations of the conciliar commission on the liturgy as these were conveyed to the fathers of the council by Bishop J. Albert Martin—were suggesting that some of the intercessions (preces) of Prime be transferred to Lauds.[196] They also proposed that a form of the prayer of the faithful be inserted in Vespers.[197] Reasons given for including some of the preces from Prime in the revised format for Lauds were (1) a number of bishops at Vatican Council II were opposed to the suppression of Prime precisely because the preces capituli seemed to be a very suitable prayer for the beginning of the day; (2) the conciliar commission recommended to the postconciliar commission (Consilium) the transfer of some of these prayers to another Hour; (3) the character of Morning Prayer better fits Lauds, and thus some of the preces would be suitable as prayer at the beginning of the day.

The reasons given by a minority of the consultors *(periti)* for excluding these prayers from Lauds were (1) Lauds is an Hour of praise and ought not to focus on human needs and (2) other formularies, for example, the morning collects preserved in some ancient Sacramentaries, seem to be better intercessory forms for Lauds.[198] But these reasons were not persuasive to Group 9. Furthermore, the nearly universal tradition of intercessions at Vespers, still represented in the Roman tradition by the rarely used *preces feriales* and, according to Canon Martimort, the insistence by Msgr. Balthasar Fischer from the early 1950s to refashion the ferial prayers along the lines of the universal prayer, prompted the consultors of Group 9 to recommend to the Consilium that a common prayer or prayer of the faithful *(oratio communis seu fidelium)* be restored to Vespers.[199]

Two questions, then, regarding intercessions at Lauds and Vespers were proposed by Group 9 for presentation to the Consilium at its fourth plenary session (September 28–October 9; November 16, 1964):

"Question 2: Should some of the prayers that were once said in the Chapter after Prime be inserted in Lauds?
"Question 8: Should a common prayer or prayer of the faithful be inserted in Vespers?"[200]

The Consilium responded favorably but not unanimously to both questions as these were reworded somewhat, probably as a result of discussion in the Group of Relators prior to the fourth session:

"2. Should the prayers taken or adapted from Prime be placed in the Breviary as prayers to be said fittingly before work (in the manner of devotional prayers such as grace before meals)?
"8. Should a common prayer or prayer of the faithful be inserted in Vespers even in recitation without the people present?"[201]

To the first question (no. 2) fourteen of twenty-nine voting members of the Consilium responded yes; seven, no; eight, yes with reservations. Of those who voted with reservations, five wanted the *preces* obligatory; one wanted them inserted immediately after Lauds; one suggested they be part of Lauds; and one had no recommendation. To the second question (no. 8), twenty of twenty-eight voting members responded yes and eight no.[202] More difficulty, obviously, attended the question of the *preces* in conjunction with Lauds than the question of the universal or "common" prayer *(oratio communis)* in Vespers.

The qualified approval given by the Consilium in 1964 to the use of some form of *preces* in conjunction with Lauds and of a universal prayer in Vespers was only the beginning of a difficult process lasting some three years to determine more precisely the exact placement and form of these prayers in the structure of the Office as a whole. The difficulty seems not to have originated or been exacerbated by the objections in 1965 to the lines of reform of the Office—objections prompting the questionnaire of December 1965. That questionnaire contains no queries regarding the prayers at Lauds or Vespers.[203]

Only in September 1966 did Group 9 raise the question again about the placement of intercessions in or after Lauds and within Vespers.[204] At its meeting of September 6–8 the group, uncomfortable with the vote of the Consilium in 1964 on the question regarding the *preces* in or after Lauds but without posing a new question, informed the Consilium that the mind of the group was to fashion intercessions to be inserted *within* Lauds, having a *form* different from that of the universal prayer to be inserted into Vespers and retaining the same *elements* as found in the then-current *preces*.[205] With respect to the intercessions at Vespers, Group 9, apparently assuming that the question of the inclusion of a universal prayer in Vespers had been settled in the affirmative, turned its attention to the *form* such prayers should take. This concern regarding form will be considered at greater length in the next chapter in the discussion of Vespers.[206]

The question, however, of the existence of a universal prayer within Vespers was not yet settled in some peoples' minds, as is evident from the definitive text of the report *(relatio)* submitted by Canon Martimort on behalf of Group 9 to the sixth plenary session of the Consilium (October 19–26, November 22–26, December 1, 1966).[207] The text of this report was essentially that of Schema 185 (September 19, 1966) with some additions from discussion in the Group of Relators' meeting prior (September 26–27) to the sixth session. The following question was to be put to the Consilium regarding the intercessions at Vespers: "Should the universal prayer be inserted into Vespers in the manner and for the reason described above?" The intercessions, it was suggested, should have a form different from that used in the Mass so as to avoid causing weariness and to be suitable for use in private recitation.[208] The vote by the Consilium was apparently unanimously in favor of the insertion of the universal prayer (oratio universalis) into Vespers but with a form different from that of the prayer of the faithful in the Mass.[209]

The question as to the inclusion of preces in or after Lauds was still not settled by the time of the use of the first specimen of the reformed Office (SCDO) at the eighth plenary session of the Consilium (April 10–19, 1967). For that volume Group 9 had agreed to the inclusion in Vespers of a form of intercessions found in the ancient Sacramentaries. No intercessions were provided for Lauds.[210]

Although a specific question regarding the insertion of intercessions seems not to have been presented to the eighth session of the Consilium, the members, on the basis (at least for Vespers) of their use of SCDO, did approve on April 17 the inclusion of intercessions in both Lauds and Vespers, on condition that those for Lauds be concerned with the offering of the day and of work to God and those for Vespers be in the form of a universal prayer.[211] Thus the inclusion of intercessions in some form in both Lauds and Vespers was assured, even though the nature of the intercessions at Lauds continued to be discussed. But that is a matter to be considered in chapter 5.[212]

The question of whether to conclude each Hour with an oration, another element in the category of "Prayers," did not enter the discussion of Group 9 until its meeting of February 6–8, 1967. At that time the various possibilities were simply discussed. For the minor Hours the options seen were two: (1) use of the special prayers in the Gelasian Sacramentary for the different Hours, and (2) use of the Lord's Prayer only to conclude each Hour. Some members of Group 9 wished to see both options used; others, one or the other option. For the major Hours three possibilities were proposed: (1) conclude with the prayer of the Mass as was the current practice; (2) use proper prayers on feasts and days of great importance; (3) on other days use prayers specific to the Hours. The only decision reached was to give the questions over to the competent study group, Group 18*bis* (prayers and prefaces [for Mass and Office]), to be studied further.[213]

With nothing definitively established regarding the use of orations in the Office, Canon Martimort announced to the Consilium in March 1967 that the specimen (SCDO) of the Office for use by the Consilium at its eighth plenary session would contain for Lauds and Vespers on Sundays and feasts the customary orations from the Mass. On ferial days the prayers proposed for these Hours would be formulae found in the ancient Sacramentaries.[214] In SCDO the minor Hours had orations appropriate to each Hour provided as options to the recitation of the Lord's Prayer. The oration concluding the Office of Readings was the same as that given for Lauds, and the concluding oration for Compline, likewise appropriate to the Hour, was identical each night.[215]

Immediate reaction to this arrangement among members and consultors of the Consilium centered on the option of Lord's Prayer *(Pater)* or oration at the "middle Hour." A few wanted the *Pater* obligatory; the majority wanted the oration in order to highlight the special character of the Hour. Msgr. Joseph Pascher suggested a compromise: Let the Lord's Prayer remain optional *(ad libitum)* and the oration be obligatory.[216]

At the meeting of Group 9 in Munich, July 20–23, 1969, several questions regarding the orations were considered. These can be reduced to two categories. First, as to whether the major Hours of Lauds and Vespers should be concluded after the intercessions with an oration or the Lord's Prayer, Group 9 agreed unanimously that an oration—either that of the Mass of the day or a prayer appropriate to the Hour—should conclude the intercessions but did not rule out entirely the use of the *Pater*. Acknowledgment was made, in fact, that conclusion with the Lord's Prayer, as witnessed in the *Rule of St. Benedict* and in the Visigothic tradition, might be a more ancient practice.[217] Second, since the discussion in the meeting of Group 9 concerning orations at the Hours other than Lauds and Vespers was about the *kind* of oration to be used, it was presupposed that there would be concluding orations in these Hours at least experimentally for the next specimen of the Office (SDO) to be used by the Consilium in its ninth plenary session in November 1967. Thus with the exception of the Office of Readings (in which the concluding oration was that of the Mass of the day), there were included for all the Hours in SDO orations appropriate in some way to the times of day corresponding to the respective Hours.[218]

From November 1967 until the appearance of LH there does not seem to have been any major questioning of the existence of orations at the conclusion of each hour. It is worth noting, however, that the question of the *existence* of concluding orations in the Hours seems never *explicitly* to have been presented to the Consilium for a discussion. Group 9 was still debating the existence of a concluding oration at Lauds and Vespers at its meeting in Genoa from February 27 to March 1, 1968. Some consultors at that time still favored concluding the intercessions with the *Pater* only. At conclusion of the discussion, however, the vote in favor of concluding the intercessions on a feast day, the memorial of a saint, a Sunday, or during special times in the year with the corresponding proper oration used in the Mass was unanimous. This decision, of course, said nothing about what should be done to conclude the intercessions in Ordinary Time, but the discussion in Group 9 indicated that there were tendencies to favor orations that would either relate to the intercessions or to the time of day corresponding to either Lauds or Vespers.[219] The question of the position of the oration in the structure of a given Hour is another matter and will be discussed for each Hour in chapter 5.

In the discussions of Group 9 and of the Consilium, a question closely tied to that of the concluding oration was the one regarding the use of the Lord's Prayer at the conclusion of all or some of the Hours. In the schema of the Constitution on the Sacred Liturgy (72c) it was proposed that the Lord's Prayer be recited at the conclusion of the minor Hours. This was opposed on the council floor because it did not pertain to the fundamental principles (*altiora principia*), which alone were to find expression in SC. Thus article 72 was eliminated and the recommendation made that such matters as it mentioned be considered for implementation by the postconciliar commission.[220] No discussion of the use of the *Pater* in the Office seems to have occurred in Group 9 before February 1967. At that time, during the meeting of the group in Genoa, the possibility was raised, as stipulated in the schema for SC, of concluding the minor Hours with the *Pater*.[221]

The following month, while introducing the specimen of the

Office (SCDO) to be used by the Consilium in its eighth plenary session, Canon Martimort made only one mention of use of the Lord's Prayer in the experimental scheme, and that in the minor Hours. He noted that there would have to be discussion of the use of the *Pater* and concluding oration in the future but that in the specimen the option would be given of praying the Lord's Prayer or an oration to conclude each of the minor Hours. In SCDO itself, outside the minor Hours, there is no indication of using the Lord's Prayer at the conclusion of an Hour.[222]

Some immediate reaction to the use of the *Pater* surfaced in the discussion of the Office by the Consilium on April 17, 1967, following the experiment with SCDO. Generally, there was dissatisfaction with the option of *Pater* or oration.[223] The dissatisfaction prompted Group 9, at its meeting in Munich during July 1967, to discuss more extensively the conclusion of the minor Hours as given in SCDO. Msgr. Pierre Jounel wished to see a choice offered between *Pater* and oration for the reason that the orations in the minor Hours were not of great euchological quality and the *Pater* would allow relief from them. Besides, recitation of the *Pater* three times a day would restore an ancient tradition of Christian prayer. Fr. Pelagio Visentin would retain only the *Pater*. Fr. Antoine Dumas, relator of Group 18*bis* (revision of prayers and prefaces) wanted both *Pater* and oration obligatory. Others (Msgrs. Salvatore Famoso and Joseph Pascher; Canon Andre Rose; Frs. Agostino Amore, Ansgar Dirks, Burkhard Neunheuser, and Anselmo Lentini) favored omission of the *Pater* and retention of the oration only, since the oration, together with the hymn, favored the "sanctification of time" *(sanctificatio temporis)* by expressing the sense of an Hour.[224]

In further discussion regarding the use of the Lord's Prayer in the Office as a whole, there was general agreement that an honorable place should be found for it and that the solution in SCDO (the April specimen) was not at all acceptable. Father Dumas suggested placing it at the conclusion of each Hour. Others opted for recitation at one Hour a day. (Monsignor Famoso suggested the Office of Readings, since that Hour had no suitable prayer; Monsignor Pascher suggested Vespers, since numerous orations for Lauds were available from ancient Sacramentaries but few for Vespers.) The majority, however, thought that the *Pater* would best conclude Lauds and Vespers. The recitation of the prayer at these Hours coupled with its use at Mass would thus allow the ancient tradition of a threefold daily praying of the Lord's Prayer to emerge again for all the faithful.[225]

At its meeting in July 1967 after further inconclusive discussion on the place of the *Pater* in Lauds and Vespers, Group 9 put to itself this simple question: "Do you wish the inclusion of the Lord's Prayer in Lauds and in Vespers?" The vote was unanimously in favor.[226] That decision effectively insured the use of the *Pater* in the Office. The question of the placement of that prayer in the Office seems never to have been put to the Consilium itself. Once Group 9 had decided that the prayer should be included in Lauds and Vespers, the questions regarding its position in relation to the intercessions and oration within the structure of each of those Hours became a major concern. These questions resisted solution for over a year and were the subject of prolonged discussion in the group. They will be considered in chapter 5 in the discussion of the structure of Lauds and Vespers.[227]

Commemoration of the Faithful Departed

Following the eighth plenary session of the Consilium (April 10–19, 1967) and the experiment with SCDO, some consideration was given to how the dead should be prayed for within the Office. In SCDO the customary "May the souls of the faithful departed through the mercy of God rest in peace" (the *Fidelium*) was included as an option at the end of each Hour. In relating a summary of the opinion received following its use, Canon Martimort noted that all responses indicated that some place must be found in the Office to pray for the dead. Reactions were diverse as to how this should be done: Two persons favored retention of the *Fidelium* as obligatory, but Canon Martimort noted that this verse was a late introduction into the Office by Pope Pius V when he suppressed the obligation to the Office of the Dead, and it does not coalesce well with the structure of the Office. Three other solutions were proposed: (1) Find a formula that brings together a commemoration of the saints, absent brethren, and the dead; (2) at the conclusion of the whole Office after the antiphon to the Blessed Virgin Mary, make some commemoration of the dead; (3) introduce a commemoration of the dead in the universal prayer at Vespers. The majority of Group 9 opted for the last solution.[228]

At its meeting in Munich July 20–23, 1967, Group 9 formally adopted the solution that the commemoration of the dead should occur in the last of four petitions in the universal prayer at Vespers.[229] This solution was submitted to the Consilium at its ninth plenary session (November 14–20, 1967) both in SDO for use during that session and in a formal question to the Consilium: "Is it agreeable that the commemoration of the dead be made in the universal prayer and that the verse *Fidelium* be omitted after the individual Hours?"[230] In the discussion, Fr. Joseph Gelineau, a consultor, proposed that two questions ought to be considered here: (1) Should the dead be commemorated in the universal prayer at Vespers? (2) Should this be done daily? His proposal was accepted, and after a brief discussion in which the majority favored the solution proposed by Group 9, the vote for the question as to whether commemoration of the dead should be made in the universal prayer at Vespers received a majority of yes votes with six members opposed. The vote in favor of the second question was unanimous. Thus the commemoration of the faithful departed, formerly made at the conclusion of each Hour of the Office, was to be limited to the final petition in the intercessions at Vespers.[231]

Most of the structural elements, then, of the former Roman Office found in each of the Hours were retained in LH. Psalmody, readings, and hymns were assured by virtue of prescription in SC. The conviction that the Office is by its nature communal prayer ultimately prevailed in preserving antiphons for all modes of its use. Antiphons were even allowed use as refrains in a responsorial mode of psalmody, though the content of some antiphons disallowed that use in practice. Responsories were retained in their truncated form without that kind of historical investigation that might have restored them to their original form and to a position of different and greater significance within the structure of an Hour than they had had in the former Office. Blessings and absolutions disappeared without any significant objection, as did most versicles. With regard to prayers, intercessions were not only retained but given greater scope and significance in Lauds and Vespers. Orations were maintained and in many instances made to relate the Hour of the Office better to its respective time of day and the Christian significance of that time. Although use of the Lord's Prayer was reduced in the Hours, its significance was enhanced by its confinement, ultimately, to the major Hours of Lauds and Vespers. Its competition with the oration as the concluding prayer of those Hours is, as noted above, a matter for further consideration in the next chapter. Finally, the commemoration of the faithful departed was given a more modest place at the conclusion of the intercessions of Vespers only.

The major structural element of all the Hours is, of course, psalmody. The long process by which the psalmody was restructured for LH is the subject of consideration next.

THE DISTRIBUTION AND DIVISION OF THE PSALMS

A major work in the reform of the Office was that of redistributing the psalms over a period longer than one week, as SC 91 demanded. This redistribution posed questions regarding the structure of the Office: (1) If distribution of the psalms is throughout a period longer than one week, should the psalmody of individual Hours be reduced? (2) Is it advisable, given a greater amount of time in which to employ the psalms, to divide in some way longer psalms at given Hours? A number of other questions certainly had to be considered in redistributing the Psalter; for example, are all 150 psalms to be retained? If not, can the so-called imprecatory psalms or verses in the psalms be omitted? Can the historical psalms be omitted or used as biblical readings? These other questions, however important and however lengthily discussed, do not pertain directly to the structure of the Office and so will not be considered at length here.[232] Since the structural questions regarding the reduction of the number of psalms in the Hours and those regarding the division of lengthy psalms are inextricably entwined, they are discussed together in what follows.

Between April and June of 1964 Group 3 (distribution of the psalms) deliberated on how to implement SC 89 and 91, which set the general principles for reform of the individual Hours (89) and decreed a redistribution of the Psalter throughout a period of time longer than one week (91). The relator of Group 3, Msgr. Joseph Pascher, and its secretary, Canon André Rose, drew up a number of schemata for the distribution of the psalms. These were examined by the other members of Group 3.[233] Monsignor Pascher and

Canon Rose reported on the work of their study group at the meeting of Group 9, June 20–21, 1964, and together with the other members of Group 9 agreed on principles that would govern the redistribution of the psalter.[234] The relator and the secretary then devised two new schemata based on these principles for the distribution of the psalter. Those affecting the structure of the Office were, (1) the length of the psalmody is to be reduced in the entire *cursus*, (2) the length of the psalmody is to be determined by the spirituality possible to a cleric *(sic)* today, and (3) the psalms are to be distributed over four weeks with the exception of Lauds, Vespers, and Compline.[235]

In submitting the two schemata (tables 3 and 4 below) to Group 9, Monsignor Pascher also presented a commentary on the principles governing their compilation. Regarding the reduction of the psalmody in the entire *cursus* and not just in Matins as SC 89c stipulates, Monsignor Pascher noted that SC 91 looks to the whole of SC 89, so the whole Psalter must be distributed over a longer period of time. Such extension entails fewer psalms or divisions of psalms in Hours other than Matins. The relator emphatically supported the principle that length of psalmody was to be determined by the spirituality possible today to clergy with pastoral care. It is possible, he said, for the busy cleric today to hear the Word of God in the psalms and to utilize these ancient poems as prayer only if their number in any one Hour is less than in the former Office.[236]

Regarding the distribution of the Psalter over four weeks, Monsignor Pascher noted that although abbreviation of the *incisa* (psalms or psalmic divisions in a given Hour) and extension of the *cursus* over four weeks was thought necessary in order to provide what was deemed an appropriate measure of psalmody for spiritual profit, it could render choral celebration difficult. He does not offer a reason for this observation, but presumably a greater number of *incisa* might pose a greater musical challenge, calling perhaps for an increased number of psalm tones over the four weeks. Lest the number of *incisa* be excessively increased and single *incisa* be excessively abbreviated, a *cursus* of one week is retained in Schema I for Lauds and Vespers, and at Compline Psalms 4, 90, and 133 are proposed for use daily. Sundays and Fridays would have the same setting of psalms each week to commemorate, respectively, the resurrection of the Lord and his passion.[237]

In Schema II the number of psalms in Vespers is reduced from five to three for all—clergy and laity. Monsignor Pascher and Canon Rose preferred this schema because it did not set up a division between the Office of clergy and that of the people, and despite the preference of most in Group 9 for Schema I, they asked that the Consilium itself discuss the merits of Schema II.[238]

Since a basic question, however, affecting distribution and division of the psalms, namely, whether all 150 psalms were to be retained in the *cursus*, remained disputed among the members of Group 3, Monsignor Pascher in the name of Group 3 submitted the question to Group 9 at its meetings during the fourth plenary session of the Consilium (September 28–October 9, November 16, 1964). All in Group 9 agreed that according to SC all the psalms are to be retained in the Office, but some thought SC 91 would allow placement of some psalms (e.g., imprecatory) outside the *cursus* (e.g., among the readings). Those who believed this was possible said that before the council met this question had been discussed. If the council had wished all psalms included within the *cursus*, it would have indicated this explicitly. It did not so indicate, and thus liberty is left to remove some psalms from the *cursus*. Those who opposed this view said that article 91, in referring to a redistribution of the psalms over a period of time longer than one week, refers to the Psalter as currently distributed. Since all psalms are distributed over one week in the current arrangement, all psalms must be used in the reformed *cursus*. All the members of Group 9 with one exception voted in favor of retaining all the psalms in the *cursus*.[239]

There was, however, continued discussion on whether the question of the interpretation of article 91 should be submitted to the Consilium. Finally, Canon Martimort suggested that the question of interpretation be left aside and that the Consilium be asked simply "whether or not everyone would be pleased to retain all the psalms in cyclical recitation within the *cursus* of the Office."[240] Among the twenty-five members of the Consilium present when this question was presented during the fourth plenary session, twenty-one voted in favor of retention and four against it. Thus the Consilium upheld the decision of Group 9 that all the psalms should be used in the *cursus* of the Office.

At the same series of meetings of Group 9, Monsignor Pascher also submitted from the many proposed arrangements for the dis-

TABLE 3

SCHEMA I OF PROPOSED DISTRIBUTION OF PSALMS
IN A FOUR-WEEK CYCLE
FOR THE REFORMED ROMAN OFFICE
1964

			Week 1								Week 2			
H[a]	Sun.	Mon.	Tue.	Wed.	Thu.	Fri.	Sat.	Sun.	Mon.	Tue.	Wed.	Thu.	Fri.	Sat.
M	1	6	12	18a	27	21a	101a	*	37a	41a	44a	48a	*	104a
	2	7a	13	18b	29a	21b	101b		37b	41b	44b	48b		104b
	3	7b	14	19	29b	21c	101c		37c	42	45	48c		104c
L	62	5	35	66	89	91	Ca.[b]	*	*	*	*	*	*	*
	Ca.	Ca.	Ca.	Ca.	Ca.	Ca.	Ca.							
	148	148	148	148	148	148	148							
	149	149	149	149	149	149	149							
	150	150	150	150	150	150	150							
T	118a	118b	118c	118d	118e	118f	118g	*	118h	118i	118j	118k	*	118l
	117a	8	16a	20	26a	79a	77a		36a	38a	28	51		55a
	117b	10	16b	22	26b	79b	77b		36b	38b	31	52		55b
S	92	9a	17a	23	32a	34a	77c	*	36c	39a	43a	49a	*	56
	65a	9b	17b	25a	32b	34b	77d		36d	39b	43b	49b		67a
	65b	9c	17c	25b	32c	34c	77e		36e	39c	43c	49c		67b
N	95a	9d	17d	24a	33a	68a	77f	*	30a	40a	46	50a	*	67c
	95b	9e	17e	24b	33b	68b	77g		30b	40b	47a	50b		67d
	99	11	15	24c	33c	68c	77h		30c	40c	47b	50c		67e
V	109	111	112	116	131a	129	140	*	*	*	*	*	*	*
	110	114	120	123	131b	128	136							
	113a	115	121	124	126	130	137							
	113b	119	122	125	127	132	139							
	Ca.	Ca.	Ca.	Ca.	Ca.	Ca.	Ca.							
C	4	4	4	4	4	4	4	*	*	*	*	*	*	*
	90	90	90	90	90	90	90							
	133	133	133	133	133	133	133							

			Week 3								Week 4			
H[a]	Sun.	Mon.	Tue.	Wed.	Thu.	Fri.	Sat.	Sun.	Mon.	Tue.	Wed.	Thu.	Fri.	Sat.
M	*	54a	70a	73a	75a	*	106a	*	83a	93a	98	138a	*	102a
		54b	70b	73b	75b		106b		83b	93b	100	138b		102b
		54c	70c	73c	81		106c		86	93c	107	138c		102c
L	*	*	*	*	*	*	*	*	*	*	*	*	*	*

140

TABLE 3 *(cont.)*

H[a]	Week 3							Week 4						
	Sun.	Mon.	Tue.	Wed.	Thu.	Fri.	Sat.	Sun.	Mon.	Tue.	Wed.	Thu.	Fri.	Sat.
T	*	118m	118n	118o	118p	*	118q	*	118r	118s	118t	118u	*	118v
		58a	64a	74a	78a		88a		84a	103a	141	143a		105a
		58b	64b	74b	78b		88b		84b	103b	142	143b		105b
S	*	57	71a	60	80a	*	88c	*	85a	103c	134a	144a	*	105c
		61a	71b	63	80b		88d		85b	103d	134b	144b		105d
		61b	71c	69	80c		88e		90	103e	134c	144c		105e
N	*	53	72a	76a	82a	*	88f	*	87a	96a	135a	145	*	108a
		59a	72b	76b	82b		88g		87b	96b	135b	146		108b
		59b	72c	76c	82c		88h		87c	97	135c	147		108c
V	*	*	*	*	*	*	*	*	*	*	*	*	*	*
C	*	*	*	*	*	*	*	*	*	*	*	*	*	*

SOURCE: Schema no. 23, supplement.

[a]In this column H = Hour; M = Matins; L = Lauds; T = Terce; S = Sext; N = None; V = Vespers; C = Compline.

[b]Ca. = Canticle. Specific canticles were not designated for any of the hours.

*Psalms are for the corresponding day in Week 1.

TABLE 4

SCHEMA II OF PROPOSED DISTRIBUTION OF PSALMS
IN A FOUR-WEEK CYCLE
FOR THE REFORMED ROMAN OFFICE
1964

	Week 1								Week 2						
H[a]	Sun.	Mon.	Tue.	Wed.	Thu.	Fri.	Sat.	Sun.	Mon.	Tue.	Wed.	Thu.	Fri.	Sat.
M	1	6	12	19	28	21a	104a	*	39a	43a	47a	58a	30a	105a
	2	7a	13	20	29a	21b	104b		39b	43b	47b	58b	30b	105b
	3	7b	14	22	29b	21c	104c		39c	43c	51	60	30c	105c
L	62	5	35	66	89	50	Ca.[b]	*	*	*	*	*	*	*
	Ca.	Ca.	Ca.	Ca.	Ca.	Ca.	Ca.							
	148	148	148	148	148	148	148							
	149	149	149	149	149	149	149							
	150	150	150	150	150	150	150							
T	117a	18a	18b	118a	118b	118c	118d	*	118e	118f	118g	118h	118i	118j
	117b	9a	16a	23	31	79a	36a		38a	44a	55a	59a	79a	67a
	117c	9b	16b	25	45	79b	36b		38b	44b	55b	59b	79b	67b
S	92	9c	15	24a	32a	34a	36c	*	40a	48a	54a	61a	34a	67c
	65a	9d	17a	24b	32b	34b	36d		40b	48b	54b	61b	34b	67d
	65b	9e	17b	24c	32c	34c	36e		46	48c	54c	63	34c	67e
N	99	8	17c	26a	33a	53	37a	*	41a	49a	52	64a	53a	70a
	95a	10	17d	26b	33b	87a	37b		41b	49b	56	64b	53b	70b
	95b	11	17e	27	33c	87b	37c		42	49c	57	81	87	70c
V	109	111	112	116	131	129	140	*	*	*	*	*	*	*
	113a	110	115	120	131	124	121							
	113b	114	119	122	123	125	132							
C	4	4	4	4	4	4	4	*	*	*	*	*	*	*
	90	90	90	90	90	90	90							
	133	133	133	133	133	133	133							

	Week 3								Week 4						
H	Sun.	Mon.	Tue.	Wed.	Thu.	Fri.	Sat.	Sun.	Mon.	Tue.	Wed.	Thu.	Fri.	Sat.
M	*	71a	80a	81	91	68a	106a	*	Ca.	Ca.	Ca.	Ca.	Ca.	Ca.
		71b	80b	83a	96a	68b	106b		Ca.	Ca.	Ca.	Ca.	Ca.	Ca.
		71c	80c	83b	96b	68c	106c		Ca.	Ca.	Ca.	Ca.	Ca.	Ca.
L	*	*	*	*	*	*	*	*	*	*	*	*	*	*

TABLE 4 *(cont.)*

H	Sun.	Mon.	Tue.	Wed.	Thu.	Fri.	Sat.	Sun.	Mon.	Tue.	Wed.	Thu.	Fri.	Sat.
				Week 3							Week 4			
T	*	118k	118l	118m	118n	118o	118p	*	118q	118r	118s	118t	118u	118v
		72a	74a	75a	78a	79a	85a		107a	126	128	136	79a	143a
		72b	74b	75b	78b	79b	85b		107b	127	130	137	79b	143b
S	*	73a	77a	82a	88a	34a	93a	*	101a	103a	134a	138a	34a	144a
		73b	77b	82b	88b	34b	93b		101b	103b	134b	138b	34b	144b
		73c	77c	82c	88c	34c	93c		101c	103c	134c	138c	34c	144c
N	*	76a	77d	84a	88d	53a	97a	*	102a	108a	135a	139	53	145
		76b	77e	84b	88e	53b	97b		102b	108b	135b	141	87a	146
		76c	77f	86	88f	87	100		102c	108c	135c	142	87b	147
V	*	*	*	*	*	*	*	*	*	*	*	*	*	*
C	*	*	*	*	*	*	*	*	*	*	*	*	*	*

SOURCE: Schema no. 23, supplement.

[a]In this column H = Hour; M = Matins; L = Lauds; T = Terce; S = Sext; N = None; V = Vespers; C = Compline.

[b]Ca. = Canticle. Specific canticles were not designated for any of the hours.

*Psalms are for the corresponding day in Week 1.

tribution of the psalms three that were judged eminent and a fourth proposed as a via media incorporating elements of the other three. These schemata, in summary, were (1) a four-week cycle for Matins, Terce, Sext, and None; one-week cycle for Lauds and Vespers, and Psalms 4, 90, and 133 daily for Compline (as in Schema I or II in tables 3 and 4 above); (2) a two-week cycle for Matins, Terce, Sext, and None; one-week cycle for Lauds and Vespers, and Psalms 4, 90, and 133 daily for Compline; (3) a two-week cycle for all the Hours except Compline, and Psalms 4, 90, and 133 daily for Compline; (4) a four-week cycle for Matins; a two-week cycle for all the other Hours except Compline, and Psalms 4, 90, and 133 daily for Compline.

After discussion on all four proposals the group was of a mind that the third and fourth proposals had the most merit. Nine members thought Group 3 should draw up schemata for both these proposals, but four members thought only the last should be developed. Monsignor Pascher proposed that a decision from the Consilium on the number of psalms for each Hour should be received before attempting to determine a scheme of distribution. So several questions on the number of psalms for each Hour were submitted to the Consilium at its fourth session. These and the results of the Consilium's voting were as follows:

"1. Are five or three psalms to be said in Lauds? [Of 29 members present, 23 favored five psalms; 5 favored three; and 1 favored three with a canticle.]

"5. Should one schema for Vespers be retained whether clergy celebrate this Hour with or without people present, and should this schema have five psalms with the understanding that two may be omitted in celebrations with the people? [Present, 28; all, yes.]

"9. Should three psalms be assigned to Compline? [Present, 28; all, yes.]

"12. Should three psalms be used at Terce, Sext, and None? [Present, 28; all, yes.]

"13. Should the psalms at Terce, Sext, and None be variable? [Present, 28; all, yes.]

"19. Should three psalms be said at Matins? [Present, 24; yes, 22; no, 1; null vote, 1.]"[241]

So again the Consilium supported the desires of Group 9 and in sanctioning five psalms for Lauds and Vespers (but three at Vespers "with the people") and three psalms for the other Hours, gave Group 3 the parameters it desired for constructing arrangements for distribution of the Psalter.

Group 9, on the basis of a majority of its members favoring the third proposal for distribution of the psalms as noted above, agreed at this same series of meetings that once the decision had been made by the Consilium on the number of psalms for each Hour, Group 3 should prepare a schema in which the psalms were distributed over a two-week cycle for all the Hours except Lauds and Vespers. In these Hours the psalms would be distributed throughout a one-week cycle.[242]

To Monsignor Pascher himself privately and to the Consilium publicly, Cardinal Confalonieri, vice president of the Consilium, expressed his desire that the psalmic *incisa* of the Office be each about ten verses. A number of members of the Consilium supported him in this wish. Monsignor Pascher explained to the Consilium that this would be difficult to do if the psalms were distributed over a two-week cycle, for some 336 *incisa* would then be required, and only 273 (including the entire Psalter and seven canticles, all divided into approximately ten verses) were available. If Lauds and Vespers could be put on a weekly cycle, however, 273 *incisa* would be sufficient. Cardinal Confalonieri's opinion was discussed, and in the end the Consilium agreed that Group 3 should arrange a schema in which the psalms, each divided into segments of approximately ten verses, were distributed over a period of two weeks for all the Hours except Lauds and Vespers. For these latter Hours a one-week cycle would prevail.[243]

Before March 1965 Monsignor Pascher was ready to present from Group 3 to the members of Group 9 two schemata for the distribution of the Psalter along the lines recommended by the Consilium. Only one of these, Schema "A," was actually presented, however, since it was the only one that all but one of the members of Group 3 endorsed. This schema (table 5 below) was presented to Group 9 at its session in Rome on March 1 and 2, 1965.[244]

In his presentation of Schema "A" to Group 9, Monsignor Pascher noted that the attempt to adhere to the use of approximately eight to twelve verses for each of the *incisa* had especially

TABLE 5

SCHEMA "A" OF PROPOSED DISTRIBUTION OF PSALMS IN A TWO-WEEK CYCLE FOR THE REFORMED ROMAN OFFICE
1965

H[a]	Week 1							Week 2						
	Sun.	Mon.	Tue.	Wed.	Thu.	Fri.	Sat.	Sun.	Mon.	Tue.	Wed.	Thu.	Fri.	Sat.
M	1	9a	9c	17a	17d	21a	24a	117a	25	20	36a	36d	34a	39a
	2	9b	9d	17b	17e	21b	24b	117b	27	32a	36b	37a	34b	39b
	3	13	14	17c	19	21c	24c	117c	45	32b	36c	37b	34c	51
L	92	46	95	96	97	50	98	*	*	*	*	*	*	*
	99	5	42	64	89	142	91							
	62	28	100	66	35	84	63							
	Ca.[b]	Ca.	Ca.	Ca.	Ca.	Ca.	Ca.							
	150	148	149	150	148	149	150							
T	8	18a	118a	118c	118e	118g	118i	75	118k	118m	118o	118q	118s	118u
	15	18b	118b	118d	118f	118h	118j	80a	118l	118n	118p	118r	118t	118v
	22	26	29	38	47	53	55	80b	56	57	59	74	78	81
S	23	43a	44a	48a	49a	68a	68d	88a	88d	77b	77e	73a	132	105c
	65a	43b	44b	48b	49b	68b	71a	88b	88e	77c	77f	73b	105a	105d
	65b	43c	83	86	49c	68c	71b	88c	77a	77d	77g	107	105b	105e
N	103a	54a	58a	67a	72a	143	104c	135a	79a	82a	134a	106a	106d	108a
	103b	54b	58b	67b	72b	104a	104d	135b	79b	82b	134b	106b	93a	108b
	103c	136	137	67c	72c	104b	104e	135c	145	146	147	106c	93b	108c
V	109	111	112	115	131a	129	140	*	*	*	*	*	*	*
	110	114	120	123	131b	138a	141							
	113a	116	121	124	126	138b	144a							
	113b	119	122	125	127	139	144b							
	Ca.	Ca.	Ca.	Ca.	Ca.	Ca.	Ca.							
C	4	6	10	16a	30a	33a	101a	4	41a	52	61	69	87a	102a
	90	7a	11	16b	30b	33b	101b	90	41b	70a	76a	85a	87b	102b
	133	7b	12	31	30c	40	101c	133	60	70b	76b	85b	128	130

SOURCE: Schema no. 73, *addendum*, 6.

[a]In this column H = Hour; M = Matins; L = Lauds; T = Terce; S = Sext; N = None; V = Vespers; C = Compline.

[b]Ca. = Canticle. Specific canticles were not designated for any of the hours.

*Psalms are for the corresponding day in Week 1.

affected nine psalms: Psalms 9, 17, 36, 68, 77, 104, 105, 106, and 118. These had to be divided into more than three *incisa*. Several results emerged from discussion on Monsignor Pascher's report: Six of eleven members of Group 9 were pleased with the division of the psalms even, where necessary, into more than three *incisa*. Fr. Pelagio Visentin, however, said that division should occur only when absolutely necessary and that division into some eight to twelve verses seemed too mechanical. Fr. Anselmo Lentini cautioned against a lack of sense or meaning in single *incisa*; Msgr. Igino Rogger asked that the literary nature of the psalms be respected, with division admitted only in cases of true necessity; and Fr. Vincenzo Raffa thought only Psalms 118 and 77, as the longest, should be divided in the way proposed.[245]

To Monsignor Pascher's presentation of a two-week *cursus* in Schema A for all the Hours except Lauds, Vespers, and Compline, Group 9 responded favorably but with some reservations. Both Fathers Lentini and Raffa thought the omission of a large number of psalms (almost one-third of the Psalter) by those who would choose to pray only one of the minor Hours was unacceptable. Father Raffa also affirmed that the one-week cycle for Lauds and Vespers was tied to the division of psalms at the minor Hours. He preferred a one-week cycle for the minor Hours to reduce the number of psalms omitted by those praying only one of these Hours, and he opted for a two-week cycle for Lauds and Vespers.[246]

Schema "A" was then submitted to the fifth plenary session of the Consilium (April 26–30, 1965) with a number of questions and notes detailing the rationale or problems underlying the questions. First, it was noted that there was a two-week *cursus* for Matins because the Consilium had voted in its previous autumn session for three psalms only at this Hour. Those responsible for the distribution thought the psalms suitable for Matins would have to be distributed over a two-week cycle—one week being insufficient and three or four weeks, too long. The question submitted to the Consilium on this matter was, "Is the *cursus* of two weeks for Matins acceptable?" To this the Consilium gave a unanimously favorable response.[247]

Second, if longer psalms were divided into three parts only and these were assigned to one Hour, the equilibrium of the Hours might be disturbed if the parts were each longer than approximately ten verses. The normal length of psalmody in an Hour is about thirty verses. Furthermore, if the longer psalms were divided into more than three *incisa* they would less fittingly be assigned to Vespers, which, when celebrated with the people, is to have three psalms or *incisa* only. Besides, such an arrangement would disrupt the ancient tradition of using Psalms 109 through 147 for Vespers. It was thought best to assign the longer psalms in Schema "A" to the minor Hours and, when there were not more than three *incisa*, to distribute the remaining ones horizontally at the same Hour on different days. Where one psalm would not be recited entirely at one Hour, care was taken to provide *incisa* that each has internal unity. The question asked of the Consilium was, "Is it acceptable to divide the longer psalms enumerated above (9, 17, 36, 68, 77, 104, 105, 106, 118) into more than three *incisa*?"[248] The response of the majority was favorable.

Regarding the two-week *cursus* for the minor Hours, it was observed that one-third of the Psalter would be lost for those selecting only one Hour, that being the same Hour every day. This consequence was known to the bishops of the council when SC 89e was accepted. Even if an individual priest, it was said, would skip some psalms, the whole Psalter would nevertheless be sung as the prayer of the Church by the Church universal. To offset the difficulties arising from the proposed arrangement, however, Groups 3 and 9 had discussed a one-week *cursus* for the minor Hours and a two-week *cursus* for Lauds and Vespers. Great inconveniences were seen to result from such an arrangement, however. First, it would be impossible to find enough suitable psalms for Lauds. Second, the tradition of beginning with Psalm 109 in a *lectio continua* of "very beautiful" psalms for Vespers would have to be omitted. Some of these psalms were considered very fitting for celebration with the people. Finally, some relatively brief psalms (e.g., Pss 91, 89, and 131) would have to be divided and sections of Psalm 118 used at Lauds and Vespers—a practice that would be untraditional and not in keeping with the character of those Hours.[249] The Consilium was asked, then, "Is the *cursus* of two weeks for the minor Hours acceptable?"[250] The affirmative answer supported, yet again, the position of Group 9.

Two more acceptable solutions to the problem of omission of psalms in the minor Hours had been discussed by Groups 3 and

9. The first was to allow in the case of a one-week *cursus* for the minor Hours a choice of psalms for Terce during the first week of a month, for Sext during the second and fourth week, and for None during the third week. This solution was rejected as being exceedingly complex and possibly contributing to "confusion of conscience in priests' minds and a certain aversion to the Divine Office."[251] The second solution was to allow a priest *(sic)* who would recite only one of the minor Hours to take the psalms of any one of these Hours of the same day. That possibility was presented to the Consilium thus: "Is it acceptable that a rubric may allow a priest saying only one of the minor Hours to choose the psalms of another minor Hour of the same day? Is it acceptable that such a rubric may simply permit this, not obligate it?"[252] To both questions the Consilium responded favorably. The members of the Consilium, then, appeared at this stage of the reform to be relatively strong in their support for the positions adopted by Groups 3 and 9 regarding the division, distribution, and use of the psalms in the Hours.

The searching questions, however, on the direction of the reform of the Office raised at the sixth plenary session of the Consilium (October 19–26, November 22–26, December 1, 1965) included several on the number, distribution, and division of the psalms. Some of those formulated in the questionnaire of December 1965 regarding the number of psalms at Lauds and Vespers were considered above.[253] Others, regarding the psalms as they affect the structure of the Office were,

"11. Does what the Consilium has already accepted suffice, namely, that in the new distribution of the Psalter the psalms or their *incisa* should usually consist of no more than ten verses?

"12. Does the number of psalms already foreseen for the individual Hours seem acceptable, namely,
    —Matins: three psalms,
    —Lauds and Vespers: five psalms with the option of reducing the number to three when the people celebrate the Hour,
    —The minor Hours and Compline: three psalms?

"13. Should the complete Psalter, that is, 150 psalms, be retained in the Ordinary cycle as has been done up to the present time even if that cycle is no longer only one week?

"16. Should the ordinary cycle of the Psalter be two weeks?"[254]

The meager response to the questionnaire yielded the following results (I.M. = *iuxta modum,* or yes with reservations) for these questions:

	Yes	No	I.M.
Question 11 (*Incisa* about ten verses)			
Members	14	4	3
Consultors	12	11	-
Question 12 (Number of psalms)			
Three psalms for Matins:			
Members	18	2	2
Consultors	15	[no response, 8]	
Five psalms for Lauds and Vespers:			
Members	14	4	4
Consultors	10	8	5
Three psalms for minor Hours:			
Members	15	3	4
Consultors	10	9	-
Three psalms for Compline:			
Members	13	5	3
Consultors	12	7	-
Question 13 (Retention of entire Psalter)			
Members	8	13	1
Consultors	12	2	7

	Yes	No	I.M.
Question 16 (Two-week cycle for Psalter)			
Members	15	3	2
Consultors	5	3	15

Although the results were acknowledged as generally inconclusive, the difference between the responses of consultors and members for Questions 13 and 16 is noteworthy. Regarding Question 13 on retention of the whole Psalter, members had less difficulty in abandoning some psalms (notably imprecatory and historical) than consultors did. Consultors, generally, foresaw more than members did that a number of questions presupposed by Question 16 needed solution before the length of the cycle could be determined.[255]

Without attempting here to consider at length the long and major controversy over the retention of historical and imprecatory psalms (and verses of such)—a question, as noted above, deserving a separate study—it must be remarked that arguments for and against retention of these psalms were the major consideration in whether the whole Psalter should be retained in the Office. The length of the cycle of distribution, in turn, would depend to some extent on the number of psalms preserved.[256] Here only major elements of the discussion as it affected the structure of the Hours—particularly the establishment of the length of the cycle of distribution of psalms—will be considered.

After his study following publication of the December 1965 questionnaire, Canon Martimort devoted almost fifteen pages of his report (RG) to Group 9 on the question of retention of the entire Psalter in the Office.[257] He first summarized the situation of the Psalter before the time of the council (i.e., from 1911 to 1962), noting on the one hand an increase in devotional use of psalms and on the other hand, widespread difficulty with use of many of them due to a lack of ''biblical culture.''[258] At Vatican Council II, he noted, a number of bishops had called for elimination of some psalms, especially the so-called imprecatory ones, because they represent a stage in revelation insufficient to employ in Christian prayer. Others had countered with the argument that all Scripture is inspired, that difficult psalms when prayed with a Christian interpretation are spiritually profitable, and that omission of selected psalms is made according to principles that could be termed "rationalistic"—a procedure dangerous in that it invites human tampering with divine revelation.[259]

After the council, Canon Martimort said, both the suppression of Prime and the option allowed of choosing only one of the minor Hours (an option extended progressively to choir religious and even monks) had resulted in the omission of some psalms in the Office even before the *cursus* had been reformed. The allowance, too, of using the vernacular languages had rendered more acute the problem of understanding and fruitfully praying the psalms.[260]

Turning to the use of the Psalter among various Protestant groups, Canon Martimort noted that the Anglican Office, the Swiss Office (*L'Office divin de chaque jour*), and the Office of Taizé all omit some more difficult psalms. He saw, particularly in the Office of Taizé, a progressive elimination of psalms once the principle that not all psalms need be employed was admitted.[261]

Arguing for retention of all 150 psalms in the Office, Canon Martimort appealed for support to tradition, theology, spirituality, and the danger of arbitrary choice. Even if traditionally not all psalms were used in the Office, they were all judged worthy of comment by writers of the early Church such as Origen, Chrysostom, and Augustine. If psalms were omitted from liturgical use, he said, they were not excluded simply on grounds of the sentiments expressed in them. He acknowledged that there was selective use of psalms in the ancient cathedral Office as attested, for example, by Egeria, but in that tradition the selectivity was governed by appropriateness of certain psalms for a given Hour, not by a judgment that the content of a psalm was incompatible with Christian revelation. Theologically, he said, all Scripture (as the author of 2 Tim 3:16-17 has acknowledged) is inspired and useful even if the Church has selectively chosen portions of Scripture for liturgical use due to lack of time to include all or the incapacity of some people to grasp certain portions of it. It would be quite another thing to exclude some psalms because they are judged unsuitable in themselves for Christian use. The lack, generally, of biblical culture and formation before the council is supposed to be rectified in the postconciliar period (see SC 90) so a better understanding of psalms from a Christian perspective could yield better spiritual profit. Finally, a subjective and arbitrary choice of what are suitable psalms could not only vary according to persons and places but would, as at Taizé, lead to mutilation and discard of authentic elements of Christian piety.[262]

Recognizing that many, psychologically, have difficulty with some psalms, the canon proposed the following: (1) Maintain all the psalms in the Office, but put in parentheses or brackets certain verses that could be omitted optionally as is done in the *Book of Common Prayer* (1928). On this point the canon explained that although use of the integral Psalter was monastic in origin and that many argue that use of selected psalmody in the cathedral tradition of the Office is more suitable for parochial clergy and laity, nevertheless, in antiquity all the psalms were susceptible to liturgical use. (2) Make certain psalms optional either by putting them in an Hour of the Office that is not obligatory or by providing an alternative psalm. (3) Have a system of distribution of psalms that allows certain ones to appear relatively rarely, as in the system of R. Paquier for the Swiss Reformed Church. (4) Reserve certain psalms to certain times—a solution utilized at Taizé.[263]

At its meeting of September 6, 7, and 8, 1966, Group 9 reviewed and discussed Canon Martimort's rationale and proposals in RG. In the discussion it was maintained that even if the integral Psalter in the Office is a monastic invention, that fact alone does not necessarily make the custom unsuitable for the whole Church. Monks, it was said, have continually contributed to progress in doctrine and spirituality within the Church.[264] The members finally agreed to the following: (1) All psalms with all verses should be retained in the liturgical edition of the Psalter. Some liturgical use should be provided for all the psalms. (2) Imprecatory formulas that arouse wonder in non-Christians and poorly educated Christians should be avoided in popular liturgical celebrations. (3) Care should be taken for the many priests lacking a biblical and liturgical mentality who experience insuperable difficulties in reciting psalmodic imprecations in the same sense the Church has recited them. So that these three objectives might be achieved practically, Group 9 proposed that (1) some of the more difficult verses be put in italics with a rubric advising that such verses could be omitted; (2) other psalms be substituted for a few that are wholly imprecatory. The vote on the first proposal was fourteen in favor, one opposed, and one approving with reservations. On the second proposal seven were in favor and five opposed.[265]

These two proposals were formulated into questions for the Consilium at its seventh plenary session (October 6–14, 1966):

"1. Is it acceptable that some of the more difficult verses of the psalms be set off in parentheses with a rubric saying that these verses may be omitted if desired, especially when the Office is recited with the people?
"2. Is it acceptable to substitute other selected psalms for those few of which the greatest part, upon careful examination, is truly imprecatory, so that placing a few verses in parentheses would not suffice?"[266]

The first question was answered affirmatively by the Consilium (yes, 20; no, 11; yes with reservations, 1) as was the second (yes, 24; no, 5). This decision of the Consilium was an important one, for while it left intact the integral Psalter for the Office, by allowing optional use of some psalms and verses of psalms it opened the way for further consideration of their outright elimination.[267]

Group 9 also considered at its meeting in September 1966 how the *cursus* of psalmody might be adapted to render more fruitful use of the psalms. Responding to Question 6 in the questionnaire of December 1965, "Should the custom of reciting psalms one after the other with several in a given Hour be retained?"[268] twelve bishops replied affirmatively; two, negatively; two, affirmatively with reservations. Twenty-two consultors replied affirmatively but called for a fitting number of psalms in each Hour, introduction of silence after psalmody, or abandonment of mathematical and artificial divisions of the psalms. One consultor replied negatively. With reference to these responses Group 9 concurred in two matters that might affect the structure of the Office. The first was that while maintaining all 150 psalms, the reformed Office could employ some psalms more than once in the *cursus* by reason of their intrinsic worth or the more popular character of an Hour in which they might be used. It was also agreed (in response to Questions 11 and 12 of the questionnaire regarding the length of psalms or *incisa* and the number of psalms in each Hour) that the quantity of psalmody in each Hour generally should be abbreviated so that it could be prayed "with a tranquil and quiet mind."[269] Division of a psalm, however, should not violate its literary unity. Better, it was said, to use one undivided long psalm approximately equal to several short ones than to divide the long psalm (as did St. Benedict and Pope Pius X) to give the impression that a certain number of psalms were being used.[270]

The Consilium at its seventh plenary session (October 6–14, 1966) apparently was not asked directly questions dealing specifically with these proposals. It did, however, approve the introduction of a canticle from the New Testament (a proposal considered in Groups 3 and 9 almost from the beginning of their work) into the corpus of psalmody for Vespers.[271] This decision coupled with the suggestions of Group 9 that the quantity of the psalmody in each Hour be abbreviated, that psalms be repeated, and that possibly the gradual psalms be used for the nonobligatory minor Hours rendered difficult if not impossible the distribution of the Psalter over two weeks.[272] Thus Group 3 proceeded to devise a distribution of the Psalter over a four-week period in accordance with principles approved by the Consilium and with the suggestions of Group 9 as found in Schemata 185 and 194.[273]

At its meeting of February 6–8, 1967, Group 9 reviewed and approved the work of Group 3. It also for the first time considered providing psalm prayers for each of the psalms to aid in their Christological interpretation. There was agreement that such would be valuable but that they should be for optional use. Structurally they could occur after each psalm and its antiphon and in the new edition of the Office could be printed after psalm and antiphon or in an appendix or even in a separate volume. Fr. Jorge Pinell was asked to prepare a selection of these prayers.[274]

Group 9 then turned its attention to the preparation of SCDO, the first experimental edition of the revised Office, for the spring (eighth) session of the Consilium (April 10–19, 1967). SCDO contained the new distribution of the Psalter over four weeks devised by Group 3 (table 6 below), even though only one week would actually be used by the members and consultors of the Consilium from April 9 to 15.[275]

TABLE 6

PROPOSED DISTRIBUTION OF PSALMS AND CANTICLES IN A FOUR-WEEK CYCLE FOR THE REFORMED ROMAN OFFICE APRIL, 1967

	Week 1							Week 2						
H[a]	Sun.	Mon.	Tue.	Wed.	Thu.	Fri.	Sat.	Sun.	Mon.	Tue.	Wed.	Thu.	Fri.	Sat.
O	1 2 3	9a 6	9b 11	24	17a	21	104	103	30	33	36a	43	34	105
L oc	62 (8)[b] 149	5 (2) 28	23 (3) 32	35 (4) 46	56 (5) 47	50 (6) 99	118s (12) 116	117 (1) 150	41 (7) 18a	42 (10) 64	76 (11) 66	79 (13) 80	50 (9) 147	91 (14) 8
M	117	18 7	118a 12 13	118b 16	118c 17b	118d 25 27	118e 38 51	22 75	118f 39	118g 52 53	118h 54	118i 55 57 [56][d]	118j 58	118k 59 60
V nc	109 113a (1)[c]	10 14 (2)	18b 19 (4)	20 29 (3)	26 (5)	31 40 (6)	118n 15 (7)	109 113b (1)	44 (2)	45 61 (4)	48 (3)	71 (5)	111 114 (6)	115 112 (7)
C	4 90 133	85	142	30a 6	15	89	120 122	*	*	*	*	*	*	*

	Week 3							Week 4						
H	Sun.	Mon.	Tue.	Wed.	Thu.	Fri.	Sat.	Sun.	Mon.	Tue.	Wed.	Thu.	Fri.	Sat.
O	144	49	67	70	88a	37	106	23 65	72	101	102	108 [33]	68	77a
L oc	92 (8) 148	83 (15) 95	84 (16) 96	85 (17) 97	86 (18) 98	50 (23) 99	118s (26) 116	117 (1) 150	89 (19) 145	100 (20) 134a	107 (21) 143a	142 (22) 146	50 (25) 147	91 (24) 8
M	117	118l 63 69	118m 73	118n 75	118o 88b	118p 74 78	118q 82 [83]	22 75	118r 81 119	118s 87	118t 93	118u 127 128	118v 132 139	77b
V nc	109 110 (1)	120 123 (2)	122 124 (4)	126 130 (3)	131 (5)	134 (6)	121 129 (7)	109 125 (1)	135 (2)	136 137 (4)	138 (3)	173 (5)	144 (6)	140 141 (7)
C	*	*	*	*	*	*	*	*	*	*	*	*	*	*

TABLE 6 *(cont.)*

SOURCE: Schema no. 212, pp. 12–13.

[a]In this column H = Hour; O = Office of Readings; L = Lauds; oc = Old-Testament canticle; M = Middle Hour; V = Vespers; nc = New-Testament canticle; C = Compline.

[b]Old-Testament canticles are indicated here as (1) Dan. 3:52-57; (2) 1 Chr. 29:10-13; (3) Tob. 13:1-10; (4) Jdt. 16:15-21; (5) Jer. 31:10-14; (6) Is. 45:14-26; (7) Sir. 36:1-16; (8) Dan. 3:57-88, 56; (9) Hab. 3:2-4, 12-19; (10) Is. 38:10-20; (11) 1 Sam. 2:1-10; (12) Ex. 15:1-13, 17-19; (13) Is. 12:1-6; (14) Dt. 32:1-12; (15) Is. 2:2-5; (16) Is. 26:1-10, 12; (17) Is. 33:13-18; (18) Is. 40:10-17; (19) Is. 42:10-16; (20) Is. 49:7-15; (21) Is. 61:10-11, 62:1-5; (22) Is. 66:10-14; (23) Jer. 14:17-21; (24) Ez. 36:24-28; (25) Tob. 13:10-15, 17-19; (26) Wis. 9:1-12. Numbers (1) through (14) were utilized in the then current Roman Office; numbers (15) through (25) were selected from the monastic Office, and number (26) was newly proposed. (Schema n. 212, pp. 8, 11.)

[c]New-Testament canticles are indicated here as (1) Rev. 19:1b-2a, 4b, 5b, 6b-8a; (2) Eph. 1:3-10; (3) Col. 1:12-20; (4) Rev. 4:11, 5, 9-10, 12; (5) Rev. 11:17-18, 12:10b-12a; (6) Rev. 15:3-4; (7) Phil. 2:6-11.

[d]Psalm numbers in brackets indicate psalms which may replace those considered imprecatory and indicated immediately above the bracketed numbers.

*Psalms are for the corresponding day in Week 1.

At the April session Consilium members were asked a series of questions based on the proposed Office as shown in SCDO. Those questions pertaining to the proposed distribution and division of the psalms and canticles were as follows:

"1. Should the psalms, excluding those of Compline, be distributed throughout an ordinary course of four weeks?

"2. Should Compline have an ordinary course of one week?

"4. Should Lauds have in first place traditional morning psalms and others similar to them; in second place canticles from the Old Testament; in third place psalms of praise or similar selections of a hymnic genre?

"5. Should the number of Old Testament canticles be increased to suffice for four weeks?

"6. Should the twenty-two parts of Psalm 118 be distributed throughout the weekday middle Hour as was done in the sample?

"7. Should gradual psalms be used for the "optional minor Hours," as was suggested in the report?

"9. Should canticles from the New Testament in an ordinary course of one week take third place in Vespers?

"11. Besides Psalm 118, should Psalms 17, 77, and 88 be divided and distributed between the Office of Readings and the middle Hour?"[276]

All these questions received an affirmative response from the members of the Consilium.[277]

Thus the Consilium approved (1) the distribution throughout a four-week cycle of the psalms for all the Hours except those for Compline, (2) a one-week cycle for the psalms of Compline, (3) morning psalm, Old Testament canticle, and psalm of praise in that order for Lauds, (4) expansion of the then-current repertoire of Old Testament canticles to suffice for four weeks, (5) the division of Psalm 118 into twenty-two parts and their distribution throughout the weekday midday or middle Hours, (6) the provision of a selection from the gradual psalms (Pss 119–33) for use at the optional minor Hours, (7) a one-week series of New Testament canticles each for use at third place in the psalmody for Vespers, (8) the division besides Psalm 118 of Psalms 17, 77, and 88 and their distribution between the Office of Readings and the middle Hour.

With the exception of the last mentioned, all these decisions ultimately prevailed even though there were modifications in the distribution of some psalms and a reduction in the number of psalms at Compline, as will be considered below.

Three suggestions from members and consultors at the April session are worthy of note. Father Bugnini objected to the division of long psalms into two different Hours (Office of Readings and the middle Hour) of the same day with a complex rubric indicating that the first part of the divided psalm should be said at whichever Hour is used first. He proposed a simpler solution: Put the divisions of such psalms on different days. He also proposed dividing long psalms by introducing a *Gloria Patri* at the end of each division to allow a "little pause of the mind." Bishop Boudon (Mende) suggested a similar division but by means of an antiphon. Msgr. Pierre Jounel also objected to the division of psalms over the course of a day. He saw a problem in that one part of a psalm could be repeated and another omitted if one section were recited communally and the other privately.[278] Father Bugnini's and Monsignor Jounel's objections, it should be noted, prepared the way for a reconsideration later of the manner in which the longer psalms were divided.

At the meeting of Group 9 in Munich from July 20 to 23, 1967, a number of questions concerning the distribution and division of the psalms were considered. Regarding the long psalms, particularly Psalms 17, 77, and 88, Monsignor Pascher noted there were three possibilities: (1) division of a psalm between the Office of Readings and the middle Hour on a given day with a rubric advising that the order of parts of the psalm be kept (as was the case in SCDO); (2) division between the same Hours without the aforesaid rubric, since neither theological nor literary unity need be harmed; (3) distribution of parts over two subsequent days at the Office of Readings. After agreeing (12 to 2) that Psalms 17, 77, and 88 should be divided, Group 9 itself was split (7 to 7) on whether these psalms should be divided at different Hours of the same day or at the same Hour on different days. After more reflection and with note made that division of a psalm over two days at the same Hour would enable those regularly using only part of the Office to pray the whole psalm and that the Benedictines have used this practice for a long time, Group 9 voted 13 to 1 in favor of dividing

Psalms 17, 77, and 88 over two days at the Office of Readings.[279]

Division of psalmody within a given Hour was also discussed again at this meeting of Group 9. Since SCDO had presented most psalms and canticles without division, allowing any number of verses from roughly fifteen to fifty for a given Hour, the question was raised again as to whether Cardinal Confalonieri's request that psalms be divided into *incisa* of no more than eight to twelve verses should be agreed to. Against adoption of such a principle was the reason that such a division is artificial and without respect for the objective sense of a psalm. The major principle *(lex suprema)* ought to be an arrangement such that those praying the psalms be aided in their understanding of them. However, pauses would seem to favor reflection and in choral celebration allow for necessary changes in tone. Divisions could be made that would respect the objective sense of a psalm. Some members proposed that the *Gloria Patri* be used at the end of each of these *incisa*. Others objected—some seeing this as fitting only at the end of all the psalmody of an Hour; others, at the end of an entire psalm only. The discussion raised other concerns: the need to foresee what would happen when psalms or *incisa* are prayed communally and privately, in Latin and in a vernacular, with strophic division and without, with minor pauses as well as major. Pauses within the psalmody could be signified by *Gloria Patri* or antiphon or silence or psalm prayer.

Finally, Group 9 posed to itself six questions. To the first— Should each Hour have a ternary structure for psalmody?—ten agreed and four disagreed. To the second—Should strophic divisions be used within the ternary division?—twelve agreed and two objected. The third question—Should the *Gloria Patri* and antiphon be used at the end of an entire psalm?—was favored by thirteen and opposed by one. The fourth question—Should a division of psalmody, more or less like those in the current Breviary, conclude with the *Gloria Patri* and exist without an antiphon unless it is a different psalm or a division carrying a different sense from the other psalms or *incisa* in the Hour?—was favored by twelve and opposed by one. To the fifth question—Should the *Gloria Patri* or a moment of silence be employed between the divisions of psalmody in private recitation?—twelve responded affirmatively and two, negatively. The final question was, Can the psalms, especially when sung in the vernacular, be sung in a responsorial mode with the antiphon interjected after each strophe and the *Gloria Patri* used at the conclusion? To this Group 9 agreed unanimously.[280] So Group 9, in effect, accepted Father Bugnini's and Monsignor Jounel's suggestions regarding the distribution and division of long psalms and, additionally, agreed to ternary structure, strophic division, pauses within, and responsorial use of the psalmody for a given Hour.

Another question affecting at least the appearance of the structure of the psalmody in the Hours was raised at this meeting of Group 9. Monsignor Pascher communicated the wish of most in Group 3 for including titles for the psalms, but he said that one member of Group 3 objected to them on the grounds that such would limit the Christological interpretation of a psalm. It was stated, however, that titles should in no way be understood as exhausting all signification and meaning of the psalms. They would be offered simply as aids to intelligent and devotional praying of them. After a discussion that, among other things, noted that even in the council a desire was expressed for such titles and that there had been since the time of the council an expression of eagerness for inclusion of these, Group 9 agreed that two titles should be provided for each psalm, one for the literal sense and another for the Christian sense. These should be printed in red, one after the other, at the beginning of each psalm.[281]

A final question on psalmody to arise in the course of this meeting of Group 9 concerned the manner of marking at various times of the year the beginning of the four-week cycle of psalmody. The mode proposed was to have the first week of the Psalter begin on the first Sunday of Advent, the first Sunday after Christmas, the first Sunday of Lent, and the first Sunday after Pentecost. There was acknowledgment, however, that more refinement of this mode would be needed.[282]

Between the eighth and ninth plenary sessions of the Consilium, Group 3 worked to modify the schema of distribution of psalms and their division according to the suggestions and voting in both the Consilium and Group 9. Group 3 also selected special psalms for feasts and compiled two series of titles for the psalms.[283]

Before the meeting of the ninth plenary session of the Consilium (November 21–28, 1967), the Synod of Bishops at its session of

October 26, 1967, discussed and voted on one question—Question 5—that pertained indirectly to the distribution of the psalms: "Should all the psalms, including the imprecatory and historical, be retained in the ordinary course of four weeks proposed for the Psalter in the Divine Office?"[284] The results of the voting were yes, 117; no, 25; yes with reservations, 31. This question was the only one posed to the synod regarding the psalmody in the Office as a whole. The bishops had been informed before their session that the Consilium favored the four-week distribution of the Psalter, repetition of some "better loved" psalms, reduction of the quantity of psalmody in each Hour, retention of all the psalms including imprecatory and historical, the bracketing of more difficult verses for optional use, and the optional substitution of alternate psalms for a few of the more difficult imprecatory ones.[285]

When the Consilium met for its ninth session, it had to consider (1) the result of the synod's response to Question 5, (2) suggestions of Group 9 for division of the psalmody in the Hours and the insertion of the four-week cycle in the annual cycle, and (3) another experimental edition of the Office (SDO) for use during the session. SDO contained the new distribution of the psalms arranged by Group 3 after the eighth session of the Consilium. This arrangement is given in table 7 below.

With respect to the synod's vote on Question 5, the Consilium apparently had little to say, since the result was favorable (although only by a simple majority) to its own decision at its eighth session.[286] The suggestions of Group 9 for division of the psalmody within the Hours had been (1) use of the *Gloria Patri* at least at the conclusion of a whole psalm, (2) some signification of the ternary structure of the psalmody in each Hour, (3) provision for the option of observing the ternary structure of the psalmody in each Hour, (3) provision for the option of observing the ternary division either by triple *Gloria Patri*'s or by silence, (4) provision for the freedom (especially in private recitation) to recite a divided psalm throughout, (5) provision for antiphons not only at the beginning and end of a complete psalm but also with parts of a psalm when these parts have different senses, (6) provision for strophic division and responsorial execution of psalms in vernacular tongues. With these recommendations of Group 9 the Consilium had no major difficulty.[287] The proposed insertion of the four-week cycle into the annual liturgical cycle received no action pending further study on how to reconcile this proposal with a proposed monthly cycle of readings for the Hours.[288]

SDO, the experimental edition of the Office used by the Consilium at its ninth session, incorporated some of the features desired by Group 9 and the Consilium for the structure of the psalmody. These features included a ternary structure for the psalmody itself of each Hour as provided in the latest distribution of the Psalter (table 7 above), although parts were not always clearly distinguished.[289] No titles were included, nor was there any attempt to arrange each psalm according to strophes. Imprecatory verses were bracketed and antiphons provided between divisions of a psalm within a given Hour.[290] There were apparently no objections from the Consilium to the distribution and division of the psalmody as presented in SDO.[291] That structure, with some minor changes in specific psalms used at specific Hours rendered necessary principally by the later omission of three imprecatory psalms (57, 82, and 108), became the definitive structure of distribution and division (table 8 below).[292]

One other matter—apparently not discussed at the ninth session of the Consilium but considered by Group 9 and the Group of Relators at the time of the ninth session—was the question of the psalm prayers that Fr. Jorge Pinell and a corps of his students and colleagues had been collecting.[293] Father Bugnini expressed his objection to their inclusion in the Office as rendering it burdensome and contrived. Canon Martimort agreed but felt they should be provided in a separate booklet (libellum) for those who like them and want to recite them privately, since many have petitioned for them. Fr. Pierre Marie Gy indicated that from his personal experience with these prayers they would be helpful, and the door should not be closed to their use even though they present some difficulties. Reciting one psalm after another presents its own problems, he noted, and psalm prayers might obviate them. Father Bugnini called for a study edition of these prayers before a decision would be made on their value and on the criteria of their distribution in the Office.[294]

When Group 9 met next from February 27 to March 1, 1968, the only structural question regarding the psalmody that it considered concerned the disposition of the four-week cycle of the Psalter.

TABLE 7

PROPOSED DISTRIBUTION OF PSALMS AND CANTICLES IN A FOUR-WEEK CYCLE FOR THE REFORMED ROMAN OFFICE
NOVEMBER, 1967

	Week 1							Week 2						
H[a]	Sun.	Mon.	Tue.	Wed.	Thu.	Fri.	Sat.	Sun.	Mon.	Tue.	Wed.	Thu.	Fri.	Sat.
O	1	9a	9c	17a	17d	34a	104a	103a	30a	36	38a	43a	37a	105a
	2	9b	9d	17b	17e	34b	104b	103b	30b	51a	38b	43b	37b	105b
	3	6	11	17c	17f	34c	104c	103c	30c	51b	38c	43c	37c	105c
L	62	5	23	35	56	50	118s	117	41	42	76	79	50	91
oc	(8)[b]	(2)	(3)	(4)	(5)	(6)	(12)	(1)	(7)	(10)	(11)	(13)	(9)	(14)
	149	28	32	46	47	99	116	150	18a	64	96	80	147	8
M	117a	18	118a	118b	118c	118d	118e	22	118f	118g	118h	118i	118j	118k
	117b	7a	12	16a	24a	25	33a	75a	39a	52	54a	55	58a	59
	117c	7b	13	16b	24b	27	33b	75b	39b	53	54b	57 [56][d]	58b	60
V	109	10	19	26a	29	40	118n	109	44a	48a	61	71a	111	115
	113a	14	20	26b	31	45	15	113b	44b	48b	66	71b	114	112
nc	(1)[c]	(2)	(3)	(4)	(5)	(6)	(7)	*	*	*	*	*	*	*
C	90a	85a	142a	30a	15a	89a	120	4a	*	*	*	*	*	*
	90b	85b	142b	129a	15b	89b	122a	4b						
	90c	85c	142c	129b	15c	89c	122b	133						

	Week 3							Week 4						
H	Sun.	Mon.	Tue.	Wed.	Thu.	Fri.	Sat.	Sun.	Mon.	Tue.	Wed.	Thu.	Fri.	Sat.
O	144a	49a	67a	88a	88d	68a	106a	23	72a	101a	102a	108a	77a	77d
	144b	49b	67b	88b	88e	68b	106b	65a	72b	101b	102b	108b	77b	77e
	144c	49c	67c	88c	89	68c	106c	65b	72c	101c	102c	108c [33]	77c	77f
L	92	83	84	85	86	50	118s	117	89	100	107	142	50	91
oc	(8)	(15)	(16)	(17)	(18)	(23)	(26)	(1)	(19)	(20)	(21)	(22)	(25)	(24)
	148	95	66	97	98	99	116	150	145	134a	143a	146	147	8
M	117a	118l	118m	118n	118o	21a	118p	75a	118q	118r	118s	118t	118u	118v
	117b	63	70a	73a	74	21b	82a	75b	81	87a	93a	127	132	44a
	117c	69	70b	73b	78	21c	82b [33]	75c	119	87b	93b	128	139	44b
V	109	120	122	126	131a	134a	121	109	135a	136	138a	143a	144a	140
	110	123	124	130	131b	134b	129	125	135b	137	138b	143b	144b	141

TABLE 7 (cont.)

	Week 3							Week 4						
H	Sun.	Mon.	Tue.	Wed.	Thu.	Fri.	Sat.	Sun.	Mon.	Tue.	Wed.	Thu.	Fri.	Sat.
nc	(1)	(2)	(3)	(4)	(5)	(6)	(7)	*	*	*	*	*	*	*
C	90a 90b 90c	*	*	*	*	*	*	4a 4b 133	*	*	*	*	*	*

SOURCE: Schema no. 244, 2–3.

[a]In this column H=Hour; O=Office of Readings; L=Lauds; oc=Old-Testament canticle; M=Middle Hour; V=Vespers; nc=New-Testament canticle; C=Compline.

[b]Old-Testament canticles are indicated here as (1) Dan. 3:52-57; (2) 1 Chr. 29:10-13; (3) Tob. 13:1-10; (4) Jdt. 16:15-21; (5) Jer. 31:10-14; (6) Is. 45:15-26; (7) Sir. 36:1-16; (8) Dan. 3:57-88, 56; (9) Hab. 3:2-4, 12-19; (10) Is. 38:10-20; (11) 1 Sam. 2:1-10; (12) Ex. 15:1-13, 17-19; (13) Is. 12:1-6; (14) Dt. 32:1-12; (15) Is. 2:2-5; (16) Is. 26:1-10, 12; (17) Is. 33:13-18; (18) Is. 40:10-17; (19) Is. 42:10-16; (20) Dan. 3:26-45; (21) Is. 61:10-11, 62:1-5; (22) Is. 66:10-14; (23) Jer. 14:17-21; (24) Ez. 36:24-28; (25) Tob. 13:10-15, 17-19; (26) Wis. 9:1-12. Numbers (1) through (14) were utilized in the then current Roman Office; numbers (15) through (19) and (21) through (25) were selected from the monastic Office, and numbers (20) and (26) were newly proposed. (Schema no. 244, 2.)

[c]New-Testament canticles are indicated here as (1) Rev. 19:1b-2a, 4b, 5b, 7-8a; (2) Eph. 1:3-10; (3) Rev. 4:11, 5, 9-10, 12; (4) Col. 1:12-20; (5) Rev. 11:17-18, 12:10b-12a; (6) Rev. 15:3-4; (7) Phil. 2:6-11. Two other canticles were proposed: 1 Peter 2:21-24 for Sundays in Lent and 1 Tim. 3:16 for the feasts of Epiphany and Transfiguration. (Schema no. 244, 3.)

[d]Psalm numbers in brackets indicate psalms which may replace those considered imprecatory and indicated immediately above the bracketed numbers.

*Psalms are for the corresponding day in Week 1.

TABLE 8

DISTRIBUTION OF PSALMS AND CANTICLES IN THE FOUR-WEEK CYCLE OF *LITURGIA HORARUM* 1971

	Week 1[d]							Week 2[d]						
H[a]	Sun.	Mon.	Tue.	Wed.	Thu.	Fri.	Sat.	Sun.	Mon.	Tue.	Wed.	Thu.	Fri.	Sat.
O	1	6	9c	17a	17d	34a	104a	103a	30a	36a	38a	43a	37a	105a
	2	9a	9d	17b	17e	34b	104b	103b	30b	36b	38b	43b	37b	105b
	3	9b	11	17c	17f	34c	104c	103c	30c	36c	51	43c	37c	105c
L	62	5	23	35	56	50	118s	117	41	42	76	79	50	91
oc	(8)[b]	(2)	(3)	(4)	(5)	(6)	(12)	(1)	(7)	(10)	(11)	(13)	(9)	(14)
	149	28	32	46	47	99	116	150	18a	64	96	80	147	8
M	117a	18b	118a	118b	118c	118d	118e	22	118f	118g	118h	118i	118j	118k
	117b	7a	12	16a	24a	25	33a	75a	39a	52	54a	55	58	60
	117c	7b	13	16b	24b	27	33b	75b	39b	53	54b	56	59	63
V	109	10	19	26a	29	40	118n[e]	109	44a	48a	61	71a	114	112
	113a	14	20	26b	31	45	15	113b	44b	48b	66	71b	120	115
nc	(1)[c]	(2)	(3)	(4)	(5)	(6)	(7)	*	*	*	*	*	*	*
C	90	85	142	30a	15	87	4	*	*	*	*	*	*	*
				129			133							

	Week 3							Week 4[d]						
H	Sun.	Mon.	Tue.	Wed.	Thu.	Fri.	Sat.	Sun.	Mon.	Tue.	Wed.	Thu.	Fri.	Sat.
O	144a	49a	67a	88a	88d	68a	106a	23	72a	101a	102a	43a	54a	49a
	144b	49b	67b	88b	88e	68b	106b	65a	72b	101b	102b	43b	54b	49b
	144c	49c	67c	88c	89	68c	106c	65b	72c	101c	102c	43c	54c	49c
L	92	83	84	85	86	50	118s	117	89	100	107	142	50	91
oc	(8)	(15)	(16)	(17)	(18)	(23)	(26)	(1)	(19)	(20)	(21)	(22)	(25)	(24)
	148	95	66	97	98	99	116	150	134a	143a	145	146	147	8
M	117a	118l	118m	118n	118o	21a	118p	22	118q	118r	118s	118t	118u	118v
	117b	70a	73a	69	78	21b	33a	75a	81	87a	93a	127	132	44a
	117c	70b	73b	74	79	21c	33b	75b	119	87b	93b	128	139	44b
V	109	122	124	125	131a	134a	121	109	135a	136	138a	143a	144a	140
	110	123	130	126	131b	134b	129	111	135b	137	138b	143b	144b	141
nc	*	*	*	*	*	*	*	*	*	*	*	*	*	*
C	*	*	*	*	*	*	*	*	*	*	*	*	*	*

TABLE 8 (cont.)

SOURCE: A. Rose, "La répartition des psaumes dans le cycle liturgique," LMD 105 (1971) 66–102; LH, 4 vols.

[a]In this column H=Hour; O=Office of Readings; L=Lauds; oc=Old-Testament canticle; M=Middle Hour; V=Vespers; nc=New-Testament canticle; C=Compline.

[b]Old-Testament canticles are indicated here as (1) Dan. 3:52-57; (2) 1 Chr. 29:10-13; (3) Tob. 13:1-10; (4) Jdt. 16:2-3, 15-19; (5) Jer. 31:10-14; (6) Is. 45:15-26; (7) Sir. 36:1-7, 13-16; (8) Dan. 3:57-88, 56; (9) Hab. 3:2-4, 13a, 15-19; (10) Is. 38:10-14, 17-20; (11) 1 Sam. 2:1-10; (12) Ex. 15:1-4a, 8, 17-18; (13) Is. 12:1-6; (14) Dt. 32:1-12; (15) Is. 2:2-5; (16) Is. 26:1-4, 7-9, 12; (17) Is. 33:13-16; (18) Is. 40:10-17; (19) Is. 42:10-16; (20) Dan. 3:26-29, 34-41; (21) Is. 61:10-11, 62:1-5; (22) Is. 66:10-14a; (23) Jer. 14:17-21; (24) Ez. 36:24-28; (25) Tob. 13:10-15, 17-19; (26) Wis. 9:1-6, 9-11. Numbers (1) through (14) were utilized, some in expanded form, in the former Roman Office; numbers (15) through (19) and (21) through (25) were selected (and some adapted) from the monastic Office, and numbers (20) and (26) were newly proposed. (Schema no. 244, 2.)

[c]New-Testament canticles are indicated here as (1) Rev. 19:1b-2a, 4b, 5b, 6b-7; (2) Eph. 1:3-10; (3) Rev. 4:11, 5:9-10, 12; (4) Col. 1:12-20; (5) Rev. 11:17-18, 12:10b-12a; (6) Rev. 15:3-4; (7) Phil. 2:6-11. Two other canticles are given: 1 Peter 2:21-24 for Sundays in Lent and Common of Martyrs and 1 Tim. 3:16 for the feasts of Epiphany and Transfiguration. (LH[2] 1:1381, 2:1907, 4:1762)

[d]At Office of Readings during Advent, Christmas, Lent, and Easter, the psalms given in this table are replaced by historical psalms as follows: Saturday of Week 1, Ps. 104; Saturday of Week 2, Ps. 105; Friday of Week 4, Psalm 77 (first three parts); Saturday of Week 4, Psalm 77 (last three parts).

[e]Saturday evening psalmody is for Sunday Evening Prayer I.

*Psalms or canticle of the corresponding hour in Week 1.

Monsignor Pascher proposed a system in which the four-week Psalter should begin (1) on Easter Sunday and continue to Pentecost (including its octave—still part of the calendar at the time of this proposal); (2) on the first Sunday after Pentecost; (3) on the first Sunday after Epiphany; (4) on the first Sunday of Lent; (5) on the first Sunday of Advent. The distribution during the Christmas season would be computed separately. While this arrangement represented a refinement of that proposed earlier, it presented the problem to some members of Group 9 of incomplete cycles at various times in the year.[295] Monsignor Pascher, however, did not see this problem as bringing any great harm. Group 9 then accepted his proposal, notwithstanding the difficulties inherent in it.[296]

The proposal was submitted to the Consilium at its tenth plenary session (April 16–30, 1968). Here Canon André Rose pointed out that with the proposed numerical designation from one to thirty-four of the Ordinary Sundays of the liturgical year, it might be advisable to start the four-week cycle on the first Sunday per annum and have it run continuously in accordance with this enumeration. With this major modification, the proposal was accepted.[297] The decision brought to an end the major work of redistributing the Psalter, dividing the psalms, and situating the new four-week cycle within the reformed liturgical calendar.

One remaining question affecting the structure of the psalmody in the new Office remained: whether psalm prayers should be provided on an optional basis. Group 9, of course, had discussed their inclusion in the Office in November 1967. In submitting the first draft of IGLH to the members of Group 9 in June 1968 Canon Martimort asked if anyone knew whether Father Pinell's work on the prayers had been completed. He had heard nothing for almost a year regarding it.[298] In the draft itself, however, a paragraph on the psalm prayers was included that was essentially the same as that in all the following drafts and in the definitive text of IGLH.[299] Since the final draft of IGLH was approved by the Consilium, there was no objection to the inclusion of the psalm prayers; but, as IGLH indicates, they were to be printed in a supplementary volume for optional use following a pause for silent prayer at the conclusion of a psalm.[300]

The major work, then, of revising the structure of the psalmody in the Office had these important results: The Psalter was distributed over four weeks and most of the Hours assigned reduced amounts of psalmody, often achieved by careful division of psalms into several *incisa*. Greater scope was given to selective use of psalms appropriate to hour, day, or season without abandoning at least the semblance at times of their semicontinuous arrangement. New Testament canticles from books other than the gospel accounts were introduced into Vespers to enhance the Christian character of the psalmody. In addition to antiphons, new aids were supplied for the Christian interpretation of the psalms, namely, titles and psalm prayers, and encouragement was given for personal prayer by provision for moments of silence following the psalms. Strophic division of the psalms was introduced, allowing for their responsorial use. Finally, although a disappointment to the consultors who fought against it, the omission of three imprecatory psalms and a number of verses offensive to some sensibilities effectively breached a major organizing principle of the Roman and other monastic Offices, namely, use of the integral Psalter. While the restructuring of the psalmody was perhaps the greatest and most troublesome work of the reform, another structural matter that concerned choral or communal celebration of the Office also became problematic to consultors and members of the Consilium, namely, the structural union of an Hour of the Office with another liturgical action. To that matter attention is now turned.

STRUCTURING OF AN HOUR
JOINED TO ANOTHER LITURGICAL ACTION

The question of whether to attempt to provide a structural ordering of the elements in an Hour of the Office whereby an organic union of an Hour with some other liturgical act (another Hour of the Office, or Mass) would be achieved seems to have arisen following the reevaluation of the progress in reform of the Office initiated by the questionnaire of December 1965. Canon Martimort raised the question in his lengthy *relatio* (Schema 185) of September 19, 1966. Noting that the practice had often been to join Lauds or Vespers to another liturgical action, especially Matins or Mass, he suggested that the rubrics for the Office should provide for such joining in order to avoid repetition of prayers and readings and in order to have all elements arranged in a fitting organic union, as is found in other liturgies, notably the Oriental.[301]

In June 1967 Canon Martimort related to the members of Group 9 a summary of opinion he had received to date on the question of joining an Hour to another liturgical action. He first noted that the Office of Readings could not be joined to the Mass "because the Mass is another office of readings."[302] He then explained that there were divergent views on how the Office of Readings could be joined to Lauds or Vespers. Some (consultors Famoso, Lengeling, Amore, and Dirks) thought the Hours should remain distinct, although they would admit some adaptations within each Hour when both are joined. Others (consultors Pascher, Rose, Jounel, Visentin, and Dumas) favored making one Hour of two combined. Monsignor Jounel, however, would limit such union to communal celebration lest the adaptation simply serve convenience in private recitation. Canon Rose warned that such conjunction could only exist between two Hours of the same ferial or festal Office. One should not attempt, for instance, to combine the ferial Office of Readings for one day with festal First Vespers of the following day.[303] Three different solutions were proposed for joining the Office of Readings with Lauds or Vespers:

Scheme "A"
1. Invitatory (in the morning)
2. Hymn from Office of Readings or from Lauds (Vespers)
3. Psalmody from Office of Readings
4. Psalmody from Lauds (Vespers)
5. Biblical reading and responsory from Office of Readings
6. Patristic reading and responsory from Office of Readings
7. Gospel canticle
8. Intercessions
9. Oration

Scheme "B"
1. Invitatory (in the morning)
2. Hymn from Lauds (Vespers)
3. Psalmody of Lauds (Vespers)
4. Psalmody of Office of Readings
5. Biblical reading and response from Office of Readings
6. Patristic reading and response from Office of Readings

7. Gospel canticle
8. Intercessions
9. Oration

Scheme "C"
1. Invitatory (in the morning)
2. Hymn from Lauds (Vespers)
3. Psalmody of Office of Readings
4. Biblical reading and response from Office of Readings
5. Gospel canticle
6. Intercessions
7. Oration[304]

Proposals were proffered also for joining Lauds and Vespers with Mass. There was concern, articulated especially by Fathers Raffa and Dirks, that if an organic union were allowed between these Hours and the Mass it should be a simple arrangement lest rubrics be complicated and the whole liturgical action be too protracted. The proposals offered were as follows:

Scheme "A" (Lengeling)
1. All in the Hour of the Office to the oration inclusively
2. Readings of the Mass
3. Remainder of the Mass as usual

Scheme "B" (Famoso, Dumas)
1. Introit of the Mass (hymn of the Hour omitted)
2. Greeting of the Mass
3. (Penitential act)
4. Psalmody (short reading and response omitted)
5. Gospel canticle
6. Opening prayer of the Mass
7. Remainder of the Mass as usual

Scheme "C" (Famoso): For Vespers with Evening Mass
1. All as in Mass up to Communion
2. Hymn
3. Psalmody (short reading omitted)
4. Gospel canticle
5. Prayer after Communion
6. Blessing and dismissal

Scheme "D" (Pascher, Rose, Jounel, Visentin, Dumas)
  1. Either hymn of the Hour or introit (as the celebration requires)
  2. Psalmody of the hour
  3. (*Kyrie* or *Gloria* [unless omitted])
  4. Opening prayer of the Mass
  5. Readings of the Mass and the remainder of Mass as usual until Communion
  6. Gospel canticle
  7. Prayer after Communion
  8. Dismissal[305]

For the minor Hours opinions also were varied. Two members of Group 9 believed Mass should take the place of any of these Hours when both Mass and Office might occur at the same time. Canon Martimort himself expressed the fear that if Mass replaced a minor Hour daily, many psalms in the Office would be lost by those adopting the arrangement and, since the Mass is tied to no Hour of the day, nothing would remain for sanctifying the Hour. Other members of Group 9 thought that the procedure for conjunction here should be the same as that adopted for the major Hours.[306]

Group 9 did not consider this question of organic union at its next meeting of July 20–23, 1967, apparently because there was consensus that it would be better to wait until the lines of the reformed Office and Mass were clearer before doing so.[307] Many requests, however, were being received by the Consilium and the SCR from religious orders and congregations for immediate action on the matter, according to Canon Martimort, so on November 20, 1967, he presented to the Group of Relators, meeting before the ninth plenary session of the Consilium (November 21–28, 1967), ways in which the Hours could be combined with Mass without prejudicing the final solution to this question still under study. It is not clear what role, if any, the other members of Group 9 had in formulating this interim solution. For modes of union the canon suggested the following arrangements:

A. Union of a minor Hour and Mass
  1. *Deus in adiutorium*
  2. Hymn of the Hour or introit chant and entrance procession
  3. Psalmody

4. *Dominus vobiscum (Pax vobis)*
5. Prayer of the Hour or of the Mass
6. Readings of the Mass and the remainder of Mass as usual

B. Union of Lauds or Vespers with Mass (I)
  1. Introductory verse and hymn of the Hour or introit with procession
  2. Psalmody up to short reading, exclusively
  3. *Dominus vobiscum (Pax vobis)*
  4. Prayer of the Hour or of the Mass
  5. Readings of the Mass and the remainder of Mass up to and including Communion
  6. *Benedictus* or *Magnificat* after Communion
  7. Prayer after Communion and conclusion of Mass as usual

C. Union of Lauds or Vespers with Mass (II)
  1. Mass as usual to Communion, inclusively
  2. Psalmody of the Hour (reading and short response or versicle omitted)
  3. *Benedictus* or *Magnificat* (intercessions omitted)
  4. Prayer after Communion and conclusion of Mass as usual

Generally, Lauds ought to precede Mass as the first prayer of the day, and the union of Office of Readings with Mass is to be excluded. Exceptions are foreseen, as when the Office of Readings might coincide with celebrations of Mass at night (e.g., on Christmas). No mature decision seemed possible, said Canon Martimort, regarding the union of Office of Readings with Lauds or Vespers, so the current practice for such conjunction is, in the interim, recommended for retention.[308]

Apparently as a result of discussion in the Group of Relators, some modifications were made in Canon Martimort's report before it was presented to the Consilium. First, it was stated that union of an Hour of the Office with Mass could harm the faithful, so pastoral considerations should primarily guide the adoption of this arrangement. For the conjunction of a minor Hour and Mass the changes were that (1) one could use *either* the introductory verse of the Hour *or* the hymn as one option or the introit chant with procession as the other; (2) after the psalmody, the *Kyrie* being omitted, the *Gloria* would be said if it occurs in the Mass. For uniting Lauds or Vespers with Mass the arrangement was basically the same as that given earlier except that (1) the *Gloria* would be included after the psalmody and (2) the universal prayer of the Mass would be used in its proper place, with the option given of using instead the morning intercessions *(preces matutinales)* of Lauds in morning Mass on ferial days.[309]

At its ninth plenary session the Consilium approved these methods for union by voting yes, 23; no, 5; yes with reservations, 1. The approval, however, came not without some objecting to *any* attempt at organic union. Several of the many interventions by both members and consultors on the topic are worthy of note. Msgr. Johannes Wagner, director of the Liturgical Institute at Trier and relator of Group 10 (Ordinary of the Mass), acknowledged the general acceptability on his part of the proposals for organic union of Office and Mass but thought that if Vespers followed Mass, harm would come to those who leave before Vespers begins in that they would miss the prayer after Communion. Also harmful, in his opinion, would be the replacement in the Hour of its introductory parts by those of the Mass, or those of the Mass by those of the Hour. He and others preferred to see the two (Office and Mass) kept distinct, especially when the faithful were present. Several (consultors Smits, Franquesa, Dumas, and Gy) wanted Mass simply to replace a minor Hour rather than be organically united to it. Father Dirks thought that psalmody at the beginning of Mass should be avoided, since it would make the Liturgy of the Word burdensome. If it could be avoided in a conjunction of Lauds and Mass, it should be avoided in a union of Vespers and Mass. Psalmody should follow the Communion of Mass. Father Gy also strongly urged the adoption of a way to unite the Office of Readings with Lauds and Vespers.[310]

Before Group 9 met again Canon Martimort recalled to the members the substance of his report in June 1967 and the actions taken by the members and consultors of the Consilium at the ninth plenary session.[311] When the group actually met in Genoa from February 27 to March 1, 1968, the discussion turned first to the difficulty of uniting Mass and an Hour of the Office. The "audience," it was said, is different for each. Those who come for one may leave for the other. An organic union, however, would be of profit in seminaries and monasteries. A major difficulty was seen in attempting to unite the Office of Readings with Lauds or Vespers. To the question "Should the Office of Readings and the Office of a major Hour be kept distinct?" ("Placetne ut Officium Lectionis et Horae maioris distinctae retineantur?") almost all agreed. Several reasons persuaded the consultors to answer affirmatively. Since the Office of Readings is not tied to any given Hour, it could be said with any other Hour. A combination of Office of Readings and another Hour, however, could be either exceedingly artificial, reducing the simplicity and beauty the reform is attempting to achieve, or the length of the combined Offices would be perceived as burdensome and ways would be sought to abbreviate them further. Thus the only abbreviation Group 9 would admit for combining the Office of Readings with another Hour was the omission of the conclusion of one Hour and the introduction of the other.[312]

For the meetings of the Group of Relators and of the tenth plenary session of the Consilium (April 14–30, 1968), Canon Martimort reviewed for all what had been approved at their ninth session and, taking into consideration some of the *modi* made at that time, offered some modifications in the proposed structures for organic union: (1) Vespers should regularly not be celebrated before Mass but rather after it. When this is done, the order for Vespers and the minor Hours, too, if celebrated following Mass would be *(a)* prayer after Communion, *(b)* psalmody, *(c)* *Magnificat* (in Vespers), *(d)* concluding prayer, and *(e)* blessing. (2) On the feast of the Nativity of the Lord, at the end of the Night Office if Mass is to follow immediately the prayer and *Benedicamus* could be omitted. With the exception of this case, the Office of Readings should not be combined with Mass. In monasteries, however, where it is seen fit to celebrate Mass after a ferial night Office, the Benedictine practice could be followed of beginning the readings of the Mass immediately after the psalmody of the second nocturn.[313]

In the meeting of the Group of Relators, only the question of uniting the Office of Readings with another Hour was of major concern. Father Gy again became a strong proponent of a way to unite the Office of Readings with another Hour because he foresaw the disappearance of the Office of Readings if it were not possible to use it in conjunction with another Hour. Canon Rose and

Monsignor Jounel supported him. Monsignor Wagner, however, not only opposed this but took a stronger stand than he had taken in the ninth plenary session against any organic union of Lauds or Vespers with Mass. He opposed such unions on the grounds that these arrangements were simply bad mixtures. To the question of whether the matter of organic union of the Office of Readings and another Hour should be further pursued, ten agreed, nine disagreed, and two abstained. The almost equally divided opinion on the matter may explain why the question was apparently not brought to the impending plenary session.[314]

For the meeting of Group 9 at Verona from July 16 to 19, 1968, Canon Martimort provided the first draft of IGLH, in which the modified proposals regarding organic union made to the Group of Relators the previous April were incorporated. One further modification had to be made, however, in view of the revised structure of the Office of Readings. If, aside from the night of the Nativity, it would be necessary to join the Office of Readings with Mass, then immediately after the second reading of the Office with its responsory, Mass would begin.[315]

Until the autumn of 1969, the provisions for organic union remained essentially as presented in 1968 at the time of the tenth plenary session of the Consilium.[316] In preparation for the twelfth plenary session (November 4–8, 1969), however, Canon Martimort conveyed to the members of the Consilium his view of the difficult road traveled in pursuit of a solution to organic union and his proposals for modifying some aspects of the ways to amalgamate Hours of the Office and Mass:

"We have examined again and again Title XII [of the proposed IGLH], *Concerning the Way of Combining the Hours of the Office with Mass.* Altogether contradictory opinions are continually presented even in our group, and it must be admitted that a solution entirely satisfactory to all simply cannot be found. It seems that we should not prolong this discussion so that the substance of this important section is not somehow kept intact. We think, however, that some changes must be made not only so the directives conform to the new Order of the Mass, now in effect, but also so the celebration of Vespers before evening Mass can be provided for under certain conditions."[317]

Thus, in the final draft of IGLH, dated March 1, 1970, there appeared an additional paragraph permitting Vespers to be joined to Mass in the same way as Lauds could be on the condition that Vespers and Mass were of the same Office. First Vespers of solemnities, Sundays, and feasts of the Lord could not be celebrated in this way, however, unless Mass of the previous day or of the Saturday had already been celebrated.[318] Missing from this draft is the general provision, found in all earlier drafts, for uniting any Hour of the Office with Mass by simply omitting the prayer and conclusion of the Hour when it immediately precedes the Eucharist.[319] It is unclear what role, if any, Group 9 or the Consilium had in the making of these decisions, which were the final ones affecting organic union of an Hour of the Office with another liturgical action.

So without general satisfaction on the part of consultors and members of the Consilium but with a desire to meet a practical need experienced particularly in some religious communities, the Consilium and those unspecified persons arranging final details made provisions for uniting an Hour of the Office to Mass and for uniting the Office of Readings to another Hour of the Office. Evaluation of these provisions is reserved for chapter 6, but it must be noted here that in the process leading to the establishment of the provisions there does not seem to have been any serious questioning of the assumed link between Office and Mass nor of the anomaly of making one of the traditional Hours, namely, Vigils (Matins) into a "roving Hour," such that, as Office of Readings, it could coincide with the time appropriate to another Hour. The seeming lack of critical examination of the very basis of a liturgical practice not only characterized deliberation on this question but also on the one to be examined next—the position of the hymn in all the Hours.

THE POSITION OF THE HYMN IN ALL THE HOURS

Since SC 93 seemed to presume that hymns would remain as structural elements in the reformed Office, Group 7, whose responsibility it was to restore and enlarge the repertoire of hymns for the Office, undertook its task from the first days of the reform, and by the time of the meeting of Group 9 from September 25 to

26, 1965, had produced a collection of 108 hymns for all the Hours both *per annum* and for the special seasons of the liturgical cycle.[320]

At its meeting in September 1966 however, Group 9 seems for the first time to have scrutinized at some length both the collection of hymns and the place of hymns in the Office. The collection itself is not of concern here except to the extent it affected structural considerations. Group 9, acknowledging the great work Group 7 had undertaken, questioned the appropriateness of many of these hymns in vernacular translations. This question led to another regarding the appropriateness of hymns at all in the Office. The group, apparently thinking primarily (if not exclusively) of a recited Office and ignoring the poetic nature of psalms and canticles along with the possibility of their selected use, seems to have been of one mind that an almost purely scriptural Office would be rather severe and that hymns, as ecclesiastical compositions, helped relieve that severity. Some of the Latin hymns, it was admitted, could also be pleasing in vernacular translation.[321] So Group 9 agreed (1) that a place in the Office should be found for some hymns, (2) that better traditional hymns should be retained through a very careful selective process, (3) that for the Office in the vernacular languages SC 38 should prevail and episcopal conferences should allow both the adaptation of the Latin hymns and the creation of new hymns.[322]

When these proposals were submitted to the Group of Relators in preparation for the seventh plenary session of the Consilium (October 6–14, 1966), an additional consideration emerged. Eighteen relators thought the hymns should be optional for private recitation while fourteen would have them obligatory. The Consilium, consequently, was asked four questions regarding hymns:

"15. In the structure of the Office should some place be found for hymns?
"16. Are hymns to be kept as obligatory or optional in private recitation?
"17. Is it acceptable that from those Latin hymns that are sound and traditional, those that seem apt for today may be kept?
"18. Should the aforesaid faculty be given in the rubrics to the episcopal conferences?"

The members of the Consilium unanimously assented to Questions 15, 17, and 18. For Question 16, twenty-four members wished to see the hymn obligatory and eight, optional.[323] Thus while the existence of hymns in the structure of the Office was assured as well as a corpus of suitable Latin hymns and others approved by the various episcopal conferences, there was some hesitation about their obligatory use in private recitation.

In preparing SCDO for the meeting of the Consilium in April 1967, Group 9 in February 1967 considered moving the hymn in Lauds and Vespers from its position after the short reading *(capitulum)* to the beginning of those Hours. Canon Martimort made the proposal, and the reasons offered for this change were to give "color" to the Hours at their outset and to provide an effective way to begin them, especially when celebrated with the people. The hymn at the beginning of the Hour could set the tone or the mood for the entire celebration, as was the case for Vespers in the Ambrosian liturgy. All the members of Group 9 agreed to this.[324] Thus for SCDO, used by the Consilium from April 9 to 15, 1967, each Hour had a hymn, and each hymn except that at Compline occurred at the beginning of the Hour.[325]

On April 17, 1967, after a week of using SCDO, both the members and consultors of the Consilium discussed among other matters regarding the hymn the change of position for the hymns in Lauds and Vespers. Msgr. Balthasar Fischer was not pleased with the move. He thought it unwise to make identical all the Hours (the case of Compline apparently forgotten) by placing the hymn first. In Sunday Vespers, he noted, the outstanding beginning of the Hour is Psalm 109 with its vision of the Messiah. The hymn at the start of the Hour would obscure this. Furthermore, not all the hymns of Lauds and Vespers are able to give color or create a mood, as for example, the hymns on feasts of the saints. Prof. Emil Lengeling, however, compared the hymn to the introit of the Mass. As the introit sounds the theme of the day, so could the hymn at the beginning of an Hour give the theme of that Hour. In its traditional place the hymn does not fit well with the other parts. Msgr. Ernesto Moneta Caglio, president of the Pontifical Institute of Ambrosian Sacred Music in Milan, vouched for the suitability of the hymn in first place in the Ambrosian Office. Fr. A. M.

Roguet, O.P., of the Institut Supérieur de Liturgie in Paris, was concerned about the inferior quality of hymns in the vernacular tongues and thus about their suitability for beginning the Hours. Bishops Pichler (Banjaluka, Yugoslavia) and Boudon (Mende) asked for experimentation before a definitive decision was made. Cardinal Lercaro was favorable to the move, especially in the Office *per annum* because the character of the Hours would be better highlighted. He recalled that Dante's naming Compline "Te Lucis" showed that an Hour is characterized by the hymn. When the vote of the Consilium was called for, almost all members favored the change. When the consultors had voted in the meeting of the Group of Relators, twenty-three of thirty-one were in favor, seven preferred to keep the hymn in its then current position, and one wished that its position be left optional.[326]

For the second experimental edition of the Office, SDO, utilized by the Consilium from November 12 to 25, 1967, the hymns were in the same positions as in SCDO. In the meeting of the Group of Relators of November 14 to 20 a lengthy discussion occurred on the position of the hymn. The discussion arose in the midst of debate on the proposed introduction of short responses to the readings at Lauds and Vespers. Fr. Joseph Gelineau, S.J., saw need for a fitting chant after the reading but considered a responsory, canticle, and intercessions to be an excessive accumulation of elements following the reading. Why not, he asked, use the hymn as response after the reading? Its move to the start of the Hour, in his opinion, was a pastoral and liturgical error. Canon Martimort reminded him that the move had already been agreed to and was judged opportune from the Ambrosian experience. Father Gelineau, however, considered introductory verses and hymn to be too much for the beginning of an Hour. Experience indicated to him that the hymn would serve best after the reading. Monsignor Jounel did not like the idea of having two chants, hymn and canticle, following the reading. Monsignor Fischer, however, agreed with Father Gelineau, claiming that hymn and canticle were of different genres, but Monsignor Jounel disputed this claim. Canon Martimort noted a difficulty in providing hymns as responses to the readings: there would be need of as many hymns as there are readings if the hymn were to function as a special response to the reading. Fr. Joseph Patino, S.J., director of the

Secretariado Nacional de Liturgia in Spain, considered Canon Martimort's contention to be an exaggeration. It would suffice, he said, for the hymn to provide, generally, some kind of meditation after the reading. Father Gy thought the arguments heretofore, both for and against, were simply theoretical and lacking an experiential base. Some, however, maintained that experience showed that a hymn served best at the beginning of a service. Professor Lengeling and Msgr. Theodor Schnitzler of Cologne offered their experience with the German pious exercise called "Andacht," which begins with a popular hymn and without which there would not be a good disposition of the other elements of the service. Others noted that experiences differ from community to community due to their diverse natures and needs.

Canon Martimort finally asked if the relators would favor the retention of the hymn at the beginning of the Hours at least during a period of experimentation, with the possibility allowed of considering the matter again later. Short optional responses rather than hymns would follow the readings during the experimental period. Apparently this was agreeable to the relators, for no questions regarding use of the hymn as response to the reading were offered to the members of the Consilium.[327]

In his communication to the members of Group 9 preparatory to its meeting from February 27 to March 1, 1968, Canon Martimort recalled the controversy among the relators in the previous November and expressed confidence that experimentation would indicate the appropriateness of moving the hymn at Lauds and Vespers to the beginning of those Hours. He reported that Monsignor Schnitzler had promised in November to conduct experiments using the hymn at the start of Lauds and Vespers in the Office of religious and laity under his care in Cologne. The monsignor had reported that the results were exceptionally good. The hymn at the beginning brought together those praying ("sie singen sich zusammen!"), and the wider separation of hymn and gospel canticle allowed each its due emphasis. Canon Martimort also reported that Monsignor Pascher had suggested that the hymn at Compline also be moved to the start of the Hour.[328]

Group 9 at its meeting in February–March 1968 left unchanged what had been decided regarding shift in position for the hymn at Lauds and Vespers. With respect to Compline, ten of the eleven members present favored Monsignor Pascher's suggestion to place the hymn at the beginning of the Hour.[329]

In preparation for the tenth plenary session of the Consilium (April 23–30, 1968), Canon Martimort reminded consultors and members that the Consilium had already approved the transfer of the hymn at Lauds and Vespers to the beginning of those Hours. Nothing was said about the place of the hymn in Compline.[330] At its tenth session the Consilium apparently did not consider either the place of the hymn at Lauds and Vespers or its place in the structure of Compline.[331] All the drafts of IGLH and the definitive text itself of that document indicate that the hymn is at the beginning of Lauds and Vespers.[332] At Compline, also, it occurs near the start of the Hour. In all drafts of IGLH the hymn follows immediately the *Deus, adiutorium* opening the hour, but in the definitive text the hymn is to follow the examination of conscience inserted optionally after the introductory verses. The latter change, proper to the structure of Compline, will be discussed in the next chapter.[333]

Noteworthy in all the discussion of the position of the hymn in the Hours, especially in Lauds and Vespers, is the apparent absence of any consideration of reasons why the hymn at Lauds and Vespers occurred after the short reading *(capitulum)* in the former Roman Office. The possible seriousness and implications of this oversight will be considered in chapter 6.[334] One other, less-controversial matter affecting the structure of all the Hours remains to be considered, namely, the provision for periods of silence within each Hour.

THE INTRODUCTION OF SILENCE

In the questionnaire of December 1965 the members and some consultors of the Consilium had been asked, "Does it seem fitting to provide through the rubrics for some time of silence and meditation even in common recitation and in choir, for example, after one or another psalm or after readings?"[335] The members responding to this question had voted 15 to 7 in favor of allowing silence at certain times, and consultors had favored its introduction by a vote of 21 to 2.[336]

Not until the eighth plenary session of the Consilium (April 10–19, 1967), however, did there seem to be any discussion on the matter. Some of the members, apparently noting that no provision had yet been made for moments of silence in the Office, asked that it be introduced. Bishop Pellegrino (Turin) attested to the good experience he and others had with such moments in the celebration of the sacred triduum in his diocese. He thought, however, that such moments ought to be left to the prudent judgment of the one presiding at the Office or of the one reciting it. Bishop Guano (Leghorn) attested to the fruitfulness of moments of silence in his own experience of common prayer many times with university students. Canon Martimort reassured the assembly that a provision for moments of silence within the Office would be mentioned in a general decree (the future General Instruction), but such provision, he said, would be left optional.[337]

In all but the first draft of IGLH, the text of the three articles (201–3) in the definitive edition providing for and describing the value of moments of silence is found. Nothing was included about silence in the first draft of IGLH because Canon Martimort had not heard from any consultors or members as to what should be said about it "as becomes silence" ("sicut decet silentio"), he adds. The purpose of these moments of silence, say the later drafts and IGLH 202, is to allow the Holy Spirit "to be heard more fully in our hearts and to unite our personal prayer more closely with the Word of God and the public voice of the Church." Such moments are appropriate after a psalm especially if a psalm prayer is to follow, after a reading, and before or after a responsory.[338]

Thus was introduced—perhaps reintroduced—into the Roman structure an element essential to the ancient monastic Office, for as Fr. Adalbert de Vogüé has observed with respect to psalmody:

"In reading [the *Rule of Benedict*] today we do not suspect that the ancient monastic office was composed of psalms *and prayers*. Yet these prayers, of which nothing remains in our modern office, were an essential part, or to say it better, the very essence of the ancient prayer. Each psalm of the office ended with a time of silence in which those present rose and prostrated themselves to pray. . . . While the psalmody required only a respectful bearing and an attentive mind, the prayer demands an intense effort of supplication. . . . The very contrast of attitudes invites us to see in it the supreme act of the office."[339]

Leaving these essential moments of silence optional in LH is puzzling, at least from the point of view that the reformers felt obliged to restore or maintain as requirements so many other elements from the monastic tradition—elements meant to serve the prayer *(oratio)* in silence.

From the foregoing considerations on the Consilium's efforts to reform the structure of the Office as a whole, it is clear that while radical reform opposed to a literal interpretation of SC was rejected and a relatively conservative line of reform and the needs of clergy and private recitation of the Office were clearly of major concern throughout the reform, there was nonetheless some shift in 1966 to a more pastoral concern to provide for all—diocesan clergy, monks, other religious, laity. This concern was revealed especially in the restructuring of Lauds and Vespers to make both Hours the same for and more accessible to all and in the redistribution and more selective use of the psalms to provide for more fruitful prayer. The matter for consideration next is to see how each of the Hours underwent structural modification.

Chapter 5

The Structure of the Individual Hours

The examination in chapter 4 of the process by which the Hours of the Office as a whole were restructured did not touch on the reform of many structural elements peculiar to each of the Hours. It is the purpose of this chapter to describe the process by which the structure of each Hour of the Office was reformed and to indicate what was done with respect to the various elements in each Hour. The focus will be on elements and procedures not considered in detail in the previous chapter. Those Hours that have an identical structure and that were usually grouped together in the process of the reform will be considered together here. Thus, examined in chronological sequence of their structural reform will be (1) Lauds and Vespers; (2) Terce, Sext, None; (3) Matins or Office of Readings (including the invitatory); and (4) Compline. As in the previous chapter, the proposals and deliberations of Group 9 and the action of the Consilium or other groups and individuals regarding them will form the bases of the description.

LAUDS AND VESPERS

A structural reform of Lauds and Vespers was not explicitly demanded in SC 89a. That article simply stated that Lauds and Vespers were to be *considered* and to be *celebrated* as the chief Hours. SC 90, however, in decreeing an adaptation of the Roman Office so that all might profit better from it, and SC 100, in prescribing that the chief Hours, especially Vespers, be celebrated communally in churches on Sundays and solemn feasts, might be said to call implicitly for structural reform of those Hours. Resistance to reforming the structure of the chief Hours, especially that of Lauds, was evident in the early stages of the reformers' work. This resistance, as described in chapter 4, centered principally on the questions of whether to reduce the psalmody in Lauds and Vespers and, if done, how and for which Hours such a reduction should be accomplished.[1] Those questions grew out of a general *questio* put by Canon Martimort to the second plenary session of the Consilium (April 17–20, 1964), with the request that the Consilium accept it as a proposition for consideration by Group 9: "Is it fitting to adapt Lauds and Vespers especially when they are celebrated with the people or in the parish church? (art. 100; *Emendat.* p. 11, 1; *Modi* p. 9 n. 11)."[2]

With the Consilium's approval of the appropriateness of the question, Group 9 entered into a protracted discussion in several meetings and by correspondence among the consultors as to just what, if anything, should be done with Lauds and Vespers. Advice from some outside Group 9 was not lacking. As discussed in chapter 4, for example, Fr. Juan Mateos attempted to elucidate the nature of cathedral Lauds and Vespers and to recommend to Group 9 a radical revision of these Hours along the lines of their ancient forms in the cathedral Office. By September 1964 Canon Martimort was at least able to present to the Consilium for its fourth plenary session (September 28–October 9, November 16) another series of questions under discussion on specific elements in Lauds and Vespers. Besides the questions, considered in chapter 4, on the number of psalms in Vespers and on the structure of Lauds and Vespers in relation to the other Hours, the members and consultors of the Consilium heard the following, to which they were asked to respond: (1) Should some of the intercessions *(preces capituli)* that occurred at the end of Prime be inserted into Lauds? (2) Should a canticle from the New Testament be added to Vespers? (3) Should a longer reading be proposed for Vespers when the people are present? (4) Should an *oratio communis*, or "prayer of the faithful," be inserted in Vespers? Canon Martimort reported that the majority of Group 9 favored the insertion of some of the *preces* of Prime into Lauds to enhance its character as Morning Prayer. The minority preferred other ways to emphasize this character such as inserting into Lauds some morning collects from the ancient Sacramentaries.

As to the insertion of a canticle from the New Testament into Vespers, an original unanimity in favor of this, said the canon, gave way when it was understood that exegetes may not agree that certain passages in the New Testament are indeed canticles. If a canticle were introduced, he said, it might best be put after the *capitulum* so as to preserve the traditional order of the use of Scripture in the Roman Liturgy, namely, passages from the Old Testment (some of which might appear as *capitula*), passages from the New Testament other than those from the Synoptics or John, and finally, passages from any of the four accounts of the gospel. In any case, the fifth psalm in Vespers could be dropped if a canticle were introduced.

Group 9 agreed that a longer reading than the current *capitulum* should be introduced into Vespers but only when the people were present. According to Canon Martimort, however, there was concern that Vespers not be turned into a "celebration of the Word of God" such as those services recommended in SC 35.4, because Vespers is and ought to remain Evening *prayer*. As to introducing a "universal prayer" or "prayer of the faithful" into Vespers, Group 9 was apparently unanimously in favor.[3]

A majority of the members of the Consilium responded affirmatively to each of the four questions regarding Lauds and Vespers. The greatest number of negative votes and reservations attended the question on inserting *preces* from Prime into Lauds. Of twenty-nine voting seven responded negatively and eight, yes with reservations. A number of the suggestions *(modi)* asked to have the *preces* put after Lauds, not within it. Two other questions garnering some (seven to eight) negative votes but no reservations were those concerned with insertion of a New Testament canticle and intercessions *(oratio communis)* into Vespers.[4]

Preoccupied with the major questions of the number and selection of psalms for Lauds and Vespers, Group 9 did little to act on the positive response of the Consilium to the other four questions before the sixth plenary session (October–December 1965). At its meeting of March 1–2, 1965, however, Group 9 briefly entertained the idea of restoring a rite of *lucernarium* and offering of incense, presumably with Psalm 140 or other "evening psalms." Impetus for this suggestion may have come from Father Mateos' proposal, which was rejected at this meeting as contrary to SC. Canon Martimort has told this author that he was unhappy with the then-current provision for use of incense at the *Magnificat* and would have liked to have seen restored the use of incense with

Psalm 140, but not on a daily basis. Psalm 140, he said, is too long for daily use. He would have preferred to see Psalm 140 with incense reserved for Sunday Vespers. It was Father Bugnini, according to the canon, who was adamant in preserving the use of incense with the *Magnificat*. In the end, Group 9 put off to another time consideration of restoring the *lucernarium* and oblation of incense. In fact, however, no further serious consideration of this proposed restoration seems ever to have been made. But Fr. Jorge Pinell had proposed before this meeting that the first psalm in Vespers every evening be a vesperal psalm *(lucernarius psalmus)* in accordance with the ancient universal tradition for such. These psalms were, he said, 109, 111, 112, 115, 129, 131, and 140. Msgr. Joseph Pascher and the others in Group 3 had, in fact, incorporated most of these psalms as the first for Vespers in the earliest schemata of distribution of the Psalter (see tables 3 and 4 above), and in the schema (table 5 above) presented at this meeting included all of them. Group 9 endorsed Father Pinell's proposal along with the schema of Group 3, as described more at length in chapter 4.[5]

At its meeting of September 25–26, 1965, Group 9 agreed to the insertion of a New Testament canticle in Vespers and examined ten texts proposed by Group 3 as such canticles. When the Group of Relators met on September 28, however, there was more hesitancy to accept the proposal to adopt the canticles. Fr. Burkhard Neunheuser objected that canticles of this kind in Vespers would simply be against tradition, and if they were introduced the New Testament would no longer be the culmination of the Hour. Furthermore, those canticles from the Pauline epistles would be put to chant with difficulty. Fr. P. M. Gy did not think the canticles would connect well with the *Magnificat*. Fr. Bernard Botte thought the passages selected pertained more to a homiletic genre than to that of canticles, and Msgr. Johannes Wagner said he would rather see examined the possibility of structuring Vespers on the Benedictine model of four psalms, reading, responsory, and versicles. To Father Neunheuser's objection that the New Testament would cease to culminate the Hour it was said that the *Magnificat*, a canticle from the gospel, would remain as the high point of Vespers. Monsignor Joseph Pascher thought that even if the proposed canticles were untraditional they ought to be introduced. Priests *(sic)* ought not be deprived of the joy these canticles can induce. There should be no difficulty, he said, in moving from the Old Testament psalms to the New Testament canticle because the psalms should be read in the light of the New Testament. To Father Gy's objection that the canticles would not go well with the *Magnificat* it was maintained that just as the epistle at Mass went with the gospel, so the New Testament canticle at Vespers could go with the gospel canticle, the *Magnificat*. Fr. Herman Schmidt favored the addition of the canticles because they would render Vespers more solemn and, just as the use of an evening psalm in first place at Vespers (as had been proposed) might open up the possibility of introducing a ritual of light (such as the ancient lamp lighting in cathedral Vespers), so the New Testament canticle in last place could lead into "the evening sacrifice" *(sacrificium vespertinum)*, by which he may have meant, in this context, evening Mass. Fr. A. M. Roguet also favored the introduction of the canticles into Vespers because they would help show better the connection between Old Testament and New.[6]

The sixth plenary session did not act on the proposal for New Testament canticles in Vespers or on any other specific proposals regarding Lauds and Vespers because it had to discuss what should be done in response to the widespread protest (discussed in chs. 3 and 4) against the general lines of reform of the Office. In the questionnaire issuing from that session, one question (no. 4) pertained specifically to Lauds and Vespers. Besides asking, as indicated above in chapter 4, if reduction of the number of psalms to three in Lauds and Vespers where the people were present would be appropriate, it queried whether a long reading and homily should be introduced into these Hours when they are celebrated with the people. Sixteen members replied affirmatively; four, negatively, and three, yes with reservations. The consultors were split, twelve in favor, ten against. The majority of the negative votes of the consultors were against the proposed double arrangement of psalmody (one for clergy using the Office by themselves, the other for use when laity were present) and not specifically against the introduction of a long reading and homily.[7]

While the questionnaire was in circulation, Canon Martimort was engaged, as noted above, in his own personal study of the issues raised in the sixth plenary session. One of these issues, of course, was the structure of Lauds and Vespers. His own study of the tradition of the Office, some Protestant forms of Morning and Evening Prayer, Pope Paul VI's suggestions (three psalms and long reading in both Hours) in his letter of April 5, 1966, and the results of the questionnaire prompted him to write some ten pages of reflections on the structure of Lauds and Vespers in his report (RG) to Group 9 at the end of July 1966. The substance of this report as it pertains to Lauds and Vespers and the aftermath in the meetings of Group 9 (September 6–8, 1966), of the Group of Relators (September 26–27, 1966), and of the seventh plenary session of the Consilium (October 6–14, 1966) have already been discussed in chapter 4. The principal result of the lengthy reexamination of the reform of Lauds and Vespers, it may be recalled, was the approval by the Consilium of a threefold structure of psalmody (including canticles from Old or New Testaments) in both Lauds and Vespers rather than the formerly proposed fivefold structure with provision for a threefold structure in Vespers only when the laity were present.[8]

Besides the psalmody, three other structural elements proposed for Lauds and Vespers were subjects of discussion at the seventh plenary session. These elements were (1) readings in both Hours, (2) *preces* in Lauds, *oratio communis* in Vespers; and (3) New Testament canticle in Vespers. With respect to readings in Lauds and Vespers the questionnaire of December 1965 had asked, "Is it fitting that a reading from Sacred Scripture be admitted into the other Hours, especially Lauds and Vespers, except Matins, since it is an Hour of reading?"[9] The response of Consilium members had been twenty to two in favor; the response of the consultors, twenty-two to one in favor of readings. In his first intervention into the Consilium's process of reforming the Office by his letter of April 5, 1966, the Pope, too, had gone on record in favor at least of a long reading at Lauds and Vespers when the people were present. When at its meeting from September 6 to 8, 1966, Group 9 considered the response to Question 7 and that to Question 4, alluded to above, as well as the Pope's suggestions and the comments of some of the members of the Consilium with respect to these questions, it was noted that sixteen respondents among the members of the Consilium had asked that the long reading be used not only when laity participated in Lauds or Vespers but also when these Hours were used only by clergy so that they might better profit spiritually. This request was attributed, however, by some in Group 9 to a desire to substitute a celebration of the Word of God or spiritual reading for the prayer and praise of God, which are the more important dimensions of Lauds and Vespers. Besides, Group 9 said, there is a danger of unduly lengthening Lauds and Vespers by incorporating a long reading; and, perhaps the greatest difficulty, there already exist two other cycles of readings (one for Matins, the other for Mass), so that adding two others (one for Lauds, one for Vespers) would seem excessive.

Nonetheless, Group 9 unanimously agreed to propose that a long reading be used, if desired, in Lauds and Vespers when the laity were participants, but that the reading would be drawn from already existing cycles (that for Office of Readings or that for Mass). The group also unanimously agreed to propose that in the private recitation of Lauds and Vespers a long reading could be used optionally, but a *capitulum* or short reading should be provided for those not choosing the long reading. Four questions were presented to the Group of Relators and the members of the Consilium on these proposals:

"*Question 12:* Should a longer reading be provided in Lauds and Vespers when these Hours are celebrated with the people?
"*Question 13:* Should this reading also be allowed optionally without the people present?
"*Question 14:* Do you agree that a new course of readings should not be created, but that the reading should be drawn from cycles already existing in the manner described above?
"*Question 15:* When the longer reading is not used, should a short reading be provided?"[10]

A majority in the Group of Relators responded affirmatively to these questions during the group's meeting on September 26 and 27. The questions received a unanimous affirmative reply from the members of the Consilium at the seventh plenary session.[11]

The second structural element discussed in the seventh plenary session was the insertion in both Lauds and Vespers of intercessions. It will be recalled that in 1964 the Consilium had been asked whether some of the the *preces* of Prime should be introduced into Lauds and whether an *oratio communis* should be inserted in Vespers. Group 9 did not consider the answers to these questions clear enough at the time, and no questions on these issues had been asked in the questionnaire of December 1965. The Pope, however, had suggested in his intervention of April 5, 1966, that some elements of Prime that referred to the offering and sanctification of daily work should be inserted into Lauds. At its September 1966 meeting Group 9 agreed that just as it was appropriate to add a universal prayer to Vespers, so it would be fitting to have some form of *preces* in Lauds. But the form should be different from that used in Vespers. The *oratio communis* at Vespers, in turn, should be different from that to be used in the Mass in order to avoid weariness. Significantly, the group also recommended that, at least for Vespers, the form of the prayer should lend itself to both communal and private use. The group thus indicated once again its penchant for compromised structures. No question was posed for the Group of Relators and the members of the Consilium regarding the *preces* for Lauds, but regarding the universal prayer for Vespers the Consilium was asked, "Should a universal prayer be inserted into Vespers in the manner and for the reason described above?"[12] The Group of Relators seems to have expressed no opposition to the proposal, and the Consilium in its seventh session was unanimously in favor of it.[13]

Finally, the third structural element considered by the seventh session, namely, the insertion of a New Testament canticle into Vespers, had been debated, as previously indicated, by both Group 9 and the Group of Relators prior to the sixth plenary session. Group 9 considered the matter again at its meeting in September 1966. Group 3 (distribution of the psalms), which, with the assistance of Group 4 (biblical readings) and Group 8 (chants), was primarily responsible for work on the proposed canticles, had offered three reasons for their introduction into Vespers. The first reason was that there is a liturgical tradition for the use of such canticles. Although the Roman Rite has never used them, they are found in the Mozarabic liturgy. The second reason was one of usefulness. Recent biblical studies have revealed that some passages of the New Testament are of a hymnic literary genre. These passages resemble in their literary form the psalms of praise in the

Old Testament. That form, which invites to praise and gives motives for doing so, is especially favorable to fostering the spirit of liturgical prayer. Besides, although the psalms ought always to be prayed in the spirit of the New Testament, many have difficulty in doing so. Canticles from the New Testament with their specifically Christian focus could assist in fostering a Christian understanding of the Psalter. Finally, these canticles could provide a transition from the Old Testament psalmody to the culmination of Vespers in the gospel canticle, the *Magnificat*. From that point of view it would seem best to put the New Testament canticle in the last place of the psalmodic section rather than after the reading. New Testament canticles may not always serve well as responsories to the readings because responsories are relatively short passages having a function different from the psalmody. It would be well to enhance the psalmody itself with New Testament passages of a nature like the psalms themselves.

There was agreement in Group 9 on the appropriateness of these canticles in Vespers, and the majority in the group thought they should be included in the body of psalmody. Some, however, suggested that their insertion not follow a rigid daily pattern. A question was formulated for the Group of Relators and the Consilium to which the former group had no objection and the latter group gave a unanimously favorable reply: "Should a New Testament canticle be inserted into the psalmody of Vespers in the manner described?"[14]

Supplied with the results of the questionnaire of December 1965, principles adopted in Group 9 at its meeting of September 6-8, 1966, and directives from both the sixth and seventh plenary sessions of the Consilium, Group 3 (distribution of the psalms) reworked, as described in chapter 4, their former proposals for the psalmody of all the Hours. For the meeting of Group 9 from February 6 to 8, 1967, Msgr. Joseph Pascher, relator of Group 3, was able to present a new scheme for the psalmody of both Lauds and Vespers. Using the ternary structure of psalmody for these Hours, as had been agreed, he proposed on behalf of Group 3 that in Lauds, respecting the tradition of the *laudate* psalms in last place at this Hour but acquiescing to the desire for fewer and more varied psalms, one psalm of praise culminate the set of three. He acknowledged that some had wished to see a psalm of this type begin Lauds followed by a psalm in the genre of lamentation. He had argued for the reverse as more appropriate, since there could be observed a progression from the attitudes in a psalm of lament to those expressed in a hymnic or laudatory psalm. But between the first psalm, generally a lament type, and the last should occur a canticle from the Old Testament, since such canticles were traditional at Lauds in the Roman Office. A firm principle followed here and in the psalmodic structure of all the Hours was that never are two psalms of the same literary genre joined side by side on the same day and at the same Hour. For Vespers, said Monsignor Pascher, generally psalms from those traditional for Roman Vespers (Pss 109–47) were proposed for the first two in the group. Their sequence in the Psalter would be retained, but no two of the same literary genre would stand together. The third place would be given to the New Testament canticle for the reasons already indicated. Group 9 accepted the proposals presented by Group 3 and incorporated them into the experimental edition of the Office, SCDO, being prepared for the eighth plenary session of the Consilium.[15]

The preparation of SCDO demanded that Group 9 consider in some way all the elements that were to constitute Lauds and Vespers. Those not common to the other Hours, about which some discussion was held in the meeting of February 5–8, 1967, were the *capitula* or short readings, short responses, the gospel canticles (*Benedictus* and *Magnificat*), the *preces* for Lauds and the *oratio communis* for Vespers, and the conclusion of these Hours. In connection with the proposal considered at the seventh plenary session that a long reading be placed optionally in Lauds and Vespers, some attention had been given in Group 9 and the Group of Relators to *capitula* or short readings. A consensus was apparently reached in those groups that the *capitula*, preferably to be termed "short readings," ought to be retained in Lauds and Vespers when these Hours were said privately. The current *capitula* would need revision, but readings not much longer than these that would be true proclamations of the biblical word focusing on a particular idea would be acceptable alternatives to the long reading.

At its meeting, then, in February 1967 Group 9 charged Group 4 (biblical readings) with preparing a set of short readings drawn from the New Testament and encompassing one week for inclusion in Lauds and Vespers (as well as in the minor Hours) of SCDO. It was proposed and accepted, however, that for each short reading an indication be given of the long or complete text from which it had been taken. Group 9 also agreed by a vote of ten to four *not* to allow the liberty of selecting texts other than those assigned. On the basis of the decisions made at the seventh plenary session that responsories should follow long readings in the Office even in private recitation, Group 9 was unanimously agreed that a response or responsory should follow even the short readings at Lauds and Vespers. The use of responsories at Lauds and Vespers in both the Benedictine Office and the Office of Taizé was cited as precedent. At the same meeting, after some discussion in which certain ones apparently proposed alternatives to the daily use of the *Benedictus* at Lauds and the *Magnificat* at Vespers to avoid weariness, a final, unanimous agreement was reached to retain both canticles on a *daily* basis. Cited as reasons for retaining the *Magnificat* daily were its popular association with Vespers and its superb expression of thanksgiving. While, it was said, the *Benedictus* was less popular than the *Magnificat,* it was singularly fitting for the morning Hour and was a summary of the expectation of the holy people of the Old Testament. In Canon Martimort's explanation of these reasons to the Consilium preparatory to the eighth plenary session, he noted that very grave reasons would be necessary for abandoning daily use of both canticles.

No decision had yet been made by the Consilium regarding insertion of intercessions in Lauds, but Group 9, favorable to the idea, simply noted at the February meeting that it seemed that a special study group should be constituted to deal with the structure and content of these prayers for both major Hours. A place for the intercessions immediately following the gospel canticle was tentatively agreed to in the structure of Lauds and Vespers. No attempt was made to provide *preces* for Lauds in SCDO, but two forms of an *oratio universalis* were composed to be used alternately at Vespers. Each form consisted of five or six petitions addressed directly to Christ, each of which could stand alone when said privately or could be followed either by a short pause or by a suitable acclamation when said publicly. In his explanation to the Consilium of SCDO before the eighth plenary session, Canon

Martimort said that these two forms were offered not as exemplars of what was to come but as items for discussion.

With respect to the concluding elements for Lauds and Vespers, Group 9 agreed to a final prayer followed by a blessing. The group was unable to decide, however, if the final prayer should be that of the Mass of the day or a prayer specific to the Hour or a combination of these two options, with the prayer of the Mass used on feasts of saints and major feasts and the prayer related to the Hour used on all other days. The question was remanded for further study to the group (18bis) concerned with orations common to Mass and Office. At least Group 9 agreed that in SCDO the concluding prayer would be "according to custom" (de more) the same as that in the Mass of the day. As to the blessing, there was agreement it should be a brief form from the Pauline epistles if "the people" were present. If "the people" were not present, each Hour could be concluded with "Let us bless the Lord" (Benedicamus Domino) or "May the divine assistance . . ." (Divinium auxilium).[16]

Thus in the first experimental edition of the new Office (SCDO) used at the eighth plenary session of the Consilium, Lauds and Vespers had the following structure:

LAUDS	VESPERS
Deus in adiutorium and *Gloria Patri* (except at Lauds if invitatory used)	
Hymn	
Morning psalm O.T. canticle Psalm of praise (all with antiphons)	2 short psalms in sequence or one long psalm N.T. canticle (all with antiphons)
Short Reading	
Responsory	
Benedictus (with antiphon)	*Magnificat* (with antiphon)

Oratio universalis

Prayer of the day

Benedicamus Domino

Fidelium animae . . .
(optional)[17]

Among the questions on the Office considered at the meeting of
the Group of Relators (April 3–8, 1967) and at the eighth plenary
session (April 10–19, 1967) after the members and consultors had
used SCDO for a week were several pertaining to Lauds and Vespers. Asked if the *Benedictus* and the *Magnificat* should be retained
daily, the members agreed unanimously and the consultors were
favorable (29 to 3). Fr. Joseph Patino had objected to them on the
grounds that they became routine, and Fr. Jacques Cellier, director
of the Centre National de Pastoral Liturgique and consultor, would
omit them for the sake of brevity. Fr. Burkhard Neunheuser countered that these canticles were both the psychological and theological summit of the Hours in which they were used, that they
were age-old elements in the Roman tradition, and that his personal experience with them for some fifty years indicated to him
that they need not become routine or tedious. Msgr. Balthasar
Fischer also saw the canticles as the summit of their respective
Hours, and Fr. A. M. Roguet noted that as the psalms represent
the prophetic phase (of the mystery of redemption), so the canticles represent the phase of realization.

Questioned as to whether the structure of the psalmody at Lauds
was acceptable, a majority of the members replied favorably. Although no formal question was apparently asked about the short
readings, note was made that both consultors and members were
pleased with those in SCDO.

Some controversy, however, surrounded the use of responses
after the short readings. In the Group of Relators, before use of
SCDO, Father Bugnini submitted that a responsory, unless
chanted, seemed to be an artificial thing. He would rather see liberty left to use either responsory or some other chant in the sung
Office. Fathers Patino and Gy voiced similar recommendations.

Father Cellier thought responsories would be put into the modern languages only with difficulty. Canon Martimort finally asked if the relators could agree that (1) there would be a responsory in Lauds and Vespers with "the people," (2) specimens of responsories would at least be provided by the appropriate study group, and (3) the possibility be allowed of using the responsory optionally in private recitation. To these the relators agreed. In the plenary session, after use of SCDO, Bishops Jean Bluyssen ('s-Hertogenbosh, Holland) and C. Guilford Young (Hobart, Australia) repeated Father Bugnini's earlier objection. But Bishop Hermann Volk (Mainz, West Germany) thought some element of meditation was needed after the scriptural reading, and Bishop Emilio Guano (Leghorn, Italy) and Archbishops Henri Jenny (Cambrai, France) and Michele Pellegrino (Turin, Italy) spoke in favor of retention of responsories on grounds that private recitation needed a link with choral celebration and that responsories, if well chosen, give poetic color and foster meditation. Archbishop Pellegrino noted that some good examples can be found in Greek euchological texts. Msgr. Joseph Pascher also thought that even a recited responsory had a spiritual utility.

Finally, with respect to the *oratio universalis* at Vespers, Father Gy observed that the forms given in SCDO seemed to be very similar to a series of orations. He asked that different forms be included in a second specimen of the Office. Monsignor Fischer proposed a form similar to the *preces* in the current Office to be used with the triple invocation *Kyrie eleison, Christe eleison, Kyrie eleison.*[18]

Before Group 9 met again in preparation for the ninth plenary session, its members (and other advisors, consultors, and members of the Consilium) submitted to Canon Martimort their opinions on three questions still undecided about Lauds and Vespers: (1) Should there be a response or responsory after the short reading? (2) What should be done about the intercessions? (3) What should be proposed about the blessing when the Hours are celebrated communally? With respect to the response after the short reading, a variety of opinion still prevailed. Some (Bishop Guano, Monsignor Famoso, Father Neunheuser) wanted an obligatory responsory. Others (Canon Rose, Monsignors Pascher and Benedetto Cignitti, an advisor) would have the responsory obligatory in communal celebration but optional in private recitation.

Still others (consultors Jounel, Raffa, Dumas, Amore, Lentini) thought a responsory pointless, since the gospel canticle would follow immediately. They proposed a short verse, psalmodic or otherwise, of a laudatory and festive character to provide a transition between the reading and the canticle. Fr. Ansgar Dirks thought that if the reading were brief then a moment of silence after it would be sufficient. Regarding the intercessions a consensus seemed to be emerging that the traditional place for such intercessions, after the gospel canticle, should be retained and that the form of these intercessions would best be that of the traditional Roman *capitella de psalmis*. The forms should be brief. Many had the same objection as did Father Gy at the eighth plenary session to the form used at Vespers in SCDO. It seemed to be a series of orations, each appropriate in itself but when strung together, detrimental to the concluding oration. As for the blessing at communal celebrations, many opinions favored a short formula like the one at Mass or one drawn from a few verses of Scripture.[19]

When Group 9 met at Munich from July 20 to 23, 1967, the two major concerns regarding Lauds and Vespers were the responsories or responses after the reading and the concluding prayers of the Hours. Regarding responsories, it was reported that Group 8 (chants of the Office) was having great difficulty in preparing suitable texts for these despite the suggestions made at the eighth plenary session. So the question was raised anew as to whether a responsory or some short response should follow the brief reading at Lauds and Vespers. Thirteen in Group 9 still favored this; one abstained from voting. Asked if they still supported the notion that the responsory or response should be optional in private recitation, ten said yes, and four would have it obligatory. In view of the difficulty in supplying texts for these responsories or responses, Group 9 agreed that they should serve primarily popular celebration in the modern tongues, so some could be taken from current repertoires and others created in the mode of acclamations.

Regarding the concluding prayers, Fr. Vincenzo Raffa, relator of Group 12*bis* (prayers in Lauds and Vespers), gave an extensive report on the work of his group. He first discussed the scope of intercessions in tradition and then noted that special formulae to sanctify the day and work would not necessarily be required at Lauds, since the Hour itself fulfills that function. Besides, special prayers offering the day and its work to God need not occur in Lauds, since tradition associates this action with the Mass. Furthermore, into Mass (more likely than not to be celebrated in the morning) intercessions would be inserted. Father Raffa submitted, however, that in his view intercessions should be included in Lauds for a number of reasons, among which were that Lauds and Vespers should have parallel structures; intercessions are traditional in both Hours; Protestant Offices include them at Lauds; and the popular character of Lauds would be enhanced by their inclusion, since the faithful like to have various intentions expressed in communal prayer. This last reason would seem to be a reference to popular devotions—a reason seldom if ever proffered before and unusual in that most reasons heretofore had been based on what is traditional, ecumenical, or beneficial to the spiritual nourishment of clergy. After lengthy discussion of the matter, in which it was pointed out that the Consilium had already asked that some *preces* of Prime be placed in Lauds and that universal intercessions in Lauds would be tedious if followed by the same at Mass, a question was proposed as to whether *preces* for sanctification of the day should be placed in Lauds, leaving to Vespers the prayer of the faithful. Group 9 favored this solution by a vote of 13 to 1.

The next concern was whether the Lord's Prayer should appear in Lauds and Vespers, and if so, whether it should come before or after the intercessions. As was discussed in chapter 4, its use at the end of the major Hours had been suggested in the eighth plenary session as a more honorable place than that given it in SCDO, namely, as an optional element at the conclusion of the minor Hours. If the intercessions followed the Lord's Prayer, they would serve as a kind of embolism of the fundamental intentions expressed in it. However, if the Lord's Prayer followed the intercessions, it would act as a conclusion or synthesis of them. But when it was noted that the Lord's Prayer was no longer, as formerly, a presidential prayer in the liturgy, many would exclude the latter solution on the grounds that a presidential prayer should conclude the Hours and that it would be unwise to make the Lord's Prayer presidential in the Office when it was no longer that in the Mass. Another problem some saw was whether it was fitting for the Lord's Prayer to appear in both Lauds and Vespers or in only one of those Hours, since it would appear in the Mass daily. Others saw it as fitting in both Hours and Mass because it would correspond to the ancient tradition of the Lord's Prayer said three times a day. Finally, two questions were posed: (1) Should the Lord's Prayer appear in both Lauds and Vespers? (2) Should the *preces*, or intercessions, function as a kind of embolism of the Lord's Prayer? To the first question all members of Group 9 responded affirmatively. To the second, the vote was ten in favor, three opposed, one vote blank. It was recommended that several forms of intercessions be prepared for the next specimen of the Office to be used at the next plenary session.

One other item was a matter of concern. To those who preferred the Lord's Prayer after the intercessions it seemed no concluding oration should follow. To the majority, who favored the intercessions as an embolism of the Lord's Prayer, it seemed an oration should conclude them, since this practice would be in keeping with later Roman tradition. The group accepted this view unanimously. As to the kind of oration, although the question is not entirely germane to consideration of the structure of the Office, it should be noted that many possibilities were considered. Group 9 generally agreed that on feasts the oration of the Mass should be used at both Lauds and Vespers. For other days the question of using orations pertaining to the respective Hours was left open.[20]

Before the ninth plenary session (November 21–28, 1967) the Synod of Bishops, meeting from September through October 1967, gave its collective opinion on what had been decided to that time regarding Lauds and Vespers. Of the 180 bishops voting, 144 were pleased, 7 were not, 23 voted yes with reservations (*iuxta modum*), and 6 abstained. Among the *modi* were three that asked that the long reading be obligatory at Lauds and Vespers and three that called for omission of responsories after the readings in these Hours.[21]

The second specimen of the Office, SDO, for November 12–25, 1967, was ready for use both by the Group of Relators meeting from November 14 to 20 and the plenary session held from November 21 to 28. In it the structure of Lauds and Vespers was the same as that in SCDO through the gospel canticles. The conclusion of the Hours had been modified thus:

Kyrie, Christe, Kyrie
Lord's Prayer (aloud)
Intercessions (*preces*)

Prayer *(oratio)*
"Let us bless . . ." *(Benedicamus Domino)*

In both Hours all of the above elements were under the heading
"Concluding Prayers" *(Preces conclusivae)*. The *preces* in Lauds were
concerned with sanctification of the coming day and its work;
those in Vespers, with universal needs. Both series, however, had
identical constructions. During the first week the construction of
the intercessions for both Lauds and Vespers was a series of four
or five versicles and responses. In the second week, series of intentions, either petitionary or laudatory, with an identical short response to be said after each intention were given for both Hours
from Sunday through Tuesday. From Wednesday through Saturday each set in Vespers was again constructed of a series of versicles and responses while those in Lauds alternated between the
two types, undoubtedly to enable both members and consultors to
judge on the basis of experience which of the formulations was
more viable.[22]

In both the Group of Relators and the plenary session the
responsories, position of the Lord's Prayer, and the intercessions
were the major considerations. The Group of Relators had an extensive debate, discussed in chapter 4, on allowing the hymn of
Lauds and Vespers to function as the response to the reading in
those Hours. In the plenary session at least Cardinal Pellegrino
and Bishops Pichler, Boudon, and Guano spoke of their reservations about allowing a hymn to function in this manner. Their
principal concern seemed to be to insure that the response be of
perennial and profound meaning. Hymns or various options for
hymns as responses were less likely to insure that condition unless episcopal conferences controlled the selection and the options.
When the matter was put to a vote, once again, as is to be expected from a committee, compromise was in order so that the
many might be satisfied. A unanimous affirmative reply was given
to two questions: "(1) In the public celebration of the Office
should responsories be used after the readings, even if brief, in
Lauds and Vespers? (2) Should responsorial chants, which are not
strictly obligatory, be proposed for public celebration in such a
way that other chants of a similar kind and function may be used
provided they are properly approved?"

Discussion among the relators regarding the position of the Lord's Prayer was protracted. Msgr. Balthasar Fischer was not pleased with the solution, found in SDO, of positioning the prayer before the intercessions because in that spot it does not have an honorable place. Furthermore, the notion of the intercessions functioning as an embolism is not traditional. He suggested putting the *Pater* in the middle Hour. Canon Martimort replied that it would be better to have an oration to characterize the middle Hour itself rather than the *Pater* there. The Lord's Prayer would seem to be placed more appropriately in the major Hours, and its common recitation by all in public celebrations would in itself give it more honor than it had had in the previous usage of silent recitation. But Monsignor Fischer saw no reason why the *Pater* could not be a commonly recited prayer in the Mass and a presidential prayer in the Office. Canon Martimort said that would be impossible. There simply must be one manner of praying the *Pater* in both Mass and Office lest, as Father Raffa, summarizing Canon Martimort's remarks has it, "the faithful wonder" (*ne fideles mirentur*). Father Bugnini interjected that the manner of its recitation ought to be left optional. Fr. Joseph Patino thought joining the *Kyrie* to the *Pater* made it penitential when it really has an eschatological sense and ought to function as a companion of the concluding oration, not of the intercessions. Fr. Joseph Gelineau, who claimed it was his idea in the first place to put the *Pater* before the *preces*, now had a change of mind and favored the order of *preces*, *Pater*, concluding oration. Msgr. Pierre Jounel, apparently trying to find a way to leave the *Pater* in the last, most honorable place, suggested putting the oration immediately after the hymn. Precedent for this could be found in the Ambrosian tradition, he said. However, Msgr. Joseph Pascher did not see that the Lord's Prayer would have importance if placed last. Max Thurian, an observer from the ecumenical community at Taizé, submitted a written observation on the matter based on the experience at Taizé. This experience, he said, had convinced him that the order of *preces*, *oratio*, *Pater* is the correct one. *Preces* after the *Pater* seem to be a falling back. There should be a respect for a kind of ascent in the prayer climaxing in the *Pater*, after which only the blessing of the presider should detain the assembly. Canon Martimort finally suggested that perhaps a solution would emerge from experiment.

A question was put to both relators and members as to whether the Lord's Prayer should have a place in Lauds and Vespers. Both groups agreed it should. The members only were asked if the *Pater* should come somewhere after the psalmody and before the concluding oration. The reply was affirmative. Canon Martimort asked both relators and members for a straw vote on whether the *Pater* should precede or follow the intercessions. Members and relators parted company on this one. Members voted twenty-four to nine, with two indifferent, in favor of the *Pater* preceding the intercessions. Relators voted seventeen to seven, with two abstentions, in favor of the *Pater* following the intercessions. There the matter was left for the time being.

Canon Martimort's call for experiment was heeded. According to Father Raffa, the members of Group 9 utilized various forms of intercessions, presumably in varying relationships with *Pater* and oration, with their respective communities. Fr. Adalbert Franquesa of the Abbey of Montserrat had already been experimenting in his monastery for two months prior to the ninth plenary session. He reported, in fact, that the order in Vespers of prayer of the faithful or *preces*, *Pater*, and oration of the day was fruitful and acceptable to those using it.[23]

Discussion on the intercessions among both relators and members was also lengthy at the November 1967 session. It had to do mostly with content and internal structure, and so it may simply be summarized here, since it had less direct bearing on the structure of the Hours. In general both members and relators were pleased that intercessions, whether universal intentions at Vespers or *preces* for the coming day at Lauds, be placed after the gospel canticle. There was general agreement that the series of intentions should not exceed four or five, that one or two intentions might be added optionally, that the series vary at least throughout one week, that they be addressed to God so that they may be suitably prayed in communal or private recitation, and that possibilities for adaptation be permitted for popular use.[24]

At its next meeting from February 27 to March 1, 1968, Group 9 focused its attention again on the short reading, responsories, intercessions, orations, and the order of the concluding elements in Lauds and Vespers. Additional matters emerging were the final blessing and the manner of commemorating a saint in these Hours during the season of Lent. The questions regarding short readings, responsories, and orations had more to do with content than structure, and the primary question regarding the intercessions was whether the principle adopted by Group 12bis, namely, that the intercessions in some way should recall a salvific event in a laudatory way, was acceptable. Group 12bis was of the mind that even though the laudatory dimension is evident in other elements of Lauds and Vespers, it ought also be present in the intercessions. Group 9 accepted the principle but advised that, given the proper character of intercessions or *preces* as petitionary and the general laudatory character of Lauds and Vespers, the principle should be applied with great latitude. Group 9 agreed, too, to the recommendations of Group 12bis that episcopal conferences be allowed the faculty to approve special *preces* for their respective regions and that allowance be made at the conclusion of a given series for one or two intentions pertaining to local or individual needs. To Group 9, Group 12bis also proposed its unanimous preference for the ordering of the final elements in Lauds and Vespers. The group's preference was for the sequence of *preces*, concluding oration, Lord's Prayer, and blessing. The reasons were historical on the one hand and psychological and theological on the other. Not only is such an order traditional in Roman and Benedictine practice, but the Lord's Prayer can and should be experienced as the high point of the Hour only if it occupies the final place before the blessing.

Furthermore, Group 12bis proposed that the oration be linked closely with the intercessions as their concluding element. It might also be appropriate, submitted the group, to have an introduction to the intercessions. Once again, not all in Group 9 were persuaded. Some held that the *Pater* can just as well be the culminating element in the Hour if it comes after the *preces*, is recited or chanted solemnly by all (communal celebration being assumed), and is followed by the oration. The oration, recited by the presider only, would not detract from the *Pater* simply by its position following it. Group 9 rejected the proposal to link the oration closely with the intercessions because such linkage would undermine the traditional use of the Mass oration as the concluding oration of Lauds and Vespers during special seasons and on feasts.

With respect to the final blessing, the tendency in former discussions to provide a variety of forms was reversed in favor of a very few fixed forms. Father Raffa's suggestion of using either the formula from Prime or one from the Mass was accepted.

Finally, a lengthy discussion ensued on insertion of a structure into Lauds and Vespers whereby saints whose optional memorials occurred during Lent might be commemorated. Canon Martimort had, before the meeting, expressed his opinion that since the new calendar, already approved by the Consilium, had placed the memorials of most saints on the dates of their deaths but had also, fittingly, taken measures to insure the use of the seasonal propers during Lent, some saints' memorials would be impeded *in perpetuum* unless provision were made for some kind of commemoration of them in the Office. It would be important, he said, to find a mode of celebration that satisfies the devotion of those to whom it is pleasing to celebrate the memorials of the saints without destroying the spirit of the season rightly preserved in the new calendar. The discussion in Group 9 yielded two modes by which such a commemoration could be made in Lauds and Vespers: (1) The addition of a "little Office" *(parvum Officium)* consisting of an antiphon and oration commemorating the saint; (2) the simple insertion of some mention of the saint in the intercessions. Group 9 preferred the first alternative by a vote of eight to two with three abstaining. It was left to a later time to determine the precise placement of this *parvum Officium* in the structure of Lauds and Vespers.[25]

The proposals of Group 12*bis* as modified by Group 9 regarding the intercessions were accepted without difficulty by the Consilium in its tenth plenary session (April 23–30, 1968). The seemingly ever troublesome question of the position of the Lord's Prayer occupied considerably more attention in both the meeting of the Group of Relators (April 14–22, 1968) and in the plenary session following it. The relators were able to maintain their majority opinion, expressed in the straw vote at the time of the previous plenary session, in favor of the *Pater* following the preces. In the plenary session, since most attention had to be given to the problem of the imprecatory and historical psalms (discussed in ch. 4), a special group of members and consultors considered the problem of the placement of the Lord's Prayer. In that group Fr. Joseph Patino strongly maintained the position that the order should be *preces*, oration, *Pater* so that the Lord's Prayer might have the most honorable, that is, the last, place. But Bishop Guano said he believed solemnity did not depend on position but on manner of use. He preferred the order *preces, Pater*, oration. Others maintained one or other of these positions, Canon Martimort insisting all the while that experience would reveal which is the better arrangement. No vote was taken, no decision reached, and the matter was not presented to the full assembly. On other matters (responsories, final blessing) too, no full-scale discussion or voting was held.[26]

In all editions of the General Instruction, the first draft of which emerged shortly after the tenth plenary session, and in the specimen of the Office (DSOD) sent to the bishops in 1969, the concluding elements of Lauds and Vespers were arranged in the following order:

Intercessions *(preces)*
Lord's Prayer
Oration
Blessing

At the twelfth plenary session (November 4–8, 1969), following the experiment with DSOD, the Consilium was finally asked to approve this sequence. It is that order that has entered into LH for Lauds and Vespers.[27]

As to the *parvum Officium* for commemorating a saint whose memorial is impeded by Lent or another privileged season, what Group 9 considered as a first alternative, namely, the use at the conclusion of Lauds and Vespers of an antiphon and oration commemorating the saint, was incorporated into all the drafts of the General Instruction and into the definitive version of IGLH. There it was stipulated that these elements would follow the concluding oration of the day.[28]

THE MINOR HOURS

For the minor Hours of Terce, Sext, and None no structural reform was specifically decreed by SC. The stipulation, however, in SC 89e that outside choir one might select any one of the three Hours according to the respective time of day led to consideration of abandoning two of the minor Hours altogether, as described in chapter 4, and of radically restructuring the remaining Hour, as will be described below. The only question regarding the minor Hours deemed necessary to present to the second plenary session of the Consilium (April 17–20, 1964) among the thirty-three questions for the direction of the work of the study groups was, "Article 89e remaining in force, should Terce, Sext, and None be adapted or remain as they are now?" The Consilium, of course, accepted the question as a starting point. Initially the question of how to distribute the psalmody so that those bound to only one minor Hour would not omit any psalms in the *cursus* and the question of omitting altogether two of the minor Hours were the only structural matters considered by Group 9 and the Consilium. These have already been discussed in chapter 4. It was not until after the settlement of these questions in the seventh plenary session (October 6–14, 1966) that attention was given to the internal structure of the minor Hours.[29]

The elements that might constitute the minor Hours were first considered explicitly at the meeting of Group 9 from September 6 to 8, 1966. For the obligatory Hour were proposed one or more psalms from the current Psalter and a hymn with, perhaps, a prayer suited to the Hour. The optional Hours would consist of the same elements, but the psalms would be invariable. With the unanimous approval of Group 9 and the approval of the majority (twenty-five of twenty-eight) of the relators in their meeting of September 19–October 1, 1966, these proposals were presented to the seventh plenary session of the Consilium and were accepted unanimously.[30]

It was in the process of preparing SCDO for the eighth plenary session that Group 9 was faced with providing a detailed structure for the minor Hours. In addition to the psalmody, hymn, and prayer already explicitly approved, a short reading, a versicle, and the Lord's Prayer were included. The reading seems to have been included on the basis of the positive response to Question 5 in the questionnaire of December 1965, which had asked if the Office composed of traditional elements—psalms, readings, and other formulae—was able still to nourish the piety of the priest *(sic)*. Group 4 had been given the task of preparing for the minor Hours as well as for Lauds and Vespers a week-long selection of short readings drawn from the New Testament. Group 9, according to Canon Martimort in his presentation of SCDO to the eighth plenary session, had not yet agreed on a way to respond to the reading. The short responses of the current Office seemed to many inappropriate, so it was decided to provide, provisionally, a versicle as a response. The Lord's Prayer was included because in the schema for SC (72c) recitation of the *Pater* had been recommended at the conclusion of the minor Hours. Group 9 had been unable to decide if an oration or the *Pater* should conclude a minor Hour, so it was proposed and agreed that a choice of one or the other would be provided. Thus the structure of the minor Hours provisionally agreed to by Group 9 and incorporated into SCDO was

"God, come to my help . . ." *(Deus in adiutorium)*
Hymn of Terce, Sext, or None
Threefold psalmody under one antiphon
Short reading of Terce, Sext, or None
Versicle of Terce, Sext, or None
Lord's Prayer *or* final prayer of Terce, Sext, or None
Blessing or *Benedicamus Domino*
"May the souls . . ." *(Fidelium animae;* optional)[31]

In the discussion following the use of SCDO in the eighth session, both consultors and members were generally pleased with the minor Hours. Recommendations focused on the *Pater* and oration. The Brazilian consultor, Msgr. Joaquim Nabuco, wanted the *Pater* obligatory, but Canon Martimort, Monsignor Pascher, and Father Gy spoke for leaving it optional. Father Patino, with Canon Martimort and Monsignor Pascher in agreement, said the oration should be obligatory in order to help highlight the specific characteristic of each Hour. Some time after the session (May 8, 1967) Father Bugnini wrote to Canon Martimort and gave him a number of personal suggestions, which he claimed were those of others, too, about the reform of the Office. He recommended there be only one brief, easily memorized psalm in the midday Hour because this Hour would ordinarily be used by priests and religious communities at noon, the time at which some religious communities usually have a series of prayers and spiritual exercises such as *Veni, Sancte Spiritus*, examination of conscience, and Angelus. If the middle Hour is brief, he said, it can be included, but if it is

209

not something will disappear. This ought not be the examination of conscience, so useful at midday, nor the Angelus, a prayer in common use.

Moreover, Father Bugnini raised again the issue that seemed to have been resolved in the seventh plenary session of reducing the minor Hours to one midday Hour. Noting that since contemporary reckoning divides a day into three, not six, parts, he asked why reality as it is could not be respected and the illusion of living in the fourth century abandoned. The presence together of three readings, three verses, and three orations (one of each to be selected appropriate to the time the midday Hour is used, as had been the case in SCDO) will give the impression of a love for tradition out of touch with the reality of life.[32]

Despite his displeasure with Father Bugnini's proposal, which he attributed to the secretary's attachment to *devotio moderna,* Canon Martimort presented it along with other communications he had received regarding the conclusion of the minor Hours to the meeting of Group 9 from July 20 to 23, 1967. After a lengthy discussion in which some noted that reduction of the psalmody to one psalm in the midday Hour would enhance the major character of Lauds and Vespers, it was concluded that (1) any reduction would be ill taken by bishops who had been complaining about excessive abbreviation of the Office; (2) the distribution of the Psalter would have to be extended over many months and the whole equilibrium in the cycle of the psalms would be destroyed; (3) one psalm or a few verses of a psalm would be insufficient to foster necessary recollection; (4) the addition of private devotions to the Office may seem good, but the mind of the constitution is that devotions be subject to the liturgy, not liturgy to devotions; (5) restricting the middle Hour to one at noon would remove the liberty given by the council of selecting, as opportunity allows, that minor Hour that suits the time of day at which it can be prayed; (6) religious and faithful who observe the middle Hour as desired in the proposal and do not use the Office of Readings would be deprived of a major portion of psalms; (7) use of one fixed psalm would not be in keeping with the wish of a majority of Consilium members, who desire a variety in the psalmody to avoid weariness; (8) placing together readings, versicles, and prayers can be considered again, but the arrangement in SCDO was due to the urgency to produce the specimen quickly; and (9) for distinguishing the major Hours from the minor, the prayers, canticles, and sense of the formulae suffice. With all of these matters considered, Group 9 unanimously agreed that the structure of the minor Hours as it appeared in SCDO should be retained.[33]

When the Synod of Bishops in the autumn of 1967 considered the question of whether what was proposed by the Consilium regarding the minor Hours was acceptable, 141 of 180 voting said it was; 13 were displeased; 6 abstained, and 20 voted yes with reservations *(iuxta modum)*. Of the *modi*, only three concerned the structure of the Hours, and these proposed increasing their length.[34]

Shortly after the synod, the Group of Relators, meeting from November 14 to 20, and the ninth plenary session (November 21–28, 1967) made use of the second specimen of the Office. This arrangement, SDO, retained the same structure for the minor Hours as was found in SCDO except that the optional *Pater* had been omitted altogether, the oration made obligatory at the end of each Hour, and the *Fidelium animae* dropped for the reasons explained in chapter 4. As in SCDO the three psalms or their equivalent were placed under one antiphon. There seems to have been no discussion of the structure of the minor Hours specifically during the ninth session.[35]

After the ninth session and before the meeting of Group 9 in February 1968, the only questionable item in the structure of the minor Hours mentioned by Canon Martimort in his presentation of the agenda for the upcoming meeting was the response after the short reading. At the meeting itself (February 27–March 1, 1968) no decision seems to have been reached on the matter. One proposal was to retain the versicle, but this after the response *Deo gratias* to the short reading. Another suggestion was to use a strophe of some hymn or simply have a moment of silence. Still another question considered at this meeting regarding the structure of the minor Hours but dealt with in the larger context of the other Hours was that of using one or several antiphons for the psalmody. The decision was made, as discussed in chapter 4, to provide each psalm or section of psalm with its own antiphon except in certain special cases.[36]

The tenth plenary session of the Consilium (April 23–30, 1968) considered nothing on the structure of the minor Hours in themselves. In preparation for the meeting of Group 9 from July 16 to 19, 1968, Canon Martimort reminded the members of the group that a decision was still needed on what if anything should function as a response to the short reading in the minor Hours. In the first draft of IGLH, which he submitted to them for consideration at that meeting, the indication in the description of the minor Hours was that there would be no response at all to the readings. At the meeting, however, there was apparently agreement to retain the versicle after the reading, for in the second draft of IGLH, produced in late July and early August 1968, the versicle is explicitly mentioned as response to the reading.[37]

The later drafts of IGLH and the experimental edition of the Office, DSOD, sent to the bishops of the world in 1969, retained the structure proposed in the summer of 1968 and given below. It was this structure that entered the definitive edition of LH:

"God, come to my assistance . . ." (*Deus in adiutorium*)
Hymn
Three psalms (with antiphons)
Short reading
Versicle
Oration
"Let us bless . . ." (*Benedicamus Domino*, at least in communal celebration)[38]

THE OFFICE OF READINGS

SC 89c gave some very specific directives regarding Matins. That Hour was to retain its character of nocturnal praise when celebrated in choir but, made up of fewer psalms and longer readings, was to be adapted for use at any Hour of the day. A question asking precisely how this should be done was among the thirty-three submitted by Canon Martimort to the second plenary session of the Consilium (April 17–20, 1964) for approval as a starting point for the reform of Matins. The question also referred to *modi* presented at the council when the schema for SC, chapter 4, was discussed. Principal among these was the wish of fifty-three fathers that outside of more solemn feasts, priests could substitute for Matins a determined time of spiritual reading and meditation. Bishop J. Albert Martin, relator of the conciliar liturgical commission, had advised that whatever provision was to be made for a priest's spiritual reading and meditation would be dealt with in other documents of the council. Matins, however reformed, was to keep its form of public prayer with psalms. Other *modi* that the conciliar liturgical commission believed should be dealt with by the postconciliar commission gave some detailed suggestions on the structure of the Hour. One proposed the Hour consist of invitatory, hymn, five psalms, ten-minute reading (in Latin) from the New Testament, no response, and *Te Deum*. Another would have only three psalms and three readings. Bishop Martin had said just before the approval of SC by the council that such suggestions would be given to the postconciliar commission to act on. While not himself suggesting that the postconciliar commission change the name of the Hour, Bishop Martin had, in presenting the first revision of the schema for SC, chapter 4, referred to reformed Matins as an "office of readings."[39]

In its first meetings from April to September 1964 Group 9 discussed numerous suggestions submitted on the reform of Matins, often referred to as "Office of Readings," and reached tentative conclusions on the invitatory; hymn; number of psalms; number, kind, and extent of readings. Suggestions and conclusions regarding the invitatory and the psalms considered both at these early meetings and throughout the course of the reform have already been discussed in chapter 4.

With respect to the hymn, there was question as to whether a hymn, particularly the hymn for use at nocturnal celebration of the Hour, should be retained for use at any Hour of the day. Some consultors thought composition of new hymns for daytime use would be very difficult, but Group 9 agreed on maintaining the hymn as an element in the structure of Matins no matter when the Hour was used. The principal question regarding the readings had to do with length: Should the amount of reading be fixed so that the Hour has the same length it currently has? Group 9 consented to this principle: Let the Hour be increased in readings to the extent it is diminished in psalmody.

As to the kind of readings, Group 9 unanimously agreed, after a discussion in which one consultor opted for alternation of scriptural and patristic readings, that every day should have its own scriptural reading. The majority of the group also agreed that each day should have its own patristic reading, too. Readings from the Fathers of the Church should be preferred, it said, even though SC 92b had foreseen the inclusion of writings of doctors and ecclesiastical writers in this Hour. In opting for this preference, it was noted, Group 9 accepted the opinion of Fr. Bernard Capelle offered to the Pian Commission not for the reason that antiquity is to be preferred but because the Fathers of the Church are more suited to opening up for priests *(sic)* the riches of the faith and are excellent witnesses to primitive Christian tradition. It was proposed, moreover, that besides a *cursus* of patristic readings there be compiled a patristic Lectionary from which one could, optionally, choose readings. In this Lectionary could be included writings of some who were neither saints nor, in all respects, orthodox Christians. Furthermore, Archbishop Michele Pellegrino proposed that the patristic selections be drawn up by the method of "centonization," that is, a weaving together of texts from various writers. Group 9, however, was generally opposed to this and opted for selections having textual unity. After a long discussion on the advisability of admitting hagiographical readings, Group 9 agreed to their use provided they were brief and trustworthy, as SC 92c had directed. There was general agreement that such readings could replace patristic readings on saints' feasts, but it was remarked that sometimes a patristic text either composed by the saint whose feast it was or speaking about the saint might be more worthwhile than a hagiographical text of the kind existing in the then-current Office.[40]

Among the twenty-eight questions on the Office submitted to the fourth plenary session of the Consilium (September 28–October 9, November 16, 1964) ten pertained to the Office of Readings. Five of these had bearing on the structure of the Hour. With the one on the number of psalms (considered in ch. 4) omitted, the others were as follows. Voting results in the order of affirmative, negative, and null votes are given after each question:

"18. Even though the traditional hymns would be retained for recitation at night, should other hymns also be provided for recitation outside of nighttime? [21-2-1]
"21. Should the amount of reading be such that the Office has the same length as it has now? [23-0-0]

"22. Should the norm be established that no day is without a scriptural reading and no day is without a patristic reading? [23-0-0]

"24. Should a patristic Lectionary be compiled containing readings that are not in the Breviary but that can be used either obligatorily or optionally? [23-0-0]

"28. Should a hagiographical reading be provided in the Office of Readings when it seems fitting? [23-0-0]"[41]

Other than questions pertaining to the psalmody and responsories (already discussed in ch. 4), nothing was considered by Group 9 or the Consilium on the structure of the Office of Readings until the autumn of 1966. Even the questionnaire of December 1965 avoided any direct queries on the structure of this Hour. But as part of Pope Paul VI's first intervention into the work of the Consilium after distribution of the questionnaire was his suggestion that in Matins (Office of Readings) the readings should be the principal part of the Hour and should present a rich selection of biblical, patristic, and hagiographical texts. It would seem preferable, he said, to alternate psalms with the readings and to keep responsories in the form found in the Office of Corpus Christi, that is, with texts of the Old Testament and New Testament woven together.[42]

In his reflection on the results of the questionnaire and in his own personal study between December 1965 and July 1966 Canon Martimort became concerned that the reform of the Office was tending too much in the direction of providing for the special needs of clergy in pastoral care and of active religious. In the communication of his thoughts to Group 9 in July and August he noted that some of the characteristics of the Roman Office that catered to contemplatives needed to be preserved. These characteristics were to be found primarily in the minor Hours and in Matins. For the minor Hours he proposed a solution (discussed in ch. 4), but for Matins, he said, something more than has been proposed must be provided for the sake of contemplatives using the Roman Office lest they be constrained to adopt the Benedictine Office, which retains those elements suited to monks.[43]

To the seventh plenary session of the Consilium (October 6-14, 1966) Canon Martimort revealed the germ of his proposal for an adaptation of the Office of Readings to better suit contemplatives and others who might desire more than the standard offering. He had apparently discussed his proposal in the meeting of Group 9 held September 6–8, 1966, but there is no record of how it fared there. What he proposed was an optional expansion of the ordinary structure of the Office of Readings (which would consist probably of invitatory, hymn, psalmody, and two readings) by allowing the addition of six or nine psalms from the four-week cycle and the use of additional scriptural and patristic readings from an optional Lectionary. It would be important to provide for this expansion, understood as a nocturnal Vigil, because primitive spiritual writers had exhorted the faithful to nocturnal prayer with such effect that prescriptions for such prayer had entered all monastic rules. Vigils were important for giving expression to the desire to imitate the "everlasting praise" *(laus perennis)* of heaven and for fostering the expectation of the Lord who will come again. If the liturgy does not provide for such prayer, he maintained, extraliturgical forms of it will be created because the sense of "vigil-keeping prayer" *(oratio vigilaris)* is deeply rooted in people. He advocated the restoration of a Vigil Office for Sundays and feasts, available to all, and a daily Vigil available primarily to contemplatives. No decisions on this proposal were asked of the Consilium, and the matter did not come up again until early summer of 1967.[44]

Meanwhile, at the meeting of Group 9 in Genoa (February 6–8, 1967) three elements in the Office of Readings were discussed preparatory to the issuance of SCDO for the eighth plenary session. The first pertained to the invitatory: Should the antiphon to the invitatory psalm be kept and used as a refrain after each strophe of Psalm 94, or should the psalm, in choir, be said directly without chant *(sine cantu in directum),* as in some monasteries? There was unanimous agreement it should be retained. Omission of it would be an impoverishment. Nevertheless, a careful selection of antiphons would be needed so that even in private recitation and in the vernacular languages the sense of the antiphon and its beauty could be retained. The second item had to do with the content of hymns and is not relevant here. The third concerned the *Te Deum.* According to some consultors, since this hymn refers in the words "Dignare, Domine, die isto" to the morning Hour, it should not be included when the Office of Readings is used at another Hour. Others, however, maintained that the words can apply to any time of the day. Group 9 accepted the principle that the *Te Deum* should be included after the response to the patristic reading but only in the Office for Sundays and feasts whose rank, according to then-current terminology, was first or second class.[45]

When Canon Martimort presented his report introducing SCDO to the eighth plenary session (April 10–19, 1967) he explained that more study was needed on a number of ways in which the Office of Readings might be utilized: on solemnities, feasts, and in celebrations with the people; by contemplatives; by priests exercising a pastoral ministry; and by all so that its "traditional treasury" is preserved. In SCDO, he explained, the invitatory (now designated *introductio officii*) would be used to begin the Office of Readings if this were the first Hour of the day, otherwise the Hour would begin with "God, come to my assistance . . ." *(Deus in adiutorium)*.

Following the hymn and psalmody there would be a versicle, because it was the judgment of Group 9 that some kind of transition to the readings was needed. Since the semicontinuous biblical readings would be relatively short, all in Group 9 had agreed that some way should be provided, for those who so desire, to read longer passages in order that the whole of a biblical book could be read over a given period of time. It was deemed unnecessary to provide such indication in SCDO, since the Acts of the Apostles would be read in its entirety between Mass and Office in the Easter season. He noted that to the question of whether more individual liberty should be allowed in the selection of biblical texts for the Hour, ten in Group 9 had said no and four, yes. The reasons against providing such liberty were that certain books go with certain seasons; the readings of the Office would be arranged in conjunction with those for the Mass and with the patristic readings; and subjective criteria might be employed in selecting readings.

With respect to the patristic reading he explained that selection would either illustrate the liturgical season, comment on the biblical reading of the Hour, or refer to one or other of the readings in the Mass of the day. Generally only those pertaining to a liturgical season or commenting on the biblical text in the Office would be included in the breviary *(sic)* itself. Others would be inserted in the optional Lectionary. A criterion established by Group 9 was that the patristic reading would be no longer than the three sections of the patristic reading in the current Office or the equivalent of one column in Migne's edition of the works of the Fathers of the Church.

The responsories differed in that the one following the biblical reading would either throw new light on that text, insert the reading in the history of salvation, lead from the Old Testament to the New, or aid in turning the reading into prayer and contemplation; whereas the one following the patristic reading would recall the sense of the whole biblical book to which the reading referred or the sense of the liturgical season. There would always be a responsory after the patristic reading, even when the *Te Deum* occurred.

As to the hagiographic reading, Group 9 agreed, said Canon Martimort, that on obligatory memorials (according to the terminology of the new calendar) such a reading would replace the patristic reading and have its own responsory. For optional memorials occurring in Ordinary Time *(per annum)*, five members of Group 9 wanted the same procedure as used for obligatory memorials. Eight members objected, fearing that many priests *(sic)* celebrating these saints' memorials would frequently abandon the patristic readings or, even if rarely celebrating the saints' memorials, would lose the continuity of the patristic readings, which, perhaps, would be arranged semicontinuously over several days. These consultors proposed adding the hagiographic as a third reading. That procedure, it was agreed, would be followed for optional memorials occurring in privileged times (Lent and late Advent) on the precedent of the *processio ad martyrium* at the conclusion of the Visigothic and Milanese Offices. But time was lacking, said Canon Martimort, for Group 9 to resolve the problem of the patristic and hagiographical readings on optional memorials *per annum*. In SCDO the hagiographic reading could take the place of the patristic reading. Whatever the ultimate solution, the canon observed, certain hagiographic readings would be from the Fathers or acts of the martyrs, and so could very well be taken as patristic readings. Then, indicating his own objection to a third reading, he added that it is to be feared lest by "aggravating the burden of the celebration of the saints, their cult may disappear or, at least, their deeds and virtues may pass into oblivion."[46]

Thus the structure of the Office of Readings as it appeared in SCDO was as follows:

Introductio Officii or *Deus in adiutorium*
Hymn
Three psalms (under one antiphon)
Versicle
Biblical reading
Responsory
Patristic or Hagiographical reading
Responsory
Hagiographical reading (on optional memorials)
Responsory (on optional memorials)
Te Deum (on Sundays)
Oration (from Lauds)
Benedicamus Domino
Fidelium animae . . . (optionally)

In SCDO there were only two optional memorials, that of St. Hermenegild on April 13 and that of St. Justin on April 14. In the Office of Readings for each memorial both patristic and hagiographical readings appear. Presumably one could substitute the hagiographical for the patristic, as Canon Martimort had indicated in his report, but no directives or recommendations were given in the text of SCDO to that effect.[47]

In the discussion on Canon Martimort's report *(relatio)*; on the *relationes* made of the work of Groups 4 (biblical readings), 5 (patristic readings), and 6 (hagiographic readings); and on the experience of using SCDO, both members and relators generally acknowledged themselves satisfied. Prof. Emil Lengeling, relator of Group 4, explained that the seasons of Easter, Advent, Christmas, and Lent would each have its own cycle of readings. For the time *per annum* (Ordinary Time), Group 4 proposed a two-year cycle of readings, forty-one from the Old Testament and twenty-seven from the New Testament. Books of the Bible read in the Mass in a given year would not appear in the cycle of readings for the Office that year. At the end of each year in the two-year cycle, between the readings for Mass and those for Office of Readings almost the whole of the Scriptures would be read. A question about allowing greater liberty of selection was asked: "With the freedom to select readings disallowed for the reasons already set forth (namely, lest the harmony between the readings of Mass and Office be lost, lest the wisely chosen order based on the history of salvation be arbitrarily disturbed, and lest a number of texts from Holy Scripture be omitted), should the cycle of connected biblical readings be observed?"[48] Twenty-nine relators voted affirmatively; three, negatively. All of the members accepted the proposal. Furthermore, no one opposed the principle that complete pericopes of biblical readings of which only parts are contained in the Breviary might be read in the Office.

Fr. Umberto Neri, relator of Group 5, explained to the eighth plenary session the criteria used in selecting patristic readings. Summarily these were that selections from the Fathers of the Church are given priority and that writings of different ages, however, even those of modern times, will also be included if they are theologically and spiritually important, appeal to the modern mind, and befit the liturgical character of the Breviary. Both members and relators accepted these principles unanimously. In the discussion on the patristic readings Bishop Hermann Volk (Mainz), Msgr. Joseph Pascher, and Msgr. Joaquim Nabuco, a consultor from Brazil, asked that liberty be left to the episcopal conferences to compile collections of patristic readings supplementary to the patristic Lectionary and suitable to their regions. Canon Martimort agreed but added that such liberty should exist even for smaller geographical locations. Fathers Bugnini and Ildefonso Tassi, an Italian consultor, recalled that current patristic readings are no more than 100–120 words per section. Each new reading, then, which would correspond to three sections of a current one, should be no more than 300–360 words.[49]

Also at the eighth session, both members and relators approved six principles to govern the selection of hagiographic readings. The principles, as presented by Fr. Agostino Amore, relator of Group 6, were the following: (1) Legends are to be expunged altogether; (2) true "acts" are to be used if available; (3) if acts are not available, an exposition from the Fathers regarding the saint will be used, or (4) a writing of the saint, if available, will be presented; (5) for saints of the Middle Ages or of modern times, a new reading, historically true and spiritually profitable, will be provided;

and (6) at the beginning of a reading, in the manner of a rubric and as related to the reading, will be put some chronological and biographical elements regarding the saint. Father Amore also noted the difficulty, presented already by Canon Martimort, regarding the use of hagiographic readings on optional memorials. The discussion focused on that problem. Frs. Joseph Lecuyer and Gaston Fontaine, French and Canadian consultors respectively, maintained that both patristic and hagiographic readings should be used on optional memorials. Canon André Rose held that the hagiographic should substitute for the patristic if the saint's memorial were celebrated. Canon Martimort, in support of that position, noted that it was essential to find a solution whereby the cult of the saints would be retained in the Office and yet the Office would not be burdened by this retention.[50]

Discussion at the eighth session about retention of the invitatory has already been considered in chapter 4. Discussed also was the possibility of substituting psalms, such as Psalms 80, 91, or 99, for the usual Psalm 94 (perhaps abbreviated) in the invitatory. Members agreed to the substitution and abbreviation if the invitatory were retained.[51]

Finally, a question was raised in the eighth session about the suitability of the words "Dignare, Domine die isto . . ." in the *Te Deum* if the Office of Readings were used after midday. Msgr. Giovanni Lucchesi, an Italian consultor, suggested terminating the hymn at "in gloria numerari," as in the original composition, thus avoiding the difficulty. No decision, however, was made on the matter.[52]

Between the eighth and ninth plenary sessions both old and new questions regarding the Office of Readings received considerable attention. In preparation for the meeting of Group 9 in July 1967 Canon Martimort attempted to summarize the many opinions he was receiving from members of Group 9 and other consultors, members, and advisors of the Consilium. First was the matter of how to arrange the Office of Readings for Sundays and feasts. Group 9, said the canon, seemed to be agreed that the Hour should be no longer than it currently was for those engaged in pastoral ministry. But concern was also expressed that the "liturgical treasury" (*thesaurus liturgicus*) of feasts not be lost. No one solution to the difficulty was yet at hand, he noted. Opinions were not very clear on what should be done for popular vigils before special feasts, nor were they much clearer on how the Office of Readings could be extended to provide a vigil, especially for contemplatives. Canon Martimort himself had refashioned his suggestion for an expansion of the Office of Readings made to the seventh plenary session, and he had proposed it to the members of Group 9 in a letter on April 19, 1967. After the Hour is completed but before the *Te Deum*, he suggested, canticles may be added, then a Gospel passage sung in a solemn mode, a homily delivered (either a passage from the Fathers or the words of the homilist), and finally, the *Te Deum* sung. This matter, too, would need further discussion.

Next was the question of the hagiographic reading on optional memorials. One advisor *(consiliarius)*, Msgr. Benedetto Cignitti, and four consultors (Monsignor Pascher, Professor Lengeling, Fathers Amore and Raffa) wanted both the hagiographic and patristic readings maintained on the grounds that celebrations of the saints should not be multiplied nor should the patristic reading be disregarded. Monsignor Pascher, however, thought that if a cleric *(sic)* had a special devotion to a saint, he would not mind the addition of the hagiographic reading to the patristic. If the devotion is not present, then better that the hagiographic reading be skipped and the patristic read. Professor Lengeling, too, would have the hagiographic reading optional. Canon Rose and Father Dumas thought a choice between patristic and hagiographic readings should be allowed, while Monsignors Famoso and Jounel as well as Fathers Dirks, Neunheuser, and Lentini opted for the hagiographic reading to replace the patristic reading as on obligatory memorials. Monsignor Jounel, for example, was concerned lest the patristic reading be put on the same footing with the biblical reading. There would be no harm, he said, in letting the hagiographic reading replace the patristic, especially since the former would often be an extract from the works of the saint being celebrated. Father Dirks observed that the value of "continuous" patristic reading ought not be exaggerated.[53]

Two other questions regarding the Office of Readings received attention after the eighth plenary session. One was the manner of joining the Office of Readings with another Hour of the Office. This matter has already been considered in chapter 4. The other was the question of the order of psalmody in the Hour. Pope Paul VI had earlier suggested alternating psalmody with readings, and Canon Martimort reported that one of the members of the Consilium had suggested the same procedure. Two ways of accomplishing this alternation had been proposed: (1) Put all the psalmody between the biblical and patristic readings; (2) put part of the psalmody before the biblical reading and part before the patristic reading. The first mode was rejected, he believed, by all who had examined it as being untraditional and as rupturing the movement of prayer. Fathers Raffa, Lentini, and Dirks seemed to have considered the second alternative seriously. But Monsignors Famoso, Pascher, Cignitti, Professor Lengeling, Canon Rose, and Fathers Jounel, Amore, Visentin, and Dumas rejected it with a number of reasons against its adoption. First, the psalmody has already been so abbreviated that division into two parts would render it rather tenuous. In fact, since the longer psalms have been reserved to the Office of Readings, and often only one is said daily, it would be necessary again to divide them in sections. Besides, responsories would lose their force, since after the responsory for the first reading psalmody would begin again. Furthermore, as Father Dumas had observed, psalmody is another kind of thing than reading, requiring a different cast of mind. Finally, Father Raffa observed that a psychological difficulty might occur with some people if the Hour appears to have two nocturns rather than being one unit. Such, then, was the state of opinion on some major questions regarding the Hour prior to the summer 1967 meeting of Group 9.[54]

When Group 9 met in Munich (July 20-23, 1967) a few of the aforementioned questions were discussed along with concerns raised in the eighth plenary session regarding the Office of Readings. Two of the foremost questions pertained to the readings. The first had to do with their length. It was noted that someone had proposed reducing each reading to no more than 150 words. But Group 9 seemed agreed that since the three readings of the current Office were, in sum, about 300 words, such a reduction would seem opposed to the mandate of the council, which called for fewer psalms and longer readings in Matins (SC 89c). A solution had been proposed: Add to readings what is removed from the psalmody. Thus, when asked if it were pleasing that the length of a new reading have the same measure as three readings in the current Office, all in Group 9 replied affirmatively. This measure, it was understood, would apply to biblical, patristic, and hagiographic readings.

The second question concerned, once again, the substitution of the hagiographical for the patristic reading on optional memorials. The two solutions already considered in the eighth plenary session were discussed again: (1) Substitute the hagiographic for the patristic reading, or (2) add the hagiographic reading obligatorily to the patristic reading. The reason offered in support of the first solution was that the cult of the saints is to be fostered. If the hagiographic reading were added to the patristic many would be led to neglect it, and so the accusation would be made that the reformed Office does not foster veneration of the saints. In support of the second solution, it was said that the argument supposing the patristic readings, arranged in semicontinuous manner, would be interrupted on optional memorials by the substitution of the hagiographic reading was invalid because the patristic readings were not going to be arranged in semicontinuous fashion. Furthermore, since the hagiographic is generally a more vivid reading than the patristic and since saints' memorials are numerous and increasing, the hagiographic would undoubtedly more often be preferred to the patristic reading if the first solution were adopted. But if one prefers the celebration of a saint's memorial to the ferial day, that person should find no difficulty in adding the hagiographic to the patristic reading. History shows, it was said, that the patristic reading tends to be put aside in favor of other elements, so caution is needed here. When put to a vote the question produced one of the sharpest divisions ever in Group 9. Eight opted for optional substitution (the first solution), and six supported obligatory addition (the second solution). One absent member (Fr. Jean Gribomont) had submitted by letter his support for the second solution.[55]

Other matters pertaining to the structure of the Office of Readings discussed at some length at the July meeting of Group 9 were the inclusion of a versicle between psalmody and readings, the exclusion of absolutions and blessings, and retention of the invitatory. All these matters were considered above, in chapter 4. With respect to the invitatory there was discussion on whether the whole of Psalm 94 should be retained. Some regarded the last verses of the psalm ("Today, if you shall hear his voice . . .") as not having the character of invitation, but others said the final part of the psalm was necessarily connected to the first part and of importance to the Christian in the light of its use in the Epistle to the Hebrews inviting to the "rest" of the Lord. Group 9 voted 12–2 in favor of retaining the whole of Psalm 94 in the invitatory.[56]

The Synod of Bishops, meeting in September–October 1967, was informed that the Office of Readings would consist of about a third of the psalmody in the current Office and of longer readings. The cycle of biblical readings was to be coordinated with those of the Mass, and a patristic reading (or reading from a Christian author) equal in length to the three sections of the current offering would be provided daily as a commentary on the liturgical season or on a biblical text. The option of selecting a patristic reading from a Lectionary would be provided. To the question "Are the fathers pleased with those things proposed in the report regarding Matins or the Office of Readings?" 139 of the 180 bishops present replied affirmatively; seven voted no; and twenty-eight, yes with reservations. Regarding the suggestions or *modi* pertaining to structure, four called for a free choice of readings, and five wanted the psalmody in the Hour suppressed altogether.[57]

When the Consilium assembled soon after the synod for its ninth plenary session (November 21–28, 1967), the *modi* calling for greater liberty in choice of the patristic reading became the focus of discussion on the bishops' response to the question given them on the Office of Readings. Fr. Jacques Cellier, a French consultor, and Bishop Isnard (Nova Friburgo, Brazil) spoke in favor of greater liberty. Canon Martimort conceded that such liberty could be allowed occasionally but not habitually lest the official character of the reading, the integrity of the cycle, and the connection with the biblical reading be lost. Father Neunheuser agreed, but Monsignor Pascher, with Cardinal Pellegrino in agreement, thought sufficient liberty would be provided through the patristic Lectionary and collections of readings to be made by the episcopal conferences. Fr. Joseph Patino, a Spanish consultor, accused Canon Martimort of having a "monolithic conception" that "responds neither to tradition nor to the desire of clerics." He wanted no obligation to read predetermined passages. Father Bugnini suggested that since there was "a conflict of opinions" *(conflictus sententiarum)* among the members and relators of the Consilium on the matter and lest their efforts be wasted, a fundamental structure for the readings allowing a certain flexibility of choice should be established in the proposed General Instruction for the Office. Bishop Boudon (Mende) spoke in favor of this arrangement, and with most of the members acquiescing, there the matter was left.[58]

SDO, the second specimen of the proposed Office utilized during the ninth session, contained the same structure for the Office of Readings as that in SCDO except that the prayer for the dead, *Fidelium animae*, had been omitted (in accordance with the decision of Group 9 at its meeting in July 1967); and an arrangement was provided for optional memorials whereby the hagiographic reading was substituted for the patristic reading if the Office of the saint were used rather than the Office of the day.[59]

To the members of Group 9 before their meeting from February 27 to March 1, 1968, Canon Martimort sent a compilation of opinions he had received on some provision for popular festive Vigils and Vigils for contemplatives. All agreed, said the canon, that the Office of Readings should be equal in length on both feasts and ordinary days for clergy obliged to it. But reasons exist for an expansion of the Hour in certain circumstances. People keep vigil, he observed, not only at Easter, but in the night of Christmas and on pilgrimage. Contemplatives and some priests (e.g., the infirm and aged) desire a protracted celebration of Sunday Vigils and Vigils of feasts. But Fathers Lentini and Amore were opposed to any such provision. Father Lentini had written that the Consilium ought to prepare "a Roman Breviary for the secular clergy and for those who accept it wholly." This undertaking would not prevent religious orders or other institutes from preparing their own Breviaries that follow their traditional customs or even adopt something new. The Roman Breviary, he maintained, "ought not to become heavy and intricate with these various Offices." Conversely, Bishop Guano (Leghorn, Italy) and Fr. Pelagio Visentin supported Canon Martimort's position that provision for Vigils should be made. Bishop Guano submitted that a richer offering would be desired by some religious communities not only for Sundays and feasts but everyday. If this were not provided, a way would be left for the multiplication of less nourishing devotional practices.

Canon Martimort presented two ways of providing Vigils for contemplatives. One was his own solution, previously proposed, of adding canticles (as in the Benedictine or Milanese traditions), solemn reading of the Gospel, and homily to the Office of Readings. The other was use of psalmody from the old Office along with the third reading (biblical or homiletic), thus preserving the "traditional treasury" (thesaurus traditionalis). Monsignor Cignitti had said he favored Canon Martimort's proposal for Sunday Vigils but thought a Vigil of three nocturns would best serve contemplatives. Canon Rose had submitted a detailed outline of an extension of the Office of Readings that corresponded to Canon Martimort's proposal: one or three Old Testament canticles, gospel (on Sunday, of the resurrection; on feasts, gospel of the feast from an alternate cycle for the Mass), homily, and hymn (Te Deum or Te decet). Monsignor Jounel had proposed that those using the Office of Readings in a modern language would want more reading, not more psalmody. He was opposed to the solemn reading of the gospel because this would be done at Mass. Father Raffa had suggested that for those not aware of tradition, preserving some of the ancient treasures of the Office is a matter of secondary importance. For providing a Vigil he would allow the choice of from three to nine psalms in addition to those given for the Office of Readings and the selection of additional readings from the Scriptures and Fathers according to the desire of those celebrating the Vigil.[60]

At the February–March meeting itself, after discussion of the matter of providing for Vigils Group 9 concurred that for popular Vigils it would suffice to prolong Lauds or Vespers by using a longer reading and adding a homily and intercessions. On the Vigils of the Nativity and Pentecost, to the Office of Readings could be added the readings from the Masses of those days. On the Vigil of Easter for those not participating in the Easter Vigil itself, the Office of Readings would consist of the Old Testament readings, responsories, prayer, Gloria, epistle, gospel, and prayer of the faithful from the Liturgy of the Easter Vigil. As to a Vigil for contemplatives, Group 9 agreed to an addition to the Office of Readings consisting of one or several Old Testament canticles, a gospel reading (on Sundays, of the resurrection; in other cases, of the Mass of the feast or day), and possibly a homily. Some doubts were expressed on the suitability of a gospel passage on the resurrection for the Sundays of Lent and Advent, but no decision seems to have been made to exclude such passages in those seasons. Group 3 (distribution of the psalms) was given the task of preparing a collection of canticles for the Vigil, and Group 9 was in agreement that something should be said about all this in the proposed General Instruction.[61]

Group 9 also appears to have agreed at this meeting to the arrangement presented in SDO for use of patristic and hagiographic readings on optional memorials outside privileged times of the liturgical year: If the Office of the saint is selected, the hagiographic reading is to replace the patristic reading. But another problem presented itself: What should be done in the Office of Readings during Lent and on other days on which the optional celebration of the saint is impeded? Some, out of respect for the importance of the seasonal Office, wanted to exclude all reference to the saint. Others, desiring to maintain some reference to the cult of the saints at these times, wanted the norms governing the Office for optional memorials at other times to apply to privileged times as well. Father Raffa, reporting on the meeting, says that in the course of discussion many solutions were proposed. Finally, a question was put to all: "For the celebration of saints' memorials should a hagiographic reading be added after the patristic reading to be used optionally in privileged times, for example, Lent?" Twelve replied affirmatively; one had reservations and requested that the additional reading not be too long. To another question as to whether the prayer pertaining to the saint should be added after the hagiographical reading, Group 9 was evenly divided: six in favor and six against. One voted yes with reservations, asking that there be only one prayer (presumably for the Hour) if the choice to commemorate the saint were made.[62]

One other matter concerning the Office of Readings occupied the attention of Group 9 at its spring meeting. The question proposed in the eighth plenary session regarding the suppression of the final part of the *Te Deum* was taken up with some who had investigated the structure of the hymn suggesting that, indeed, the conclusion of the hymn should be omitted. They maintained there was no organic bond between the first part and the last, which consisted of a series of psalmic verses (*capitella ex psalmis*) and which showed many variants in various texts of the hymn.

They also maintained that the "Dignare, Domine, die isto . . ." did really suit only the morning well and that there would be no musical difficulty in terminating the hymn, presumably at "in gloria numerari." Ten voted in favor of suppression; four wanted the final part retained for reasons not specified.[63]

Because the tenth plenary session (April 23–30, 1968) was preoccupied with the question of the imprecatory and historical psalms, the matters concerning the Office of Readings, after being considered at the meeting of the Group of Relators (April 14 to 22) were remanded to a special group of members and relators. Decisions were made on several items. First, informed by a statement of Fr. Pelagio Visentin on the importance of placing a versicle between the psalmody and reading as an element dispositive to hearing the Word of God, both the relators and special group approved its insertion.

On the second item, the suppression of the last part of the *Te Deum*, there was disagreement in both the Group of Relators and the special group. In the former, Father Neunheuser called for its being optionally omitted; Monsignor Fischer, for retention of the whole hymn; Monsignor Jounel, for its omission because of the words "Dignare, Domine, die isto . . ."; and Monsignor Fischer, again, for at least adaptation so that it suits any hour of the day. Eighteen favored suppression; eleven, retention; and one voted favorably but with reservations asking that the final part be omitted optionally. In the special group the concern was with the musical rendition of the hymn. Msgr. Theodor Schnitzler, a German consultor, wanted the final part retained because of the beauty of its melody. Canon Martimort suggested, then, that a decision should be made to omit the conclusion only when the hymn is not sung. But Father Visentin again noted there was no difficulty regarding the Gregorian melody if the last part were suppressed. Father Patino regretted its suppression because he saw in these verses an example of petition rising from praise. In the end, the special group agreed that the concluding verses could be omitted optionally.

Finally, concerning the extension of the Office of Readings as a Vigil, the Group of Relators agreed to the proposal accepted by Group 9 in which the Vigil would consist of the ordinary Office of Readings (through the final responsory) plus Old Testament canticles, gospel passage, possibly a homily, and *Te Deum*. In the special group, however, Bishop Kervéadou (Saint Brieuc, France) thought the matter of sufficient importance to present it to the full assembly of the Consilium. He asked if religious had been consulted about this proposal and was told that they had not been. Monsignor Schnitzler thought the mode proposed was excessively complicated. He thought it better if the Office of Readings of the previous Sunday were added to that of the current one to create an extended Vigil. Father Visentin and Monsignor Pascher vouched for the good experience of monks in using Old Testament canticles of the third nocturn, but Bishop Spülbeck (Meissen, East Germany) thought the added elements might not be sufficient. Bishop Pichler (Banjaluka, Yugoslavia) objected to inclusion of the gospel of the resurrection as breaking the connection he would want between the Office of Readings and Mass. Furthermore, he saw no precedent in the Roman Liturgy for such provision. No decision was reached, nor was the matter brought to the full assembly. This group could not decide, either, on the proposal of Group 9 to utilize most elements of the Liturgy of the Word in the Easter Vigil for the Office of Readings on Easter Sunday. Objections were raised that such an arrangement would violate *veritas temporis*, the principle that the Hours of the Office should be celebrated at their respective times of the day or night. If the Office of Readings were used during the day Hours of Easter Sunday the principle would be violated, since the elements to be utilized are those of a nocturnal Vigil. This question was to be brought to the full assembly, but if it was, a vote was not taken, and the matter remained, as Father Raffa observed, in suspense. As to what Group 9 proposed regarding the popular Vigil (i.e., the extension of Lauds or Vespers), the special group advised that this arrangement be explained in the General Instruction.[64]

The structure proposed for the Office of Readings remained basically the same in all the drafts of the General Instruction. The first draft, appearing in June–July 1968, proposed the optional omission of the last part of the *Te Deum* beginning with the words "Per singulos dies." The Hour was to end with the prayer of the Mass of the day and *Benedicamus Domino* in all cases. The second draft (July 1968) allowed the omission in the *Te Deum* to begin with "Salvum fac populum tuum," and the third draft (August 1968) restricted use of *Benedicamus Domino* to common recitation.

In January came the printed specimen of the Office (DSOD) for February 1 and 3. No directions were given for the *Benedicamus Domino,* and surprisingly, a *Dominus vobiscum* (or *Domine, exaudi orationem meam* for private recitation) appeared before the final prayer. The structure of the Hour was otherwise as it had appeared in SDO and as described in the drafts of the General Instruction. At the twelfth plenary session of the Consilium (November 4–8, 1969), at which the responses of the bishops to DSOD were considered, no proposals directly affecting the structure the Office of Readings were made. The fifth draft of the General Instruction (March 1970) further specified that *Benedicamus Domino* was to be used *at least (saltem)* in common recitation. These relatively minor changes affecting the concluding elements of the Hour seem to have been made by Group 9 without recourse to plenary sessions of the Consilium. As to the provisions for the extension of the Office of Readings to provide for protracted Vigils, they, too, remained the same throughout the drafts of IGLH and as had been proposed by Group 9 at the tenth plenary session.

Thus, as presented in IGLH, the definitive structure of the Office of Readings and its extension to provide a lengthy Vigil is as follows:

OFFICE OF READINGS   EXTENDED VIGIL

Invitatory (if first Hour)
or *Deus in adiutorium*
and *Gloria Patri*

Hymn

Three psalms (or sections
of psalms) with antiphons

Versicle

Biblical reading

Responsory

Patristic or hagiographic reading

Responsory

EXTENDED VIGIL

Three Old Testament canticles

Gospel from series on paschal mystery
or from Mass of feast

Homily (optional)

Te Deum

Oration (from Mass)

Benedicamus Domino
(at least in common recitation)[65]

COMPLINE

Only a general directive that Compline be drawn up as a suitable prayer to end the day (SC 89b) provided the starting point for
the Consilium's structural reform of that Hour. To the Consilium
at its second plenary session (April 17–20, 1964) and for its approval as governing the work of the study groups, Canon Martimort put only one question regarding Compline: "How may
Compline be drawn up to fit the end of the day suitably (89b)?"
As part of the complete plan presented by the canon, this question was accepted by the Consilium as that which should direct
the reform of Compline.[66]

The structural reform of Compline received scant attention from
Group 9 in its early sessions. The first concern about the Hour
was its psalmody. In presenting the initial work of Group 9 to the
fourth plenary session of the Consilium (September 28–October 9,
November 16, 1964), Canon Martimort related that some consultors
originally opted for one psalm rather than three in Compline on
the model of that Hour as described by St. Basil (*Longer Rules*
37.2–5). Bishop J. Albert Martin in his report on behalf of the conciliar liturgical commission had also suggested that only Psalm 90,
the same used in Basil's Compline, might constitute the entire
psalmody of Compline. But after discussion all in Group 9 were
agreed that three psalms should be retained according to the
Roman and Benedictine traditions. It had also been proposed that
the current daily variation in psalmody be abandoned in favor of

an invariable scheme so that the psalms could be said from memory. Seven consultors favored the use of Psalms 4, 90, and 133 every day, as was the case in ancient Roman and Benedictine practice and as was favored by the Pian Commission and several bishops of the Vatican Council. Two consultors, however, had argued for variety in the psalmody in order to avoid tedium. As a compromise solution, three consultors favored a combination of two variable psalms and one (Ps 133) fixed every day. One consultor, reported Canon Martimort, wanted the short reading at the beginning of Compline expanded to aid recollection, as was the case in many monasteries. When it was pointed out to him that this reading was done during "collation," not after it, and that this was not originally a part of Compline itself, he withdrew his suggestion. The majority of Group 9, in fact, desired the suppression of the short reading (1 Pet 5:8-9) because it duplicated the *capitulum* and was a remnant of a monastic reading.[67]

The members of the Consilium at this fourth session responded to three questions put to them regarding Compline. The first concerned the number of psalms and was considered in chapter 4. The other two and the results of the voting were as follows:

"10. Should Compline be drawn up with variable or invariable psalms? [variable, 20; invariable, 6; null votes, 2]
"11. Should the short reading in Compline be suppressed? [for suppression, 17; for retention, 10; null vote, 1]"[68]

Not until Group 9 met from September 25 to 26, 1965, was anything concerning Compline discussed again. At that meeting, as part of the reaction to the report from Group 3 on its new proposal for daily variation in the psalms for Compline, the members of Group 9 accepted the recommendation that the psalms for Sunday Compline could be used optionally in place of the given psalms for the other days of the week. Nevertheless, the group wished that the rubric giving that option should include a reminder that "the mind of the Church" was that all psalms should be said and that the reason for the option was a pastoral one.[69]

In the questionnaire issued after the sixth plenary session (October 19-26, November 22-26, December 1, 1965) only one question concerned Compline. To that, which asked if Compline should have three psalms, thirteen members said yes. Seven wanted fewer. Pope Paul VI, expressing his views on reform of the Office during the time the questionnaire was in circulation, said of Compline only that the Consilium should decide whether an invariable or variable scheme for the Hour should be used. Canon Martimort, after his period of study and reflection at this same time, said nothing of Compline in his report (RG and SRG) to Group 9 in July–August 1966.[70]

In his lengthy report to the Consilium, however, in preparation for the seventh plenary session (October 6–14, 1966), Canon Martimort stated that Group 9 and Group 3, apparently still faced with the desire of a number of people for an invariable scheme of psalmody in Compline, were prepared to offer a via media: Let Compline have two psalms, one varying daily, the other taken from Sunday Compline. A rubric could, moreover, indicate that Sunday Compline could be used daily as an option. But, he said, lack of time prevented (at the meeting of Group 9 from September 6 to 8, 1966) thorough consideration of the matter. A definite proposal would be forthcoming later. Group 9, in fact, found its solution at its meeting from February 6 to 8, 1967. There it accepted the proposal of Group 3 for a one-week cycle of psalms, all of which were used elsewhere in the four-week distribution for the Hours other than Compline. Acceptance of the one-week cycle meant a reduction in the number of psalms in Compline on most days. Sunday retained its traditional three; Wednesday had one and a half; Saturday, two. On all other days only one psalm was assigned to the Hour. If the psalms for Sunday Compline were chosen for a weekday, as would be allowed, use of the integral Psalter would still be maintained.[71]

In his report to the eighth plenary session (April 10–19, 1969), Canon Martimort outlined the structure of Compline as it appeared in SCDO, the specimen of the Office to be used during that session. Structurally, it was for the most part the current form of Compline without the initial short reading and with a slightly revised introduction:

"Our help . . ." (*Adiutorium nostrum*)
Examination of conscience
Confiteor and absolution
"Convert us, God . . ." (*Converte nos, Deus*)

Psalm(s) under one antiphon
Hymn
Short reading *(capitulum)*
Responsory: "Into your hands . . ." *(In manus tuas)*
Canticle of Simeon *(Nunc dimittis)* with antiphon
Oration *(Visita, quaesumus)*
Blessing
Antiphon to the Blessed Virgin
"May the divine assistance . . ." *(Divinum auxilium)*[72]

Generally, the structure of Compline was acceptable to both members and relators at the eighth session. In the discussion concerning the Hour, however, both Msgr. Emmanuel Bonet (Spanish consultor) and Bishop Isnard (Nova Friburgo, Brazil) wanted the *Nunc dimittis* removed. Bishop Isnard thought Compline as presented was complicated, and to simplify it he would, besides omitting the canticle as a daily element, abbreviate the hymn, drop the responsory, and use shorter psalms. In a written opinion submitted after the eighth session, Msgr. Pierre Jounel also advocated removal of the *Nunc dimittis* from Compline but suggested its use as the gospel canticle in Vespers for Saturday or Sunday. Bishop Guano (Leghorn, Italy), however, pleaded for retention of the canticle as something essential to the "suggestivity" that characterizes Compline. Father Bugnini, in a written submission to Canon Martimort after the session, suggested there be one psalm only in Compline because those praying Compline, being tired at the end of a day, need something brief in order for the prayer to be fruitful. Besides, he said, in a religious community there are other exercises to be performed such as preparing the meditation for the next day.[73]

Meeting from July 20 to 23, 1967, Group 9 considered the foregoing and other requests regarding Compline. As to omitting the *Nunc dimittis*, the members of the group were unanimously opposed for the reason that the canticle was a very special element of Roman Compline. Those, it was said, who use the monastic Office, which lacks the *Nunc dimittis*, have shown themselves envious of this very beautiful element in Roman Compline.

Suggestions for reducing the psalmody on weekdays were considered. It was noted that there was in the arrangement of Compline in SCDO some disparity between the Sunday and weekday psalmody. If that of the weekdays were reduced further, a greater disparity would be evidenced, and this would certainly displease clerics who have pastoral obligations, especially on Sunday. It seemed, rather, that some change should be made in the quantity of the Sunday psalmody. It was proposed to divide the Sunday psalmody into two series—on the one hand, Psalm 90 and on the other, Psalms 4 and 133. The series would be alternated week to week. Group 9 accepted this arrangement by a vote of 11 to 1.

Objections to the introduction to Compline as it had appeared in SCDO were also discussed. Some complained of the period of silence after *Adiutorium nostrum*. It appeared to them unseemly to begin vocally and move immediately to silence for the examen. Postponement of the examen and confession to a position after the psalmody was suggested because those actions, it seemed, ought to constitute the last acts of the day, and a precedent for this order could be found in the Ambrosian Office. The discussion was inconclusive, however, and this matter, which was to become the thorniest of solution for Compline, was put aside for another time.[74]

The bishops gathered for the synod in September–October 1967 were informed that Compline would consist of the three customary psalms on Sunday and varying psalms, already used elsewhere in the *cursus*, on weekdays so that the Sunday psalms could be used, optionally, every day. The other major elements as they had appeared in SCDO were outlined for them. The bishops received no question regarding Compline specifically, but some who submitted *modi* regarding the minor Hours offered their views on Compline as well. None was significant for the structure of Compline save three at the most, which asked for its abolition, and this request was dismissed as being against SC and probably against "the universal sense of priests and the faithful."[75]

At the ninth plenary session (November 21–28, 1967) the only item discussed regarding Compline was the matter of whether to retain the *Nunc dimittis*. By a show of hands, all agreed to retention of the canticle. In SDO, the second specimen of the Office, which the Consilium used at this session, the structure of Compline was identical to that in SCDO save for the two newly accepted alternating schemes of Sunday psalmody.[76]

The unresolved questions regarding the structure of Compline were thoroughly reviewed at the meeting of Group 9 from February 27 to March 1, 1968. Some opinions on these questions had been submitted to Canon Martimort before the commencement of the meeting. On the major question concerning the beginning of the Hour with examen and confession, there were a number of opinions. Consultors Famoso, Dumas, Lentini, and Visentin thought the proposed structure should be retained. Monsignor Pascher wanted the examen and confession placed before the final oration in the mode of *preces* as in the Premonstratensian Office. Fathers Dirks and Raffa preferred them after the antiphon to the Blessed Virgin, as in the Milanese Liturgy. Either Father Dirks or Father Raffa (it is not clear who) withdrew this suggestion on the belief, not otherwise explained, that the examen after the *Nunc dimittis* would not be fitting. Other solutions proposed were to put the examen after the hymn and before the psalmody or immediately before the *Nunc dimittis*. In an attempt to resolve the matter, three possibilities were put to vote. Five favored examen and confession after the hymn; five, before the hymn; and one opted for placing them after the antiphon to Mary. This impasse was presumably resolved when ten members accepted Monsignor Pascher's suggestion to move the hymn to the beginning of the Hour. Then, eight favored examen and confession after the hymn, while three maintained they should precede the hymn.

Before the meeting objections had also been made to the use of *Adiutorium nostrum* to begin Compline either because it was rather isolated, especially if examen followed, or because historically it was a concluding, not an initial element. In the meeting the same objection was made against the position of *Converte nos* in the proposed structure. No decision, however, was reached on these matters. Group 9 was generally agreed that the formula of confession should be invariable, perhaps one of those proposed for the penitential rite at the beginning of Mass. A verse or an antiphon could signal the start of the examen. Since no clear resolution to most of the difficulties could be reached, Canon Martimort simply reported the situation regarding the structure of Compline to the tenth plenary session, at which no action was taken concerning it.[77]

In submitting the first draft of the General Instruction to his colleagues of Group 9 in June 1968 Canon Martimort offered still other changes in the structure of Compline. In his introduction to the draft he said: "The structure of Compline still remains very uncertain and must be decided. In the draft of the instruction, I have been so bold as to propose to you yet another solution that may have to be rejected." He proposed that the Hour begin, like the others, with *Deus in adiutorium*, followed by the hymn, psalmody, short reading, *Nunc dimittis* (with its antiphon), concluding oration, *Dominus vobiscum* (if appropriate), blessing *(Noctem quietam)*, and the antiphon to the Blessed Virgin with its verse and prayer. The examen he left optional—either before or after the Hour.[78]

At its meeting from July 16 to 19, 1968, those in Group 9 apparently found most of their relator's proposal acceptable, the exception being what was suggested for the examen. In the second and third drafts of the instruction (July and October 1968) the examen was put *before* the hour began as an optional item and allowance made in communal celebration for optional use of a penitential act not otherwise specified. This structure was basically that in the specimen (DSOD) sent to bishops in January 1969. In the text of Compline there, however, the *Confiteor* and *Misereatur* were given as the penitential act optional before the Hour; the traditional responsory appeared after the short reading, and *Divinum auxilium* appeared after the antiphon to Mary with its verse and prayer.[79]

Mention of the responsory, *In manus tuas*, was included in the fourth draft of the instruction, and no mention was made either of *Dominus vobiscum* before the concluding oration or of anything following the antiphon to the Blessed Virgin. In his report to the Consilium for its twelfth plenary session (November 4–8, 1969), Canon Martimort specifically called attention to the retention of the responsory and the omission of verse and prayer after the antiphon to Mary. He also noted that for solemnities occurring within a given week, the psalms proposed for Compline after First Vespers were those of the preceding Sunday, while those for Compline after Second Vespers were those of the following Sunday. The fifth and final draft of the General Instruction (March 1970) contained these changes for Compline as well as a stipulation that the concluding prayer would be that given in the Psalter (thus varied from day to day) rather than that given in the ordinary, as previous drafts had specified.[80]

The tortured matter of the place of the examen and confession, however, had not yet seen its definitive solution. The draft of the General Instruction, as explained above in chapter 3, underwent a thorough scrutiny by Pope Paul VI, who conferred with Father Bugnini on a number of its items. It thus appears that the repositioning of the examen and penitential act *within* the structure of Compline is due to the Pope's action with the possible assistance of the secretary of the Sacred Congregation for Divine Worship. In any case, the definitive structure of Compline given in the IGLH puts the examen and penitential act *after* the introduction to the Hour. The IGLH contains one other modification of the fifth draft: The psalmody that was to alternate between Sundays now alternates between Compline following First Vespers and that after Second Vespers of Sundays and solemnities. As explained in chapter 3, a last-minute realization while texts were being prepared for the printer that nothing had been provided for *Sunday* Compline on Saturday evening necessitated this change. Thus, the definitive structure of Compline as it appears in IGLH and LH itself is as follows:

"God, come to my assistance . . ." *(Deus, in adiutorium")*
"Glory to the Father . . ." *(Gloria Patri)*
Optional examination of conscience
    (in common celebration either in silence or within a penitential
    act according to one of the formulae of the Roman Missal)
Hymn
One or two psalms with antiphons
Short reading
Responsory *(In manus tuas)*
Canticle of Simeon *(Nunc dimittis* with antiphon)
Concluding variable oration (initial *Oremus* only)
Blessing *(Noctem quietem)*
Marian antiphon[81]

One must conclude, then, that the structural revision wrought in all the Hours was greater in some than in others. The Office of Readings, made uniform on all days, festive or not, with all division into nocturns abandoned, certainly stands out in one respect as that Hour having undergone the most radical change. From another perspective, however, the provisions for reduction of the minor Hours in many cases from three to one represent just as radical a revision. While these major revisions along with the shortening of the other Hours occupied months, sometimes years, of the working time of Group 9 and the Consilium, it is remarkable that some less significant structural changes internal to each of the Hours consumed great amounts of the time and energy of consultants and members of the Consilium. Such changes would include the position of the *Pater* and intercessions in Lauds and Vespers, the use of the hagiographic reading on optional memorials in the Office of Readings, and the position of the examen within or outside the structure of Compline. It remains now to evaluate not only these and the other structural changes but also the process by which the structure of the Office was reformed.

Chapter 6

Evaluation of the Reform

The process by which the Consilium, both members and consultors, reformed the structure of the Roman Office was indeed a long and complex one. Likewise, the options considered and choices made regarding the structure of the Office were not only numerous but of varied importance. Some were basic to the direction of the reform; others affected the structure of the Hours as a whole; still others had to do with both major and minor adaptations in the individual Hours themselves. In this chapter, as a conclusion to the history of the structural reform of the Office, both the process of the reform, on the one hand, and the options entertained and decisions reached regarding structure, on the other hand, will be evaluated. Evaluation of the process will be in terms of persons involved and procedure followed. Evaluation of the options and choices will be made in the light of (1) an interpretation of the pertinent norms in SC that reflect the Church's tradition on the Office as its common prayer actually to be prayed in common, as far as possible, by all in the Church and (2) contemporary needs for viable forms of prayer as evidenced in practice and writing current both at the time of the reform and after it. This evaluation will culminate in a conclusion on the structural reform and its significance for the future.

THE PROCESS OF REFORM

The Consilium established by Pope Paul VI was supposed to include both pastors and scholars drawn from numerous areas of the international Church. Such was, in fact, the case to some extent, but with respect to the membership of the Consilium, the bishops who formed the overwhelming majority of the membership and who were considered to fulfill a pastoral role in the reform can be said to have done so only to a limited degree. Bishops, as heads of local Churches, certainly can perceive needs in these Churches, but their pastoral perceptions are not necessarily those of the clergy, religious, and laity over whom they preside. That the membership of the Consilium should have been more inclusive of the Church as a whole was probably unthinkable in 1963, but the fact that the membership was constituted mostly of an international selection of residential bishops (forty-nine of sixty-one from thirty-one countries throughout the life of the Consilium) can certainly be considered a more pastoral and representative body than a small group of curial bishops to whom the reform could have been entrusted. Likewise the number (approximately 220) and international character (twenty-two nations represented) of the group of *consultores* and *consiliarii* undoubtedly constituted a more representative group of scholars within the international Church than might have been selected by the Pope or curial congregation acting without the consultation that in fact marked the selective process. But because the selection of consultors and advisors was primarily the responsibility of the Italian secretary of the Consilium, Fr. Annibale Bugnini, it is perhaps no wonder that almost 30 percent of the *consultores* were Italian—the largest number (forty-two) from any nationality. Archbishop Bugnini has admitted he relied on scholars he knew personally in the formation of the corps of consultors; and these might be expected to be people, for the most part, of his own nationality. It is certainly questionable, however, that the best liturgical expertise in the Church was confined to such an extent within the boundaries of one nation. Moreover, the group of *consultores* was overwhelmingly clerical and male. There were, at the most, four lay consultors among whom was only one woman, Dr. Christine Mohrmann (University of Nijmegen, Holland). Still, any lay representation at all was an advance over the exclusively clerical constituency of the group of consultors to the preparatory liturgical commission for the council. More particularly with respect to the Office, the composition of Group 9 reflected that of the main body of consultors. Eight nationalities were represented in the totally clerical group with Italians constituting approximately 40 percent of the membership. Thus views on the Office as these are culturally conditioned by geographic place and circumstances almost certainly found less adequate expression within Group 9 than they would have had if the group had been more nationally diverse.[1]

One certainly cannot exclude from the number of those who participated in the reform of the liturgy and, particularly, in the reform of the Office the many people who experimented with parts of the Office or with a complete arrangement of it. But aside from a statement of CNPL regarding the French experiment with *Prière du temps présent* very late in the reforming process, there is no evidence to suggest that persons experimenting elsewhere had any significant impact on the course or substance of the structural reform. Neither can a large percentage of the episcopate nor superiors of religious congregations be disregarded as contributors to the reform, since DSOD was sent them precisely for their critical comments and those of at least some in their respective constituencies. Participants in the episcopal synod of 1967 also contributed their opinions on the reform up to that time. But in all these cases ordinary participants in the Office would have had to submit their observations through bishops, religious superiors, or an institution such as CNPL. Neither the Consilium nor Group 9 seem ever to have conducted a consultation or an experiment in which there would have been direct access to the multitudes who regularly prayed the Hours. That the consultation and experimentation was as wide as it was is, of course, commendable. Hindsight of some twenty years suggests it might have been even wider.[2]

Pope Paul VI was a contributor to the reform in more than an authoritative way of giving definitive rejection or approval to the Consilium's work. Most of his interventions were offered as personal opinions or suggestions, even though misconstrued as papal directives by some. This character of the papal interventions is significant for what might have been—a point to be considered below.[3]

Finally, the presence of six Protestant observers at sessions of the Consilium beginning in 1966 was certainly a welcome ecumenical gesture, but their contribution to the reform itself must be termed very minimal, since they had neither voice nor vote in the sessions, although they could and did offer observations outside them. Perhaps the most notable and direct contribution of an observer, that of Max Thurian of Taizé, who became an active participant in Group 12bis (*preces* for Lauds and Vespers) and who contributed the intercessions for the major Hours of LH during Holy Week, attests at least to the advantage enjoyed by the Consilium of a loose juridical structure allowing an enriching arrangement such as this to occur. It is simply unfortunate that the Consilium did not follow up on a suggestion to invite an Orthodox observer, for one of the weaknesses of the reform of the Roman Office seems to have been a lack of attention to Eastern liturgical forms as these impinge on Western ones, the consequences of which will be considered below. A judicious selection of Eastern (Catholic and Orthodox) observers with voice in the meetings both of the study groups and in the plenary sessions might have offset some of the limitations necessarily present if Western liturgical traditions were considered, as they were, almost in isolation.[4]

With attention turned now to the procedure by which the structural reform of the Office was accomplished, the first consideration will be the process of interaction between the members and consultors of the Consilium. It is evident from the history of the reform that it was the custom of Group 9, at least, to seek from the members of the Consilium in their plenary sessions some specific directives for their work before undertaking it and to ask for direction when disagreement occurred within the study group. Such a way of proceeding is understandable from the point of view that the consultors served in an advisory capacity to the membership of the Consilium, who had the responsibility for shaping the reform. But by seeking the advice of the membership at almost every step of the way for almost every structural element of the Office, Group 9 put itself in the position of utilizing the membership of the Consilium as a consultative body to itself. A group of scholars who, theoretically at least, had a grasp of the tradition of the Office, of the norms of SC, and of the recommendations of the conciliar liturgical commission might have drafted a scheme for the structure of the Office without initial and extensive continuing recourse to the members for direction. The original plan for the *modus operandi* of the Consilium as devised by Father Bugnini seems to have envisioned just such a procedure—drafting of material by the study groups to be examined and approved or rejected by the membership. That befuddlement attended at least some members when they were asked to give direction was clearly evident at the fourth and fifth plenary sessions of the Consilium (September–November 1964, April 1965). Time and effort might have been better spent had Group 9, perhaps in conjunction with the Group of Relators, simply developed among themselves drafts of the structure and of the contents of the Hours and then presented them to the members for review and decision rather than so often seeking their direction before drafting any such schemes. Most members, after all, were not liturgical scholars. Only a few, like Bishop Anton Hanggi (Basel, Switzerland), were such, and the latter for a good part of the reform (i.e., until his ordination to the episcopacy in 1967) was a consultor. To say this is not to deny that the members had a unique pastoral role to fulfill in judging the acceptability of the work of the study groups. The voting record of the Consilium would seem to bear out that the members accepted almost every proposal made to them, at least regarding the structure of the Office, that had the support of a majority of those in Group 9 or in the Group of Relators. Indeed, the relatively unchallenging acceptance of these proposals by the members might be indicative of an inordinate reliance on the scholarly views of the consultors and a lack of confidence in their own pastoral expertise.[5]

On the positive side, however, the mutual exchange allowed in the plenary sessions between members and consultors was undoubtedly beneficial to both groups. If any advance was made from the time of the council itself in an understanding of the Office as communal prayer in which all in the Church had a right to participate—and there was such an advance, evidenced, for example, by a comparison between SC, chapter 4, and IGLH, chapter 1—it certainly must be attributed in part to the interchange possible among experts and bishops both within and outside the plenary sessions. As noted above in chapter 4, even minority opinions among the consultors, such as Father Mateos' proposals for Lauds and Vespers, had an effect in shaping the structure of these Hours so that they were more accessible to all.[6]

Another feature of the procedure of reform was interruption. This unforeseen, unplanned interruption assumed various forms—papal interventions, interventions by the secretary of the Consilium, consolidation of the Consilium with SCR, the major reexamination of the whole project of reform for the Office from

December 1965 to October 1966; and the submission of the work of the reform to the Synod of Bishops in 1967 together with its judgment on that reform. While these forms of interruption could be considered as hardly facilitating the task of careful rethinking and reformulation of the structure and content of the Office by means of the established, normal process, each of them, by confronting the Consilium, Group 9, and the other study groups with questions or situations perhaps not adequately being dealt with, induced beneficial results that undoubtedly would not have been obtained had the process moved on without them.

The papal interventions, particularly those advocating reduction of the minor Hours to one and the abandonment of imprecatory and historical psalms, not only contributed to the evocation of major reconsideration of the structure of the Hours as a whole and the role and distribution of psalmody in the Office but, perhaps more significantly, also revealed that Pope Paul VI was willing to go beyond the norms of SC with respect to reform of the Office. That the Consilium and Group 9 did not, in the name of fidelity to the constitution and for the sake of avoiding a semblance of fickleness, seize that offer and propose more radical structural reforms has been and continues to be the disappointment of many. Nevertheless, the reconsideration, induced in part by the Pope's interventions, led to what must be termed a major modification in the structure of the Roman Office. Because of the papal recommendation and then insistence on the exclusion of three so-called imprecatory psalms and of difficult verses in some others from the *cursus* of the psalmody, a fundamental and traditional principle of the Roman Office, namely, the use of the integral Psalter, has been breached. However slight the evidence of this is in the revised *cursus*, the abandonment of the principle in practice sets a precedent that will undoubtedly render easier a decision for more selective use of psalms in some future reform of the Roman Office. Group 9, of course, cited the abandonment of the principle as a dangerous one allowing the introduction of subjectivism as a criterion in determining what is to constitute the Office. Yet it is a matter of history that selective use of psalmody was one of the distinguishing marks of the cathedral Office. A revival of some form of cathedral Office for secular clergy and laity was, during the reform and after it, the desire of many.[7]

Besides the papal interventions and perhaps connected with some of them were the interventions of the secretary of the Consilium, Fr. (later, Archbishop) Annibale Bugnini. His advocacy of one middle Hour in place of the three minor Hours might have been more persuasive to Group 9 had he not linked his proposals to the safeguarding of religious practices springing, as Canon Martimort would have it, from his attachment to *devotio moderna*. But Father Bugnini's support for one middle Hour as well as for the elimination of the imprecatory psalms and verses, as disconcerting as may have been the manner in which that support was shown at times, challenged Group 9 and, particularly, its relator, Canon Martimort, to reconsider on several occasions in the light of contemporary needs the appropriateness of the insistence on maintaining both the three minor Hours and the integral Psalter and to develop a defense of that position. This defense, be it noted, was cogent enough to win the support of the membership of the Consilium and, with respect to the preservation of the imprecatory psalms, might have succeeded ultimately had not Father Bugnini intervened directly with the Pope against retention of those psalms.[8]

The gradual consolidation of the Consilium with SCR was not as interruptive of the reforming process for the Office as were the other events considered here. The establishment (in 1968) of Cardinal Gut in the presidency over both bodies simultaneously was intended to ease the tension between them but seems not to have affected much the actual process of reform. More critical was the later absorption (1969) of the Consilium by the Congregation for Divine Worship—a move that radically altered the *modus operandi* of Consilium members and consultors. Although the major lines of the structure of the Office were in place by this time, the notable decrease in at least official communications regarding reform and the inability of consultors to meet and to discuss with members might have provided some of the conditions for the hasty and admittedly unsatisfactory arrangements (e.g., reduction of the two cycles of biblical readings to one cycle) that had to be made as LH was readied for publication.[9]

The reexamination of the proposed reform of the Office following the objections made against it in 1965–66 fulfilled a function similar to that of the interventions considered above. The paramount effect of this reexamination was certainly a shift, particularly in Group 9, from a conception of the structural reform of the Office as primarily designed to foster better private use by secular clergy to a conception of the reform as intended to restructure the Office, at least both major Hours, as viable public prayer for all in the Church.[10]

Despite a shift in perspective on the purpose of the reform, some members of Group 9 seem to have maintained their disbelief that popular participation in the Office was a serious prospect for the future. When speaking in sessions of the Consilium or in meetings of Group 9, they continued to address issues primarily in terms of their effects on clerics. Canon Martimort, though an energetic and conscientious leader of the reform of the Office, never demonstrated conviction on the need to restructure the Office primarily for public celebration by clergy and people together. He nevertheless manifested, particularly in the face of the criticism that gave rise to the questionnaire of December 1965, a creative sensitivity to that criticism and a diminishing skepticism regarding the possibility of popular participation in Lauds and Vespers.[11]

Finally, the examination by the 1967 Synod of Bishops of the reform of the liturgy to that time was interruptive of the process of reform to the extent that information had to be prepared for it and the Consilium had to consider its observations and the requests of those submitting *modi*. The synod seems to have provided at least some impetus to the reconsideration of the use of the integral Psalter in the Office, since it approved by only a simple majority the retention of all the psalms in the *cursus*. As noted above, the struggle over inclusion of imprecatory psalms and verses, certainly the most explosive of the reform, issued in a breach of the principle traditional in the Roman Office since at least the sixth century requiring use of the entire Psalter over a determined period of time. Thus while the interruption caused by the synod in the normal process of reform of the Office may be termed insignificant on most issues, since the synod supported by a two-thirds majority the positions adopted by the Consilium, on the issue of retention of the integral Psalter the synod's support by only a simple majority of the Consilium's position provoked, at least in part, a reconsideration of that issue. This reconsideration led eventually to a radical decision to abandon some imprecatory psalms and verses and, in effect, moved the Roman Office a very small step in the direction of the selective psalmody so characteristic of cathedral Offices.[12]

A major characteristic of the process of reform was compromise. The most important area of compromise was undoubtedly that of the users of the Office and their needs. Those few who saw the Office as the public prayer of the entire Church had, if they wished to succeed, to yield to or to reach agreements with those who regarded clerics and religious as the primary users of the Office and as representatives of the entire Church when they prayed it. But those others who held the "realistic" views that the needs of secular priests and religious needed to be the focus of concern or that preservation of the *thesaurus traditionalis* should be primarily in view during the reform process had to acknowledge, if they wished to succeed, the legitimate aspects of the positions adopted by those arguing for radical reform so that the Office might become once again the prayer of the entire Church. Fr. Juan Mateos, for example, seemed unwilling to compromise his radical position and thus withdrew from any further major input on structural reform when his initial proposals were rejected. In contrast, Canon Martimort and Father Bugnini, when faced with criticism or rejection of their and their colleagues' preferred line of action, were at least willing to incorporate or to accept something of their opponents' desires in a proposed solution. By dint of compromise the structural reform was achieved. It is questionable whether without it the reform would have been brought to term, and from that perspective one can appreciate Canon Martimort's claim that compromise was a strength, not a liability of the reform. Yet the great disadvantage of the compromising process insofar as structural reform was concerned was the establishment of one arrangement of the Hours and one arrangement of elements within each of the Hours for all individuals and groups using the Roman Office and, as shall be seen, very limited provision for adaptability. This disadvantage will be discussed in connection with the consideration of the major choice presented to the reformers in 1964–65 for either radical revision, perhaps going beyond the prescriptions of SC, or modification of the Roman Office well within the obvious limits imposed by the constitution.[13]

What often characterized the process of reform, too, were certain a priori assumptions upon which decisions for or against reform were based, at least until such assumptions were challenged by others within or without the Consilium. Such assumptions included the notions that reform of the Office was primarily intended to render it more serviceable for clergy with pastoral care; that communal celebration of Lauds would never be frequented by laity in any great number; that if Vespers were to be celebrated with "the people," it must include longer readings and homily; that daily use of incense with Psalm 140 could not be restored to Vespers because of the lengthiness of the psalm; that most priests would continue to recite alone Lauds and Vespers. Whether dispelled later or not, these assumptions, especially evident in Group 9, which had the principal responsibility for structural reform, reveal a mentality comfortable with the status quo. They suggest a lack of vision of what might be, an unwillingness to risk moving much beyond current practice in order to achieve the major, general goals of liturgical reform as stated in SC 14, 26–27, namely, communal celebration of all liturgical rites by all members of the Church. It was precisely the perception of this mentality in the reformers that discouraged Father Mateos from offering continuing major input on reform of the Office. His remarks in this regard, whether one can agree with them in their entirety or not, are at least corroborated by the evidence cited above and indicate why this consultor, who might have moved the structural reform in a direction different from that in which it went, was silent throughout most of the reforming process:

"You know, there was the French Institute for liturgy in Paris and they thought . . . their views must be accepted. . . . I think San Anselmo was not yet known as a school of liturgy . . . and so, the only [other] one was Trier. That was very pastoral but not very scientific. Paris claimed to be really scientific. I say "claimed to be" because actually they publish very little [besides] *La Maison-Dieu*. . . . The group, the team in Paris was not especially scientific. They were very pastoral, very interested in the new needs and people and very openminded for the time. But they didn't see some great revolution for the future that was *to be* foreseen. . . . And so, they wanted to impose those views. But, you know, it was insufficient.

"I have taught in old Congo, and I knew a little of central Africa. I saw that there, for instance, the situation is that they have no electric light very often. So, in the villages after sunset they are absolutely free. People have nothing to do, and so they get together, they talk. Seeing that, I proposed . . . for those people something easy to pray. . . . [I saw this same] situation in Asia—in Manila and also in Hong Kong. I visited Thailand and Cambodia. In Manila [I] met people from the whole Orient—from Japan, India, New Zealand, Australia, all the islands, Indonesia. There were seventy or eighty students every year. . . . We had meetings about the different cultures. . . . The problems were the same especially in rural areas—and that's most of the world. . . . And so we proposed [the radical reform of the Office] with this great, bigger horizon of the missions and also rural life [in view]. . . . Of course, it was based on the old tradition. . . . But they [the group charged with reform of the Roman Office] didn't think that way, you know. And so, the thing was decided. I left. I had nothing more to do."[14]

Aligned with the penchant for a priori assumptions were two other related characteristics of the reforming process. One was what might be termed an eclectic traditionalism and the other, a distrust of liturgical scholarship without distinguishing the various types of this scholarship. By eclectic traditionalism is meant a justification of proposed reforms on the basis of isolated precedents found either in the Roman Liturgy or in any other pre-Reformation Christian liturgical rite. For instance, the insertion of New Testament canticles was justified on the basis of their use in the Mozarabic Liturgy; placement of the hymn at the beginning of an Hour, on the basis of a precedent for such in the Ambrosian liturgy; a proposal to put the oration of Vespers after the hymn, also on the basis of the practice in the Ambrosian liturgy. But none of these precedents, it seems, was ever contexualized in its proper tradition. The mere existence of an element in a liturgical tradition seemed sufficient justification for its use, if desired, in the Roman reform. A certain distrust of liturgical scholarship, especially evident in Canon Martimort, to serve as a major criterion in the reform process may have abetted this traditionalism. In the canon's view former structures of the Office revealed by scholarly research, although certainly helpful to understand and to utilize, could not function as criteria for reform without being carefully nuanced because doctrinal and liturgical developments may have rendered them obsolete or less appropriate today. In making this judgment Canon Martimort does not distinguish between various types of scholarly research. He rightly accuses Fr. Louis Bouyer of inexactness in the latter's reconstruction of ancient, popular Vespers. But Father Bouyer's general, sometimes arbitrary and unsubstantiated views can hardly be compared to those offered by, for example, Father Mateos and his colleagues, whose hypotheses and conclusions were set forth only after a meticulous, comparative, structural analysis of liturgical units in many traditions. The latter type of research is perhaps the only means by which the structures of the Roman Office as it may have existed before its monastic modification may come to be known, at least in part. Restoration of these traditional structures, not out of some motive of archeologism but from a pastoral one, as structures that might well meet the communal prayer needs of a broad range of people today, clergy and laity alike, would then rest on solid traditional grounds—not only of the Roman liturgy but of universal or widespread liturgical traditions.[15]

OPTIONS AND CHOICES

As a prelude to an evaluation of the major options considered and choices made by Group 9 and the Consilium regarding the structure of the Office, consideration will be given first to the interpretation of the norms of SC and the major contemporary needs in light of which the reform was undertaken. As stated above, these norms, as consonant with the Church's tradition of the Office, along with contemporary needs for its revision as expressed before, during, and (to some extent) after the time of reform, will serve as references from which to evaluate the options and choices. Next, the options and choices regarding the structure of the Office as a whole will be evaluated. Finally, the options and choices regarding the arrangement of major or much debated structural elements within the various Hours will be critiqued.

The Norms of SC and Contemporary Needs

It could hardly be expected that the bishops of Vatican Council II would produce in SC norms for the reform of the Office that would clearly give a priority to its communal, ecclesial celebration.

As discussed above in chapter 2, the overwhelming majority of the interventions made regarding chapter 4 of the schema for SC betrayed an understanding of the Office as primarily the preserve of clergy and religious and the reform as that which should benefit primarily private recitation by the secular clergy. It is remarkable, then, that some articles in chapter 4 pointing to a broader, more traditional understanding of the Office and serving to link its projected revision to the major principles of reform of the entire Roman liturgy, expressed especially in SC 14, 21, 26–27, were utilized to modify the direction the postconciliar reform of the Office was taking from 1963 to 1965, namely, a direction toward an Office primarily suitable for clergy engaged in pastoral care.

SC 14 demands that the "full and active participation by all the people" be "the aim to be considered before all else" in the reform of the liturgy. SC 21 calls for restoration of texts and rites to express clearly the "holy things" (*sancta*) they signify so that "the Christian people" might easily understand them "and take part in them fully, actively, and as befits a community." SC 26 states that liturgical actions "are not private functions, but are celebrations of the Church," and article 27 asks that preference be given to "communal celebration involving the presence and active participation of the faithful" over "individual and quasi-private" performance. These articles certainly must be linked with SC 90, 98, and 100, which were cited by Father Bugnini as containing the principles in light of which the members and consultors of the Consilium were to answer the questionnaire of December 1965. The secretary first quoted the pertinent section of article 90: "In revising the Roman Office, its ancient and venerable treasures are to be so adapted that all those to whom they are handed on may more extensively and easily draw profit from them." He then suggested that the "all" in article 90 referred, in addition to secular clergy and religious obliged to the Office, to all religious (as indicated in SC 98) and laity (as indicated in SC 100). Thus, from an interpretation of SC itself, a more traditional conception of the Office as ecclesial liturgy was proposed as that which must govern its reform. Father Bugnini's remarks laid the emphasis in the section of article 90 quoted above on "are to be so adapted that all those to whom they are handed on may more extensively and easily draw profit from them," whereas the reformers, up to that point in time, had been emphasizing (and were never completely to cease from stressing) the need to preserve "the ancient and venerable treasures of the Roman Office" and to adapt it to serve primarily the clergy engaged in pastoral care.[16]

The major contemporary needs expressed before and during the reform that a revised Office was expected to meet were numerous. Among the principal concerns were spiritual nourishment of clergy in pastoral care; allowance to those engaged in apostolic work better to meet the pastoral demands facing them (thus abbreviation of the Office in various ways); sanctification of the day by prayer at various times throughout it (thus a return to an Office respecting the "truth of the Hours," *veritas horarum*); variety and liberty of choice with respect to some elements of the Office; nourishment for the prayer of monks and other contemplatives; and participation of "the people" in the prayer of the Church. Many, of course, believed that a number of these needs could not be met by one form of the Roman Office and thus called for at least a "monastic Breviary" for communal or choral use and a "pastoral Breviary" for private recitation by clergy in pastoral care. The priority to be given these needs and their interrelationship were perceived so differently both among the reformers and among those outside the Consilium that a revision of the Office answering them all to the full satisfaction of all would seem a virtual impossibility. Following the reform a concern for structures (and content) to meet the multiple and differing needs, cultures, styles, and so on of a variety of geographic, ethnic, and other social groups emerged more strongly. This concern, to put it simply, was with adaptation and inculturation.[17]

The Structure of the Office as a Whole

As evidenced in chapters 3 and 4 above, without ever making a formal decision on the matter Group 9 and the Consilium began the structural reform of the Office with the notion that it was primarily intended for the secular clergy. Canon Martimort's and perhaps others' primary concern was larger only in that they did not want the needs of contemplatives and those obliged to the choral Office overlooked. Rendering the Office more accessible to the laity was of quite secondary importance. There was to be no reform of Lauds, and Vespers was to have a special structure when "the people" were present, which would probably not occur frequently. Father Mateos' proposal for restoration of a cathedral Office was rejected on the grounds that it went beyond the norms of SC and that the role of the Consilium was to implement SC, not to forge new paths. Only with the reexamination of the direction of the reform beginning in December 1965 were Group 9 and the Consilium seriously confronted with the choice of radical reform or modification according to a strict, not to say narrow, interpretation of the norms of SC. In the end it was the latter they opted for, and in doing so paradoxically effected, on the mandate of the council, the most radical structural reform of the Roman Office since its known beginnings. Father Vincenzo Raffa has observed:

"In the memorial which the Spaniard, Juan de Arze, presented to the Council of Trent in criticism of the Santa Croce Breviary, he attacked Quignones for daring to tamper with a divine ordinance, for such, in Arze's view, were the three nocturns on Sunday. What would Arze have thought of anyone daring to change the Horarium itself which certainly had behind it a tradition no less ancient than the three Sunday nocturns? And yet Vatican Council II, in its global revamping of the liturgy in the light of new conditions and lifestyles, decided to change even the Horarium. . . .

"Unlike any of the prior reforms, the Council has . . . intervened even in the Horarium, despite the fact that for over a millennium the latter had been one of the most stable institutions in clerical and monastic life."[18]

Any criticism of the options and choices of Group 9 and the Consilium must indeed be viewed in the light of the major reform that was accomplished. No more, in fact, than that which they did achieve might reasonably have been expected from them given the general preconciliar and conciliar mentality regarding the Office.

Yet, another road, which might have led to a better result, was open, and it was not taken. In his response to the criticism of the direction the reform was taking in 1965–66, Canon Martimort noted with respect to the first question of the December questionnaire that the demand many were making for a "normative Breviary" could be interpreted in two ways. It could mean the preparation of an essential structure of the Office allowing for adaptations by different groups using the Office, or it could mean preparation of a uniform Office to be used by all. He rejected the possibility of the latter as against the principles of SC 38, which called for regional and cultural variations and adaptations in the liturgy. The canon's and the Consilium's decision was to opt for the former, but in a way that provided far more than an essential structure for the Office and greatly restricted the possibilities for adaptation. It seems that the Consilium could have taken the route followed by the Benedictine Confederation in their provision for reform of the monastic Office. Beginning in 1968 while the reform of the Roman Office was still in progress, the Benedictine reformers, faced with the differing needs of the many monasteries of the confederation, rejected a single solution such as a common Breviary. In the words of Henry Ashworth, ''. . . the Liturgical Commission produced not a breviary, composed for choral or private recitation, like the *Liturgia Horarum* of the Roman Rite, but a collection of possibilities intended to serve the needs of many. It provides an aid both for those houses which desire to keep the disposition of Rule, yet feel the need to bring it up to date, as well as those who wish a deeper and more radical adaptation to their circumstances. Hence the title of the work was given as the *Thesaurus Liturgiae Monasticae Horarum.*''[19]

The widely differing needs of monastic communities facing the Benedictine reformers were multiplied many times over, *mutatis mutandis*, for the reformers of the Roman Office. Surely if Group 9 and the Consilium had provided only an essential structure and "a collection of possibilities," not only could the full "liturgical treasury," the *thesaurus liturgicus* of the Roman Office (so often invoked by the reformers), have been preserved but regional episcopal conferences, monasteries, houses of apostolic religious, dioceses, parishes, families, and groups of all kinds could have provided for themselves Offices varying even structurally and better meeting their needs than the one Roman form with full advantage taken of its limited options. But as has so often been indicated in the foregoing chapters the overriding concern to provide for clerical spirituality, the fear to risk abandonment altogether of private recitation in favor of communal celebration lest clergy cease to pray, the fear of showing inconsistency ("today liturgists want this; tomorrow, something else"), and an interpretation of

SC that displaced in importance or largely ignored the implications of the articles cited above prevented Group 9 and the Consilium from opting for, perhaps even from ever considering, this approach—an approach that need not have gone beyond the norms of SC in that structures and content of the Roman Office would have been offered as models or resources.[20]

Even if such an approach were considered too bold there could have been offered at the conclusion of IGLH a series of provisions such as is found at the conclusion of the *praenotanda* to the other reformed rites. The latter explicitly provide for regional and cultural adaptation by episcopal conferences, and this they do sometimes quite liberally, as, for instance, in the rites for Christian initiation. No such provisions are found in IGLH. A limited choice of texts is allowed on certain occasions, but there is no clear provision for adapting structures such as allowing for abbreviation (or extension) of the psalmody at Lauds or Vespers, excluding reading of Scripture at those Hours, inserting the *lucernarium* in Vespers, using incense anywhere else but during the gospel canticle of the major Hours, or reversing the positions of intercessions and Lord's Prayer in those same Hours (a matter of prolonged debate in Group 9). Canon Martimort himself has acknowledged that providing for a just equilibrium between the given and the adaptable is difficult to realize. But it would seem that an excessive fear of what individuals or groups might do if left to make choices within broad norms has motivated the limited provision for adaptation in IGLH. Canon Martimort has written:

"Indeed, the liturgy being a common work as well as the celebration of the Christian mystery, it cannot be organized according to subjective motives, however laudable these may be. The great events of salvation, their preparation and their repercussions, which are the subject of the liturgical year, must absolutely engage every baptized Christian. Even the structure of liturgical celebrations responds to an internal logic that must not suffer disfigurement by arbitrary changes. One must not, for example, replace a biblical reading or psalm by a nonbiblical text, whatever its quality may be. That is why the General Instruction recalls very clearly some evident principles. In number 246 we read: 'The general arrangement of each Hour is not to be disturbed.' In numbers

245-47 it is clear which celebrations exclude any variation in the texts given. These particulars established, the General Instruction does allow some options within the Office provided those things that might provoke hesitation or uncertainty or degenerate into arbitrariness or bad taste are avoided."[21]

Canon Martimort adds that the final period of the Middle Ages was marked in many places by a serious liturgical decadence, which was partly the cause of the Protestant Reformation. This decadence, he says, was due to the biblical ignorance of clerics, the invasion of private devotions, the absence of a historical sense, bad taste, and an ignorance of liturgical structures. While there is no need today to remain in the rigidity of the Counter Reformation, the canon believes, yet to prevent such abuses from occurring again "the freedom to organize the liturgy ought to be contained within strict limits." The concern is certainly a valid one, but the means proposed to deal with it is questionable, for there existed generally in the Church, even in 1971 as IGLH was promulgated, sufficiently widespread sensitivity to and understanding of liturgical structures, the Scriptures, a historical sense, the place of private devotions in Christian life, and good taste to counter effectively over a period of time the arbitrariness and subjectivism feared by Canon Martimort. To say this is not to deny that widespread ignorance and lack of sensitivity also existed among both clergy and laity. But the corps of people educated in the history of the liturgy, liturgical theology, and pastoral liturgical practice was sufficiently large and strategically placed (in seminaries, diocesan offices, religious communities, etc.) to influence benignly the course liturgical practice would take in the years ahead. In fact, the spread by this corps of understanding of the liturgy and sensitivity to its structures and dynamics would seem to have done more than juridical norms, so often disregarded anyway, to curb abuses.[22]

With respect to what was accomplished regarding reform of the general structure of the Office, that is, the *horarium*, or arrangement of the Hours as a whole as well as the elements of the Hours and their arrangement within or distribution throughout the Hours, there can be little quarrel that it is simpler and more deferential to the needs, generally, of people in modern urban society than was the lengthy and complex general structure of the former Office. The very positive response, for example, to DSOD and to *Prière du temps présent* bear witness to this. But it would seem that this positive response was derived somewhat from a contrast between the burdensome effect the former Office produced and the less burdensome one of the reformed version. As sensitivity increases to the need for local and cultural adaptation or indigenization, there may be less satisfaction with aspects of the given structure and the limited provisions for its adaptation.

One witness of this dissatisfaction, which obviously reflects a broader discontent, is the rescript given by the Sacred Congregation of Religious and Secular Institutes to mendicant orders on recitation of the Office in common (May 31, 1969). While this rescript has to do with obligation to the entire Office and precedes the completion of the Roman reform, it implicitly witnesses to the lack of compatibility between maintenance of the structure of all the Hours (the minor Hours being almost certainly the focus) for some orders and congregations bound to choir and the contemporary demands made on these groups. The rescript acknowledges that the congregation "has received many petitions concerning the choral recitation of the divine office" and that it was necessary to set up "a commission expressly for this purpose and made up of five superiors general or their deputies." It then provides that (1) special general chapters may decide that the Office may be recited "in common" rather than "in choir"; (2) if a general chapter wishes to retain the obligation to choir, it may grant particular exceptions to that obligation and designate which Hour "may be recited in common rather than in choir"; (3) if any community is not able to pray all the Hours in choir or in common, the superior general with his council and according to circumstances and reasons approved by the general chapter can state which Hours must be recited in choir or in common, the individual religious remaining under the obligation to recite the other Hours in private.[23] Such tortured provisions would probably be unnecessary if a more radical revision of the *horarium* had been effected (such as the reduction of the three minor Hours to one middle Hour for all). Legislation regarding obligation, of course, could solve the problem, while reduction to one minor Hour would perhaps deprive some groups of a desired full complement of minor Hours. All this will be considered below in the evaluation of the structural reform of the minor Hours. The point here is that evidence of a grave difficulty in maintaining the traditional *horarium* existed at the time of the reform, and radical structural reform (e.g., abandonment of two minor Hours) might have eased that specific difficulty.

The essential structure of each of the Hours—hymn, psalmody, reading, prayers—has found few objectors to it. It is a traditional structure of Christian worship in that elements predominantly of praise and thanksgiving (hymn, psalmody) precede those that are primarily intercessory (prayers). But two difficulties arise from an examination of the work of Group 9 and the Consilium. The first concerns the decisions that rendered all the Hours uniform in structure, and the second has to do with the statement in IGLH that "the essential structure of this liturgy is a dialogue between God and people."[24]

What effectively rendered the structure of the Hours uniform was the decision, first for Lauds and Vespers, then for Compline, to move the hymn to the beginning of those Hours. The reasons cited for this move seem pastorally sound: to give "color" to the Hour and to set its tone or mood. Precedent was found for the move, at least for Lauds and Vespers, in the Milanese liturgy. But no consideration seems ever to have been given to why, structurally, the hymn at Lauds and Vespers came *after* (and in Compline, just before) the reading *(capitulum)*, whereas the hymn *began* the other Hours. Had the reformers taken more seriously the results of comparative structural analysis of liturgical units in the liturgies of East and West, they might have grasped the strong probability that the elements of traditional Roman Vespers in the first part of that Hour (variable psalmody and reading) derive from the monastic tradition of the Office, whereas elements in the latter part (responsory, hymn, versicle, intercessions) derive ultimately from the cathedral tradition. At the time of the reform Father Mateos (and later, Prof. Gabriele Winkler) made a strong case, on the basis of these elements in Roman *Vespers* and of their counterparts in other traditions, for the existence in Rome of a cathedral form of Vespers prior to the hybridization wrought by the urban monks. The first part of ancient Roman *Lauds*, however, retained a stronger link with the cathedral tradition by its use of selective, invariable psalmody. The hymn at Lauds, too, though introduced (as was the hymn at Vespers) through Benedictine influence, derived from the cathedral tradition, where it was usually not the first element of the Hour but followed at least the first part of the psalmody. By ignoring the findings of comparative analysis that were available to them and relying on an eclectic traditionalism (the precedent of the hymn beginning Milanese Vespers, the first part of which, incidentally, derives from the cathedral tradition, unlike Roman Vespers), the reformers showed themselves more innovative than traditional in repositioning the hymn at Lauds and Vespers. More significantly, however, they deprived themselves of a traditional basis in the Roman Rite itself for reestablishing, as was desired in some quarters, at least two forms of Vespers to meet the differing conditions of life for contemplative religious on the one hand and pastoral clergy and laity on the other. Certainly SC 89a (prescribing celebration of Vespers and Lauds as chief Hours) in conjunction with SC 90 (prescribing adaptation to profit *all*) and SC 14, 21, 26–27, with their emphasis on communal celebration and participation of all, might have been better fulfilled had serious and considered attention been given to the evidence of cathedral and monastic units already present in the structure of those Hours and had the suitability of their separation, revival, and enhancement in view of the multiplicity and variety of contemporary needs been debated. Professor Winkler has pointed out that, with the structure of Roman Vespers now identical to that of all the other Hours, the basic difference between the monastic and cathedral forms formerly reflected in the two parts of that Hour has been obscured. This obfuscation, wrought perhaps most notably by the transfer of the hymn to the beginning of the Hour, will not prevent future reform in which there is greater cognizance of monastic and cathedral units, but it continues the hybridization begun by the urban monks of Rome before Benedict's time—a hybridization common enough in the development of liturgical rites but often contributing to their popular irrelevance and eventual decay, as in the case of the Roman Office.[25]

The uniformity of structure in all the Hours is also the basis in IGLH 33 for a statement that "the essential structure of this liturgy is a dialogue between God and people." The final draft of IGLH, issued as Schema 362 (March 1970), expanded on this notion:

"The Liturgy of the Hours is structured according to its own laws. In a special way it combines those elements which are in other Christian celebrations, *namely, manifestation of God in the readings, praise and confession of God in psalms and hymns, supplication in prayers,* and so it is always arranged as follows: the opening hymn; psalmody; a shorter or longer reading of Sacred Scriptures; prayers.

"Whether it is celebrated in common or in private, the essential structure of this liturgy is a dialogue between God *who is revealed* and people *who by praising and beseeching respond."*[26]

It remains unclear why the additional (emphasized) phrases in this text were dropped from the definitive version in IGLH. Since the definitive text is not explicit about which elements "manifest God" and which are those manifesting human response, Canon Martimort and Professor Lengeling were asked if the reason the earlier phrases were eliminated was that they stated a theology that did not neatly fit the structure of the reformed Office. Did Group 9 proceed (as reports of their and the Consilium's sessions would seem to indicate) without much advertence to the underlying dynamics of the structure they were reforming? Professor Lengeling's response was negative. The dialogical conception, he said, was a principle guiding the whole reform from the beginning. He noted that this conception is expressed in SC 7, which affirms that the liturgy is an exercise of the priestly office of Jesus Christ in which God sanctifies and humans respond in worship. SC 5 indicates the priority of God's sanctifying action, and if the structure of the Office were to signify that ideally, readings (as manifesting that action) would precede hymn, psalmody, and prayers (manifesting human response) as in the ancient Liturgy of the Word for Good Friday. The reason some elements manifesting response (hymn, psalmody) precede that element manifesting God's action (reading) is psychological. People need to be motivated to celebrate the mystery. Canon Martimort, however, maintained that this dialogical conception cannot be pressed too far. There is a dialogue within the psalms themselves, he noted. In fairness to Professor Lengeling, it must be noted that he, too, had expressed a view similar to the canon's in acknowledging that each of the two aspects of the dialogue cannot be attributed exclusively to certain elements in the structure of the Office, although each element emphasizes one or other of those aspects.[27]

Without denying the essentially dialogical character of all Christian liturgy and thus of the Office, one must take note of some statements that suggest that differing needs of monastic communities and people (laity, pastoral clergy, active religious) may well demand differing structures for extraeucharistic communal prayer. Those for monks and other contemplatives would emphasize the sanctifying divine action, reflection on, and reception of it; those for people more actively engaged in the secular would emphasize worship as human response to God. With respect to the monastic Office and its relationship to monastic life, Father Adalbert de Vogüé has observed:

"The whole life of the monk is in essence a search for God, and effort at prayer. But in this continual search and effort the hours of the office mark the beats at which the monk can recollect himself. If need be, they relaunch the impetus of incessant prayer. Seen this way, the office is not one act of the monk among many, not even the principal or the essential one; it is simply a particular way of doing the unique spiritual activity which fills his whole day—a discontinuous, collective, regulated way which should sustain a life of prayer that is continual, private, and spontaneous.

"This organic relationship of the office to the rest of the monk's day appears more clearly still if we examine the contents of each. . . . [T]he ancient office was made up of psalms and *prayers*. Similarly, the monastic day consisted of manual work accompanied by 'meditation' and interspersed with prayers. It was customary for the cenobite and hermit always to accompany the activity of their hands with that of their mouths, that is, with the oral repetition of scriptural texts, which they called *meditatio*. The psalter was one of the favorite texts used for this exercise. Thus the monk was doing the same thing at work as at the office; in both the time flowed by in the continual recitation of Scripture, and especially of the psalms. Prayer was the response, both at work and at office, to *this incessant hearing of the word of God* [emphasis added]. At the office the prayer was said after each psalm during a period of time determined by the superior who concluded it; at work prayer came and went more freely as it pleased the one praying, and according to the possibilities his work allowed. . . .

"For analogous reasons the office is also in basic continuity with *lectio divina* and meals. During the two or three hours of daily *lectio* what is the monk doing but reading and listening to Scripture, learning it by heart or preparing to decipher it? The purpose of these studies is to furnish the memory with inspired texts to recite continually, either at the office or at work. Meals we know included reading then as now. But perhaps we do not grasp immediately the analogy established between the refectory, the oratory, and the workshop. The monk ate to the sound of reading, just as he worked while reciting texts, and what he did while eating and working, he continued at the work of God. From morning to night, during diverse activities, *hearing the word of God* [emphasis added] went on, arousing responsive prayer at more or less close intervals. The office was no exception to this rule. Rather than the irruption of the sacred into a profane time, it was the privileged moment when all business ceased and the *word was listened to more attentively* [emphasis added], and prayer responded more frequently and fervently."[28]

This view, in which the psalmody is Word of God to be heard, while modified somewhat, as Father de Vogüé acknowledges, in *The Rule of the Master* and in Benedict's *Rule*, would make the structural elements of the monastic Office, with the exception of silence, serve primarily to signify the divine action in its dialogical character. Is such a view significant for monastic life today? It would seem Father de Vogüé thinks so:

"The fact that Benedict does not refer to 'Pray without ceasing' in order to establish the prayer of the Hours, changes nothing in regard to the origin of this prayer. Even if relatively late authors such as the Master and Benedict make no mention of it, the scriptural word remains historically at the origin of the system of the Hours of the office. . . . This scriptural word has . . . played a decisive role in searches which were bound to end in the constitution of our office, and we must return to it if we wish to find again its profound meaning."[29]

In some contrast to the foregoing understanding of the Office in monastic circles, Fr. Carl Dehne has surfaced seven characteristics of modern popular devotions that also seem to have characterized the ancient cathedral Office from which the devotions seem to have derived and for which they substitute. Popular devotions, he says in his widely acknowledged study of the same, tend to be expressive, person centered, Christocentric, clear in expression, circular or spiraling in structure, highly ceremonialized, and invariable in form. With respect to the first of these characteristics he observes:

"The worshiper is the subject rather than the object. The devotional service is a vehicle which enables the worshiper to do something; it is not primarily a means of doing something to him. Its purpose is not to inform or to enthuse the Christian, but to provide a medium in which the reality of the Christian life already received and already enjoyed may resonate and be enhanced. The worshiper is a privileged person—a chosen and a choosing one. . . .

"Christians know what God has done in Jesus; they know his name. And so their praise and thanksgiving can be explicit, specific and personal. Christians know that they form the body of Christ, united in the triumphant Son of God. And so their intercession is privileged."[30]

After a description of the other characteristics, he concludes that popular, communal, extraeucharistic prayer must spring from the cathedral rather than the monastic tradition if the work of the Spirit throughout the centuries in the Church is to be taken seriously. He concludes:

"The services of the future will be celebrational rather than didactic, highly ritualized and with much song, obviously Christocentric, with relatively little text. They will be circular in structure, repetitious, with little variety. In other words the communal extraeucharistic prayer of ordinary Christians—if it is to exist at all—will look and feel more like the robust and gracious popular devotions of the recent past than the monumental and—for purposes of popular prayer—almost entirely useless books of the liturgy of the Hours."[31]

If this contrast in the *emphases* of monastic and cathedral communal prayer is correct, then the reformers of the Roman Office, by failing to scrutinize the structures they inherited for monastic and cathedral units, further monasticized reformed Lauds and Vespers rather than popularized them when they called for expansion of Vespers (and eventually of Lauds) by long reading and homily, especially when "the people" were present. And this they did in the mode of eclectic traditionalism by an appeal to practice in Byzantine Great Vespers and Milanese Vespers. But the presence of readings, at least, in these Offices would seem to be in units inherited either from cathedral Vigils (and thus not a *daily* popular Office) or from monastic practice.[32]

Thus, rendering Lauds and Vespers uniform in structure with the other Hours, which are of monastic origin, showed an inattentiveness to distinctive units within them, some monastic, some popular, the rehabilitation of which in two distinct structures, one for contemplative religious communities, the other for more actively engaged folk (laity, clergy, and religious), might have responded better to the nature and basic needs of these different groups than an obviously welcome simplification and more logical ordering (hymn, psalmody, reading, prayers) that glossed over those distinctions.

Options and choices regarding three elements pertaining to the structure of the Office as a whole call for some evaluation here—psalmody, readings, and responsories. Group 9 and the Consilium, by establishing the four-week cycle of psalms, faithfully executed the demand in SC 91 for their redistribution over a period longer than one week. In striving for this in several tentative arrangements, resulting finally in the four-week cycle, and in reducing the number and length of psalms in the individual Hours, they also undoubtedly fulfilled the needs of pastoral clergy and even monastic communities, so often expressed, for a reduction in the daily "task" (*pensum*) so that apostolic concerns might be better served and that a greater serenity in celebration of the Hours might foster richer prayer. The maintenance of antiphons and provision for psalm prayers and titles as aids to the Christian interpretation of the psalms cannot be disputed, at least theoretically, as structural elements helpful to most. The strophic division of the psalms and encouragement (IGLH 125) to use the antiphon given with a psalm as a refrain after each strophe can be welcomed as a mode favorable to popular celebration of the Hours. One cannot help but conclude, however, that the preservation of some lengthy antiphons (e.g., some of those for Lauds and Vespers in the Christmas season) not at all suitable for repeated refrains indicates that the desire for preservation of the "liturgical treasury" *(thesaurus liturgicus)* tended to obscure the implementation of the reforming principles in SC 14, 21, 26–27, and 90. Titles may be helpful to those who have Office book in hand, but book in hand may not be the most appropriate way for ordinary people to celebrate the Hours. Psalm prayers, too, may assist in uncovering meaning hidden in the psalms, but relegation of them for optional use to a supplementary volume that after twenty years still awaits publication as part of the *editio typica* of LH hardly suggests the reformers attached much importance to them.[33]

Preservation of the semblance of an integral Psalter and of the "continuous Psalter" *(psalterium currens)* in a minimally semi-continuous arrangement of psalms, especially in the Office of Readings and Vespers, undoubtedly pleased those who wished to see preserved these two traditional, monastic characteristics of the Roman Office. Msgr. Joseph Pascher has maintained that keeping the psalms as far as possible in their numerical order is a valuable principle "insofar as it eliminates arbitrary and subjective distributions." But this preservation coupled with limitation on choice of which and how many psalms one might use to replace those given for an Hour (IGLH 252) may hinder the development of forms of Lauds and Vespers appropriate to the needs of groups celebrating only those Hours if such limitations are adhered to literally. Adherence to the principle seems to have denied to Vespers a kind of progression in its structural elements that is more readily observable in Lauds, where the principle is hardly in evidence. This matter will be discussed below in the evaluation concerning Lauds and Vespers. But certainly the increase in selective psalmody in all the Hours, especially in Lauds and Compline, has obscured the semicontinuous arrangement and moved the Roman Office closer to the cathedral tradition, at least in this respect. The abandonment of three so-called imprecatory psalms and of difficult verses in other psalms has breached, as noted above, the age-old monastic principle that the integral Psalter be used over a determined period of time. The move indeed answered, at least partly, the desires of many for a Psalter cleansed of phrases difficult for a modern Christian to pray. While one can sympathize with the reformers' concern that this omission may further the use of a rationalistic principle of judgment on what is appropriate or not for Christain prayer and may lead to abandonment of more of the Psalter as at Taizé, one can also be comforted that this omission, too, has strengthened the precedent in the Roman Office for selective psalmody in keeping with the nature of the Hours and the condition of those praying the Hours. The establishment of precedent, which seems so important for any change in Roman tradition, may facilitate future reform of the Office for more popular celebration in accordance with the norms of SC cited above.[34]

There can be no disputing that retention of both short and long readings in the reformed Office with revision to render them somewhat more extensive and varied has answered the desire of many for better nourishment from the Scriptures within the Office. But one of the criticisms directed against the reformed Office by those using the experimental *Prière du temps présent* was that it provided a system of readings unrelated to those of the Mass, making unification in their spiritual life and assimilation of the Scriptures difficult. The critics asked that the possibility be given of utilizing in the Office the texts of the Lectionary for Mass to better achieve this unification and assimilation. While the criticism and suggestion are more a matter of content than of structure, it is interesting to note that in IGLH 46 such a possibility is allowed for the optional long reading at Lauds or Vespers. Group 9 and the Consilium in opting for the two-year cycle of scriptural reading to be used primarily in the Office of Readings but available also for Lauds or Vespers maintained another ancient principle of the Roman Office: the reading of the entire (or almost entire) Bible over a determined period of time. In the ancient Roman Office this period of time was a year. In the revised Office with the two-year cycle it is two years if the cycle is considered by itself and one year if, as intended by the reformers, it is used in conjunction with the cycle for Mass (with which that in the Office is coordinated). Despite the fact that readings are primarily from the monastic tradition of the Office, little objection has been offered to their modest use in popular celebration, since better acquaintance with the Scriptures among Catholics was a goal of the liturgical reform (SC 24, 35, 92). It is unfortunate, then, that the two-year cycle was reduced to one year for the sake of producing a manageable Breviary encouraging private recitation. This concern to provide a set of books, each of which might easily be held in hand for private use, thus had a deleterious effect on one of the more notable gains of the reform.[35]

Closely associated with the scriptural readings, of course, are the responsories. The decision to maintain them after scriptural readings in the Office of Readings and to provide them for the readings in Lauds and Vespers on the grounds of facilitating assimilation of the reading or transforming it into prayer is certainly laudable and perhaps serves that purpose for many. Objections to retention of responsories, as discussed in chapter 4, came first from those who found them, understandably, incongruous in private recitation. The proposal to introduce them into Lauds and Vespers brought protest and pleas for other types of response (simple verse, hymn, silence) even from those who appreciated the communal nature of the Office, a reminder of which responsories would be in private recitation. An effort to search out the original form and function of responsories by comparative analysis of units in various traditions might have yielded a consensus on their restoration as responsorial psalmody, perhaps in some instances entirely independent of readings or rehabilitated as responsorial psalms in cathedral forms of Lauds and Vespers or abandoned altogether. Fr. Paul Jasmer, for instance, has recently suggested on the basis of comparative analysis that the responsory following the reading in monastic Lauds and Vespers may be the remnant of responsorial psalmody from the *cathedral* tradition, which originally began those Hours. It was seen as related to the readings only when cathedral elements were juxtaposed with monastic elements putting responsory after reading. In its new position the responsory could be seen as related to the reading and an entirely new function assigned it. The reformers may be excused for not having determined the original function or functions of responsories, since scholarship had no definitive conclusions on this matter at the time of the reform. The point is, there is no evidence they even tried to ascertain their original meaning or function in order to see whether a more ancient practice might better serve the needs of their contemporaries than the current practice inherited from a more recent past in which responsories had degenerated to very brief forms.[36]

Another consideration regarding the structure of the Office as a whole has to do with the options and choices for organic union of the Hours among themselves or with Mass. With respect to union of one Hour with another, Group 9 rightly, out of respect for "the truth of the Hours" *(veritas horarum)*, would consider only union of the Office of Readings with another Hour. The time-consuming effort (1966–70) to find a way to unite the structure of an Hour with that of the Mass in order to satisfy the need many religious communities had of praying an Hour (usually Lauds or Vespers) at the time of the community's Mass produced a mode of organic union that must be said to truncate the structure of the Hour in favor of that of the Mass. While such an arrangement may serve convenience and even be found agreeable, it respects neither the proper character of the Hour nor that of the Mass. Group 9, of course, found none of the options it considered entirely satisfactory. In the option it finally and reluctantly accepted, two structural elements of the Hour (hymn and concluding oration) that can best serve to relate the Hour to its proper time of day may (in the case of the hymn) or must (in the case of the oration) be eliminated when the Hour is joined to Mass. The introductory rite of the Mass, already overburdened in the opinion of some with too many elements, can become increasingly so (even with penitential rite omitted) when the psalmody of an Hour is added. A thorough reconsideration of the relationship of the Liturgy of the Hours to Eucharist in the whole tradition, East and West, might better have served the reform of both Office and Mass than an unquestioning assumption of the medieval and modern practice of daily celebration of both and, consequently, of an intrinsic connection understood to exist between them. But such a reconsideration could not be expected from Group 9 (and perhaps not from Group 15 [general structure of the Mass]) given Canon Martimort's and others' assumption about the necessity of daily Mass in conjunction with Office.[37]

Finally, a word must be said about provision for periods of silence as structural elements in the Hours. Although apparently not much discussed in Group 9 and plenary sessions of the Consilium before it was reached, the decision to allow, even to encourage, short periods of silence after psalms and readings was widely appreciated, according to CNPL, by users of the French experimental Office. Silence after the psalms is, according to Father de Vogüé, an essential element in the monastic Office, and thus its reintroduction into the Roman Office even on an optional basis contributes to its monastic cast. But periods of silence undoubtedly are a boon to personal prayer and provide a more peaceful rhythm within an Hour than a continuous verbal utterance can. This would seem to be the case even in popular celebrations, as the experience of many with regard to periods of silence in the Liturgy of the Word at Mass can attest.[38]

The Structure of the Individual Hours

In the evaluation of the options and choices available to or considered by the reformers of the Office with respect to the structure of the individual Hours, those Hours that have an identical structure and that were considered together in the process of the reform will be considered together here: (1) Lauds and Vespers, and (2) the minor Hours. The evaluation will conclude with (3) Office of Readings, and (4) Compline.

Lauds and Vespers. The initial effort of Group 9 to fulfill SC 89a, which called for Lauds and Vespers to be considered and to be celebrated as the "the double hinge" *(duplex cardo)*, the chief Hours of the entire Office, was justly challenged in 1965, and the responsiveness of the Group to the criticism did produce a basic structure (hymn, psalmody, reading, prayers) for these Hours that could lend itself to varied use, including communal celebration in religious communities, popular celebration, and private recitation. The movement from a proposed twofold structure for Vespers and an unrevised form for Lauds in which the number of psalms (five) was seen to constitute them as major Hours to a simpler structure in both Hours for all uses seems to have satisfied or at least mollified the critics. But a number of aspects of the reformed structure may be questioned in terms especially of their fulfilling the needs of ordinary people for communal prayer.

There is first the matter of provision for the differing needs of monastic or semimonastic communities and communities more actively engaged in the secular (parishes, communities of apostolic religious, etc.). This matter was addressed above in the discussion of the repositioning of the hymn in Lauds and Vespers, thus rendering these Hours identical in structure to the others, Compline initially excepted. Ironically, the original proposal for two forms of Vespers, one for the clergy and one for use with "the people," may not have been so far from the mark as critics thought in 1965. Certainly a grave misunderstanding on the part of the reformers as to what constituted the cathedral tradition led them to propose a form of popular Vespers that emphasized proclamation and exposition of the Scriptures (long reading, homily). Had they understood the different *emphases* and styles of the monastic and cathedral traditions well, they might have proposed two structures not only for Vespers but also for Lauds, with the difference that one, more reflective and emphasizing proclamation of the Word would be intended for monastic, contemplative communities and the other, more expressive and emphasizing worship as response to God would be intended for pastoral clergy and laity (including apostolic lay religious). But it would have undoubtedly been inconceivable for the reformers to have seriously entertained such an option when there was conviction that the Roman Office was one and must be reformed as one. Even the original proposal for two forms of Vespers suggested that underlying it was an understanding of the structure for popular participation as a modification only, for pastoral reasons, of the standard structure for clergy. The basic structure for Lauds and Vespers finally accepted might well have served both monastic and popular needs had it been left as a basic structure. It became problematic, especially for popular celebration, when details of this structure (number of psalms, form of intercessions, necessary inclusion of reading, ordering of concluding prayers) were spelled out for all uses—monastic, popular, private—and little room was given for adaptation in these details.[39]

The psalmody in Lauds and Vespers, for instance, must include three pieces. Certainly, the reduction to three from the originally proposed five pieces was welcome to most, but why no less or no more? The reformers initially thought five was too much for "the people" and three not enough for clergy. In reducing the psalmody to three pieces they seem to have been guided principally by the employment of a ternary structure of psalmody in Lauds and Vespers of the "short Breviaries" successfully used by many religious communities. But for those many for whom the language, style, and imagery in much of the psalmody is quite foreign, one judiciously selected psalm may be all that is profitable. If, as was stated by Monsignor Pascher and Canon Rose to the Consilium as early as 1964, there is nothing sacred about the number five, neither is there anything sacred for psalmody (despite precedents for ternary psalmodic structures) about the number three. Yet no provision to allow reduction in the psalmody to fewer than three pieces on the basis of local need and circumstances seems ever to have been considered, nor is any made in IGLH.[40]

Because traditionally Lauds has been less influenced by the monastic tradition, the reformers utilized selected psalmody for that Hour more strikingly than they did for Vespers and gave it a definite thematic progression. In first place is a morning psalm with reference to light, confidence, or repentance, climaxing in the third placed psalm of praise. The Old Testament canticle in second place seems to have been included more for the sake of tradition than of meaningfulness in the perceived progression from first psalm to third. In contrast, the structure of the psalmody at Vespers appears to have little thematic progression. Its traditional monastic form was respected in the final revision to the extent that the semicontinuous arrangement of psalms is more in evidence than at Lauds. With one exception a numerically lower psalm precedes a numerically higher psalm in the four-week cycle for Vespers, whereas there are six exceptions to that kind of arrangement in the same cycle for Lauds. Furthermore, in weeks 3 and 4 of the cycle only psalms from the traditional, monastic vesperal unit (109–46) are utilized. The eventual abandonment of Father Pinell's proposal (1965) that a traditional evening psalm always come first in Vespers undoubtedly contributed to a sense that there is little progression in the psalmody of Vespers in a way similar to that which can be perceived in Lauds. The concern of the reformers to keep a traditional sequence of Old Testament passages preceding New Testament passages and thus in Vespers to keep the order of psalmody, New Testament canticle, and gospel canticle provides some progression in Vespers. Ironically, however, the Hour the reformers perceived would be that involving the greatest popular participation, namely, Vespers, evidences a more monastic structure in its psalmody than that of the Hour of Lauds, which they initially perceived to lack such participation.[41]

The reform of the readings (capitula) to make them coherent, short, varied proclamations of Scripture was undoubtedly an improvement over the former arrangement. But the reform pertains more to content of the readings than to structure and is thus not of concern here. The decision to retain reading in Lauds and Vespers, however, was a choice to keep an element that entered the ancient Roman structure of these Hours from the monastic tradition and thus to retain a monastic cast to these Hours, which were intended to provide (according to the interpretation of the norms of SC given above) for popular celebration. In practice, however, the decision has been found to be of profit even in popular celebration.[42]

The retention of the gospel canticles and inclusion of the Lord's Prayer and intercessions in the major Hours can hardly be disputed as advantageous. The canticles in the reformed structure can be perceived as climactic elements of praise begun in the psalmody and might have been perceived more so had the short reading and responsory been eliminated. Disconcerting, perhaps, is the length of time Group 9 spent in debate about the position of the Lord's Prayer with respect to the intercessions when other questions of structure (e.g., what elements of the Roman Office are derived from monastic and what from cathedral traditions, and how utilize them best for different groups?) really demanded careful consideration. Cogent reasons for *Pater* before intercessions and for *Pater* after intercessions were given. As it turned out, the Our Father is followed anyway by the concluding oration, which, from a perspective of ancient Roman usage, gives to Lauds and Vespers two concluding prayers, one *(Pater)* derived from the practice of the basilican Office of the urban monks, the other (oration) derived from cathedral usage. Thus the conclusion of Lauds and Vespers, from a structural point of view, retains redundant elements. Of course, the inclusion for ferial days of orations derived from the ancient Sacramentaries for Morning and Evening Prayer, besides answering several preconciliar requests, served to relate the Hour to its respective time of day and thus to underscore nicely "the truth of the hours" *(veritas horarum)*, especially important for Lauds and Vespers, since they were the chief Hours in the cathedral tradition in which such relationship was emphasized. But this relationship derives more from the content of the prayers than from their position within the structure of the Hours, and so it is of less concern here.[43]

The intercessions in Lauds and Vespers, however, are of concern. The decision to restore them daily to the major Hours was certainly well taken in that this structural element, which served in cathedral Lauds and Vespers and in popular devotions following the demise of the cathedral Office, aids in restoring to the chief Hours a kind of prayer in keeping with their popular nature. A difficulty, however, attends their internal structure. Designed primarily on the model of "psalmic verses" *(capitella de psalmis)* in order to be congruous in both communal use and private recitation, they can also be used (fittingly only in communal celebration) after the model of a litany with an invariable response after each intercession. The attempt to blend two modes of intercessory prayer (*preces* and litany) was roundly criticized by Clement de Bourmont, monk of Bellefontaine, on the basis of experiment with the form before the definitive edition of LH. After noting the complexity in the intentions of the new intercessions conceived of as *preces* on the model of *capitella de psalmis* and the simplicity of intentions in a true litany allowing for more intense, personal prayer in the invariable response, he says:

"In choir, if there is a desire to adopt the form of refrain by the assembly and intentions by a soloist, it will be difficult to discover the characteristics of litanic prayer such as I have tried to describe and such as—I really believe—most communities expect, especially those that have the practice of the choral Office. How can a common theme of prayer be found in such diverse intentions that taken individually are excellent? A time of silence could occur after each intention before the refrain is uttered, and this practice is utilized effectively here and there. But apart from the fact that the refrain is thus rendered rather difficult and very much less natural because the rhythm is interrupted, the necessity to have recourse to a moment of silence in order to assimilate each intention shows to what mental gymnastics the community is again obliged. And if the refrain is forgone in order to utilize the intentions as given in the text, each intention being a dialogue between the president and the assembly, we are back again with the form of the *capitella*, which, practically speaking, means using the book for a prayer in which there is no freedom to follow an interior movement springing from a kind of 'resonant foundation' that a soloist can furnish in a litany."[44]

275

The difficulties Dom de Bourmont sees in the form of the intercessions are obviously the result of compromise on the part of the reformers to provide for both private recitation and communal celebration. While the form of the intercessions did please some, the validity of the monk's criticism may be corroborated by the fact that a great many unofficial forms of Morning and Evening Prayer employ a litanic form for their intercessions.[45]

The minor Hours. The major structural question regarding the minor Hours was, of course, whether they should be retained (or, at least, reduced to one) within the structure of the Hours as a whole. Aspects of this question were considered above in evaluation of the process and of the structure as a whole. A sharper focus on the question is in order here.[46]

The desire for some radical modification in the minor Hours surfaced, as described in chapter 2, in both the Pian reform and in the liturgical commission preparatory to Vatican Council II. The compromise represented in SC 89e (all minor Hours in choir; one Hour permitted outside choir) challenged Group 9 and the Consilium to produce an arrangement whereby those not obliged to all the Hours would not regularly omit the psalms in the missed Hours. Canon Martimort's solution, eventually adopted by the Consilium, whereby the gradual psalms, repeated elsewhere in the *cursus,* could be used in the optional Hours was reasonable. Although when viewed by itself this has seemed to some a complex solution, it must be considered simple when compared to the early attempts, described in chapter 4, both to preserve all the minor Hours and to provide that those bound to only one minor Hour use the integral Psalter. The radical solution, persistently advocated by Father Bugnini and supported by Pope Paul VI, of reducing the minor Hours to one would have probably answered the desires of most communities and individuals bound to the Office but would have removed the possibility (so far as the official structure of the Roman Office is concerned) of celebrating more than one minor Hour. Canon Martimort's solution respected both tradition and SC 89e in maintaining all the Hours, solved the problem of providing the integral Psalter for all, and left open the possibility for any individual or group to use one, two, or three of the Hours. It was an ingenious compromise. The difficulty it created was to require groups and individuals bound to choir to seek needed relief through juridical means. The radical structural change, however, surely would have aided in shifting attention away from obligation, with which so much thinking regarding the Office before, during, and after the council was preoccupied to the detriment, so often, of an appreciation of it as prayer and stimulus to prayerful living. That reason in itself, respecting the primacy of the pastoral principle given in SC 14, certainly outweighs arguments for maintaining a traditional practice and providing for those who want more than one minor Hour, especially when nothing prevents the latter from providing that "more" on their own.[47]

Regarding the internal structure of the minor Hours, one matter seems significant of evaluation, and that is the matter of the length of the psalmody in them. Father Bugnini's suggestion to Canon Martimort after the experiment with SCDO in 1967 to reduce the three psalms (or sections of psalms) to one fixed, easily memorized psalm in the midday Hour was rejected by Group 9 for the reasons that one psalm or a few verses of a psalm would be insufficient to foster necessary recollection and that the Consilium had favored variety in the psalmody to offset weariness born of using fixed psalms. Certainly the assumption that one psalm is insufficient for recollection is gratuitous. The "more is better" syndrome that has plagued the history of the Roman Office is obviously a difficult one to be rid of. But the compilers of the Benedictine *Directory for the Celebration of the Work of God* (1976) faced the question of the relationship of quantity in the Office to quality of prayer and concluded:

"The quality of prayer assuredly does not depend on the number of psalms recited, nor on the number of Hours celebrated, but on the inner disposition of mind and heart. For this to be perfect it is required:
(1) that all should ardently desire to put prayer at the centre of community life, because this time of prayer is the *strong moment* in which, through dialogue with God, every work and occupation becomes a means of glorifying him;
(2) that all desire with equal fervour to make prayer the means of binding the community together into that unity to which it is called."[48]

Even if the members of Group 9 had nonmonastic pastoral clergy primarily in mind in their objection to curtailment of the psalmody (as was their wont), the principle enunciated in *The Directory* ought to have guided their deliberation and decision. It is not a new principle, and its application in essentials extends to all who pray communally or individually. As to using an unvarying psalm at the midday Hour, it seems Group 9 would have done well to examine the extent of the need Father Bugnini addressed before opting for desired variety here—a variety extensively provided in other Hours of the Office. Such a course of action would, it seems, have more strongly respected the principle in SC 90 that revision of the Office was to allow all to profit "more easily" from its "treasures."

Office of Readings. The preconciliar desire for a reduction in Matins and the conciliar request for longer readings and fewer psalms as well as for use at any time for that Hour (SC 89c) allowed Group 9 and the Consilium to fashion a structure for the Office of Readings similar to that for the other Hours. This they did in the face of ongoing requests to make of Matins little more than a collection of texts for spiritual reading. Rightly, they insisted on retention of psalmody as the structural element most expressive of the prayerful character of this Hour.[49]

Perhaps the greatest structural difficulty attending reform of Matins was not in its internal structure but in its relationship to the *horarium* itself. If not used as a nocturnal Vigil, this "roving Hour," with its emphasis on reading rather than psalmody, would seem something of an anomaly in a structured series of prayers attached to specific times of day and night in order to "sanctify time." But Group 9 and the Consilium could and did bypass that difficulty, since the decision to let it be movable and composed of long readings had been made by the council. What that decision seems to have encouraged, however, was not only the desire of many to make of it simply an exercise in spiritual reading, but also the desire to allow the readings to be freely chosen by individuals or groups. If the "Hour" had to exist at all in its movable condition, Group 9 and the Consilium appropriately resisted this desire for liberty of choice in its extreme form lest the Office of Readings be at the mercy of personal whim. The provision for optional Lectionaries was some concession to the cry for free choice.

While at times the insistence of Group 9 and the Consilium on the objective character of the Liturgy of the Hours, allowing little deviation from the given, seemed excessive, here, with respect to free choice of readings, the stand seemed sensible in that the scriptural reading, at least, should be cyclic, allowing numerous aspects of the mystery it proclaimed to be assimilated over the course of a year— something a free choice of readings was not likely to achieve.[50]

What could be criticized here was the tie made between the two-year and annual cycles of readings for the Office with those for the Mass. The presupposition that Office and Mass are necessarily connected may be understandable in view of long-standing practice in which they were conceived of as closely related, but the consultors, surely, need not have maintained that connection as necessary in the face both of ancient practice (where Office and Mass are independent) and of the possibility (more and more frequently an actuality since the council) of no daily Mass.[51]

Provision for extending the Office of Readings to constitute a Vigil for Sundays or feasts undoubtedly was a boon, as Canon Martimort intended, to contemplative groups bound to the Roman Office. It also provided to some extent, as noted in chapter 4, for the possibility of a restored, popular Sunday Vigil in the cathedral tradition as Fr. Juan Mateos had suggested in the early stage of the reform. The disadvantage of the structure of the extended Vigil for popular use may lie in its abundance of readings: scriptural (other than from gospel accounts), patristic, and gospel. Neither the ancient cathedral Vigil nor the ongoing expressive style of popular worship seems to call for much reading.[52]

The concern with the internal structure of the Office of Readings after the eighth plenary session of the Consilium (April 1967) ended with a choice for psalmody to precede readings rather than to alternate with them. The choice was undoubtedly the better one, since readings were to be followed by responsories anyway. The responsory fulfilled something of the function that the proponents of one form of the alternative (i.e., psalm after each reading) seem to have foreseen for the psalmody in their scheme, namely, to act as a kind of response to the biblical or patristic reading. The other form of the alternative (psalm before each reading) was dismissed as untraditional and as rupturing the movement of prayer. But the former arrangement of Nocturns, taken together, had such an internal structure, so psalm before reading at this Hour was not without precedent. As to rupturing the movement of prayer, one might note that prayer need not be confined exclusively to psalmody, orations, and periods of silence. In the very act of listening to readings one can be praying. Some consultors in Group 9 seemed prone to link certain human activities (e.g., listening, praying) too exclusively to specific structural elements (e.g., readings, psalmody). Certainly a mixture or amalgam of several such activities can occur in one structural item.[53]

The most troublesome of the elements in the Office of Readings seems to have been the hagiographic reading. The prolonged debate on whether to let this reading substitute for the patristic reading or be added to it on optional memorials in Ordinary Time (per annum) was probably more than bickering over insignificant details. At issue was the role of the cult of the saints in the Office. Primitively, of course, outside of certain Vigils there was no role for the cult of the saints within the Hours of the Office. With all due respect to Canon Martimort's concern that remembrance of the saints be maintained and encouraged, that remembrance might better have been left to the Mass or to a special Office in order to foster an understanding of the daily Office as a Liturgy essentially related to the daily passage of time, seen both as gift of God and memorial of the paschal mystery and not as necessarily connected with feasts and seasons. But the presuppositions, strongly entrenched, as noted above, were otherwise.[54]

Finally, the problems attending the disengagement of the invitatory from the Office of Readings would probably have been nonexistent or greatly reduced had the reformers been courageous and abandoned it altogether or integrated it within the Office of Readings or Lauds. That it was made optional, finally (IGLH 35), before Lauds in the face of continuing protest to its addition to that Hour if first in the day was appropriate. In view of the essentially popular nature of Lauds, the obligatory addition of the invitatory to it might have had the burdensome effect some of the reformers thought it would if it were simply added to that Hour. The invitatory should not encumber popular Lauds with its proper style, structure, and content distinct from those of the monastic Hour of Vigils. If the invitatory psalm had been incorporated as an integral introductory element in Lauds, as in the case of many modern

Offices, and the psalmody of the Hour reduced accordingly, it would surely have been more agreeable to those who criticized its simple addition to whatever the first Hour of the day might be.[55]

Compline. The two structural elements of Compline most disputed in Group 9 were the psalmody and the examen. Members of Group 9 again showed themselves more concerned initially with replicating traditional structure in the reformed Office than with heeding the call in SC 89b to fashion Compline as "a suitable prayer for the end of the day" when they originally opted for three psalms in that Hour despite the pleas for only one. This they did simply on the basis that three psalms were traditional in Roman and Benedictine practice. Since it had once been Roman and Benedictine practice, also, to use invariable psalmody at Compline, a bare majority of Group 9 were in favor of restoring it. But the advocates of variable psalmody could and did invoke tradition too, noting how difficult it would be to maintain the integral Psalter for all if invariable psalmody were employed. The inevitable compromises in 1964 culminated in allowing the choice of invariable psalmody, so long as the rubric permitting it gave notice of the Church's preference for the integral Psalter and its concession to the use of invariable psalmody only for pastoral reasons. All this seems scarcely to focus on a revision of Compline to be "a suitable prayer for the end of the day." The decision by the Consilium in 1967 in favor of the four-week Psalter and its permission to use each psalm more than once in the cycle cleared the way for a reduction of psalmody in Compline, often to one psalm, and the exclusion of its one-week cycle from the *psalterium currens* so that optional use of invariable psalmody every day for that Hour would deprive no one, theoretically, from exposure to the integral Psalter. Many conflicting desires were thus more or less satisfied through an artful compromise. The end result more nearly satisfies both SC 89b and some expressed contemporary needs, but not through bold, determined effort from the beginning to do so.[56]

The prolonged discussion on the placement of the examen within or without the formal structure of Compline yielded, of course, a decision that seems to have been overturned by Pope Paul VI when he scrutinized the final draft of IGLH. Reasons for the final decision to place the examen within the formal structure of Compline are not apparent, but then neither are those very clear for making it optional either before or after the Hour. Once again, some in Group 9 seemed more bent on justifying a place for the examen according to a precedent in some liturgical tradition (Milanese, Premonstratensian) than on appropriateness or adequacy for current needs. In any event, it would seem that a disproportionate amount of valuable time was spent in trying to determine the place of an *optional* structural element while structural (and other) matters of greater importance (e.g., the original shape and function of responsories, the presence of "debris" from cathedral and monastic traditions in the Roman Office, whether these remnants should be restored to their pristine condition, what function they should serve and why) were largely ignored.[57]

CONCLUSION

The structure of the Roman Office has from its earliest known and principal source, the basilican Office, been primarily a monastic one. Reforms from the thirteenth to the early twentieth century have never essentially modified its monastic character, exemplified especially in its weekly *cursus* of the integral Psalter and in at least a residual annual *lectio continua* of the Scriptures. A plethora of additional and entirely secondary elements added over the years rendered the Office complex and burdensome. Desired abbreviation was sometimes (e.g., in the reform of Pope Pius X) minimally achieved, but never were the two cardinal principles of this Office, namely, use of the integral Psalter weekly and reading of the Scriptures in the course of a year, abandoned, at least theoretically. While in reforms previous to that initiated by the Second Vatican Council the integral Psalter was maintained in practice, the scriptural readings were abbreviated and often displaced by hagiographic readings. In the postconciliar reform a semblance of the integral Psalter was maintained in a four-week cycle, while an annual cycle of reading the Scriptures was restored.

Projects of reform from the eighteenth to the twentieth century (from many of which came little or no effect) never proposed a radical structural reform that would ignore altogether the two principles—use of the integral psalter over a determined period of time and annual semicontinuous reading of the Scriptures. By the time of the Second Vatican Council, however, a better understanding of the origins of the Office and of its distinct monastic and cathedral forms was possible. It could even be demonstrated then that behind the Roman basilican Office there undoubtedly stood earlier, popular forms in the cathedral tradition that had left their mark on the urban monastic Office. But this understanding was not widespread, as is evident in the majority of interventions in the preconciliar commissions and on the council floor.

The reform of the Office proposed in chapter 4 of SC, while more extensive than those reforms preceeding it and generally understood to benefit primarily secular clergy with pastoral care, was yet simply a call to modify the basically monastic structure of the traditional Roman basilican Office. In the early stage of the reform undertaken by the Consilium, the desired norm would seem to have been an abbreviated but spiritually nourishing form of this heavily monastic Roman Office for use primarily in private recitation by secular clergy with pastoral care. While pleas were made in the course of the reform (especially in late 1965 and early 1966) for the establishment of an Office more suited to pastoral clergy (and, usually secondarily, to laity), there is little evidence to show, aside from Father Mateos' interventions, that the structure of that Office was conceived of as that for clergy and laity in the cathedral tradition. Rather, the various interventions, while pointing to the need to provide for widely differing groups in the Church, served only to broaden the perspective of the reformers to develop, within a strict interpretation of the norms of SC, chapter 4, a single structure out of the traditional monastic structure of the Roman Office more likely usable, with some adaptation of content, by all in the Church.

Significant structural reform of this Office, however, was in fact achieved through an admirable even if flawed collegial process from 1964 to 1971. It can indeed be said with Fr. Robert Taft: "The renewed structure represents in many respects a courageous break with the past. Problems—of language, length, a too-full monastic cursus, too many psalms in one week—were faced with imagination and resoluteness."[58] With Father Taft, too, one can agree that failure "to make a more radical break with not just the forms, but with the mentality of this past, has marred the recent reform of the Roman Office." But his judgment that "the problem with the new Roman *Liturgy of the Hours* is not structural" is surely an overstatement.[59]

While not the only problem with the reform, the revised structure must be included as one of them. Basically, as the foregoing chapters have shown, by virtue of compromises achieved in the study groups and plenary sessions of the Consilium, the arrangement of the Hours as a whole and the essentials of the identical internal structure of each Hour do lend themselves to different uses of the Office. But taken as given, even with permitted limited options and adaptations utilized, these heavily monastic structures, albeit interwoven with elements from the cathedral tradition, fail to a greater or lesser extent to provide for those essential differences among the varying groups in the Church (e.g., monks, mendicants, apostolic religious, parishes, student groups, families) whose very life conditions and occasions for prayer would best shape coherent structures for such within the Church's various traditions—and, yes, even ancient diverse Roman practices—of daily, public, communal prayer.

Fr. Laurence Mayer, in speaking of daily prayer in the parish, has stated the desirable for communal prayer in that setting. The principles he invokes, however, can have wide application:

"A lack of coherent structure in the official forms is one of the principal difficulties in reestablishing a parish daily prayer. In order to work well as a group activity, a basic structural integrity is needed in which the ritual is unified and flows from the occasion for the prayer. In the case of a daily prayer, the occasion for prayer is simply the time of day. Text and action and material symbols must then have recognizable and appropriate links to one another. These are to be suggested from within rather than through an abstract ordering for the sake of some intended meaning.

"Parish daily prayer can flourish among contemporary Christians and still be in continuity with the larger traditions of the church. The reason *these* people gather lies in their shared experience of an event, a mystery heralded in the time of day. The event itself suggests certain actions and responses, ritual expressions and symbols, some of which are so powerful and basic to the human condition that they transcend time and place in their relevance. . . . The 'things' of prayer come from the experiences of life."[60]

No one, however, could have reasonably expected the majority of the reformers of the Office to have allowed for great diversity, especially of structure (unless as a concession to some pastoral need), given the history of the Roman Office, previous attempts at its reform, the circumstances of their time, their personal convictions, their interpretation of SC, and their admirable fidelity to that interpretation. But neither can it be denied that the possibility for radical structural reform was available to them and strongly urged. That they chose to go the way of compromise and not of boldness has been a disappointment to many, but it should not detract entirely from the substantial reform they laboriously did achieve. Imaginative implementation of the given structure together with unofficial development of new structures will provide the bases for more felicitous, official provision in the future for structural reforms within the Roman tradition.

Notes

PREFACE

1. Information given to the author by a representative of Catholic Book, New York, July 1993.

2. For a report on the initial phase of the revision of the English edition of the Liturgy of the Hours, see the *1990–1991 Report of the Episcopal Board to the Member and Associate-Member Conferences of the International Commission on English in the Liturgy*, 7.

3. *Notitiae* 1 (1965) 152–56, 206–14; 2 (1966) 3–5, 313; 3 (1967) 141–44, 415–16; 4 (1968) 99–113, 182, 350; 5 (1969) 436–41; 6 (1970) 222–31.

4. Pierre Jounel, "La liturgie des heures dans le renouveau liturgique de Vatican II," *Notitiae* 10 (1974) 310–20, 334–43.

5. E. G. Lengeling, "Les options générales de la nouvelle liturgie des heures," *La Maison-Dieu* 105 (1971) 7–33 (hereafter cited as LMD).

6. A. G. Martimort, "L'"Institutio Generalis' et la nouvelle 'Liturgia Horarum,'" *Notitiae* 7 (1971) 218–40. The section on the structure of the Hours appears on pp. 230–32.

7. A. G. Martimort, "The Liturgy of the Hours," *The Liturgy and Time*, trans. Matthew J. O'Connell, The Church at Prayer 4. (Collegeville: The Liturgical Press, 1986) 153–275.

8. Vincenzo Raffa, "Dal Breviario del Quignonez alla Liturgia delle Ore di Paolo VI," *Liturgia delle ore*, ed. Ferdinando dell Oro (Torino-Leumann: Elle di Ci, 1972) 289–363.

9. J. D. Crichton, *Christian Celebration: The Prayer of the Church* (London: Chapman, 1976). He considers the structure on pp. 12–13 and 62–75.

10. W. Jardine Grisbrooke, "A Contemporary Liturgical Problem: The Divine Office and Public Worship," *Studia Liturgica* 8 (1971–72) 129–68; 9 (1973) 3–18, 81–106. The structure of the revised Roman Office is critically examined in vol. 8, pp. 155–59.

11. Thaddaeus Schnitker, *Publica Oratio: Laudes matutinae und Vesper als Gemeindegottesdienste in diesem Jarhundert* (Münster in Westfalen, 1977) 34–69.

12. Daniel de Reynal, *Théologie de la liturgie des heures* (Paris: Editions Beuchesne, 1978).

13. Annibale Bugnini, *The Reform of the Liturgy: 1948–1975,* trans. Matthew J. O'Connell (Collegeville: The Liturgical Press, 1990). The structural reform of the Office is considered on pp. 491–516.

14. Robert Taft, *The Liturgy of the Hours in East and West* (Collegeville: The Liturgical Press, 1986) 313–17.

CHAPTER 1:
THE STRUCTURE OF THE ROMAN OFFICE
FROM THE SIXTH TO THE TWENTIETH CENTURY

1. For orations in the Verona Sacramentary see L. C. Mohlberg and others, *Sacramentarium Veronense,* Rerum Ecclesiasticarum Documenta, Series major, Fontes 1 (Rome: Herder, 1956) nos. 587–93, pp. 75–76 (= *Orationes matutinas vel ad vesperum);* for the orations in the seventh-century Gelasian Sacramentary see L. C. Mohlberg and others, *Liber Sacramentorum Romanae Aeclesiae ordinis anni circuli (Cod. Vatican. Regin. lat. 316),* Rerum Ecclesiasticarum Documenta, Series major, Fontes 4 (Rome: Herder, 1960) nos. 1576–94, pp. 230–31 (= *Orationes ad matutinas, Orationes ad vesperum).* On the distinction between the cathedral and monastic traditions of the Office see, e.g., Anton Baumstark, *Comparative Liturgy,* rev. ed. (London: Mowbray, 1958) 111–29; Juan Mateos, "The Origins of the Divine Office, *Worship* 41 (1967) 477–85; William G. Storey, "The Liturgy of the Hours: Cathedral versus Monastery," *Christians at Prayer,* ed. John Gallen (Notre Dame: University of Notre Dame Press, 1977) 61–82; Paul Bradshaw, *Daily Prayer in the Early Church,* Alcuin Club Collections 63 (London: Alcuin/SPCK, 1981) 72–149; Robert Taft, *The Liturgy of the Hours in East and West* (Collegeville: The Liturgical Press, 1985) 31–213.

2. See Pierre Salmon, "La prière des heures," *L'Église en prière,* 3rd ed., ed. A. G. Martimort (Paris: Desclée, 1965) 840 (hereafter cited as EP); *The Breviary Through the Centuries,* trans. Sr. David Mary (Collegeville: The Liturgical Press, 1962) 28–41; Juan Mateos, "La vigile cathedrale chez Egerie," *Orientalia Christiana Periodica* 27 (1961) 305–6; A. de Vogüé, *La Règle de saint Benoît,* Sources chretiénnes 185 (Paris: Les Editions du Cerf, 1972) 5:474–78 (hereafter cited as de Vogüé, RB).

3. On the possibility of the third nocturn of Sunday Vigils in RB deriving from the cathedral Vigil, see Mateos, "La vigile," 305–10; de Vogüé, RB 5:474–79. On the probable premonastic existence of the psalmody for Lauds; on the hymn, gospel canticles, and intercessions reflecting the cathedral tradition, and RM and RB as witnesses respectively to a "pre-classic" and a "classic" Roman Office, see de Vogüé, RB 5:484–98; Nathan Mitchell, "The Liturgical Code in the Rule of Benedict," *RB 1980: The Rule of St. Benedict in Latin and English with Notes,* ed. Timothy Fry and others (Collegeville: The Liturgical Press, 1981) 389–400. On the responsory and verse as possibly remnants of responsorial psalmody in the cathedral tra-

dition see Paul Jasmer, "A Comparison of Monastic and Cathedral Vespers up to the Time of St. Benedict," *The American Benedictine Review* 34 (1983) 355–60; and (for Vespers) Gabriele Winkler, "Über die Kathedralvesper in den verschiedenen Riten des Ostens und Westens," *Archiv für Liturgiewissenschaft* 16 (1974) 98–102.

4. On the monastic tradition of the Office, see Mateos, "The Origins," 481–82, 484–85. On the early Roman distribution of the psalms see Mitchell, "The Liturgical Code," 399, and Joseph Pascher, "Der Psalter für Laudes und Vesper im alten römischen Stundengebet," *Münchener theolgische Zeitschrift* 8 (1957) 255–67; Pascher, "Zur Frühgeschichte des römischen Wochenpsalteriums," *Ephemerides Liturgicae* 79 (1965) 55–88. On the modification of the primitive scheme before RM and RB, Adalbert de Vogüé writes: "The canons' office and the monks' prayer by no means fall under the sanction of ecclesiastical authority by the same title or in the same degree. In the first case, it is normal that the hierarchy control a form of worship which it has taken on. In the second, a great freedom belongs to societies whose true end is not to celebrate public worship before men in the name of the Church, but to lead their members to the secret and personal realization of 'Pray without ceasing' by means of a communitarian pedagogy.

"Admittedly these distinctions were soon more or less effaced to the extent that a type of monastery centered on serving the sanctuary and the task of worship grew up, especially in frankish, anglo-saxon, and germanic countries. Even at Rome the basilica monasteries of the fifth and sixth centuries already doubtless represent a compromise of this sort between the monastic ideal and liturgical ministry. Certain traits of the office in the Master and Benedict show the clerical influences undergone in this hybrid milieu. But the rural communities envisaged by our two rules remain the purely monastic type. There the office keeps its primitive aspect as domestic prayer, without reference to any ecclesiastical responsibility." *The Rule of St. Benedict: A Doctrinal and Spiritual Commentary*, trans. J. B. Hasbrouck, Cistercian Studies Series 54 (Kalamazoo: Cistercian, 1983) 132–33. See also de Vogüé, RB 5:545–54 on the weekly distribution of the Psalter in the Roman Office and in RB.

5. Michel Andrieu, Les *"Ordines romani" du haut moyen âge* (Spicilegium Sacrum Lovaniense, Études et documents, fasc. 24) 3: *Les textes* (suite) (*Ordines XIV–XXXIV*) (Louvain: "Spicilegium Sacrum Lovaniense" Administration, 1951) 40–41. Cf. also *Ordines XII–XIIIC*, which indicate the arrangement of readings at Vigils in the Roman monastic Office of the basilicas, probably of St. Peter's and of the Lateran in the eighth century (Andrieu, Les *"Ordines"* (fasc. 23) vol. 2: *Les textes* (*Ordines I–XIII*) (Louvain, 1948) 452–514. Cf. also Pierre Salmon, "La prière des heures," 848; A. G. Martimort, "The Liturgy of the Hours, *The Church at Prayer*, The Liturgy

and Time 4, ed. A. G. Martimort, trans. Matthew J. O'Connell (Collegeville: The Liturgical Press, 1983) 222–27.

6. On the psalmody, introduction, Old Testament canticle, *capitulum*, and hymn see de Vogüé, RB 5:484–98, 539. On the hagiographic readings see B. de Gaiffier, "La lecture des Actes des Martyrs dans la prière liturgique en Occident," *Analecta Bollandiana* 72 (1954) 134–66; Andrieu, *Les "Ordines"* 2:454, 466. Cf. also Martimort, "The Liturgy of the Hours," 226. On the *Pater* see Salmon, "La prière," 851; Martimort, "The Liturgy of the Hours," 229–30; Mitchell, "The Liturgical Code," 392, 397.

7. Salmon, "La prière," 853–55; J. D. Crichton, "The Office in the West: The Early Middle Ages," *The Study of Liturgy*, ed. Cheslyn Jones and others, rev. ed. (New York: Oxford University Press, 1992) 424–25.

8. J. M. Hanssens, ed., *Amalarii episcopi opera liturgica omnia*, Studi e Testi 139–40 (Vatican City: Biblioteca Apostolica Vaticana, 1948–50) 2 (1948) 403–57; 3 (1950) 19–37; Pierre Salmon, *L'Office divin au moyen âge: Histoire de la formation du bréviaire du IXe au XVIe siècle*, Lex orandi 43 (Paris: Les Éditions du Cerf, 1967) 33 (hereafter cited as ODMA). For *Ordo XII* see Andrieu, *Les "Ordines"* 2:459–66.

9. Summary by Salmon in ODMA, 33–38. Reference to versicle with incense at Vespers in Amalarius, *Liber officialis* 4.7.19 (Hansenns, *Amalarii* 2:435). Cf. also Amalarius, *Liber de ordine antiphonarii*, chs. 1–6 (Hanssens, *Amalarii* 3:13–15, 19–37); *Liber officialis*, bk. 4, chs. 1–12 (Hanssens, *Amalarii* 2:403–57); *Ordo XII* (Andrieu, *Les "Ordines"* 2:459–66); Winkler, "Über die Kathedralvesper," 100–101.

10. The *Officium capituli* existed at least from the time of Chrodegang (d. 766) as a monastic Office done in a chapter hall after Prime or Terce. Various forms of it apparently prevailed. Chrodegang's version involved a sermon, reading of the Martyrology, the verse *Pretiosa*, the prayer *Sancta Maria*, prayer for the sanctification of work, and chapter of faults. On this see Salmon, "La prière," 856. Regarding remnants of cathedral Vespers in the Roman scheme see Martimort, "The Liturgy of the Hours," 250; Mateos, "The Morning and Evening Office," *Worship* 42 (1968) 41–46; Winkler, "Über die Kathedralvesper," 100–101. On the introduction of the hymn into the Roman structure, see ODMA, 90; de Vogüé, RB 5:496–98.

11. Andrieu, *Les "Ordines"* 2:464. Cf. also ODMA, 36.

12. ODMA, 96–100; Salmon, "La prière," 880–61; *The Breviary*, 74–78; Martimort, "The Liturgy of the Hours," 221–22, 226.

13. ODMA, 100–101; 103; Baümer-Biron, *Histoire du bréviaire* (Paris: Letouzey et Ané, 1905) 1:367–68; Pierre Batiffol, *History of the Roman Breviary*, rev. 3rd ed., trans. A. M. Y. Baylay (London: Longmans Green, 1912) 135–45.

14. ODMA, 101–2; Baümer-Biron, *Histoire* 1:365–66.

15. ODMA, 101; Batiffol, *History*, 140.

16. See Salmon, "La prière," 857-58; S. J. P. van Dijk and J. H. Hazelden, *The Origins of the Modern Roman Liturgy* (London: Darton, Longman & Todd, 1960) 20-21; Mario Righetti, *Manuale de storia liturgica*, 3rd ed. (Milan: Editrice Ancora, 1969) 2:647-48.

17. ODMA, 149-50; Batiffol, *History*, 170-72; Martimort, "The Liturgy of the Hours," 252-53; van Dijk and Hazelden, *The Origins*, 20, 24-25.

18. ODMA, 168-69; Salmon, *The Breviary*, 77-83; J. W. Legg, *The Second Recension of the Quignon Breviary*, Bradshaw Society, vol. 42 (London: Harrison & Sons, 1912) 2:1-4.

19. Salmon, *The Breviary*, 107-12.

20. Legg, *Second Recension* 2:1-18; ODMA, 171-78; Salmon, *The Breviary*, 13-22.

21. Legg, *Second Recension* 2:39; Vincenzo Raffa, "Dal Breviario del Quignonez alla Liturgia delle Ore di Paolo VI," *Liturgia delle ore: Documenti ufficiali e studi*, Quaderni de Rivista Liturgica 14, ed. Ferdinando dell Oro (Torino-Leumann: Elle di Ci, 1972) 290-91 (hereafter cited as LDO).

22. Raffa, "Dal Breviario," 294-312.

23. For the contents of the second recension see Legg, *The Second Recension of the Quignon Breviary*, Bradshaw Society, vol. 35 (London, Harrison & Sons, 1908) 1. A detailed analysis and comparison of the various elements of both recensions is given in Legg, *Second Recension* 2:33-61.

24. Raffa, "Dal Breviario," 318-20; J. A. Jungmann, "Why Was Cardinal Quignonez' Reformed Breviary a Failure?" *Pastoral Liturgy* (New York: Herder & Herder, 1962) 200-214.

25. See Raffa, "Dal Breviario," 290-91. Canon Martimort asserted to this author that Quignonez's Breviary exerted no influence on post-Vatican II reform of the Office. Interview in Toulouse, France, April 19, 1983.

26. Raffa, "Dal Breviario," 320-40; Salmon, "La prière," 871-72.

27. Salmon, "La prière," 872-77.

28. Henri Leclercq, "Liturgies neo-Gallicanes," *Dictionnaire d'archéologie chrétienne et de liturgie*, ed. F. Cabrol and H. Leclercq (Paris, 1907-53) 9:2, cols. 1694-1705; Baümer-Biron, *Histoire* 2:330-31; Batiffol, *History*, 236-46; Prosper Gueranger, *Institutions liturgiques* (Paris: Debecourt, 1841) 2:304-12.

29. See Storey, "The Liturgy of the Hours: Cathedral Versus Monastery"; "Parish Worship: The Liturgy of the Hours," *Worship* 49 (1975) 3-5; George Guiver, *Company of Voices: Daily Prayer and the People of God* (New York: Pueblo, 1988) 115-46.

30. Batiffol, *History*, 246-83, 296-99.

CHAPTER 2:
DEVELOPMENTS IN THE TWENTIETH CENTURY
1. Salmon, "La prière," 876-77; Batiffol, *History*, 236-99.

2. Callewaert, *Liturgicae Institutiones: De Breviarii Romani Liturgia*, 2nd ed. (Bruges: Beyaert, 1939) 2:84.

3. Batiffol, *History*, 313–14.

4. Ibid., 315; Salmon, "La prière," 878.

5. Callewaert, *De Breviarii*, 84–85; Taft, *The Liturgy of the Hours*, 312; Salmon, "La prière," 877–78.

6. See Batiffol, *History*, 304–13; Callewaert, *De Breviarii*, 86. For details on these arrangements, which do not pertain directly to the structure of the Office, see Raffa, "Dal Breviario," 339.

7. Salmon, "La prière," 878; Martimort, "The Liturgy," 222.

8. A. G. Martimort, "Structure et lois de la célébration liturgique," EP, 73; A. Frutaz, *La Sezione storica della Sacra Congregazione dei Riti, origini et methodo di lavoro* (Vatican City: Tipografia poliglotta, 1963); Frederick R. McManus, *The Congregation of Sacred Rites* (Washington: The Catholic University of America Press, 1954) 23–44, 156. Cf. also Theodor Klauser, *A Short History of the Western Liturgy*, 2nd ed., trans. J. Halliburton (New York: Oxford University Press, 1979) 129–35.

9. A. Bugnini, *The Simplification of the Rubrics*, trans. L. Doyle (Collegeville: Doyle & Finegan, 1955); *The Reform of the Liturgy, 1948–1975* (Collegeville: The Liturgical Press, 1990) 6–7 (hereafter cited as RL); P. M. Gy, "Projets de reforme du bréviaire," LMD 21 (1950) 111.

10. For a listing of some of the projects and a summary of the more significant ones, see Gy, "Projets," 111–28.

11. "Il faut même dire, que l'histoire de l'office divin est actuellement un champ laissé presque entièrement en jachère par les historiens. Beaucoup de travail, et d'abord de bons ouvriers sont nécessaires avant qu'on puisse raisonnablement envisager de toucher à la structure du Bréviaire." Gy, "Projets," 126.

12. Ibid., 127. Fischer's proposal appeared first in *Trierer Theologische Zeitschrift* 59 (1950) 14–26 and was published later separately as *Brevierreform* (Trier: Paulinus-Verlag, 1950).

13. *A Short Breviary for Religious and the Laity*, ed., monks of St. John's Abbey (Collegeville: The Liturgical Press, 1941). By 1944 it was in its third edition, apparently because, as the abbot of St. John's inferred in the prefaces to the second and third editions (1942 and 1944), the world war was drawing many to pray according to the mind of the Church. By 1951 *A Short Breviary* had gone through five editions. It was reedited by William Heidt in 1954 under the same title in complete and abridged editions. These two forms were in their third edition by 1962 and continued to sell until the publication in 1976 of the one-volume English edition of the new Office entitled *Christian Prayer*.

14. This summary is based on the description and evaluation of short Breviaries provided by Herman Schmidt in his *Introductio in liturgiam occidentalem* (Rome: Herder, 1960) 472–81.

15. See ch. 4, pp. 86–90, 104–5.

16. See RL, 6–10.

17. Ibid., 7–8. The commission consisted initially of Clement Cardinal Micara, prefect of SCR; Msgr. Alfonso Carinci, secretary of SCR; Ferdinando Antonelli, relator general of the historical section of SCR; Joseph Löw, vice relator of the historical section; Anselm Albareda, prefect of the Vatican Library; Augustine Bea, rector of the Pontifical Biblical Institute; and Annibale Bugnini, editor of *Ephemerides liturgicae*. Added in 1951 was Msgr. Enrico Dante of SCR; in 1960, Msgr. Pietro Frutaz also of SCR; Luigi Rovigatti, parish priest; Msgr. Cesario D'Amato, abbot of St. Paul's; and Carlo Braga. Gaetano Cardinal Cigognanni replaced Cardinal Micara in 1953 when the latter became cardinal vicar of Rome. This commission held eighty-two meetings from June 22, 1948, to July 8, 1960, and worked in the utmost secrecy. It enjoyed the full confidence of Pope Pius XII, who was kept informed of its progress on a weekly basis, especially by Father Bea, who was the pope's confessor. The first major result of the work of this commission was the restoration by the Pope in 1951 of the Easter Vigil, then in 1955, of a restored order for the Liturgies of Holy Week. See RL, 8–10.

18. MRL, 169–304.

19. Ibid., 201–11.

20. Ibid., 212–68.

21. Ibid., 270–86. Various parts of the Roman Breviary (ordinary, Psalter, proper of time, proper of saints) were also discussed briefly. The common of saints was considered at length and proposals made to simplify and systematize it better. See especially MRL, 302. For a convenient summary of the history of elements introduced late (thirteenth century and later) into the Roman Office, see Bugnini, *The Simplification*, 75–93.

22. The responses of Jungmann, Capelle, and Righetti for those proposals of MRL pertaining to the Office were published in MRL, Suppl. 2 (1950) 40–62.

23. *Acta Apostolicae Sedis* 47 (1955) 218–24 (hereafter cited as AAS).

24. SCR, "Decretum generale de rubricis ad simpliciorem formam redigendis," AAS 47 (1955) 219. Annibale Bugnini, in his commentary on this simplification of rubrics, notes also that the simplification does not embrace all the aspects deserving reform but only those most obvious and easiest to implement. See his *Simplification*, 20–22.

25. MRL, Suppl. 4 (1957) 5–7, 12–16. When there was no response to the

first appeal, Cardinal Cicognani sent a brief letter on January 3, 1957, to the metropolitans requesting the same information he had asked for in May. See MRL, Suppl. 4, 6–7.

26. MRL, Suppl. 4, 12–16.

27. *The Assisi Papers: Proceedings of the First International Congress of Pastoral Liturgy, Assisi-Rome, September 18–22, 1956* (Collegeville: The Liturgical Press, 1957) v–viii (hereafter cited as *Assisi Papers*). The papers concerning historical questions on the Office delivered at the scholars' meeting before the Assisi Congress were published in *Brevierstudien*, ed. Josef Jungmann (Trier: Paulinus-Verlag, 1958). Topics considered were the Psalter of the Roman Office (Joseph Pascher), the premonastic morning Hour (Josef Jungmann), reform of the patristic readings (Hugo Rahner), intercessions of the people in the Office (Balthasar Fischer), The Office and popular devotions (Theodor Schnitzler), the obligation to the Office (Pierre Salmon), and the Office in the Oriental Rites (Alphons Raes).

28. Giacomo Cardinal Lercaro, "The Simplification of the Rubrics and the Breviary Reform," *Assisi Papers*, 211–12.

29. Ibid., 213.

30. On the reforms urged in the council and in the postconciliar commission, see below, pp. 70–72; ch. 4, pp. 110–16; ch. 5, pp. 207–32.

31. Bugnini, "The Simplification," 213–17.

32. See Gy, "Projets," 110–28; see also above, pp. 18–20; SCR, "Decretum generale quo novus rubricarum breviarii ac missalis Romani codex promulgatur" and "Rubricae breviarii et missalis Romani," AAS 52 (1960) 596, 622–42.

33. SCR, "Rubricae breviarii," 625–29, 631, 633–35, 639; Salmon, "La prière," 879–80.

34. F. Anderson, ed., *Council Daybook: Vatican II* (Washington: National Catholic Welfare Conference, 1965) 1:1–2; RL, 39.

35. RL, 14–28.

36. *Acta et documenta concilio oecumenico Vaticano II apparando* (Vatican City: Typis Polyglottis Vaticanis, 1968) 2.2.3:47 (hereafter cited as ADCOVA followed by series, volume, part numbers, and, where necessary, publication year of volume); RL, 16.

37. ADCOVA 2.2.3:47–48; RL, 17–21.

38. ADCOVA 2.2.3:28–41.

39. Ibid., 54.

40. Ibid., 317–18 or ADCOVA 2.3.2:48 (1969) ("De Sacra Liturgia" 70).

41. ADCOVA 2.2.3:318 or 2.3.2:48–49.

42. ADCOVA 2.2.3:318 or 2.3.2:49 ("De Sacra Liturgia" 71).

43. ADCOVA 2.2.3:319 or 2.3.2:49–50 ("De Sacra Liturgia" 74).

44. See Cardinal Larraona's remarks in ADCOVA 2.2.3:327; the *declaratio* following article 70 of "De Sacra Liturgia" in ibid., 318 (or ADCOVA

2.3.2:48–49); the discussion and voting of the central preparatory commission on ch. 4 in ADCOVA 2.2.3:336–68.

45. ADCOVA 2.2.3:328.

46. Ibid., 331–32.

47. Ibid., 336–68. Cardinal Montini's support for omitting or restricting imprecatory psalms and psalm verses is significant in view of his insistence as Pope Paul VI that such omission and restriction occur despite the opposition to this move by those responsible for the formation of the reformed Office. See below, ch. 3, pp. 69–72; ch. 4, pp. 137, 149–54, 161–62.

48. Cf. the draft ("De Sacra Liturgia") presented to the central preparatory commission by the preparatory liturgical commission in ADCOVA 2.3.2:47–53 (or 2.2.3:317–23) and the original draft ("Schema Constitutionis de Sacra Liturgia") presented to the council. See *Acta Synodalia Sacrosancti Concilii Oecumenici Vaticani II* (Vatican City: Typis Polyglottis Vaticanis, 1972) 2.3:117–23 (hereafter cited as ASSCOV followed by volume, part, and, where necessary, publication year of volume).

49. Archbishop Bugnini tells the story of this "secret" committee in RL, 25–27. Cf. also Herman Schmidt, *La Constitution de la Sainte Liturgie: Texte—Genèse—Commentaire—Documents* (Bruxelles: Editions Lumen Vitae, 1966) 68–76.

50. See Floyd Anderson, ed., *Council Daybook: Vatican II* (Washington: National Catholic Welfare Conference, 1965–66) 1:23, 47, 67; RL, 30–32, 940–41.

51. Schmidt, *La Constitution*, 74–76; RL, 26.

52. Anderson, *Council* 1:67–68.

53. ASSCOV 2.3:411–12, 457–58, 470–72.

54. Ibid., 389–474.

55. Ibid., 392–96, 403–4, 420–23, 436–39, 470–72.

56. Ibid., 392–96, 463–66.

57. ASSCOV 2.3:118–19; ADCOVA 2.2.3:317–18 or 2.3.2:48–49.

58. ASSCOV 2.3:119–20; 1.2:405–6, 420–23, 440–45, 449–50, 459–62.

59. ASSCOV 1.2:407–8.

60. ADCOVA 2.2.3:318 (or 2.3.2:48–49); ASSCOV 1.2:425–28, 440–45, 447–50, 453–55.

61. ASSCOV 1.2:409–13, 457–59.

62. Ibid., 429–31, 439, 440–45.

63. See RL, 31–32.

64. ASSCOV 2.3:113–15. The conciliar commission had also made a number of minor revisions in the text of the schema, but these were considered not to affect the substance of the original text and so were not submitted to the council members for discussion or voting. See notes in ibid., 117.

65. ASSCOV 2.3:119, 134–35.

66. Ibid.; MRL, Suppl. 4, 42–43.

67. ASSCOV 2.3:119, 132, 134.

68. Ibid., 119, 135–36.

69. Ibid., 128–33; cf. MRL, Suppl. 4, 39, 49–51; AAS 52 (1960) 594.

70. ASSCOV, 2.3:215, and 259.

71. Ibid., 290.

72. ASSCOV 2.5:701–2, 710–15.

73. Ibid., 767.

74. ASSCOV 2.6:407.

CHAPTER 3:
THE CONSILIUM, *COETUS IX,*
AND THEIR *MODUS OPERANDI*

1. RL, 49–95, 137–202, 247–54, 491–522.

2. RL, 60–68.

3. Piero Marini, "Elenco degli 'Schemata' del Consilium e della Congregazione per il Culto Divino," *Notitiae* 18 (1982) 458; RL, 54–55

4. RL, 54–55, 58–59.

5. RL, 60–62.

6. Ibid.

7. See SC 89d and e; RL, 61–62; AAS 56 (1964) 139–44, 877; International Commission on English in the Liturgy, *Documents on the Liturgy, 1963–1979: Conciliar, Papal, and Curial Texts* (Collegeville: The Liturgical Press, 1982) nos. 276–89, 294 (hereafter cited as DOL with paragraph numbers).

8. RL, 50. The names of the members, whose number was later expanded to fifty-one to provide greater international representation, appear in RL, 942–44, and in the Consilium's *Elenchus membrorum - consultorum consiliariorum coetuum a studiis* (Vatican City, 1964) 9–14.

9. RL, 51–52.

10. RL, 137–42.

11. RL, 61–66; A. G. Martimort, interview with the author, Toulouse, France, April 19, 1983. Bugnini lists Group 1 outside of the section concerned with reform of the Office in the general plan, but Group 1 was definitely placed within the section on the Office in the Consilium's *Elenchus membrorum - consultorum* (Vatican City, 1964) 39. Cf. RL, 63.

12. RL, 65–68, P. Marini, "Elencho degli 'Schemata,'" 462–64.

13. A. G. Martimort, interview with the author, Toulouse, France, April 19, 1983; RL, 491, n. 1; 493, n. 7; 526, n. 16; 533, n. 21; 538, n. 30; 545, n. 43; 548, n. 47; 551, n. 57; *Elenchus membrorum - consultorum consiliariorum coetuum a studiis* (Vatican City, 1964, 1967); J. Rotelle, "Patristic Readings in the Liturgy of the Hours: Genesis and Background" in P. Jounel and others, eds., *Liturgia opera divina e umana*, Bibliotheca "Ephemerides Litur-

gicae," "Subsidia" 26 (Rome: CLV-Edizione Liturgiche, 1983) 603–4. Relators and secretaries, respectively, of other study groups involved with the work of Group 9 were Burkhard Neunheuser, and Giuseppe Sobrero. (Group 18, revision of the commons in Breviary and Missal); Antoine Dumas, and Msgr. Giovanni Lucchesi (Group 18bis, revision of prayers and prefaces); Msgr. Salvatore Famoso (also member of Group 9) and Adalberto Franquesa (Group 19, rubrics of Breviary and Missal); Eugene Cardine and Luigi Agustoni (Group 25, revision and edition of books of liturgical chant); and Msgr. Emmanuel Bonet (Group 30, juridical matters). See Raffa, "Dal Breviario," 360.

14. RL, 73–75, 137–39. On the presidential council, see below, p. 62.

15. RL, 71, 491–92; Schema 6:1–6. On Bishop Joseph Albert Martin's *relationes* see ASSCOV 2.3:114–46; 2.5:701–24; and above, ch. 2, pp. 38–41.

16. RL, 247–48.

17. RL, 146–47, 492; Schema 31.

18. RL, 493; Schema 50:1, 14–16; A. G. Martimort, interview with the author, Toulouse, France, April 19, 1983.

19. RL, 73, 148–50, 492–94; Schemata 68, 95; *Notitiae* 1 (1965) 99–104, 150–56, 206–14.

20. RL, 152–53, 495–96.

21. RL, 495–96.

22. RL, 496.

23. RL, 153, 496; A. G. Martimort, "De quibusdam quaestionibus circa distributionem psalterii et structuram Horarum in officio divino instaurando." Mimeographed report, December 1, 1965.

24. RL, 497.

25. RL, 497; Schemata 135, and 167. While the review of the reform of the Office was in progress, another development took place. Cardinal Lercaro had presented to the Pope on December 2, 1965, a proposal for participation of Protestant observers at meetings of the Consilium. Pope Paul VI approved the request on December 14, 1965, and the Consilium together with the Secretariat for Promoting Christian Unity, the Secretariat of State, and the Congregation for the Doctrine of the Faith established directives for the participation of the observers. The following July the Anglican community nominated Rev. Can. Ronald C. D. Jasper of London, president of the Liturgical Commission of the Anglican Church of Great Britain, and Rev. Dr. Massey H. Shepherd, Jr., professor at the Church Divinity School of the Pacific in Berkeley, California, as observers. By mid-August the World Council of Churches had nominated as observer Prof. A. Raymond George, member of the Methodist Conference and director of Wesley College in Leeds, Great Britain. The Lutheran World Federation, by that time also, had nominated Pastor Friedrick

Wilhelm Kunneth of Geneva, secretary of the Commission for Worship and Spiritual Life. The Community of Taizé selected Pastor Max Thurian, subprior of the community. These nominees were approved as observers by the Secretariat of State and the Congregation for the Doctrine of the Faith on August 23, 1966. In 1968 Rev. Eugene L. Brand of New York replaced Pastor Kunneth as the Lutheran representative. Unfortunately there were no observers from any of the Orthodox Churches, and the Protestant observers, as a group, simply observed proceedings of the Consilium. Only once were they asked for their collective opinion and that was regarding the cycle of readings for the Mass. See RL, 200–202.

26. RL, 497–98, 500–501; A. G. Martimort, interview with the author, Toulouse, France, April 19, 1983. For the contents of the Pope's letter, see below, ch. 4, pp. 111–12.

27. RG, front cover, and pp. 1–33; SRG 1–8; RL, 498–501; Schemata 167, 185:2.

28. RL, 501; Schemata 185, 194. Schema 185 was apparently discussed by the Group of Relators then revised as Schema 194 for presentation to the plenary session of the Consilium. Many of the reasons cited in Schema 185 against radical reform do not appear in the revised version. It thus appears that the Group of Relators had some effect in moderating the adamancy of the stance, detected in Schema 185, against more thorough-going reform. Cf. Schema 185:19 and Schema 194:11–13. That the content of these schemata was directed as much to the Pope as to members of the Consilium was communicated to this author by Canon Martimort in an interview at Toulouse, France, April 19, 1983.

29. RL, 158–61. The charter members of the presidential council, in addition to Cardinals Lercaro (president) and Confalonieri (vice president), were Cardinal Conway (Armagh) and Bishops Boudon (Mende), Pellegrino (Turin), Spulbeck (Meissen), Enrique y Tarancon (Oviedo, then Toledo), Isnard (Nova Friburgo), and Bluyssen (s'Hertogenbosch). See RL, 160.

30. RL, 501.

31. RL, 502–5; Schemata 185, 194. For the revised principles directing the final phase of reform, see below, ch. 4, pp. 91–92, 106–7, 114–15, 118–19, 125–26, 130–31, 178–79; ch. 5, pp. 191–93, 207–9.

32. Schemata 206, 215; RL, 163, 505; interview of author with Canon Martimort, April 19, 1983.

33. RL, 76–77; 161–63, 505–6; Schema 227; "Acta Consilii," Notitiae 3 (1967) 141–43; interview of the author with Canon Martimort, April 19, 1983.

34. Schema 239; Res secretariae 28. The proposed volume of hymns was published as Hymni instaurandi Breviarii Romani (Vatican City: Libreria Editrice Vaticana, 1968). The other proposed volumes eventually published were Ordo lectionum biblicarum Officii Divini (Vatican City: Typis Polyglottis Vaticanis, 1969) and Lectiones Patrum et lectiones hagiographicae pro Officio Divino (Vatican City: Typis Polyglottis Vaticanis, 1970).

35. RL, 507–8; Schema 253; *Synodus episcoporum, De sacra liturgia: Exitus manifestationis sententiae cum recensione modorum propositorum* (Vatican City: Typis Polyglottis Vaticanis, 1967) 5, 11–16. On the questions regarding the Office considered by the synod, see below, ch. 4, pp. 161–62; ch. 5, pp. 201, 210–11, 224–25.

36. Schema 253:1.

37. RL, 169–70; see below, pp. 68–72; ch. 4, p. 114–15; ch. 5, pp. 209–11.

38. RL, 171–72.

39. SDO, 1; Schema 263:1.

40. RL, 78, 508–9. Unfortunately, the word "president" is used in RL, 508, for the Italian "presidenza" (presidency) used by Bugnini in the original edition thus conveying the notion that the note was clearly that of Cardinal Lercaro. See A. Bugnini, *La riforma liturgica (1948–1975)* (Rome: CLV - Edizioni Liturgiche, 1983) 498. For the text of *Regimini Ecclesiae universae* see AAS 59 (1967) 885–928; for the English translation of excerpt regarding the Congregation of Rites, see DOL 648–65.

41. RL, 80; rescript *Cum notae causae*, AAS 60 (1968) 50 (DOL 666); Paul VI, "Nell' atto in cui," *Notitiae* 4 (1968) 4 (DOL 667).

42. "Sembra doversi preferire la scelta dei salmi piu adatti alla preghiera cristiana, omettendo quelli 'imprecatori' e quelli 'storici' (salvo, per questi ultimi, l'opportunita di usarli in certe particolari circostanze)." The Pope's words are quoted in A. Bugnini, *La riforma liturgica*, 499; for the English translation see RL, 509.

43. RL, 509, emphases added. The excerpt presented here reads in the original Italian:

"Il Consiglio di Presidenza nella adunanza del 30 gennaio ha preso atto con riconoscenza che il Santo Padre si sia degnato di decidere un problema, costantemente dibattuto, ed ha pregato Sua Eccellenza Rev.ma Mons. René Boudon di portarLe questa mia lettera.

"La decisione del Santo Padre portera disagio al gruppo che cosi bene ha lavorato alla distribuzione dei salmi, ma sono certo che i ritocchi saranno fatti con la consueta generosita, anche se con non poco sacrificio." See A. Bugnini, *La riforma liturgica*, 499.

44. Schemata 284:6–8, 288 *addendum*; A. G. Martimort, "De psalmis sic dictis 'imprecatoriis' et 'historicis' quaestio denuo orta" (mimeographed report dated February 20, 1968; 5 pages); A. G. Martimort, interview with the author, Toulouse, France, April 20, 1983; see below, ch. 4, pp. 153–54.

45. Author's translation. The excerpt from Cardinal Gut's letter is taken from V. Raffa's typewritten "I salmi 'imprecatori,' p. 13: "Se desiderare ut omittantur e cyclo ordinario psalterii psalmi ex integro 'imprecatorii' nempe psalmi 57, 82 et 108 atque illae partes quae propositae erant ad libitum et ideo inter parentheses includendae. Psalmi autem qui 'historici' vocantur pro peculiaribus quibusdam temporibus serventur." For Archbishop Bugnini's own account of his intervention, see RL, 510–11.

46. See Archbishop Bugnini's candid judgment of Canon Martimort's report to Group 9 on July 31, 1966, as not taking seriously the Pope's wishes and as provoking a waste of the Consilium's time (RL, 500-501); his remarks on his report to the tenth plenary session in which he insisted the Pope's wishes be accepted and on the discussion regarding the psalms during the session (RL, 175-77, 510); his personal assessment of the role of the secretary of the Consilium as having two functions not always convergent: effecting the decisions of the Consilium and bringing to and having accepted by the Consilium the thought of the Pope (RL, 176-77, n. 72); his "pastoral" views in a letter to Canon Martimort on reform of the Office (RL, 506-7). The Pope himself gently chided Father Bugnini for taking his suggestions too seriously. As Archbishop Bugnini recounts the incident that occurred in the audience that members and consultors had with Paul VI during the eleventh plenary session (RL, 177, n. 72). Canon Martimort's opinions of Archbishop Bugnini's ideas and manner were related to this author during an interview in Toulouse, April 20, 1983. With respect to the Pope's own views on omission of imprecatory psalms, it should be recalled that as Cardinal Montini he had, in a meeting of the central preparatory commission for the Council, spoken in favor of eliminating or restricting use of imprecatory psalms and verses in the Office. See ch. 2, p. 295, note 47.

47. RL, 177, 509-11; Schema 294.

48. Schema 295; V. Raffa, "I psalmi 'imprecatori,' " 13 (typewritten).

49. RL, 178-81.

50. RL, 514-16; CNPL, "L'Experimentation du nouvel Office Divin," n.d. Mimeographed.

51. RL, 513-14; Consilium, *Descriptio et specimina Officii Divini iuxta Concilii Vaticani II Decreta instaurati* (Vatican City: Typis Polyglottis Vaticanis, 1969). The introduction to the sample was reproduced as "Descriptio Officii Divini iuxta Concilii Vaticani II Decreta instaurati" in *Notitiae* 5 (1969) 74-85. Use of the results to modify the General Instruction was reported by Father Bugnini at the twelfth plenary session of the Consilium. See "Schemata," *Notitiae* 5 (1969) 438.

52. RL, 78-83, 185-92, 513, 520, 522; Paul VI, "Sacra Rituum Congregatio," AAS 61 (1969) 297-305 (excerpts in *Notitiae* 5 [1969] 129-33, DOL 678-84); "Acta Consilii," *Notitiae* 5 (1969) 438; "Acta Commissionis Specialis ad Instaurationem Liturgicam Absolvendam," *Notitiate* 6 (1970) 227.

53. RL, 520-22; SCCD, *Cum edito,* and *Institutio Generalis de Liturgia Horarum* (Vatican City: Typis Polyglottis Vaticanis, 1971); Paul VI, "Laudis canticum," AAS 63 (1971) 527-35.

54. RL, 520-22; Emil Lengeling, interview with the author, Münster, West Germany, April 13, 1983; A. G. Martimort, interview with the author, Toulouse, France, April 20, 1983.

CHAPTER 4:
THE STRUCTURE OF THE HOURS AS A WHOLE

1. See below, pp. 82–83.
2. SC 89d and 91.
3. See below, pp. 110–14.
4. SC 88, and 94; see below, pp. 79–92; Schema 68:3.
5. Mateos' proposal was made initially by comments *(adnotationes)* offered on Schemata 31 (September 14, 1964) and 68 (March 26, 1965).
6. Schema 6:3.
7. See Schema 68:3.
8. See Schemata 185:21–23; 194:28–29; SRG, 1–6.
9. Père Joseph Gelineau, consultor to the Consilium has said: "The rather specific proposals of J. Mateos in favor of a cathedral-type Office with a ritualized setting and inspired by the tradition of the Eastern liturgies (light, incense, lamp lighting, etc.) were not well received. However, these proposals were important for obtaining some flexibility in the General Instruction allowing for possible adaptation for the participation of the people or of various groups." ("Les propositions, assez précises, de J. Mateos, en faveur d'un office de type cathédral avec cadre 'rituel,' inspiré de la tradition des liturgies orientales [lumière, encens, lucernaire etc.] ne furent pas bien accueillies. Pourtant cela a été important pour obtenir dans l'*Institutio generalis* des flexibilités qui ont laissé ouvertes beaucoup d'adaptations possibles pour la participation du peuple ou de groupes divers.") Letter to the author, February 9, 1982.
10. "*Quaestio:* Num et quomodo aptare oportet Laudes et Vesperas (*Const.* art. 89a), praesertim quando cum populo vel in ecclesia paroeciali celebrantur (art. 100)." Schema 6:3. Cf. also Schema 31:1.
11. An English translation with some adaptation of these *adnotationes* appeared as "The Morning and Evening Office" in *Worship* 42 (1968) 31–47.
12. "Huic quaestioni responsionem negativam proposuerunt Periti. Etenim Laudes minus populares sunt et manebunt quam Vesperae, ratione praecipue habita horae matutinalis: qui Officio Laudum intersunt pauci sunt et flos fidelium, qui possint quinque psalmos devote canere, immo, qui teste uno ex nostris, hodierna Laudum structura contenti sint. Inutile ergo esset schema speciale condere." Schema 31:3–4.
13. No indication is given in Schema 31 as to which study group the discussions and decisions summarized there are to be attributed. Presumably, since the questions are largely structural, it is the consultors forming Group 9 to whom reference is made.
14. Schema 31:5.
15. The Latin text reads: "ad structuram quae 'cathedralis' vocatur, quaeque servata est in 'magnis vesperis' ritus byzantini vel in vigiliis ritus

ambrosiani, ubi scilicet plures lectiones adsunt, reducta psalmodia."
Schema 31:5.

16. Juan Mateos, "Adnotationes ad schema 31, De Breviario, 10" (November 22, 1964) 11–12. Mimeographed. For an adapted English version of the conclusions, see Mateos, "The Morning," 46–47.

17. "In restauratione liturgica sensum eminenter pastoralem habente, videntur extolli debere officia ecclesiastica populo destinata: ea clare distinguendo ab officiis monasticis, eisque structuram conferendo primo et per se ad celebrationem cum populo aptam et ad populi aedificationem efficacem.

". . . Universale igitur et ordinarium in Ecclesia est cursus seu Breviarium constans duobus officiis quotidianis, mane et vespere. Cursus septem vel octo horarum est exceptionalis, non universalis neque ordinarius, adhibendus ab iis qui professionem vitae asceticae et contemplativae faciunt.

"Unde secunda conclusio: duo officia cathedralia esse propria non solum populi christiani, sed eodem modo cleri non monastici, dum ceterae horae monasticae non celebrantur in ecclesiis saecularibus, neque pro clero non monastico obligatoriae censendae sunt, nisi forte lectio illa spiritualis quae locum tenebit antiqui nocturni.

"Ut haec disciplina vigere posset opus esset ut officia mane et vespere non mere recitarentur, sed vere celebrarentur, cum participatione aliqua fidelium. Si enim celebratio utriusque officii cum populo locum haberet, faciliter et congruum tempus orationis liturgicae quotidianae expleret clerus, et ex altera parte magnus stimulus daretur pro usu pastorali officii divini.

"Posset concedi etiam ut aliquae lectiones sacrae Scripturae ex officio lectionum (antiquo nocturno) desumptae publice legi possent in officiis cum populo, ad libitum celebrantium et prout tempus ferret." Juan Mateos, "Adnotationes," 12 ("The Morning," 47).

In an interview with this author in Granada, Spain, April 25, 1983, Father Mateos emphatically reaffirmed his view of the ancient ecclesiastical Office as a celebration usually without readings: *Question:* In the schemata, when the cathedral Office is referred to . . . it seems to be that the understanding is that it is more of a Word service. And that is not my understanding of what the ecclesiastical Office was . . . *Father Mateos:* No, no, no, no. *Question:* They seem to be talking about it as a Word-service, that if Vespers or Lauds should be popularized, their idea was: Have extended reading and homily. *Father Mateos:* No. . . . On the contrary . . . it's singing psalms and ceremony—light, incense, and some readings sometimes, not always. It is celebration really.

18. See SC, ch. 4, especially art. 89.

19. Interview with Father Juan Mateos, Granada, Spain, April 25, 1983.

20. Ibid.

21. "Propositionem P. Mateos, de reductione Officii cleri diocesani ad Laudes et Vesperas, sodales non admiserunt, quia munus commissionis est Constitutionem liturgicam—quae cursum Horarum statuit—applicare, non mutare. Ceterum quidam dixit quod exigentiis, ex antiquo cathedralitio matutino et vespertino venientibus, iam satisfecit Constitutio, quando ut cardinem totius officii declaravit illas Horas." Schema 68:3. Reports of protracted, heated arguments at some point in time between Father Mateos and Canon Martimort or other members of Group 9 over Father Mateos' proposal cannot be substantiated. Father Vincenzo Raffa, secretary for Group 9, has asserted that "lively debate" surrounded Father Mateos' proposal. Although Canon Martimort opposed Father Mateos' proposal, said Father Raffa, he esteemed Father Mateos personally. In fact, according to Father Raffa, Father Mateos' input was much appreciated by the members of Group 9. Father Raffa claimed to still have his handwritten notes of the sessions of Group 9 but despaired of gathering and organizing them. Interview with this author, Rome, May 4, 1983. More thorough research of this aspect of the reform would not be possible without access to these notes.

22. See below on the psalmody, pp. 137-70; ch. 5, pp. 185-207.

23. "Secundum Constitutionem Conciliarem de Sacra Liturgia (cap. V, nn. 102, 106), dies dominica debet semper magis fulgere inter dies hebdomadae ut dies consecrata commemorationi mysterii paschalis, ut pascha hebdomadarium.

"Utile igitur erit considerare quid antiqua Ecclesia fecerit ad talem characterem lucem ponendum." Juan Mateos, "Adnotationes circa Officium Dominicae seu de vigilia cathedrali" (April 5, 1965) 1. Mimeographed.

24. "Non negari potest vigiliam cathedralem esse officium magni valoris pastoralis, ex simplici et profunda significatione eius. Ipsa permittit insuper servare characterem paschalem diei dominicae etiamsi, ut par est formularium Missae cyclum temporale sequatur. Brevitas eius simul et varietas elementorum eam etiam commendant. Sine difficultate posset fieri selectio canticorum et psalmorum paschalium ad quatuor saltem diversa formularia componenda, iuxta quatuor pericopas evangelicas quae narrant apparitionem mulieribus.

"Restauratio vigiliae cathedralis non esset introductio alicuius novitatis in officio romano, sed vera restitutio antiqui officii adhuc existentis, ei reddendo scopum ad quem institutum est.

"Posset commendari celebratio eius mane in dominicis, ante officium matutinum, quin tamen obligatoria consideraretur neque celebratio publica neque recitatio privata." Ibid., 5.

25. See below, ch. 5, pp. 212-32; Schemata 185:23-25; 194:14-16. Cf. also Schemata 262:3; 269:3-7.

26. Schemata 262:3; 269:3-7.

27. Schema 269:3.

28. "*Quaestio:* Utrum eadem reformatio Officii extendi debet ad officium chorale, immo monialium; an duplex Officium condere oportet, alterum chorale seu contemplativorum, alterum pro iis qui activam vitam ducunt." Schema 6:3.

29. Ibid. See the *Relatio* of Bishop Martin on the *emendationes* to articles 88–89 and 100 of SC in ASSCOV 2.3:128–35, 142; the *modi* on ch. 4 of SC and the conciliar commission's responses in ASSCOV 2.5:706–24.

30. See above, p. 80; Schema 31:4.

31. See below, pp. 93–107; Schema 31:4–7.

32. See ch. 3, pp. 54–60.

33. "Art. 90 Constitutionis praevidet ut 'in instauratione peragenda, venerabilis ille romani Officii saecularis thesaurus ita aptetur, ut latius et facilius eo frui possint omnes quibus traditur.' Ex ipsa autem Constitutione publica Ecclesiae precatio, praeter clericos in sacris constitutos et Regulares ex constitutionibus ad eam obligatos, extenditur ad omnes Religiosos (art. 98), et ad ipsos laicos (art. 100)." Schema 135:2.

34. "1. videturne sufficere parare Breviarium normativum pro tota Ecclesia postea diversimode aptandum diversis coetibus et exigentiis? *an potius* 2. opportunius videtur parare formas diversas Officii divini, nempe pro recitatione chorali, pro clero curam animarum gerente, pro laicis? 3. opportunum videtur ut praevideatur etiam alia forma ad instar 'parvi Officii' pro communitatibus paroecialibus, adhibenda a clero et laicis simul precantibus?" Ibid.

35. Schema 167:1–3.

36. See ch. 3, p. 60.

37. SRG, 1–2.

38. Ibid., 2–3.

39. Ibid., 3–4.

40. Ibid., 5.

41. "On pourrait donc se mettre d'accord sur les points suivants: *(a)* proposer au Consilium de laisser hors de son étude les Petits Offices, sans cependant accepter que, sur ce point, soit restreinte la liberté donée par la Constitution conciliaire aux Communautes;

(b) affirmer nettement la nécessité de fournir, dans le cadre de l'office romain, toutes les possibilites traditionnelles de la prière contemplative, dans le même temps que l'on dégage l'office des clercs de ses attaches monastiques.

(c) essayer d'organiser des Laudes et des Vêpres susceptibles d'être utilisées par les fidèles et les communautés non astreintes a l'Office, selon le programme que j'ai déjà resumé précédemment. Et ne parlons plus d''Office normatif.'

(*d*) ces divers points devraient suffire provisoirement, mais il sera bon de réaffirmer les principes de la Constitution pour reágir contre toute tendance à l'uniformité qui contredirait ces principes voulus solennellement par le Concile." Ibid., 5–6.

42. Interview with Juan Mateos, Granada, Spain, April 25, 1983. Emphasis added.

43. "Sint duo Officia, pro non monachis unum (pro clericis, religiosis viris et foeminis, laicis) pro monachis alterum. Hoc ultimum structuram monasticam servet, non primum." Schema 167:10.

44. "Pourquoi adopter une formule par laquelle les laïcs (religieux non clercs, religieuses et laïcs) seront encore coupes de la grande et officielle prière de l'Église, en répandant de petits offices, ou encore en restreignant artificiellement la psalmodié, comme on le propose pour les Vêpres? Une timidité excessive dans la réforme du Bréviaire aura pour conséquence qu'on retombera dans les mêmes erreurs que par le passé, où on a assisté à une prolifération de petits offices qui ont coupé un grand nombre de laïcs (religieux ou simples laïcs) de la grande prière de l'Église." Quoted in SRG, 3.

45. See Schema 185, especially pp. 21–24.

46. Schema 194:3.

47. Ibid.

48. "*Quaesitum generale:* Placetne ut structura Horarum praecipuarum, quae sunt velut cardo divini Officii, id est Laudum et Vesperarum, ita concipiatur, ut hae Horae et a communitate ecclesiali coadunata et etiam a solo celebrari possint? [*Placet*, 33; *non placet*, 0; *iuxta modum*, 1.]" Ibid., 6. Voting results are handwritten in available copy of the text. See also pp. 13–15.

49. "*Quaesitum VII:* Placetne ita instruere Horam in die obligatoriam ut constet psalmo vel psalmis e psalterio currente qui dicantur cum hymno (et forte oratione) aptis horae diei (scilicet Tertiae, vel Sextae, vel Nonae)? [*Placet, omnes.*]" Ibid., 14. Voting results are handwritten in available copy of the text.

50. Ibid., pp. 14–16, especially p. 16.

51. For Lauds and Vespers, see SC 89a; for Compline, 89b; for Matins, 89c; for Prime, 89d; for the minor Hours, 89e.

52. See below, pp. 137–69.

53. Schema 23:5 and Schema II (attached); Schema 31:2–3.

54. "Concilium diminutionem psalmodiae non solum pro Matutino prae oculis habuisse videtur. Quod patet e comparatione articulorum 89 et 91. Cum enim Constitutio Art. 91 decernat psalmos distribuendos esse 'per longius temporis spatium,' expresse pespicit ad totum Art. 89 neque ad Art. 89c tantum. Ergo non propter Matutinum solum, sed propter

totum cursum Horarum psalterium ad longius temporis spatium extendi debet. Quae autem extensio necessario abbreviationem incisorum secumfert. Quare nequaquam ex Art. 89c sequitur extra Matutinum diminutionem psalmodiae admitti non posse." Schema 23:2.

55. Ibid., pp. 2, 4.

56. "Omnes conveniunt nimios esse quinque psalmos in ea celebratione populari in qua lectio longior et homilia recitantur.

Plures dixerunt tres psalmos haud sufficere in ea celebratione in qua absente populo, lectio brevior fit et homilia omittitur. *Vesperae amitterent indolem horae maioris,* et difficulter servaretur thesaurus antiphonarum magnorum festorum." Schema 31:5-6. Emphasis added.

57. "Praeterea, si vesperae ad tres psalmos etiam in recitatione privata contraherentur, *indolem horae maioris perderent."* Ibid., p. 5. Emphasis added.

58. Ibid., p. 6.

59. "Possibilitas observandi cursum articuli 89, de qua in Art. 91 agitur, non de possibilitate quasi physica, sed de possibilitate spirituali intelligenda est. Quaeritur enim, an clerus in cura animarum constitutus in condicionibus temporis nostri possit observare cursum Horarum cum fructu spirituali. Propter hanc quaestionem Concilium Articulo 89c psalmodiam Matutini abbreviandam esse decrevit et Articulum 91 posuisse videtur.

"Psalmodia in Breviario romano valde praevalet. Quod provenit e traditione monastica et cum condicionibus monasticis convenire videtur. Nam etiam nostris temporibus viri de vita monastica periti—etsi non omnes— asserunt psalmodiam, et quidem longam, idoneam immo necessariam esse ad vitam spiritualem monachorum alendam.

"Condiciones autem cleri moderni in cura animarum constituti a condicionibus monasticis valde differunt; de quo nemo dubitat. Psalmodiam quod attinet, etiam clero magnae utilitatis esse potest, si condicionibus accomodatur. Tunc autem longa non esse debet. Sunt, qui putant psalmodiam longam clero necessariam esse, ut quietem et quasi permanentem cum Deo colloquium orationis obtineat. Sed, proh dolor, haec theoria perpulchra per circumstantias vitae durissimas irrita fit. Immo, si perseveramus insistendo in impossibilibus, damnum fortasse emerget spiritualitati." Schema 23:2.

60. Schema 31:5, 6.

61. "De cetero hoc argumentum non intelligitur: 'si vesperae ad tres psalmos etiam in recitatione privata contraherentur, indolem horae maiores perderent.' Quantitas verborum vel psalmorum non determinat momentum Vesperarum." Frederick R. McManus, "Animadversiones circa relationem de breviario (Schema 31)" 2. Typewritten.

62. "Valde displicet haec solutio. Hodie nec Laudes nec Vesperae populares sunt et radicalem instaurationem requirunt.

"Ni fallor, votum Commissionis Praeparatoriae erat quod horae praecipuae recitari possint ab Ecclesia: a sacerdotibus, a religiosis utriusque sexus, a laicis: a parocho una cum fratribus vel sororibus religiosis et etiam cum paucis fidelibus. Est gloria Anglicanorum quod sacerdotes Laudes et Vesperas (Morning Prayer et Evensong) in ecclesiis quotidie recitant cum fidelibus etiam paucissimis.

"Mihi videtur hanc relationem nimis sapere clericalismum et archaelogismum. Momentum Laudum non manifestabitur per longitudinem vel numerum psalmorum sed tantum si Hora est simplex, reapse prex matutina quae ab omnibus, etiamsi rarissime, persolvi potest." Ibid., 1.

63. "1. Omnes consentiunt quod, si Vesperae cum populo celebrantur, 3 Psalmis tantum constent.

"2. Sed dissentio est quando agitur de recitatione Vesperarum a clero, absente populo.

"I sententia optat pro *quinario* numero. Rationes:

(*a*) Nihil impedit quominus in celebratione cum populo aliquot Psalmi omittantur et duo typi Vesperarum astruantur: Primus, completus pro clero; alter, aptatus populo.

(*b*) Ratio principalis esset traditio 5 Psalmorum, quae a pluribus saeculis in liturgia romana viget.

(*c*) Servandus videtur parallelismus inter schema quinarium Laudum et Vesperarum. Insuper indoles Horae maioris in quinario numero melius servari videtur.

"II sententia optat pro *ternario* numero, etiam si a solo clero celebrantur. Rationes:

(*a*) Non convenit discrimen facere inter officium pro clero cum populo adunato et officium pro clero solo, et quidem in hora, quae, prae omnibus aliis, secundum art. 100 Constit. 'in ecclesia communiter' celebranda est.

(*b*) Reductio numeri Psalmorum non intendit abbreviationem, nam Psalmi omissi aliis elementis supplerentur: v.gr. lectione longiore, homilia et oratione fidelium.

(*c*) Traditio quinque Psalmorum non est omnino universalis et numerus 5 non est sacer." Schema 37:2.

64. "Utrum placeat retinere unicum schema Vesperarum sive pro clero, absente populo, sive in celebratione cum populo cum quinque psalmis, facta tamen facultate, per rubricas omittendi, duos psalmos in celebratione cum populo et, in hoc casu, adesset longior lectio, homilia et forsan oratio fidelium." Schema 50:4.

65. "Tertia difficultas affertur de structura Laudum et Vesperarum. Num ita instrui possint ambae illae horae, ut cum populo vel quadam parte selecta communitatis christianae quotidie persolvi valeant, ad quem finem attingendum necesse fuit exemplar imitari sive Orientalium, sive Anglicanorum vel Protestantium officiorum mane et vespere celebrato-

rum? Officium Romanum, etsi ad normam Constitutionis et Vestri suffragii abbreviatum, remanet, ut aiunt, monasticum quid, ideoque incongruum clero saeculari." A. G. Martimort, "De quibusdam questionibus circa distributionem psalterii et structuram Horarum in officio divino instaurando (1 decembris, 1965)" (mimeographed) p. 1.

66. "Celebratio Vesperarum cum populo, certis quidem diebus sapienter providenda est, immo a nobis provisa, Vobis approbantibus: quo in casu, ut recordamini, reducetur psalmodia ad tres psalmos, et loco lectionis brevis seu capituli introducetur lectio longior de qua celebrans homiliam habere possit, praeter inseretur oratio universalis seu fidelium.

"Num autem frequens et quotidiana possit esse participatio popularis ad laudes et vesperas, valde dubitatur. Interim tamen, ita instruendae sunt illae horae in quotidiano officio, ne fastidio sint sacerdoti qui jam horam lectionum persolvere tenetur ad normam art. 89 Constitutionis; sedul[o] enim observari velim, nec Anglicanos nec Protestantes officium completum retinuisse qualem Constitutio Vaticana nobis praescribit, sed solas horas matutinam et vesperalem; in Oriente vero, omnes quidem horae in libris invenitur, obligatio autem saepe cadit tantum in publica laudum celebratione." Ibid., 1–2.

67. "4. Videtur sufficere quod iam a 'Consilio' acceptum fuerat, nempe ut in Laudibus et Vesperis cum populo persolvendis praesto essent quaedam schemata communia pro aliquibus temporibus et festis, et ut psalmi ad tres reduci possent, addita lectione longiore ex sacra Scriptura necnon homilia, loco capituli?

"12bis. Placet ut Laud. et Vesp. quinque pss. habeant, cum facultate ad tres reducendi si cum populo?" Schema 167:3, 5.

68. Ibid, 3, 5–6.

69. RG, 14.

70. "Pour ce qui est des psaumes de vêpres, le Coetus III avait proposé qu'il n'y en ait que trois. Le nombre de cinq a été retenu par le Consilium eu égard surtout aux véritables offices des dimanches et fêtes et à leurs antiennes. Cette raison est rappelée dans son *votum* par notre collègue le P. Dirks: il faut donc envisager le problème technique de la conservation des éléments anciens dans la cas d'une transformation plus profonde des structures de l'office. Ceci dit, rien ne s'oppose à ce que les Coetus III et IX examinent la réduction du nombre de psaumes (pour Laudes, cette réduction n'avait pas été envisagée sérieusment en 1964) et la chose semble facile." Ibid., 23.

71. "Le futur bréviaire doit être le livre de la prière officielle du Peuple de Dieu, non pas en toutes ses parties, mais au moins dans ses Heures fondamentales, Laudes et Vêpres. Ce bréviaire doit être le livre de prière qui serve aux laïcs et aux clercs, au moins en certaines de ses par-

ties. . . ." Ibid., 25. See also the similar opinions of Cardinal Rugambwa (Dar-es-Salaam), Archbishop Botero (Medellín), Bishops Boudon (Mende) and Kerveadou (Saint Brieuc).

72. "Le sens vrai de la Constitution Conciliaire est de rejoindre ce qu'elle appelle avec raison 'la venerable tradition de l'Église universelle'. Les études de A. Baumstark ont définitivement établi l'existence de ce qu'il a appellé l'office cathedral: célébration quotidienne du matin et du soir, universellement attestée du IIIe au VIIIe siècle dans les églises non monastiques, avec la présence de l'évēque ou de son representant. . . . Allons donc à la distinction radicale entre l'office monastique et l'office de l'Église universelle: à cette seule condition on pourra realiser pleinement le voeu du Concile, à savoir que tous puissent participer, soit en commun, soit dans la prière solitaire, â l'office divin de l'Église. Le grand courant de prière liturgique qu'il faut créer ou faire naître de nouveau sera alors vivement enraciné dans l'unité de la prière universelle pour les clercs, les religieuses et les laïcs . . . Une timidité excessive dans les reforme du Bréviaire aura pour conséquence qu'on retombera dans les mêmes erreurs que par le passé, ou l'on a assisté a la prolifération de petits offices qui ont coupé un grand nombre de chrétiens de la grand prière de l'Église." Ibid., 26.

73. Ibid.

74. Ibid., 23 and 27. Canon Martimort explicitly cites the articles of Fr. Louis Bouyer in *Vie spirituelle* 114 (1966) 25–43; L. Maldonado and P. Farnes in *Phase 6* (1966) 35–45; L. Meesen in *Questions liturgiques et paroissiales* 47 (1966) 123–32.

75. RG, 27–28.

76. "Il est vrai, le Concile invite les fidèles à participer à l'office principalement aux Laudes et aux Vêpres et surtout les dimanches et les fêtes. Cette invitation s'inscrit dans une tratition législative qui remonte au moyen âge et qui se retrouve dans les documents précedant immédiatement le Concile: Encyclique *Mediator Dei*, Instruction du 3 septembre 1958. Mais il faut être très prudent: que de lois, dans le passé, sont demeurées lettre morte! Or loin de promouvoir un renouveau des Vēpres, les documents précites de 1947 et 1958 sont contemporains de leur complète disparition. Croit-on pouvoir restaurer la célébration quotidienne, ou mème seulement dominicale, des Vēpres et à plus forte raison des Laudes?

"Fréquemment, les liturgistes se réfèrent aux résultats de la science historique et appuient sur eux les projects qu'ils forment et les désirs qu'ils expriment. C'est légitime: Pie XII lui-même énumérait les progres de *l'histoire liturgique* comme une des causes du renouveau de notre époque; or Pie XII ne pouvait prévoir que ce renouveau aboutirait IIe Concile du Vatican et à la Constitution sur la liturgie. L'histoire est l'un des grands criteres qui controle l'authenticite du travail dans notre Consilium.

"Mais il faut convenir que la science historique risque d'etre utilisée de facon inexacte comme critère de réforme: ce qui était bien à une époque peut ne pas convenir à une autre; certaines évolutions sont irréversibles même du point de vue doctrinal. Par ailleurs, les résultats de la science historique, parfois, sont diffusés de façon imparfaite ou même inexacte dans les revues de vulgarisation, conférences, etc. On en arrive à fonder des requêtes sur des données historiques erronées. C'est ainsi qu'il faut mettre en garde contre les approximations dont l'histoire des laudes et des vêpres a fait l'objet dans les articles récents du P. Louis Bouyer et de Pedro Farnes déjà cites: il n'est pas exact que dans l'antiquité ces réunions, là où elles étaient quotidiennes, aient comporté habituellement des lectures; celles-ci étaient plutôt réservées aux stations plus importantes et solennelles comme les 'vigiles' des fêtes (dont il reste, entre autres, les grandes vêpres byzantines et ambrosiennes) ou le carême. Vue de près, d'ailleurs, la vie de diverses églises se prête mal à des généralisations historiques optimistes; ces réunions quotidiennes ont mis longtemps à s'implanter, leur âge d'or a été assez bref, de la fin du IVe au milieu du Ve siècle; l'un des éléments les plus populaires qui constituaient le réunion du soir, le lucernaire, serait difficilement susceptible de restauration. D'autre part au moment où ces réunions florissaient, la messe ne se celebrait quotidiennement que, peut-être, en Afrique: et ce point mérite d'être relevé car il faut désormais tenir compte de la messe quotidienne mise en honneur dans la spiritualité médiévale et surtout moderne, de la communion quotidienne à laquelle saint Pie X a rappelé les chrétiens, de la lecture courante de la Bible et de l'Evangile qui est en train de s'y instaurer actuellement." Ibid., 28–29.

77. Ibid., 29–32. Canon Martimort expresses his very strong personal view against the abandonment of daily Eucharist thus: "I know that certain liturgists would very easily take this reasoning to its logical conclusion and would abandon daily Mass. I wish to declare here very strongly my repudiation of such a view." ("Je sais bien que certains liturgistes accepteraient facilement d'aller au bout de cette logique et abandonneraient le messe quotidienne. Je tiens à declarer ici tres haut ma réprobation d'une telle mentalité" p. 32).

78. "L'office de laudes et de vêpres peut être aménagé de telle facon qu'il puisse être pratique: par le prêtre seul, par le fidèle seul, par un petit groupe (religieux, retraitants, élèves, etc.), par l'assemblée de peuple, par le choeur conventuel. Mais il est évident que ces diversités de célébration supposent des aménagements de rite à prevoir avec soin; il faut voir si c'est possible." Ibid., 32.

79. "Ut ergo de desideriis multorum et de difficultatibus mox expressis simul ratio habeatur, a nobis talis structura invenienda est, quae faveat participationi populi et a solo recitari possit, praeterea tam cum officio lectionum quam cum lectione continua Missae cotidianae componi possit. Quod vobis melius forsan patebit cum de singulis elementis Laudum et Vesperarum egerimus." Schema 185:14. Cf. also the summary in this schema of the action at this meeting on the structure of Lauds and Vespers, pp. 13–14.

80. Schema 185:14–15.

81. "Placetne ut in Laudibus et Vesperis, sive cum populo sive sine populo, tres tantum psalmi sint?" Ibid., 15.

82. Ibid., 16–18.

83. See ch. 5, pp. 185–207.

84. Schema 185, 18.

85. Schema 194, 4–5.

86. "ut clare appareant oratio totius communitatis christianae et non tantum clericorum et monachorum; ideo participatio fidelium istis Horis ne videatur esse concessio quaedam, sed ius quod fideles habent proprium. Ibid., 5.

87. ". . . maxima pars sacerdotum Laudes et Vesperas modo solitario recitabit vel saltem sine populo." Ibid.

88. "Placetne ut structura Horarum praecipuarum quae sunt velut cardo divini Officii, id est Laudum et Vesperarum, ita concipiatur, ut hae Horae et a communitate ecclesiali coadunata et etiam a solo celebrari possint?" Ibid., 6.

89. Ibid. Voting results are handwritten in copy available.

90. Ibid.

91. Interview with Canon A. G. Martimort, Toulouse, France, April 19, 1983.

92. See Schema 31:11.

93. "Si officium lectionis haud ut prima Hora recitatur, tunc placetne ut invitatorium initio primae Horae, scilicet Laudum, praeponatur et quidem obligatorie?" Schema 50:15.

94. See Schemata 135, 167. There are no questions on the invitatory.

95. Schema 206:10.

96. See, e.g., SCDO, 1–2.

97. Schema 215:6.

98. Schema 227:13.

99. Schema 231:1–3.

100. See ch. 5, pp. 221, 224–25.

101. Schema 231:3.

102. "Servandus est psalmus invitatorius ante primam Horam Officii et quidem obligatori et quotidie?" Schema 239:7.

103. ". . . in tanta procella opinionum." Schema 245:14.

104. "primae parti Officii diei semper praeponenda." SDO, 2. See ch. 3, pp. 66–67.

105. "Invitatorium fit prima ad Deum oratio, ante eam Horam (sive Officium lectionis sive Laudes) facienda, qua mane incipiat laus divina." DSOD, 6.

106. "Invitatorium locum suum habet initio totius cursus orationis quotidianae, scilicet praeponitur sive Laudibus sive Officio lectionis, prout alterutra actio liturgica diem incipiat." See Schemata 303:7; 314:7; 345:13.

107. ". . . ut admittatur . . . ubi necesse erit, etiam omitti possit Invitatorium ipsum initio Laudum celebratarum." Schema 357:3.

108. "Invitatorium locum suum habet initio cursus orationis cotidianae, scilicet praeponitur aut Laudibus matutinis aut Officio lectionis, prout alterutra actio liturgica diem inchoat. Pro opportunitate tamen, psalmus cum sua antiphona omitti poterit, quando Laudibus praeponendus est." IGLH, 35. English translation by the International Committee on English in the Liturgy (ICEL).

109. See Schemata 31:9–10; 68:2, 4, 5; 73:6–7; 95:2–5.

110. ". . . tam intricatum problema iam fuisse a concilio solutum." RG, 18.

111. ". . . standum omnino pro Constitutione ne periculum sit ut impugnatores dicant: hodie liturgistae hoc petere, cras vero aliud velle." Ibid.

112. Schema 135:5.

113. "Videturne opportunum ut, prouti hodiernae rerum condicioni et necessitati pastorali magis aptatum, distinctio aboleatur, ad Horas minores quod attinet, inter recitationem choralem divini Officii et recitationem a solo, unicam statuendo Horam inter Laudes et Vesperas, v.g. circa meridiem recitandam?" Ibid., Question 17.

114. Schema 167:8.

115. See ch. 3, pp. 10–11. With respect to the minor Hours, Paul VI said that since only one Hour is obligatory outside choir and that in choir reciting one Hour after the other is contrary to *veritas temporis,* one of the basic principles of the reform, the Consilium should consider the proposal to have only one minor Hour between Lauds and Vespers. Such an Hour would mark the pause at the end of the work of a morning and the beginning of work in an afternoon. RL, 498.

116. Canon Martimort gave as sources Tertullian, *De oratione,* cc. 23–25; *De jejunio* 10; Hippolytus, *Apostolic Tradition* 35, 41; Origen, *De oratione* 12; Cyprian, *De dominica oratione,* cc. 34–35. (RG, 16.) The summary given here of Canon Martimort's views is of the text in RG, 16–21.

117. For a discussion of the conciliar debate and decisions on the proposal for one *hora meridiana,* see ch. 2, pp. 38–39.

118. See ch. 2, pp. 31, 32–33, 39.

119. "Constitutio enim Conciliaris non eas obligat, nisi teneantur jure suo proprio." RG, 20–21.

120. Cf. Schema 185:18–21; RG, 16–21.

121. "*Quaesitum XVII:* Placetne ita instruere Horam in die obligatoriam ut constet psalmo vel psalmis e psalterio currente, qui dicantur cum hymno (et forte oratione) aptis horae diei (scilicet Tertiae, vel Sextae, vel Nonae)?

"*Quaesitum XVIII:* Placetne ut Horae minores ad libitum constent psalmis invariabilibus, in cyclo ordinario iam exstantibus, sive gradualibus sive aliis?" Schema 185:20–21.

122. "Insuper sacerdos quodam otio gaudens, vel exercitiis spiritualibus vacans, omnibus Horis traditionalibus frui poterit. Forma perfecta orationis, ad quam Ecclesia tendit in libro ostenditur." Ibid., 20.

123. Ibid.

124. Schema 194:13–14. Voting results handwritten in copy available.

125. Interview with Canon A. G. Martimort, Toulouse, France, April 20, 1983. The canon said that questions regarding the minor Hours were a "painful problem" and involved a "continual struggle" with Father Bugnini's and Pope Paul's desire. See ch. 5, pp. 208, 210–11.

126. See, e.g., SCDO, 13–17; SDO, 26–29.

127. Of 180 bishops voting, 141 replied affirmatively to the question: "Is that which is proposed in the report regarding the minor hours pleasing to the Fathers?" ("Placetne Patribus ea quae in Relatione proponitur de Horis minoribus?" Schema 253:5). Cf. also Synod of Bishops, *De Sacra Liturgia* (Vatican City, 1967) 1, 13; Consilium, "De principiis ad instaurationem Breviarii" in "Relationes ad Synodum Episcoporum," Res secretariae 28:21. Mimeographed.

128. See DSOD, 9, 36–41; IGLH 79.

129. SC 91, 92, 93.

130. Schema 68:3.

131. ASSCOV 2.3:138.

132. Schema 68:3.

133. Schema 81:2–4.

134. Schema 68:7–8.

135. "Videturne probandum principium generale, ut in novo Breviario psalmi cum aptis antiphonis canantur vel recitentur, ab his quoque qui privatim Officium persolvunt?" Schema 95:4.

136. Ibid. See the brief report on this session of the Consilium in *Notitiae* 1 (1965) 99ff.

137. Schema 136:2.

138. Ibid.

139. A. G. Martimort, "De quibusdam questionibus circa distributionem psalterii et structuram Horarum in officio divino instaurando," December 1, 1965. Mimeographed (hereafter cited as Martimort, "De quibusdam"); Schema 135:1; *Notitiae* 1 (1965) 152–56, 206–14.

140. "9. Opportunum videtur ut quaedam elementa magis stricte choralia in recitatione a solo omittantur, aut saltem omitti possint?

"10. Si vero huiusmodi elementa 'choralis' retinentur, etiam pro recitatione a solo, sufficit ut ita instituantur ut orationem personalem excitent seu dirigant?" Schema 135:3.

141. Question 9: 21, yes; 1, no; Question 10: 16, yes; 3, no. (Schema 167:4–5.)

142. See ch. 3, pp. 60–62.

143. Schema 185:11–12.

144. "Placetne ut sint in Officio antiphonae notis praedictis instructas *[sic]*?" Schema 194:2, 26.

145. Schema 206:4. While the problems regarding text are not of concern here, it should be noted that there was discussion of what should be the sources for antiphons—Old Testament and/or New Testament.

146. Schema 206:4.

147. See SCDO, 1–127.

148. Schema 215:4.

149. Compare SCDO, 19–20 or LH¹ 2:855–57 (where the antiphons are the same) with the triple "alleluia" serving as the one antiphon before and after the "setting" of five psalms in any edition of the preconciliar Breviary.

150. Schemata 215:4; 227:11.

151. See Schemata 239:12–13; 263:5; 269:8.

152. See, e.g., SDO, 27.

153. Schema 284:15.

154. See above, pp. 116–19, and Schemata 135:1; 284:15.

155. Schema 284:15.

156. See above, p. 119, and Schema 206:4; see also ch. 6, pp. 266–67.

157. "Placetne ut antiphonae provideantur pro singulis psalmis horarum minorum ac pro singulis incisioribus cum sensu proprio diverso, exceptis quidem casibus specialibus." Schema 288:9.

158. Schema 294. For a brief report on the work of this session regarding the Office, see *Notitiate* 4 (1968) 182.

159. "(f) Unusquisque psalmus vel divisio psalmi sua antiphona instruitur, quae ita delecta est ut sensum psalmi suggerat, atque in celebratione populari repeti possit post singulas strophas." DSOD, 11.

160. Ibid., 38–40, 66–67.

161. See, e.g., the four-week psalter in LH¹ 1:46–1059. On the appearance of the printed volumes, see RL, 522, n. 8. Regarding antiphons at the minor hours, the first draft of IGLH ignores mention of them except to note that on some solemnities special psalms would have proper antiphons. Schema 295:12–13.

162. See Schema 284:15.

163. "Quando psalmus pro sua longitudine in plures partes dividi potest intra unam eandemque Horam canonicam, unica antiphona ditatur, nisi partes ita diversae sint, ut sensum omnino diversum habeant." Schema 295:22.

164. "Quando psalmus pro longitudine in plures partes dividi potest intra unam eandemque Horam canonicam, singulis partibus apponitur propria antiphona, ad varietatem inducendam, praesertim in celebratione in cantu, necnon ad psalmi divitias melius percipiendas; licet tamen cui magis placuerit psalmum integrum sine interruptione persolvere, adhibita prima tantum antiphona." Schema 303:18; IGLH 115.

165. ". . . nisi aliter suo loco indicatur." See Schemata 303:10; 314:10; 345:17; 362:20; see also IGLH 82.

166. "in unaquaque Hora, una antiphona propria dicitur cum tribus psalmis e psalmodia complementari seligendis, nisi praevideantur psalmi speciales." Schema 357:4.

167. Cf. #8, Schema 357:4); #82, Schema 362:20); IGLH 82.

168. See Schema 284:15. For examples of the lengthy antiphons themselves see LH¹ 1:330, 386, 397, 459, 465.

169. IGLH 114, 123, 125. Of the eight schemata (295 [296], 303 [A], 303 [B], 314, 345, 346, 357, and 362) produced by Group 9 between June 1968 and March 1970 six are concerned entirely with the proposed instruction to precede the new Office. Only two (Schemata 346 [August 9, 1969] and 357 [October 31, 1969] relate generally what occurred at the three meetings of Group 9 between December 1968 and September 1969. In these there is nothing regarding the placement of antiphons.

170. ASSCOV 1.2:496–502, 580.

171. See above, pp. 115–17.

172. Schema 68:8. See also the brief report by Canon Martimort regarding responsories in Notitiae 1 (1965) 208.

173. Ibid. At least Prof. Emil Lengeling—relator of Group 4 (biblical readings) and one intimately involved in the structuring, selection, and composition of responsories—was aware of the ancient structure of the responsory. He acknowledges that like the graduals of the Missal, responsories are short forms (or remnants) of responsorial psalmody. See his "Le letture bibliche e i loro responsori nella nuova Liturgia delle Ore," LDO, 206–8.

174. Schema 81:5.

175. Ibid.; cf. MRL, Suppl. 4, pp. 16, 24.

176. "Placetne patribus principium generale, ut post lectionem in officio, etiam si a solo recitetur, locum habeat aliquod Responsorium." Schema 81:6.

177. Schema 95:5.

178. See Schema 135.

179. "Placetne ut huiusmodi responsoria sint obligatoria etiam in recitatione a solo?" Schema 185:11.

180. Schema 194:25. Voting results are handwritten in copy available to the author.

181. Schema 227:7–8.

182. See below, ch. 5, pp. 194–95, 197–200, 202–3.

183. Schema 68:9.

184. Schema 167:4.

185. Schema 185:10.

186. Schema 239:14.

187. Ibid.

188. "Lectiones praecedit tantum versus biblicus, ideo selectus ut mentes ad audiendum verbum Dei praeparet." DSOD, 8. See, e.g., the versicles in SCDO, 4; SDO, 2; DSOD, 26.

189. "Inter psalmodiam et lectiones dicitur de more versus, quo oratio transeat a psalmodia ad lectiones audiendas." IGLH 63.

190. Schema 239:14.

191. Ibid.

192. *Tres abhinc annos* 20; Schema 245:16.

193. "Placetne ut absolutio et benedictiones in officio lectionis ritus Romani supprimantur?" Schema 245:16.

194. Schema 263; *Notitiae* 3 (1967) 415–16.

195. See SCDO, SDO, DSOD, and LH.

196. Schema 31:3, 7. For the conciliar recommendation conveyed by Bishop Martin, see his remarks made at the 52nd General Congregation in ASSCOV 2.3:136. As Bishop Martin notes, the original schema for the Constitution on the Liturgy included a stipulation for the restoration of intercessions in both Lauds and Vespers. The conciliar commission omitted this stipulation on the grounds that it did not pertain to the "fundamental principles" *(altiora principia)*, which the constitution ought to state, and that it would restrict the freedom of the postconciliar commission in the reform of the Office. For the original stipulation see ASSCOV 2.3:120, no. 72.

197. Schema 31:7.

198. Ibid., 3.

199. Ibid., 7. See Balthasar Fischer, "Litania ad Ferialpreces in Laudes und Vesper römischen Breviers," *Liturgisches Jahrbuch* 1 (1951) 55–74. Canon Martimort indicated in an interview with this author (Toulouse, France, April 20, 1983) that Monsignor Fischer's views were influential in the recommendation of the consultors.

200. "*Quaestio 2.* Num aliquae ex Precibus quae olim in Capitulo post Primam dicebantur, in Laudes inserendae sunt?

"*Questio 8.* Nonne oratio communis seu fidelium in vesperas inseranda est?" Schema 31:3, 7. The reference to the "Chapter after Prime" seems to refer to the ancient monastic chapter *(officium capituli)* held often after the hour of Prime. In the thirteenth century it was combined with Prime in the Roman Office. See P. Salmon, "La prière des heures," *L'Église en prière,* 3rd ed., ed. A. Martimort (Paris: Desclée, 1965) 856.

201. "2. Placetne preces e Prima depromptas (accomodatas) in Breviario proponi, ut preces ante laborem pro opportunitate dicendae (quasi preces devotione propositae ut sunt e.g. nunc preces pro benedictione Mensae)?

"8. Placetne ut in Vesperis, etiam in recitatione absque populo, oratio communis seu fidelium inseratur?" Schema 50:14, 15.

202. Ibid.

203. See Schemata 135, 167.

204. Schemata 185:16, 17; 194:9, 10.

205. Ibid.

206. Schemata 185:17; 194:10; ch. 5, pp. 197–207.

207. Schema 194:10.

208. "Placetne ut in Vesperas inseratur oratio universalis, modo et ratione supra descripto?" Ibid.

209. Ibid. Results of the voting are handwritten in the copy of the schema available to the author.

210. Schema 215:12; SCDO, 12, 22–33, and passim.

211. Schema 227:1; *Notitiae* 3 (1967) 141.

212. See below, ch. 5, pp. 199–206, and Schema 245:10.

213. Schema 206:8–9.

214. Schema 215:12. See SCDO, 12, 34, passim.

215. SCDO, 31, 38–39, 45, and passim.

216. Schema 227:15. See also below, note 224.

217. Schema 239:10.

218. Ibid., 10–11. See these orations in SDO, e.g., pp. 22, 25, 28–29, 32, 34.

219. Schema 284:12.

220. See ASSCOV 2.3:120, 136.

221. Schema 206:8.

222. Schema 215:13; SCDO, passim.

223. See above, note 216.

224. Schema 231:11.

225. Ibid., 13.

226. "Vultisne ut et in Laudibus et in Vesperis fiat Oratio dominica?" Schema 239:9.

227. See below, ch. 5, pp. 200–7; and Schemata 245:9; 263:9–10; 269:15; 284:12; 288:6–7; 294:10.

228. Schema 231:14.

229. Schema 239:22.

230. "Placetne ut memoria defunctorum fiat in oratione universali, omisso versu Fidelium post singulas horas?" For a sample formula see SDO, 32. The question appears in Schema 245:6.

231. Schema 263:17.

232. The questions of whether to retain or make optional certain psalms and verses and how to dispose of the historical psalms were particularly vexing problems throughout the reform period, as discussed in ch. 3, pp. 56–57, 69–72. See Schemata 37, 135, 167, 185, 194, 212, 253; RG, 1–15.

233. Schema 23:1.

234. Schemata 23:1; 24:2, 4, 4[bis], 5–6, 8–9.

235. Schema 23:3–4. The proposal for a four-week psalter seems to derive from the decision made unanimously in Group 9 at the recommendation of Group 3 to reduce to three the number of psalms in Matins for clergy in pastoral care. A four-week cycle, then, would allow a convenient distribution of all the psalms with only three at Matins and three in the minor Hours. Lauds, Vespers, and Compline would be on a one-week cycle. For contemplatives, however, it was proposed that their night Office consist of six psalms with distribution of the Psalter, consequently, extended over two weeks only. Schema 24:8.

236. Schema 23:2–3. Cf. also above, pp. 93–95.

237. Schema 23:3.

238. Ibid., 5. See the discussion above on the proposed two schemes for Vespers, pp. 93–107.

239. Schemata 37:1; 50:3.

240. "Utrum placeat omnes psalmos nostri psalterii retineri in recitatione cyclica in cursu officii." Schema 50:3, 15, Question #14.

241. "1. Utrum quinque vel tres psalmi dicendi sint in Laudibus. 5. Utrum placeat retinere unicum schema Vesperarum sive pro clero, absente populo, sive in celebratione cum populo, cum quinque psalmis, facta tamen facultate per rubricas, omittendi duos psalmos in celebratione cum populo. . . . 9. Placetne tribus psalmis astrui Completorium? 12. Placetne Tertiam, Sextam, Nonam tribus psalmis astruendas? 13. Placetne ut psalmi Tertiae, Sextae, Nonae sint variabiles? 19. Placetne ut tres psalmi dicantur

in Matutino?" Schema 50:14–16. Another question regarding Compline—whether the hour should contain variable or invariable psalmody—was answered by twenty favoring variable and six, invariable. While this question does not affect the structure of the Hour, it is worth noting as explanation for the variety of psalms suggested for Compline in schemata proposed henceforth.

242. Schema 50:2.

243. Ibid., 6.

244. Schema 68:1–2. Schema A was described as differing from Schema B only in the placement of the Old Testament canticle in Lauds and in the daily use of one of the psalms from Psalms 148–50 at the end of Lauds. Schema 68:2.

245. Schema 68:5.

246. Ibid.

247. "Placetne cursus duarum hebdomadarum pro Matutino?" Schemata 73:5; 95:2.

248. "Placetne, ut psalmi longiores supra enumerati (9, 17, 36, 68, 77, 104, 105, 106, 118) in plus quam tria incisa dividantur?" Schemata 73:6; 95:2.

249. Schema 73:7.

250. "Placetne cursus duarum hebdomadarum pro Horis Minoribus?" Schema 95:2.

251. Schema 73:8.

252. "Placetne rubrica disponens, ut sacerdos, unam tantum Horam dicens ex Minoribus, eligat etiam psalmos alius Horae minoris eiusdem diei? Placetne talis rubrica sit permittens et non obligans?" Schema 95:2.

253. See pp. 98–99.

254. "11. Sufficere videtur quod iam a Consilio acceptum est, ut psalmi, seu eorum incisa, in nova psalterii distributione, in genere plus quam decem versiculis non constent? 12. Videturne accipi posse numerus psalmorum iam praevisus pro singulis Horis, scilicet:
- Matutinum: tres habeat psalmos
- Laudes et Vesperae: quinque habeant psalmos, cum facultate eos ad tres reducendi quando cum populo persolvuntur
- Horae minores et Completorium: tres psalmos habeant?
13. Placetne ut integrum psalterium, id est 150 psalmi, in cyclo ordinario, etsi non amplius unius hebdomadae tantum, retineantur, prouti usque adhuc factum est? 16. Videturne sufficere ut cyclus ordinarius psalterii per duas hebdomadas distribuatur?" Schema 135:4–5.

255. Schema 167:5–8. Some of the numbers in the tabulation of responses have been determined on the basis of the *modi* reportedly submitted in answer to the questions.

256. See above, note 232.

257. RG, 1–15.

258. RG, 1–2. He cites as representative of a move to drop certain troublesome psalms or verses of them from liturgical use the article of Belgian Dominican E. Bernimont, "De l'inegale valeur des psaumes," *Nouvelle revue théologique* 84 (1962) 843–52.

259. RG, 2–3.

260. Ibid., 3.

261. Ibid., 4–6. Canon Martimort notes that fifty-four psalms were eliminated from ordinary use at Taizé to accommodate Christians unfamiliar with the Psalter, agnostics not knowing or accepting a Christian interpretation of the psalms, the desires of young people frequenting the community, and members of the community itself. He does acknowledge that some of the regularly omitted fifty-four psalms are used on special occasions.

262. RG, 6–8.

263. RG, 6–7, 11–12. Canon Martimort cites as evidence for at least the possibility of liturgical use of all psalms (which would include their use as readings) a notice attributed to St. Celestine in the *Liber pontificalis* (t. 1, p. 230) in which, according to the canon, it is allowed that all the psalms could be read at Mass (RG, 6–7).

264. Schema 185:3–4.

265. Schema 185:6–7. See also pp. 1–6 which review the matter presented in RG, 1–15.

266. "I: Placetne ut aliqui versus duriores psalmorum in uncis signentur, cum rubrica quae moneat illos versus supprimi posse pro opportunitate, praesertim in recitatione.cum populo? II: Placetne ut perpauci psalmi, de quibus post maturum examen ita maxima pars est vere imprecatoria ut non sufficiat aliquos versus inter uncos ponere, sic disponantur in Officio ut substitui possint cum aliis psalmis determinatis?" Schema 185:8.

267. Schema 194:23.

268. "Usus recitandi psalmos unus post alium, plures in eadem Hora, adhuc retinendus esse videtur?" Schema 167:4.

269. See above, pp. 149–51; Schema 185:9, 15.

270. Schema 185:9.

271. Schema 194:10. The introduction of the New Testament canticle is discussed in ch. 5, pp. 186–89.

272. Schemata 185:9; 194:24. On the proposal for using the gradual psalms for the nonobligatory minor Hours, see above, pp. 113–15.

273. See Schemata 206:1–3; 212:1–2; RL, 501–5.

274. Schema 206:4.

275. Schemata 206:1–3; 215:2.

276. "1. Placetne, ut psalmi distribuantur per cursum 4 hebdomadarum excepto Completorio? 2. Placetne, ut Completorium habeat cursum unius

hebdomadae? 4. Placetne, ut Laudes habeant 1⁰ loco psalmos matutinales traditos et alios aptos, 2⁰ loco cantica Veteris Testamenti, 3⁰ loco psalmos laudatorios et similes generis hymnici? 5. Placetne ut numerus canticorum [V.T.] augeatur, ita ut sufficiant pro 4 hebdomadis? 6. Placetne, ut partes 22 psalmi 118 distribuantur per Horam Mediam feriarum, ut in schemate? 7. Placetne, ut 'Horae Minores ad libitum' instruantur psalmis graduum sicut in Relatione provisum est? 9. Placetne cursus unius hebdomadae pro canticis e Novo Testamento sumptis 3⁰ loco Vesperarum? 11. Placetne, ut dividantur, praeter Ps 118, etiam Pss 17, 77, 88, et quidem ita, ut distribuantur inter Officium lectionis et Horam Mediam?" Schema 212:10a.

277. Schema 227:2-3. Voting results are not given in detail in Schema 227 for each of the questions. Fr. Vincenzo Raffa, as secretary of Group 9, simply reports that "generally, all questions posed by Group 3 received an affirmative response from the fathers of the 'Consilium.' " ("in genere omnia quaesita posita a coetu III affirmativum responsionem habuerunt a Patribus 'Consilii.' ") Schema 227:3.

278. Schema 227:2. See the arrangement, e.g., for reciting Psalm 17 in SCDO, 77-78, 89.

279. Schema 239:2.

280. Ibid., 4.

281. Ibid., 19-20. This author was unable to ascertain the origin of the suggestion endorsed by Group 3 for titles, nor was he able to verify Monsignor Pascher's contention that titles for the psalms were requested even in the council.

282. Ibid., 21.

283. See Schema 244. The psalms chosen for feasts are not of concern here since the choice did not affect the structure of psalmody within the Hours. One series of titles suggested the literal sense of the psalms; the other series, a Christian sense.

284. "Placetne Patribus ut omnes psalmi, non exceptis imprecatoriis et historicis, retineantur in cursu ordinario quattuor hebdomadarum proposito pro Psalterio in Officio divino?" Schema 253:2; Synodus episcoporum, *De sacra Liturgia: Exitus manifestationis sententiae cum recensione modorum propositorum* (Vatican City, 1967) 11-12. This question pertained mostly to the problem of retention of imprecatory and historical psalms—a major problem in the reform of the Office. As noted above (note 232), since this problem is not directly a *structural* one, it receives but scant attention here. Cf. also RL, 507.

285. Consilium, "Relationes ad Synodum Episcoporum: De principiis ad instaurationem Breviarii," Res secretariae 28 (March 19, 1967) 23-24.

286. See above, pp. 158-59.

287. Schema 263:3. Bishop Henri Jenny (Cambrai) was concerned about the difficulty in communal celebration of deciding which of these options

to use. He suggested the establishment of an "ordinary way," which could be modified by adoption of one or more of the other options.

288. Schema 263:3. Although not specifically mentioned in the schema, the cycle of readings referred to would seem to be that of short readings for the Hours other than Office of Readings—a cycle to be coordinated with the four-week cycle of the Psalter.

289. Contrast, e.g., the divisions of Psalm 30 and of Psalm 36, SDO, 138, 156.

290. See, e.g., Psalm 20 (for bracketing of imprecatory verses) and Psalm 17 (for antiphons at divisions of the psalm), SDO, 30 and 58 respectively.

291. See Schema 263:4.

292. The decision to omit Psalms 57, 82, 108 and difficult verses from nineteen other psalms came from Pope Paul VI in May 1968, as described above in ch. 3, pp. 68–72.

293. Schemata 262:10; 263:16–17.

294. Schema 263:16–17. The decision on the inclusion of psalm prayers, however, seems to have been made or anticipated before a study edition of the prayers was available. See the first draft of IGLH (Schema 295:22 [June 25, 1968]) for provision for their inclusion in the Office and Schema 348:1–10 (September 1, 1969) for the first evidence of a collection of these prayers for study.

295. See above, p. 161; Schemata 239:21; 269:8; 284:5.

296. Schema 284:5.

297. Schemata 288:8; 294:12. Cf. also Schema 295:25.

298. Schema 295:2.

299. Ibid., 22; Schemata 303B:18; 314:18; 342:26; 345:25; 362:26; IGLH 112.

300. IGLH 112. To this date the supplementary volume has not been published. In his recent study of the Liturgy of the Hours ("The Liturgy of the Hours," *The Liturgy and Time*, The Church at Prayer 4 (Collegeville: The Liturgical Press, 1986) 204, 222, Canon Martimort seems to be reassuring his readers that this supplementary volume (to include also the two-year cycle of biblical readings) will yet be published. At least the American edition of LH, *The Liturgy of the Hours According to the Roman Rite*, 4 vols. (New York: Catholic Book, 1975; hereafter cited as LOH), includes the psalm prayers in their ICEL translation with their respective psalms in the four-week psalter. Canon Martimort indicated to this author, however, that it was clearly the mind of Group 9 that the psalm prayer occur *after* the antiphon (if used) and pause for silent prayer and not before the antiphon, as is the case in LOH. The antiphon, said the canon, may be considered as almost part of the psalm, and it is erroneous to place it after the psalm prayer. Interview at Toulouse, France, April 20, 1983. See, e.g., LOH 1:679. See also J. Pinell, "Le collete salmiche," LDO, 269–84.

301. Schema 185:17–18.

302. Schema 231:5.

303. Ibid., 6.

304. Ibid.

305. Ibid., 10.

306. Ibid., 11.

307. Schema 255:1.

308. Ibid., 2–4.

309. Schema 259:2–3.

310. Schemata 262:5; 263:14–15; *Notitiae* 3 (1967) 416.

311. Schemata 262:5; 269:12–13.

312. Schemata 284:8–9; 288:16.

313. Schema 288:15–16.

314. Schema 294:7.

315. Schema 295a:18. Neither this nor any of the drafts of IGLH specify how Mass would begin. Only in the definitive text (no. 98) is it said that Mass begins with the *Gloria* when joined to the Office of Readings on the night of the Nativity.

316. See the early drafts of IGLH in Schemata 303A:14–15; 314:14–15; 345:20–21.

317. "Titulus XII [of the proposed IGLH] *De modo uniendi pro opportunitate Horae Officii cum Missa* iterum iterumque a nobis examinatus est. Censurae omnino contradictoriae semper audiuntur, etiam in nostro coetu, fatendumque est, impossibile fore ut solutio omnibus modis perfecta inveniatur. Nec in infinitum protrahere disceptationem illam nobis licere visum est, ita ut firmam omnino retinuerimus substantiam huius tituli certe necessarii. Aliquas tamen mutationes faciendas censuimus, non solum ut praescripta de hac re conformentur novo Ordini Missae nunc publici iuris facto, sed etiam ut praevideatur celebratio Vesperarum certis conditionibus ante Missam Vespertinam." Schema 357:5.

318. Schema 362:22. The text is substantially identical to that in IGLH 96.

319. Cf., e.g., Schema 345:20 (#96) and Schema 362:22.

320. Schema 136:8–9. See also Schemata 31:11–12; 50:12; 68:6; 95:4, 6–7.

321. Schema 185:12.

322. Ibid., 12–13.

323. "15. Placetne ut in structura Officii aliquis locus hymnorum servetur? 16. Suntne retinendi tamquam obligatorii vel ad libitum hymni in recitatione a solo? 17. Placetne ut ex hymnis latinis traditione probatis serventur ii qui etiam hodie apti videantur? 18. Placetne ut Conferentiis episcopalibus in rubricis fiat supradicta facultas?" Schema 194:27. Voting results are handwritten in the copy of the text available.

324. Schemata 206:8; 215:10; interview with Canon A. G. Martimort, Toulouse, France, April 20, 1985.

325. See, e.g., SCDO, 2, 9, 13–14, 18, 25.

326. Schema 227:9–10.

327. Schema 263:6–9. No reasons other than Father Gelineau's belief that a hymn would overload the beginning of an hour are offered for the statement that he thought a hymn at the beginning of an hour was a pastoral and liturgical mistake.

328. Schema 269:15, 17.

329. Schema 284:11, 16.

330. Schema 288:4, 8.

331. Schema 294.

332. Schemata 295a:10; 303a:8; 314:8; 345:14; IGLH 42.

333. Schemata 295:13; 303a:10; 314:10; 145:17; 362:20; IGLH 86–87. See ch. 5, pp. 235–40.

334. See below, pp. 260–61. Canon Martimort saw only two reasons for maintaining the traditional position of the hymn in Lauds and Vespers: (1) force of habit and (2) need for variety. The argument for variety, in his opinion, was the only one that carried some weight. Interview, Toulouse, France, April 20, 1983.

335. "8. Opportunum videtur ut, etiam in recitatione communi et in choro facta, per rubricas aliquod tempus silentii et meditationis praevideatur momento opportuniore, v.g. post unum alterumve psalmum, post lectiones?" Schema 135:3.

336. Schema 167:4.

337. Schema 227:14.

338. See Schemata 295:30; 303:29; 314:29; 345:36; 362:39.

339. de Vogüé, The Rule, 139, 141. Cf. also the remarks of Fr. Robert Taft on the spirit of ancient monastic prayer in his Liturgy of the Hours, 66–73.

CHAPTER 5:
THE STRUCTURE OF THE INDIVIDUAL HOURS

1. See ch. 4, pp. 93–107.

2. "Num et quomodo aptare oportet Laudes et Vesperas (Const. art. 89a), praesertim quando cum populo vel in ecclesia paroeciali celebrantur (art. 100; Emendat., p. 11, 1; Modi p. 9 n. 11)." Schema 6:3. For the emendationes and modi on SC 100, see ASSCOV 2.3: 122, 142, 721. The references given by Canon Martimort regarding the emendationes and modi are to the fascicles distributed in the council hall to the bishops.

3. Schema 31:1–7. For Father Juan Mateos' proposals see above, ch. 4, pp. 78–83.

4. Schema 50:14–15.

5. Schema 68:3. For more complete information on the distribution of the psalms, see ch. 4, pp. 137–48. Canon Martimort related to this author that, in his opinion, Father Bugnini's insistence on retaining the use of incense with the Magnificat at Vespers was due to his being very much

attached to his early experience as an altar boy! Interview at Toulouse, France, April 20, 1983.

6. Schema 136:7-8.

7. For a summary of the discussion preceding and during the sixth plenary session, see above, ch. 3, pp. 55-59. On the questionnaire, see ch. 3, pp. 59-60. For the specific question on Lauds and Vespers, see above, ch. 4, pp. 98-99. See also Schema 167:3.

8. See above, ch. 4, pp. 95-107. Cf. also ch. 3, pp. 57-62.

9. "7. Opportunum ducitur ut, intacta natura Matutini prout est hora lectionis, lectio sacrae Scripturae admittatur etiam in aliis Horis, praesertim vero in Laudibus et in Vesperis?" Schema 135:3.

10. "*Quaesitum XII:* Placetne ut praevideatur in Laudibus et Vesperis lectio longior quando illae Horae cum populo celebrantur? *Quaesitum XIII:* Placetne ut etiam sine populo ad libitum adhiberi possit? *Quaesitum XIV:* Placetne ut tamen non creetur novus cursus lectionum, sed ut lectio resumatur ex cyclis iam exstantibus, modo supra dicto? *Quaesitum XV:* Placetne ut in casu quo non fiat lectio longior sit lectio brevis determinata?" Schema 185:16. Cf. Schema 194:8. On the Pope's suggestions see RL, 497-98.

11. Schema 194:8.

12. "Placetne ut in Vesperas inseratur oratio universalis, modo et ratione supra descripto?" Ibid., 10.

13. Schema 185:16-17; Schema 194:9-10.

14. "Placetne ut cantica Novi Testamenti in psalmodiam Vesperarum inserantur modo descripto?" Ibid.; Schema 185 add.:1-2, 7.

15. For a discussion of the work of Groups 3 and 9 on the redistribution of the psalms following the sixth plenary session of the Consilium see above, ch. 4, pp. 151-55; Schemata 194:24-25; 206:2-3; 212:7-9.

16. Schemata 185:16; 194:7-8; 206:2, 9, 12-13; 215:3, 10-13.

17. SCDO, 9-12, 18-23, and passim.

18. Schemata 206:2, 9; 215:3, 11-13, 15-16; 227:3, 5, 7, 12; cf. *Notitiae* 3 (1967) 141.

19. Schema 231:7-9.

20. Schemata 239:7-11, 13-14, 17; 245:7-11.

21. Schema 253:4-5.

22. SDO, 25, 32, 47, 55, 71, 78, 92, 100, 110, 117, 127, 134-35, 145, 152-53, 163-64, 171-72, 193, 237, 251, 258.

23. The original questions in Latin on the responsories were "1) In celebratione publica Officii in cantu admittenda sunt responsoria quae respondeant lectioni etsi brevi in Laudibus et Vesperis? 2) Placet ut proponantur cantus responsoriales quae sint non stricte obligatorii in celebratione publica, ita ut possint alii cantus eiusdem functionis et generis suffici dummodo sint regulariter approbati?" On the hymn serv-

ing as response to the reading, see ch. 4, pp. 180–81. Schema 263:6–10. Father Raffa's information on experiments was obtained in an interview with the author in Rome, May 4, 1983. With respect to Max Thurian's observations it should be noted that his contribution went further than submission of suggestions. As an active contributor to Group 12bis (preces in Lauds and Vespers) he was responsible for the text of the intercessions at Lauds and Vespers during Holy Week. (RL, 556, n. 64.)

24. Schema 263:11–14.

25. Schemata 269:14, 16; 284:10–12, 14; 288:4–7.

26. Schemata 288:4–7; 294:10–12.

27. See drafts of the General Instruction in Schemata 295:11; 303:9; 314:9; 345:15; 362:15–16; and DSOD, 9. On the proposals to the twelfth plenary session, see Schema 357:3. Apparently some of the replies of bishops to the use of DSOD led to some modifications in the later drafts of IGLH (beginning with that in Schema 345) regarding the concluding elements. Whereas in the early drafts the concluding oration was always to follow the *Pater* no matter who the presider might be, in the later drafts the concluding oration might be omitted if the presider were not a priest or deacon. It was this arrangement that was proposed to the twelfth plenary session. The definitive version of IGLH, however, returns to the stipulation of the early drafts. See IGLH 53.

28. Schemata 295:34; 303:37; 314:37; 345:41; 362:44; IGLH 239.

29. "Utrum stante art. 89e, aptari debent Tertia, Sexta et Nona, an remanere prout nunc sunt?" On the question of abandoning two minor hours see ch. 4, pp. 110–15; on distribution of the psalmody, pp. 113–15, 148–59. Regarding the question posed to the second plenary session of the Consilium see Schema 6:3; RL, 492.

30. Schemata 185:20; 194:14; *Res secretariae* 25:14.

31. Schemata 206:8–9, 12–13; 215:13; SCDO, 13–17 and passim.

32. Schema 227:15; RL, 506.

33. On the reduction of the minor hours to one, see ch. 4, pp. 110–15; on the conclusion of the minor hours, ch. 4, pp. 133–34; on the psalmody for the minor hours, ch. 4, pp. 148–62. For Father Bugnini's proposal see RL, 506; Schema 231:12. Canon Martimort's reaction to Father Bugnini's proposal was conveyed to the author in the interview with him at Toulouse, April 20, 1983. On the meeting of Group 9, July 20–23, 1967, see Schemata 239:5–6; 245:17–19.

34. Schema 257:5–6 (253); *Res secretariae* 28:21.

35. RL, 167; SDO, 27–29 and passim. On removal of the *Fidelium animae* see ch. 4, pp. 135–37.

36. Schemata 262:11; 284:16. On the question of the antiphons, see above, ch. 4, pp. 119–21.

37. Schemata 294; 295:2, 12; 303:10.

38. Schemata 314:9–10; 345:16–17; 362:19–20; DSOD, 9, 36–41, 65–68; IGLH, 79–83.

39. For the question presented to the Consilium, see Schema 6:3; for Bishop Martin's comments and the *modi* proposed at the council, see ASSCOV 2.3:135; 2.5:711–13.

40. On the invitatory see above, ch. 4, pp. 107–10; on the psalmody, pp. 137–69. On the early work of Group 9, see Schemata 31:10–17; 50:7–11. On Father Cappelle's position see MRL, Suppl. 2, 50–52.

41. "18. Utrum, retentis hymnis traditionalibus pro recitatione tempore nocturno, inserendi sint etiam alii hymni pro recitatione extra hoc tempus nocturnum? [21-2-1] 21. Placetne ita copiam lectionis aptare ut officium eandem longitudinem habet quam nunc habet? [23-0-0] 22. Placetne talem normam statuere ut nullus dies sit sine Scriptura, nullusque dies sine Patribus? [23-0-0] 24. Placetne lectionarium patristicum confici, lectiones etiam complectens, quae in Breviario haud inserendae sint et quo vel ad libitum vel obligatorie uti licebit? [23-0-0] 28. Num providenda est in officio lectionum lectio hagiographica, si quando opportunum videbitur? [23-0-0]." Schema 50:16.

42. See ch. 4, pp. 123–26, 137–55; RL, 497–98.

43. See ch. 4, pp. 84–92; SRG, 5.

44. Schemata 185:23–25; 194:14–16.

45. Schema 206:10–11.

46. Schema 215:5–9, 14.

47. SCDO, 2–8, 26–31, 46–51; (obligatory memorial of St. Leo the Great), 63–67, 76–85; (optional memorial of St. Hermenegild), 96–103; (optional memorial of St. Justin), 115–19.

48. "Placetne ut, exclusa libertate seligendi lectiones ob rationes espositas *[sic]* (scil. ne amittatur aequilibrium lectionum inter Missam et Officium, ne turbetur arbitrario ordo sapienter selectus de historia salutis, ne plures textus S. Scripturae omittantur) observari debeat circulus lectionis biblicae currentis?" Schema 227:5.

49. Ibid.

50. Ibid., 6; *Notitiae* 3 (1967) 142–43.

51. Schema 227:12–13.

52. Ibid., 11.

53. Schema 231:3–5.

54. On the question of uniting Office of Readings with another hour, see ch. 4, pp. 169–72; Schema 231:5.

55. Schema 239:15–16.

56. See ch. 4, pp. 108–9; Schemata 239:7; 245:14.

57. "Placentne Patribus ea quae in Relatione proponuntur de Matutino seu Officio lectionis?" *Res secretariae* 28:22; Schema 253:6.

58. Schema 263:2–3.

59. For Sunday or ferial arrangements see SDO, 17–22, 102–7, 121–23, 137–42, 155–60, 223–28; for arrangements on optional memorials see pp. 35–43, 57–67, 80–87, 173–80, 195–206, 238–47.

60. Schema 269:4–7.

61. Schema 284:3–4.

62. "Placetne ut addatur lectio hagiographica post lectionem patristicam in celebratione Memoriae Sanctorum ad libitum in temporibus privilegiatis uti est ex. gr. Quadragesima? [sic]" Ibid., 9.

63. Ibid., 6. Father Raffa, in reporting the action on the Te Deum, indicates that the question asked of Group 9 specified the part of the hymn to be eliminated as that beginning with the words, "Per singulos dies." In parentheses he asks "why not from the verse 'Salvum fac . . .' from which the psalmic cento really begins?" ("cur non a versu 'Salvum fac . . .' a quo revera incipit cento psalmodicus?"). In the definitive edition of LH, the part that may be omitted is, in fact, that which begins with "Salvum fac."

64. Schemata 288:2–4; 294:8–9.

65. Schemata 295:14–17; 303:11–13; 314:11–13; 345:18–20; 357:2–6; 362:16–18; DSOD, 8–9, 21–29, 52–58; IGLH 55–73.

66. "Quomodo Completorium instruetur, ut fini diei apte conveniat (art. 89b)?" Schema 6:3.

67. Schemata 31:8–9; 215:13. On the Pian Commission's recommendation see MRL, Suppl. 2, 44, Suppl. 4, 45–46. On Bishop Martin's suggestion see ASSCOV 2.3:134.

68. "10. Utrum placeat Completorium astrui psalmis variantibus an invariabilibus? 11. Utrum supprimenda sint [sic] lectio brevis in Completorio?" Schema 50:15; see ch. 4, pp. 144–45.

69. Schema 136:8.

70. Schema 167:6; RL, 498. Nothing is said in the English edition regarding Compline, but see the Italian edition, p. 488.

71. Schemata 185:21; 194:14; 206:3. On the psalmody accepted for Compline, see ch. 4, pp. 155–74.

72. Schema 215:13; SCDO, 24–25, 45 and passim; Notitiae 3 (1967) 142.

73. Schemata 227:15; 231:12–13; RL, 506.

74. Schemata 239:21–22; 245:12; 269:17.

75. Res secretariae 28:22; Schema 253:5–6.

76. Schema 263; SDO, 8, 34, 136, and passim.

77. Schemata 269:17; 284:16–17; 288:7.

78. "Structura Completorii adhuc nimis incerta remanet et est decernenda. In adumbratione Instructionis ausus sum aliam adhuc solutionem vobis proponere, forte vituperandam." Schema 295:2, 13.

79. Schemata 303:10; 314:10–11; DSOD, 9–10, 47–51, 74–77.

80. Schemata 357:4; 362:20–21.

81. On the decision for Saturday Compline, see ch. 3, pp. 76–77. The definitive structure of Compline is presented in IGLH 84–92 and LH (e.g., vol. 1, 537–40, 891–908).

CHAPTER 6: EVALUATION OF THE REFORM

1. See ch. 3, pp. 44–51. Statistics are derived from the listings of consultors and members in RL, 937–55. It must be noted that the number of *consiliarii* was somewhat larger than that of those officially designated such. See RL, 950, n. 5.

2. See ch. 3, pp. 65, 73–74; ch. 5, pp. 201–25, 236. Cf. also results of the synod's consideration of questions on the Office in *De sacra liturgia: exitus manifestationis sententiae cum recensione modorum propositorum* (Vatican City: Typis Polyglottis Vaticanis, 1967) 11–14.

3. On the papal interventions see ch. 3, pp. 59–60, 69–71; ch. 4, pp. 111–12; ch. 5, pp. 189–90, 215, 233–34.

4. RL, 199–202, 555–56. See above, p. 297, n. 25; ch. 5, pp. 189–90; 325, n. 22. Some of the information on the Protestant observers was furnished by Prof. Emil Lengeling, interview with this author, Münster, West Germany, April 13, 1983.

5. On the beffudlement of members, see ch. 3, pp. 53–55; on the original plan for interaction between members and consultors, ch. 3, pp. 43–44.

6. See ch. 4, pp. 83–84; ch. 5, pp. 224–27. Prof. Emil Lengeling has noted that in the first years of the Consilium when the interchange between members and consultors was possible in the plenary sessions, all learned from one another. He cited as an example his own instruction of an attentive Cardinal Felici on the link between baptism and confirmation. Interview with this author, Münster, West Germany, April 13, 1983. The difference of perspective between SC, ch. 4, and IGLH, ch. 1, can be seen especially in the overriding concern of SC (especially arts. 95–101) with the obligation of clerics, canons, monks, and nuns to the Office against the priority given in IGLH (especially nos. 20–23) to communal celebration in the local Church with bishop and clergy presiding.

7. On the papal interventions, their circumstances and effects, see besides those instances cited above in note 3, ch. 3, pp. 108, 69–71; ch. 4, pp. 111–12; ch. 5, pp. 189–91, 214–15, 234. On the question of fidelity to SC and consistency in the reform, see ch. 3, pp. 60–62; ch. 4, pp. 82–83, 110; on the danger of subjectivism, ibid., pp. 151–54. Some critiques of the reform of the Office advocating radical restructuring or revival of some form of the cathedral tradition are the following: L. Bouyer, "La réforme de l'Office Divin," *Vie spirituelle* 114 (1966) 25–43; Mateos, "The Origins," 477–85, and "The Morning," 31–47. W. G. Storey, "The Liturgy of the

Hours: Principles and Practice," *Worship* 46 (1972) 194-203, and "The Liturgy of the Hours: Cathedral Versus Monastery," *Worship* 50 (1976) 50-70; A. Ciferni, "The Structure and Content of the Church's Daily Celebration of Time," *Worship* 54 (1980) 331-35.

8. See ch. 3, pp. 70-72; ch. 4, pp. 110-15; ch. 5, pp. 209-11.

9. See ch. 3, pp. 69, 74-76. There are no schemata issued by SCCD pertaining to the reform of the Office after the final draft of IGLH (March 1, 1970) even though the printing of LH did not commence until summer of 1971. See P. Marini, "Elenco," 472.

10. See ch. 3, pp. 56-63, especially pp. 62-63; ch. 4, pp. 85-86, 91-92, 96-106, 110-15; ch. 5, pp. 189-93.

11. On the continuing reference to clerics, see, e.g., ch. 4, pp. 138, 149; ch. 5, pp. 189, 218, 222, 236. On Canon Martimort's creative sensitivity and diminishing skepticism see ch. 3, pp. 56-63; ch. 4, pp. 151-53; ch. 5, pp. 189-91, 203-4, 209-10, 215-16. See also Aimé Georges Martimort, "L'Institutio Generalis' et la nouvelle 'Liturgia Horarum,'" *Notitiae* 7 (1971) 223-25.

12. See ch. 3, pp. 65-66; ch. 4, pp. 161-62.

13. For instances of compromise see ch. 3, pp. 54, 62-63; ch. 4, pp. 88-89, 104, 106, 137-69; ch. 5, pp. 192, 204. For Canon Martimort's view on compromise see ch. 4, p. 107.

14. Interview of this author with Fr. Juan Mateos, Granada, Spain, April 25, 1983. For evidence of assumptions on reform of the Office as intended primarily for pastoral clergy, see ch. 2, pp. 32-33, 35, 40; ch. 3, pp. 52, 54, 56. For the assumptions about Lauds, ch. 4, p. 80; about use of Psalm 140 and incense, ch. 5, pp. 187-88; about continued solo recitation of Lauds and Vespers by clergy, ch. 4, p. 106; about longer readings and homily as necessary in Vespers with "the people," ch. 4, pp. 80-81; ch. 5, pp. 190-91.

15. For evidence of eclectic traditionalism see ch. 4, p. 179; ch. 5, pp. 192, 203. For Canon Martimort's view on historical scholarship see ch. 4, pp. 102-3. For Father Bouyer's views see "La réforme," 25-43. The kind of research undertaken by Father Mateos and, in a developed way by his colleagues, is described by Father Robert Taft in "The Structural Analysis of Liturgical Units: An Essay in Methodology," *Worship* 52 (1978) 314-29 (adapted version in Taft, *Beyond East and West: Problems in Liturgical Understanding* [Washington: Pastoral, 1984] 151-64).

16. On the bishops' interventions at Vatican II, see ch. 2, pp. 34-41. For Father Bugnini's remarks on the questionnaire of December 1965, see Schema 135:2; see also ch. 4, pp. 85-86.

17. See ch. 2; ch. 3, pp. 55-56; ch. 4, especially pp. 86-87, 97-98, 137-58; ch. 5; see also below, pp. 263-64.

18. Raffa, "Dal Breviario," 341 (unpublished English translation from ICEL). On the early stage of structural reform and its direction, see ch. 3, p. 54; ch. 4, pp. 78-92, 101-3; ch. 5, pp. 185-86.

19. Henry Ashworth, "The Renewal of the Benedictine Office," *Notitiae* 13 (1977) 194. On Canon Martimort's opinion and the Consilium's decision, see ch. 4, pp. 87–89.

20. On the use of the statement "Today liturgists . . ." during the reform, see ch. 4, p. 110–11. On displacement or ignoring of the implications of SC 14, 21, 26, 90, 98, and 100, see ch. 4, pp. 85–87.

21. "En effet, la liturgie étant oeuvre commune et célébration du mystère chrétien ne peut être organisée selon des motivations subjectives, quelque louables qu'elles puissent être. Les grands événements du salut, leur preparation et leur retentissement, qui font l'objet de l'année liturgique, s'imposent absolument à tout baptise. La structure même des célébrations liturgiques répond à une logique interne qui ne souffre pas d'être défigurée par des changements arbitraires: on ne peut, par exemple, remplacer une lecture biblique ou un psaume par un texte non biblique de quelque qualité qu'il puisse être. C'est pourquoi l'*Institutio* rappelle très nettement ces principes évidents: '*Ne tangatur ordinatio generalis uniuscuiusque Horae*,' dit le n. 246; les nn. 245–47 precisent quelles sont les célébrations qui excluent toute variation de formulaires. Mais ces précisions étant acquises, l'*Institutio* prévoit des facultés de choix dans l'interieur de l'Office, en évitant qu'elles provoquent hésitation ou incertitude . . ., en évitant aussi qu'elles puissent dégénérer dans l'arbitraire ou le mauvais goût." A. G. Martimort, "L''Institutio Generalis' et la nouvelle 'Liturgia Horarum,'" *Notitiae* 7 (1971) 237. For the *praenotanda* to the rites of Christian initiation see SCCD, *Christian Initiation*, "General Introduction" 30–35; *Rite of Baptism for Children*, "Introduction" 23–30; *Rite of Christian Initiation of Adults*, "Introduction" 32–35 (Roman ed., 64–67); IGLH 246–52. These documents (other than IGLH) are conveniently assembled in *The Rites of the Catholic Church*, study edition, a Pueblo Book (Collegeville: The Liturgical Press, 1990) 10–12, 44–47, 372–75. See also above, ch. 5, pp. 185–207.

22. Martimort, "l''Institutio Generalis,'" 238.

23. DOL 3411–14.

24. IGLH 33. Translation adapted from A. M. Roguet, *The Liturgy of the Hours: The General Instruction with Commentary*, trans. P. Coughlan and P. Purdue (Collegeville: The Liturgical Press, 1971) 28.

25. See ch. 1, pp. 2–3; ch. 4, pp. 177–82. The results of Juan Mateos' research was, of course, available to Group 9. His "Morning and Evening Office" is a translation of a Latin text offered to Group 9 as indicated above, ch. 4, p. 301, note 11. For later research generally supportive of Mateos' positions regarding Roman Vespers, see, e.g., de Vogüé, RB 5, pp. 483–97; Gabriele Winkler, "Über die Kathedralvesper," 97–102; Jasmer, "A Comparison," 345–48, 351–60. On the comparative analysis of liturgical units see Robert Taft, "The Structural Analysis," 314–29.

26. Translation of the portion identical with the definitive text of IGLH is adapted from Roguet, *The Liturgy*, 28, and translation of additional portions in the schema, with emphasis added, is by the author.

27. Interviews of the author with Prof. Emil Lengeling, Münster, West Germany, April 13 and 14, 1983; with Canon A. G. Martimort, Toulouse, France, April 19, 1983. For Lengeling's more nuanced view see his "Le letture bibliche e i loro responsori nella nuova liturgia delle Ore," LDO, 214–15. There he states: "The Liturgy of the Hours, too, naturally reflects this dialogical character or descending and ascending movement. The General Instruction speaks explicitly of it (nos. 10–19, especially 13–14; for the Office of Readings in particular, cf. nos. 55–56). The 'descending' aspect is to be found chiefly, though not exclusively, in the reading from Scripture. The hearing of the saving word, which God himself speaks through Christ and which by the power of the Holy Spirit is present in the Church's liturgy (cf. SC 7) and even in the liturgical Hours of the non-Catholic Churches, is fostered by prayer and in turn leads to prayer: 'God speaks to his people . . . and the people reply to God both by song and prayer' (SC 33, quoted in IGLH 14). 'And let them remember that prayer should accompany the reading of Sacred Scripture, so that God and humans may talk together; for "we speak to God when we pray; we hear God when we read the divine sayings" (St. Ambrose)' (Const. on Revelation, no. 25)." Translation adapted from unpublished version by ICEL.

28. Adalbert de Vogüé, *The Rule of St. Benedict, A Doctrinal and Spiritual Commentary*, trans. J. B. Hasbrouck (Kalamazoo: Cistercian, 1983) 135–36.

29. Ibid., 156. The Benedictine Confederation has adopted a similar view in its reform of the monastic Office. See Anne Field, ed., *Directory for the Celebration of the Work of God: Guidelines for the Monastic Liturgy of the Hours Approved for the Benedictine Confederation* (Riverdale, Md.: Exordium, 1981) 24–25, 28–31. The *Directory* prefaces the *Thesaurus Liturgiae Horarum Monasticae*, published in 1977 for the Benedictine Confederation and approved by the Sacred Congregation for the Sacraments and Divine Worship. The Latin text is found in *Notitiae* 13 (1977) 163–88.

30. Carl Dehne, "Roman Catholic Popular Devotions," *Worship* 49 (1975) 456–57; also in John Gallen, ed., *Christians at Prayer* (Notre Dame: University of Notre Dame Press, 1977) 93. For a similar set of characteristics to be seen in the ancient cathedral Office, see Storey, "The Liturgy of the Hours," 55–59.

31. Dehne, "Roman Catholic," *Worship*, 460 (*Christians*, 97).

32. See ch. 4, pp. 80–81; ch. 5, pp. 190–91; IGLH 46–47; Taft, *The Liturgy of the Hours*, 189–90, 278–79.

33. On the distribution and division of the psalms, see ch. 4, pp. 137–69; as an answer to some needs, ch. 2, pp. 36–37; ch. 3, pp. 56–57. On anti-

phons, see ch. 4, pp. 160–61; on titles, p. 161; on psalm prayers, pp. 163, 168. For examples of lengthy antiphons unsuitable for responsorial use see LH[1]1:459, 465 (*Benedictus* and *Magnificat* antiphons respectively for Epiphany); 514–15 (antiphons for Lauds on the feast of the Baptism of the Lord).

34. On the maintenance of semicontinuous psalmody and the expansion of selective psalmody see ch. 4, pp. 154–55, and the tables on pp. 140–43, 146, 156, 164, 166. That the selective arrangement has obscured the semicontinuous arrangement may account for Taft's exaggeration that "the monastic principle of continuous psalmody is *abandoned* in favor of the 'cathedral' principle of selecting psalms adapted to the hour." (*The Liturgy of the Hours*, 314. Emphasis added. For Pascher's remarks see his "Il nuovo ordinamento della salmodia nella Liturgia romana delle Ore," LDO, 168 [English translation from unpublished version of ICEL].) On the abandonment of some imprecatory psalms and verses see ch. 2, p. 33; ch. 3, pp. 56, 65; ch. 4, pp. 139, 151–54.

35. See ch. 3, pp. 76–77; ch. 5, pp. 219–20. For criticism of the disjunction between readings in the Office and those in the Mass by users of the French experimental edition, see CNPL, "L'experimentation du nouvel office divin" (mimeographed publication distributed to the Consilium, n.d.) 3. Emil Lengeling, especially, has lamented the relegation of the two-year cycle to a listing of pericopes in the yet unpublished supplementary volume of LH: "But, under these circumstances, it is impossible to satisfy the council's requirement that the readings in the Liturgy of the Hours be 'accessible in more abundant measure' (SC 92a) in order to offset the reduced psalmody in [the Office of Readings] (SC 89c). Consequently, we can only hope that when the many episcopal conferences publish editions of the Office in their national languages, they will include not the one-year cycle but the two-year cycle which was chosen by the Consilium and the Synod of Bishops, accepted by the bishops of the world, and approved by critics who saw the first draft of it. . . . Experimentation shows that it is extremely annoying and in some cases impossible (e.g., while traveling) to use a Bible for the readings of the Breviary. This is all the more true in instances in which the readings consist of several parts. It is to be feared that very few will commit themselves to the more abundant reading of Scripture which the Liturgy Constitution urges (SC 89c, 92a) and many asked for before and during the Council, as long as such reading is optional and especially as long as the texts are not printed in their entirety. How sad if once again we were to sacrifice the reading of Scripture, as happened in the twelfth and thirteenth century when the several books needed for the Office gave way to the Breviary! But won't the volumes for the Liturgy of the Hours become too big if the two-year cycle of readings is printed in them? In Volume I of the *editio*

typica, the Scripture readings in the Seasonal Proper (Advent and Christmas season), together with the responsories, occupy only about fifty-seven pages. The inclusion of a second cycle of readings would not even double this number of pages, since on five feast days the readings are the same every year. Yet the parts of the Office which are substantially the same in all four volumes occupy 722 pages of Volume I." "Le letture bibliche," 203-4. English translation from unpublished version of ICEL.

36. On responsories see ch. 4, pp. 123-26; ch. 5, pp. 198-99. As noted in ch. 4, p. 315, note 173, Prof. Lengeling was aware that the responsory was a short form of responsorial psalmody. On Jasmer's speculation see his "Comparison," 356-57.

37. For the discussion and decisions on organic union see ch. 4, pp. 169-77, and IGLH 93-99. On Canon Martimort's position regarding daily Mass and Office see ch. 4, pp. 102-3. For one statement on the overblown entrance rite of the Mass, see Ralph Keifer, "Our Cluttered Vestibule: The Unreformed Entrance Rite," *Worship* 48 (1974) 270-77.

38. See ch. 4, pp. 154-55, 182-84; CNPL, "L'experimentation," 3; de Vogüé, *The Rule*, 139-59.

39. See ch. 4, pp. 93-110. On the relative inflexibility of the structural details of Lauds and Vespers see IGLH 41-54, where it is indicated that introductory verses, hymn, three psalmic pieces, long or short reading, gospel canticle, intercessions, Lord's Prayer, concluding prayer, blessing, and dismissal are required in that order in all modes of Lauds and Vespers. Even the internal structure of the intercessions allows for only two modes of use—intention and invariable response or intention and variable response (IGLH 189-93). Of the structural elements only responsory and homily (optional anyway) may be omitted or substituted for. The choices allowed in IGLH 246-52 pertain to text only.

40. On a pre–Vatican II request for three psalms in Vespers, see ch. 2, p. 27. On the struggle in Group 9 and the Consilium over the number of psalms in Lauds and Vespers, see ch. 4, pp. 93-179; on a probable reason for the ternary structure of psalmody, pp. 104-5. In this author's experience one of the most frequently asked questions regarding the structure of Lauds and Vespers is whether it is allowable or fitting to reduce the number of psalms. The question seldom springs from motives of efficiency or distaste for communal prayer but quite the opposite, from a desire to pray well. If one has a need to rely on official directives for an answer, it seems that appeal can be made to IGLH 279, which explicitly pertains to modes of reciting the psalms but, surely, can be applied to structural and other questions: "It is very important for us to be concerned with the meaning and spirit of what we are doing. The celebration should not be rigid or artificial, nor should we be merely concerned with formalities. Above all, the thing to be achieved is to instill a desire for the

authentic prayer of the Church and a delight in celebrating the praise of God" (Roguet, *The Liturgy*, 69).

41. See ch. 4, pp. 93–106; ch. 5, pp. 185–207. On the thematic progression in the psalmody for Lauds, see, e.g., Pascher, "Il nuovo ordinamento," 169–70; IGLH 43.

42. See ch. 1, pp. 2–3; ch. 5, pp. 190–91. The continuing provision for scriptural reading in new, unofficial Roman Catholic, ecumenical, or Protestant forms of Morning and Evening Prayer is undoubtedly a witness to its effectiveness in these hours when popularly celebrated. See, e.g., W. G. Storey, F. C. Quinn, D. F. Wright, *Morning Praise and Evensong* (Notre Dame: Fides, 1973); "The Liturgy of the Hours," *Worship II* (Chicago: G.I.A., 1975), sec. 1020–71; *Lutheran Book of Worship* (Minneapolis: Augsburg, 1978) 131–53; J. A. Melloh and W. G. Storey, *Praise God in Song: Ecumenical Daily Prayer* (Chicago: G.I.A., 1979); "Morning Song" and "Evensong" in N. T. Freund and others, eds., *Peoples Mass Book* (Schiller Park, Ill.: World Library, 1984), sects. 749–62; "The Liturgy of the Hours," *Worship*, 3rd ed. (Chicago: G.I.A., 1986), sects. 1–18; Joyce Ann Zimmerman and others, *Pray Without Ceasing: Prayer for Morning and Evening* (Collegeville: The Liturgical Press, 1993). But for parochial forms without readings, see *Morning Prayer* and *Evening Prayer* (Chicago: Liturgy Training, 1985). Laurence Mayer in a commentary on these strictly "cathedral" forms notes that scriptural readings might be added for communities expressing the need for such, but he recommends utilizing such reading before the prayer formally begins. See his *Morning and Evening Prayer in the Parish* (Chicago: Liturgy Training, 1985) 28–29, 39.

43. See ch. 1, pp. 1–5; ch. 4, pp. 131–33; ch. 5, pp. 185–207, especially pp. 200–7. On the desire, previous to Vatican II, for orations related to the hour of the day see ch. 2, p. 33; on the desire during Vatican II for such, ch. 2, pp. 39–40.

44. "Si l'on veut, au choeur, adopter la forme: refrains par l'assemblée, intentions par un soliste, on aura quelque peine à trouver trace des caracteres d'une prière litanique, telle que j'ai essayé de la décrire, et telle que l'attendent—je crois bien—la plupart des communautés, surtout celles qui ont l'habitude de l'office choral. Comment trouver un thème commun de prière dans des intentions si diverses, dont chacune est d'ailleurs excellente? Il reste la resource, effectivement utilisée ca et là, de laisser un temps de silence après chaque intention, avant la reprise du refrain. Mais outre que cette reprise est ainsi rendue plus difficile et beaucoup moins naturelle, le rythme étant rompu, la nécessité même de recourir à un moment de silence pour assimiler chaque intention laisse voir le jeu cérébral auquel la communauté est, une fois de plus, obligée. Et si l'on renonce au refrain pour utiliser la mise en oeuvre, prévue par l'introduction et suggérée par la typographie, chaque intention étant alors dialoguée

entre le président et l'assemblée, nous voici ramenés aux *capitella*, c'est-a-dire pratiquement au livre, a une prière ou l'on n'a plus la liberté de suivre un mouvement intérieur sur l'espèce de 'fond sonore' que fournit le soliste de la litanie." C. de Bourmont, "Fonction et expression des prières d'intercession," LMD 105 (1971) 141–42.

45. On the compromised nature of the structure of the intercessions, see ch. 5, pp. 204–5. For favorable reaction to the intercessions (relating more to content, however), see CNPL, "L'experimentation," 2. For some popular forms of Morning and Evening Prayer employing (or supposing) a litanic form for the intercessions, see those listed above in note 42.

46. See above, pp. 245–47.

47. On preconciliar and conciliar desires regarding the minor hours, see ch. 2, pp. 27, 31–32, 39. On Group 9 and the Consilium's debate and decisions, see ch. 3, pp. 56, 59; ch. 4, pp. 110–15; ch. 5, pp. 207–12; also see above, pp. 246–47.

48. Field, ed., *Directory*, 41–42.

49. On the preconciliar desire for reduction of Matins, see ch. 2, pp. 26–30; on conciliar requests for reduction, use at any hour, and longer readings, fewer psalms, see ch. 2, pp. 38–39. For the Consilium's effort to keep the hour from becoming only spiritual reading, see ch. 5, pp. 213, 222–24.

50. See ch. 5, pp. 217, 220, 225–26.

51. Ibid., pp. 219–20.

52. See ch. 4, pp. 83–84; ch. 5, pp. 212, 215, 229–31.

53. See ch. 5, pp. 218–19, 220–21, 222–24.

54. See ch. 5, pp. 213–15. On presuppositions that Mass and Office are intimately related and that the cult of the saints must be fostered in the Office, see ch. 4, pp. 101–3; ch. 5, pp. 217–19. For a brief, tentative statement on the theological nature of the Liturgy of the Hours, see Thaddaeus Schnitker, "Das offentliche Gebet der Kirche," *Liturgisches Jahrbuch* 32 (1982) 115–18. The same article also appeared as "La prière publique de l'Église" in *Questions liturgiques* 63 (1982) 41–44.

55. See ch. 4, pp. 107–10; ch. 5, pp. 215, 216, 221. For examples of ordinary inclusion of the invitatory psalm in the proper structure of Morning Prayer in some modern Offices, see the provisions for that Hour in the Offices given in note 42 above with the exception of those in *Morning Praise and Evensong*, both editions of *Worship*, and *The Peoples Mass Book*.

56. See ch. 5, pp. 232–36.

57. Ibid., pp. 236–39.

58. Taft, *The Liturgy of the Hours*, 314.

59. Ibid., 314–15. See also R. Taft, "The Divine Office: Monastic Choir, Prayer Book, or Liturgy of the People of God? An Evaluation of the New Liturgy of the Hours in its Historical Context," *Vatican II: Assessment and*

Perspectives Twenty-five Years After (1962–1987), ed. Rene Latourelle (New York: Paulist, 1989) 2:27–46.

60. Mayer, *Morning and Evening Prayer,* 2–3. Graham Woofenden, a priest of the Roman Catholic Diocese of Liverpool, has recently offered thought-provoking suggestions for reshaping the structures of Morning Prayer and Evening Prayer along the lines of the ancient Spanish Offices. His suggestions are made not from a belief that archaic usage is somehow better than current practice but from the conviction that contemporary life patterns need to be reflected "in our liturgies of time." The structures of the Spanish cathedral Offices seem to offer possibilities that might be the bases for communal daily prayer arising from the event celebrated (i.e., the experience of morning or of evening) contextualized in contemporary experiences of life (Graham Woofenden, "The Ancient Cathedral Office and Today's Needs," *Worship* 67 [1993] 388–407). It is worth noting, also, that even Pope Paul VI in his apostolic constitution *Laudis canticum* introducing LH notes the possibilities of adapting LH to meet the circumstances of "people of different callings," and advocates adaptation of LH "to the needs of living and personal prayer" and "the spiritual needs of those who pray it" (see English version in LOH, vol. 1, 11–20, especially 13–14 and 18).

Bibliography

PRIMARY SOURCES

Published Materials
Amalarius of Metz. "Liber officialis." *Amalarii episcopi opera liturgia omnia*. Vol. 2. Studi e Testi 139. Ed. J. M. Hanssens. Vatican City: Biblioteca Apostolica Vaticana, 1948.
_____. "Liber de ordine antiphonarii." *Amalarii episcopi opera liturgia omnia*. Vol. 3. Studi e Testi 140. Ed. J. M. Hanssens. Vatican City: Biblioteca Apostolica Vaticana, 1950.
"Animadversiones scripto exhibitae quoad cap. IV schematis de S. Liturgia." *Acta Synodalia Sacrosancti Concilii Oecumenici Vaticani II*. Vol. 1. Pt. 2. Vatican City: Typis Polyglottis Vaticanis, 1970.
The Assisi Papers: Proceedings of the First International Congress of Pastoral Liturgy, Assisi-Rome, September 18-22, 1956. Collegeville: The Liturgical Press, 1957.
Breviarium Romanum ex decreto ss. Concilii Tridentini restitutum S. Pii V Pontificis Maximi jussu editum aliorumque pontificum cura recognitum Pii Papae X auctoritate reformatum juxta editionem typicam dispositum et approbatum. 4 vols. Rome: Desclée, 1914.
Bugnini, Annibale. "De principiis generalibus ad Sacram Liturgiam instaurandam atque fovendam." *Acta et documenta Concilio Oecumenico Vaticani II apparando*. Series 2. (Praeparatoria). Vol. 2: *Acta Pontificiae Commissionis Centralis Praeparatoria Concilii Oecumenici Vaticani II*. Pt. 3. Vatican City: Typis Polyglottis Vaticanis, 1968.
_____. *The Reform of the Liturgy. 1948-1975*. Trans. Matthew J. O'Connell. Collegeville: The Liturgical Press, 1990. (*La riforma liturgica [1948-1975]*. Bibliotheca "Ephemerides Liturgicae" "Subsidia" 30. Rome: CLV - Edizioni Liturgiche, 1983.)
Commissio Centralis Praeparatoria Concilii Oecumenici Vaticani II. "Disceptatio de Sacra Liturgia." *Acta et documenta Concilio Oecumenico Vaticano II apparando*. Series 2. (Praeparatoria). Vol. 2: *Acta Pontificiae Commissionis Centralis Praeparatoria Concilii Oecumenici Vaticani II*. Pt. 3. Vatican City: Typis Polyglottis Vaticanis, 1968.
Commissio de Sacra Liturgia. "De Sacra Liturgia." *Acta et documenta Concilio Oecumenico Vaticani II apparando*. Series 2. (Praeparatoria). Vol. 3:

Acta Commissionum et Secretariatum praeparatoriorum Concilii Oecumenici Vaticani II. Pt. 2. Vatican City: Typis Polyglottis Vaticanis, 1969.

Concilium Oecumenicum Vaticani II. "Sacrosanctum Concilium" ("Constitutio de Sacra Liturgia"). *Acta Synodalia Sacrosancti Concilii Oecumenici Vaticani II.* Vol. 2. Pt. 6. Vatican City: Typis Polyglottis Vaticanis, 1973.

The constitution is also printed in *Acta Apostolicae Sedis* 56 (1964) 97–138.

"Congregatio Generalis XV" and "Congregatio Generalis XVI." *Acta Synodalia Sacrosancti Concilii Oecumenici Vaticani II.* Vol. 1. Pt. 2. Vatican City: Typis Polyglottis Vaticanis, 1970. Discussion on ch. 4, Schema of the Constitution on the Liturgy.

"Congregatio Generalis LII" and "Congregatio Generalis LIII." *Acta Synodalia Sacrosancti Concilii Oecumenici Vaticani II.* Vol. 2. Pt. 3. Vatican City: Typis Polyglottis Vaticanis, 1972.

Emendations proposed for ch. 4 of the Schema of the Constitution on the Liturgy; *relatio* of Bishop Albert Martin; voting results on the emendations and on the whole of ch. 4.

"Congregatio Generalis LXXIII." *Acta Synodalia Sacrosancti Concilii Oecumenici Vaticani II.* Vol. 2. Pars 5. Vatican City: Typis Polyglottis Vaticanis, 1973.

Modi for ch. 4, Schema of the Constitution on the Liturgy; text of the revised Schema for ch. 4; *relatio* of Bishop Albert Martin on the *modi* and revised Schema.

Consilium ad Exsequendam Constitutionem de Sacra Liturgia. *Elenchus Membrorum - Consultorum Consiliariorum Coetuum a Studiis.* Vatican City: Typis Polyglottis Vaticanis, 1964 and 1967.

_____. *Hymni Instaurandi Breviarii Romani.* Vatican City: Liberia Editrice Vaticana, 1968.

Introduction to this work also printed in *Notitiae* 4 (1968) 99–113.

_____. *Descriptio et Specimina Officii Divini iuxta Concilii Vaticani II Decreta instaurati.* Vatican City, 1969.

Introduction to this work also printed in *Notitiae* 5 (1969) 74–85.

_____. *Ordo lectionum biblicarum Officii Divini.* Schemata 322; De Breviario 82. Vatican City: Typis Polyglottis Vaticanis, 1969.

Introduction to this work also printed in *Notitiae* 5 (1969) 85–99.

Consilium ad Exsequendam Constitutionem de Sacra Liturgia et Sacra Rituum Congregatio. "Inter Oecumenici" (September 24, 1964). *Acta Apostolicae Sedis* 56 (1964) 877–900.

de Vogüé, Adalbert, ed. *La Règle du maître.* 3 vols. Sources chretiénnes 105–7. Paris: Les Éditions du Cerf, 1964–65.

de Vogüé, Adalbert and Jean Neufville, eds. *La Règle de saint Benoît*. 7 vols. Sources chretiénnes 181-86 (vol. 7, *hors série*). Paris: Les Éditions du Cerf, 1971-77.

"Decima Sessio Plenaria 'Consilii.' " *Notitiae* 4 (1968) 180-84.

Directory for the Celebration of the Work of God: Guidelines for the Monastic Liturgy of the Hours Approved for the Benedictine Confederation. Ed. Anne Field and trans. John Leinenweber. Riverdale, Md.: Exordium, 1981.

"[Duodecima] Sessio Plenaria Commissionis Specialis ad Instaurationem Liturgicam Absolvendam." *Notitiae* 5 (1969) 436-41.

International Commission on English in the Liturgy. *Documents on the Liturgy, 1963-1979: Conciliar, Papal, and Curial Texts*. Collegeville: The Liturgical Press, 1982.

John XXIII, Pope. "Humanae salutis" (December 25, 1961). *Acta Apostolicae Sedis* 54 (1962) 5-13.

_____. "Rubricarum instructum" (July 25, 1960). *Acta Apostolicae Sedis* 52 (1960) 593-95.

Larraona, Arcadio. "De officio divino." *Acta et documenta Concilio Oecumenico Vaticani II apparando*. Series 2. (Preparatoria). Vol. 2: *Acta Pontificiae Commissionis Centralis Praeparatoria Concilii Oecumenici Vaticani II*. Pt. 3. Vatican City: Typis Polyglottis Vaticanis, 1968.

Legg, J. W., ed. *Breviarium Romanum a Francisco Cardinali Quignonio*. Cambridge: The University Press, 1888. Repr. ed. Westmead: Greg, 1970.

_____. *The Second Recension of the Quignon Breviary*. 2 vols. Bradshaw. Vols. 35 and 42. London: Harrison, 1908 and 1912.

Lengeling, Emil. "Les options générales de la nouvelle liturgie des heures." *La Maison-Dieu* 105 (1971) 7-33.

Lentini, Anselmus. "De hymnis Breviarii." *Notitiae* 1 (1965) 213.

Liturgia Horarum iuxta Ritum Romanum: Officium Divinum ex decreto Sacrosancti Oecumenici Concilii Vaticani II instauratum auctoritate Pauli PP. VI promulgatum, editio typica. 4 vols. Vatican City: Typis Polyglottis Vaticanis, 1971-72; *editio typica altera*, 1985-87.

The Liturgy of the Hours According to the Roman Rite: The Divine Office Revised by Decree of the Second Vatican Ecumenical Council and Published by Authority of Pope Paul VI. English trans. prepared by ICEL. 4 vols. New York: Catholic Book, 1975.

Marini, Piero. "Elenco degli 'Schemata' del Consilium e della Congregazione per il Culto Divino." *Notitiae* 18 (1982) 455-86, 548-96.

Martimort, Aimé Georges. "De lectionibus biblicis Breviarii." *Notitiae* 1 (1965) 207-9.

_____. "L'Institutio Generalis' et la nouvelle 'Liturgia Horarum.' " *Notitiae* 7 (1971) 218-40.

Mohlberg, L. C., L. Eizenhofer, and P. Siffrin, eds. *Liber Sacramentorum Romanae Aeclesiae ordinis anni circuli (Cod. Vatican. Regin. lat. 316). Sacramentarium Gelasianum*. Rerum Ecclesiasticarum Documenta. Series major. Fontes 4. Rome: Herder, 1960.

_____. *Sacramentarium Veronense. (Cod. Bibl. Capit. Veron. LXXXV* [80]). Rerum Ecclesiasticarum Documenta. Series major. Fontes 1. Rome: Herder, 1956.

"Nona Sessio Plenaria 'Consilii.' " *Notitiae* 3 (1967) 410–17.

"Octava Sessio Plenaria 'Consilii.' " *Notitiae* 3 (1967) 138–46.

"Ordo XII" through "Ordo XIII C." *Les Ordines Romani du haut moyen âge*. Vol. 2. Ed. Michel Andrieu. Louvain: "Spicilegium Sacrum Lovaniense" Administration, 1948.

"Ordo XIV" and "Ordo XXIV." *Les Ordines Romani du haut moyen âge*. Vol. 3. Ed. Michel Andrieu. Louvain: "Spicilegium Sacrum Lovaniense" Administration, 1951.

Pascher, Joseph. "De psalmis distribuendis." *Notitiae* 1 (1965) 152–56.

Pellegrino, Michael. "De lectionibus patristicis in Breviario." *Notitiae* 1 (1965) 209–12.

Pius X, Pope. "Abhinc duos annos" (October 23, 1913). *Acta Apostolicae Sedis* 5 (1913) 449–50.

Pius XII, Pope. "Mediator Dei" (November 20, 1947). *Acta Apostolicae Sedis* 39 (1947) 521–95.

"Quinta Sessio Plenaria 'Consilii.' " *Notitiae* 1 (1965) 99–104.

Prière du temps présent. Le nouvel Office divin. Texte liturgique approuvé. Paris: Desclée, 1969.

The Rites of the Catholic Church as Revised by Decree of the Second Vatican Ecumenical Council and Published by Authority of Pope Paul VI. Study edition. New York: Pueblo, 1983, 1988, 1990.

Roguet, A. M., ed. *The Liturgy of the Hours: The General Instruction on the Liturgy of the Hours with a Commentary*. Collegeville: The Liturgical Press, 1971.

The Roman Breviary in English. 4 vols. Ed. J. A. Nelson. New York: Benziger, 1950.

Rotelle, John. "De lectionibus patristicis in Breviario." *Notitiae* 5 (1969) 100–12.

The Rule of the Master (Regula Magistri). Trans. Luke Eberle. Introduction by Adalbert de Vogüé. Trans. Charles Philippi. Kalamazoo: Cistercian, 1977.

Sacra Congregatio pro Cultu Divino. *Preces ad laudes matutinas et ad vesperas officii divini instaurandi*. Schemata 348, De Breviario 92. Vatican City: Typis Polyglottis Vaticanis, 1969.

    Introduction to this work also printed in *Notitiae* 5 (1969) 458–69.

Sacra Congregatio pro Cultu Divino. Commissio specialis ad instaurationem liturgicam absolvendam. *Lectiones patrum et lectiones hagiographicae
pro officio divino.* Schemata 349, De Breviario 93. Vatican City: Typis
Polyglottis Vaticanis, 1970. Introduction also in *Notitiae* 6 (1970) 134–37.

Sacra Congregatio Rituum. "Decretum generale de rubricis ad simpliciorem formam redigendis" (March 23, 1955) and "De rubricis ad
simpliciorem formam redigendis." *Acta Apostolicae Sedis* 47 (1955)
218–24.

_____. "Decretum generale quo novus rubricarum breviarii ac mis-
salis Romani Codex promulgatur" (July 26, 1960) and "Rubricae
breviarii et missalis Romani." *Acta Apostolicae Sedis* 52 (1960) 596–685.

_____. "Tres abhinc annos" (May 4, 1967). *Acta Apostolicae Sedis* 59
(1967) 442–48.

Sacra Congregatio Rituum. Sectio historica. *Memoria sulla Riforma Liturgica.*
4 suppl. Vatican City: Tipografia Poliglotta Vaticana, 1948–57.

"Schema Constitutionis de Sacra Liturgia." *Acta Synodalia Sacrosancti Concilii Oecumenici Vaticani II.* Vol. 1. Pt. 1. Vatican City: Typis Polyglottis
Vaticanis, 1970.

"Septima Sessio Plenaria 'Consilii.'" *Notitiae* 2 (1966) 312–13.

"Sexta Sessio Plenaria 'Consilii.'" *Notitiae* 2 (1966) 3–5.

Synodus Episcoporum. *De Sacra Liturgia: Exitus manifestationis sententiae
cum recensione modorum propositorum.* Vatican City: Typis Polyglottis
Vaticanis, 1967.

"[Tertia decima] Sessio Plenaria Commissionis Specialis ad Instaurationem
Liturgicam Absolvendam." *Notitiae* 6 (1970) 222–31.

Thesaurus Liturgiae Horarum Monasticae. Rome, 1976.
The "Prefatio," "Directorium de Opere Dei persolvendo," and
"Praenotanda" of this work are also printed in *Notitiae* 13 (1977)
157–91.

"La [undecima] Sessione Plenaria del 'Consilium.'" *Notitiae* 4 (1968)
348–55.

Visentin, Pelagius. "De cantibus Officii." *Notitiae* 1 (1965) 213–14.

Unpublished Materials

Centre National de Pastoral Liturgique de France. "L'experimentation du
nouvel office divin." N.d. ICEL Collection, Washington.
Mimeographed.

Consilium ad exsequendam Constitutionem de Sacra Liturgia. "Relationes
ad Synodum Episcoporum." Res secretariae 28. March 19, 1967. ICEL
Collection, Washington. Mimeographed.

_____. "Schema completum divini Officii persolvendi a die 9 ad 15
Aprilis 1967. Psalterium Breviarii per quattuor hebdomadas distribu-

tum." Papers of Emil Lengeling, Münster, Germany. Mimeographed.
_____. "Schemata." 1964–69. Mimeographed.

Each of the schemata listed below is numbered consecutively throughout the entire series, e.g., *Schema 5*, and within major topical areas, e.g., *De Breviario 1* (= DB 1). Those produced after August 1969 are listed below, under *Sacra Congregatio pro Culto Divino*.

Schema	DB	Title and Date
5	1	"Questiones de Officio divino Consilio proponendae a Mons. Martimort." April 16, 1964.
6	2	"Questiones de Officio divino Consilio proponendae ab S. G. Martimort." April 17, 1964.
23	5	"Relatio de distributione psalmorum." July 19, 1964.
24	6	No title. Draft of *relatio* for Fourth Plenary Session of Consilium. July 20, 1964.
31	10	"Relatio generalis de reformatione Breviarii." September 14, 1964.
37	13	"Quaestiones 'Consilio' proponendae [de psalmis distribuendis]." September 28, 1964.
50	14	"Relatio de sessionibus quas Coetus a Studiis IX diebus 26, 27 septembris ac 1 octobris Romae habuit." December 1, 1964.
68	17	"Relatio de sessionibus quas Coetus a Studiis IX diebus 1 et 2 Martii 1965 Romae ad Aedes S. Marthae habuit." March 26, 1965.
73	20	"Quaestiones Consilio proponendae de distributione psalmorum (ad Const. art. 91)." April 26, 1965.
73 add.	—	"Animadversiones circa distributionem psalmorum in futuro Breviario cura D. Vincentii Raffa F.D.P." N.d.
81	24	"Quaestiones generales 'Consilio' proponendae [de cantibus Officii divini]." April 26, 1965.
95	26	"Relatio de sessione quam Coetus a Studiis IX Die 30 aprilis 1965 Romae habuit." May 22, 1965.
135	32	"Quaestiones circa Officii divini instaurationem." December 16, 1965.
136	33	"Relatio de sessionibus quas Coetus IX Romae ad Aedes S. Martae diebus 25–26 septembris habuit." December 22, 1965.

Schema	DB	Title and Date
167	38	"Exitus et computatio responsionum ad quaestionarium de Breviario (Schem. n. 135, de Breviar. n. 32) a Secreteria Consilii sodalibus et quibusdam consultoribus et consiliarii missum, die 16 decembris 1965." May 10, 1966.
185	40	"Relatio generalis de Officio divino." September 19, 1966.
185	40 add.	"De canticis Novi Testamenti." September 19, 1966.
194	41	"Relatio generalis de Officio divino." October 8, 1966.
206	43	"Relatio sessionis Coetus IX 'de structura generali Officii divini' quae Genuae apud abbatiam S. Maria 'della castagna' diebus 6, 7, 8 februarii 1967 habita est." February 15, 1967.
212	45	"Relatio de distributione psalmorum." March 7, 1967.
215	46	"Relatio generalis de structura Breviarii." March 15, 1967.
216	47	"De Officio divino. Relationes particulares." March 17, 1967.
216	47 add.	"Excursus addendus Relationi De lectionibus biblicis Officii divini." April 1, 1967.
227	48	"Acta de Officio divino in adunatione Commissionis coordinatricis et in Sessione VIII Consilii mensis aprilis 1967." May 9, 1967.
231	50	"De structura generali Breviarii." June 20, 1967.
235	53	"De precibus in Laudibus et Vesperis." May 19, 1967.
239	55	"Relatio de laboribus Coetus IX Monachii adunati diebus 20-30 julii 1967." August 25, 1967.
243	58	"De precibus in Laudibus et in Vesperis." September 18, 1967.
244	59	"De psalmis distribuendis." September 20, 1967.
245	60	"De Breviarii structura. Relatio generalis." September 28, 1967.
253	—	"De expensione 'modorum' Synodi circa questiones de sacra Liturgia." November 16, 1967.

255   61   "De unione organica Officii cum Missa."
              November 20, 1967.

257   41   "De expensione 'modorum' Synodi circa quaestiones de sacra Liturgia." November 21, 1967.

259   63   "De unione organica Officii cum Missa."
              November 22, 1967.

262   65   "Ordo agendorum in omnibus coetibus de Breviario." December 6, 1967.

263   66   "Relatio IX Sessionis Consilii et praecedentis coadunationis relatorum necnon et Coetus IX." December 10, 1967.

269   67   "De structura generali Breviarii."
              February 1, 1968.

275   68   "De precibus in Laudibus et Vesperis."
              February 15, 1968.

284   70   "Relatio Sessionis Coetus IX Genuae habitae diebus 27 februarii–martii 1968." March 15, 1968.

288   71   "Relatio generalis de labore peracto hisce ultimis mensibus ab omnibus coetibus qui Officio divino instaurando incumbunt." April 17, 1968.

288   71 add.   "De conventu Coetus IX 'De Breviario' circa thema denuo propositum: 'de Psalmis qui *imprecatorii* et *historici* dicuntur.'" April 17, 1968.

294   73   "Acta de Officio divino in X. Sessione Consilii ad exequendam Const. de S. Lit. (16–30 aprilis 1968)." May 14, 1968.

295a   75   "De generali structura Breviarii." June 25, 1968.

303a   79   "Instructio de Officio divino iussu Concilii Vaticani II reformato." July 25, 1968.

303b   79   "De generali structura breviarii." August 28, 1968.

314   81   "Instructio de Officio divino iussu Concilii Vaticani II reformato." October 3, 1968.

345   89   "Instructio de Officio divino iussu Concilii Vaticani II reformato." August 23, 1969.

346   90   "Relatio generalis de Breviario." August 9, 1969.

_____. "Specimen divini Officii pro diebus a 12 ad 25 novembris 1967." Papers of Emil Lengeling. Münster, West Germany. Mimeographed.

Gelineau, Joseph. Letter to Stanislaus Campbell, February 9, 1982. Papers
of Stanislaus Campbell. Napa, Calif.

McManus, Frederick. "Animadversiones circa relationem De Breviario,
Schema 31." Papers of John A. Rotelle. Villanova, Pa. Typewritten.

Martimort, Aimé Georges. "De psalmis sic dictis 'imprecatoriis' et
'historicis' quas denuo orta." Toulouse, February 20, 1968. Papers of
A. G. Martimort. Toulouse, France. Mimeographed.

_____. "De quibusdam questionibus circa distributionem psalterii et
structuram Horarum in officio divino instaurando." December 1, 1965.
Papers of A. G. Martimort. Toulouse, France. Mimeographed.

_____. "Rapport general sur l'Office divin." Toulouse, July 31, 1966.
Papers of A. G. Martimort. Toulouse, France. Mimeographed.

_____. "Supplément à la relation générale sur le bréviaire destinée
aux membres du Coetus IX." August 5, 1966. Papers of A. G. Martimort. Toulouse, France. Mimeographed.

Mateos, Juan. "Adnotationes circa Officium Dominicae seu de vigilia
cathedrali." Appendix ad Schema 68, De Breviario 17. Rome, 1965.
Papers of John A. Rotelle. Villanova, Pa. Mimeographed.

_____. "Annotationes ad schema 31, De Breviario 10." Rome,
November 22, 1964. Papers of John A. Rotelle. Villanova, Pa.
Mimeographed. An adapted English translation of this monograph
was published as "The Morning and Evening Office." *Worship* 42
(1968) 31–47.

_____. Letter to Stanislaus Campbell, May 14, 1981. Papers of Stanis-
laus Campbell. Napa, Calif.

Raffa, Vincenzo. "I salmi 'imprecatori' e 'storici' nell'iter della riforma
liturgica." 1983. Papers of Vincenzo Raffa. Rome. Typewritten. For a
festschrift honoring Canon A. G. Martimort.

Sacra Congregatio pro Cultu Divino. "Schemata." 1969–70.
Mimeographed.

Schemata produced before September 1969 are listed above, under
Consilium ad exsequendam Constitutionem de Sacra Liturgia. The
listing below follows the same arrangement.

Schema	DB	Title and Date
357	95	"Relatio generalis de Breviario." October 31, 1969.
358	96	"De lectionibus patristicis in Breviario." October 31, 1969.
362	98	"Institutio generalis de Liturgia Horarum." March 1, 1970.

SECONDARY SOURCES

Books

Anderson, Floyd, ed. *Council Daybook. Vatican II. Sessions 1 and 2.* Washington: National Catholic Welfare Conference, 1965.

Batiffol, Pierre. *History of the Roman Breviary.* Rev. 3rd ed. Trans. from the French by A. M. Y. Baylay. New York: Longmans, Green, 1912.

Baümer, Suitbert and Reginald Biron. *Histoire du bréviaire.* 2 vols. Paris: Letouzey et Ané, 1905.

Baumstark, Anton. *Comparative Liturgy.* Rev. by B. Botte. English ed. by F. L. Cross. London: Mowbray, 1958.

Bradshaw, Paul F. *Daily Prayer in the Early Church: A Study of the Origin and Early Development of the Divine Office.* Alcuin Club Collections 63. London: Alcuin/SPCK, 1981.

Bugnini, Annibale. *The Simplification of the Rubrics.* Trans. L. J. Doyle. Collegeville: Doyle and Finegan, 1955.

Callewaert, C. *Liturgicae Institutiones.* 2nd ed. 3 vols. Bruges: Beyaert, 1937–44. Vol. 2 (1939): *De Breviarii Romani Liturgia.*

_____. *Sacris erudiri: Fragmenta liturgica collecta a monachis S. Petri de Aldenburgo in Steenbrugge ne pereant.* Steenbrugge: Abbatia S. Petri, 1940.

Crichton, J. D. *Christian Celebration: The Prayer of the Church.* London: Chapman, 1976.

de Reynal, Daniel. *Théologie de la liturgie des heures.* Paris: Éditions Beauchesne, 1978.

de Vogüé, Adalbert. *The Rule of St. Benedict: A Doctrinal and Spiritual Commentary.* Trans. J. B. Hasbrouck. Cistercian Studies Series 54. Kalamazoo: Cistercian, 1983.

dell'Oro, Ferdinando, ed. *Liturgia delle ore: Documenti ufficiali e studi.* Quaderni de Rivista Liturgica 14. Torino-Leumann: Elle di Ci, 1972. Matthew J. O'Connell has prepared an as yet unpublished English translation of this work for the International Committee on English in the Liturgy.

Evening Prayer. Chicago: Liturgy Training, 1981.

Fischer, Balthasar. *Brevierreform.* Trier: Paulinus-Verlag, 1950. Also in *Trierer theologische Zeitschrift* 59 (1950) 14–26.

Freund, Nicholas T., Betty Z. Reiber, and Jeanne H. Schmidt. *Peoples Mass Book.* Schiller Park, Ill.: World Library, 1984.

Frutaz, A. *La Sezione storica della Sacra Congregazione dei Riti. origini e methodo di lavoro.* 2nd ed. Vatican City: Tipografia Poliglotta, 1964.

Gueranger, Prosper. *Institutions liturgique.* 4 vols. Paris: Debecourt, 1841.

Guiver, George. *Company of Voices: Daily Prayer and the People of God.* New York: Pueblo, 1988.

Heidt, William G., ed. *A Short Breviary for Religious and the Laity.* 3rd ed. Collegeville: The Liturgical Press, 1962.

Jungmann, Josef A., ed. *Brevierstudien.* Trier: Paulinus-Verlag, 1958.

Klauser, Theodor. *A Short History of the Western Liturgy: An Account and Some Reflections.* 2nd ed. Trans. J. Halliburton. Oxford: Oxford University Press, 1979.

Lutheran Book of Worship. Minneapolis: Augsburg, 1978.

McManus, Frederick R. *The Congregation of Sacred Rites.* The Catholic University of America Canon Law Studies 352. Washington: The Catholic University of America Press, 1954.

Mayer, Laurence. *Morning and Evening Prayer in the Parish.* Chicago: Liturgy Training, 1985.

Melloh, John Allyn and William G. Storey, eds. *Praise God in Song: Ecumenical Daily Prayer.* Chicago: G.I.A., 1979.

Monks of St. John's Abbey, eds., *A Short Breviary for Religious and the Laity.* 3rd ed. Collegeville: The Liturgical Press, 1944.

Morning Prayer. Chicago: Liturgy Training, 1985.

Paquier, R., and A. Bardet. *L'Office divin de chaque jour.* 3rd ed. Neuchatel: Éditions Delachaux et Niestlé, 1961.

Praise God: Common Prayer at Taizé. Trans. Emily Chisholm. New York: Oxford University Press, 1977.

Righetti, Mario. *Manuale di storia liturgica.* 3rd ed. 4 vols. Vol. 2: *L'anno liturgico - Il breviario.* Milan: Editrice Ancora, 1969.

Salmon, Pierre. *L'office divin.* Lex orandi 27. Paris: Les Éditions du Cerf, 1959.

    English trans. Sr. David Mary: *The Breviary Through the Centuries.* Collegeville: The Liturgical Press, 1962.

_____. *L'Office divin au Moyen Age: histoire de la formation du bréviaire du IXe au XVIe siècle.* Lex Orandi 43. Paris: Les Éditions du Cerf, 1967.

Schmidt, Herman. *La Constitution de la Sainte Liturgie: Texte - Genese - Commentaire - Documents.* Translated from the German. Brussels: Éditions Lumen Vitae, 1966.

Schnitker, Thaddaeus. *Publica oratio: Laudes matutinae und Vesper als Gemeindegottesdienste in diesem Jarhundert.* Eine liturgiehistorische und liturgietheologische Untersuchung. Ph.D. diss. Münster in Westfalen, 1977.

Scotto, Dominic F. *The Liturgy of the Hours: Its History and Its Importance as the Communal Prayer of the Church After the Liturgical Reform of Vatican II.* Petersham, Mass., 1987.

Storey, William G., Frank Quinn, and David Wright, eds. *Morning Praise and Evensong: A Liturgy of the Hours in Musical Setting.* Notre Dame: Fides, 1973.

The Taizé Office. Translated from the French. London: Faith, 1966.

Taft, Robert. *The Liturgy of the Hours in East and West*. Collegeville: The Liturgical Press, 1985.

_____. *Beyond East and West: Problems in Liturgical Understanding*. Washington: Pastoral, 1984.

van Dijk, S. J. P., J. Hazelden Walker. *The Origins of the Modern Roman Liturgy*. Westminster, Md.: Newman, 1960.

Worship: A Hymnal and Service Book for Roman Catholics. 3rd ed. Chicago: G.I.A., 1986.

Worship II: A Hymnal for Roman Catholic Parishes. Chicago: G.I.A., 1975.

Articles and Contributions to Collections

Ashworth, Henry. "The Renewal of the Benedictine Office." *Notitiae* 13 (1977) 192–96.

Bouyer, Louis. "La reforme de l'Office Divin." *Vie spirituelle* 114 (1966) 25–43.

Bradshaw, Paul. "What Ever Happened to Daily Prayer?" *Worship* 64 (1990) 10–23.

Ciferni, Andrew. "The Structure and Content of the Church's Daily Celebration of Time." *Worship* 54 (1980) 331–35.

Ciferni, Andrew and Laurence Mayer. "The Liturgy of the Hours." *Worship* 50 (1976) 329–36.

Crichton, J. D. "The Office in the West: The Early Middle Ages" and "The Later Middle Ages" and "The Roman Rite from the Sixteenth Century." *The Study of Liturgy*. Ed. Cheslyn Jones and others. Rev. ed. New York: Oxford University Press, 1992.

de Bourmont, Clement. "Fonction et expression des prières d'intercession." *La Maison-Dieu* 105 (1971) 134–49.

de Gaiffier, Baudouin. "La lecture des Actes des Martyrs dans la prière liturgique en Occident." *Analecta Bollandiana* 72 (1954) 134–66.

de Vogüé, Adalbert. "Origine et structure de l'office benedictin." *Collectanea Cisterciensia* 29 (1967) 195–99.

_____. "Scholies sur la Règle du Maître." *Revue d'Ascétique et de Mystique* 44 (1968) 121–59.

Dehne, Carl. "Roman Catholic Popular Devotions." *Worship* 49 (1975) 446–60.

   Also appears in *Christians at Prayer*. Ed. John Gallen. Notre Dame: University of Notre Dame Press, 1977. Pp. 83–99.

Fischer, Balthasar. "Litania ad Laudes et Vesperas, ein Vorschlag zu Neugestaltung der Ferialpreces in Laudes und Vesper römischen Breviers." *Liturgisches Jahrbuch* 1 (1951) 55–74.

Grisbrooke, W. Jardine. "A Contemporary Liturgical Problem: The Divine Office and Public Worship." *Studia Liturgica 8* (1971–72) 129–68; *Studia Liturgica 9* (1973) 3–18, 81–106.

_____. "The Formative Period. Cathedral and Monastic Offices." *The Study of Liturgy.* Ed. Cheslyn Jones and others. Rev. ed. New York: Oxford University Press, 1992.

Gy, Pierre Marie. "L'Office divin." *La Maison-Dieu 77* (1964) 159–76.

_____. "Projets de réforme du Bréviaire." *La Maison-Dieu 21* (1950) 110–28.

Jasmer, Paul. "A Comparison of the Monastic and Cathedral Vespers up to the Time of St. Benedict." *The American Benedictine Review 34* (1983) 337–60.

Jounel, Pierre. "La liturgie des heures dans le renouveau liturgique de Vatican II." *Notitiae 10* (1974) 310–20, 334–43.

Jungmann, Josef A. "Constitution on the Sacred Liturgy." *Commentary on the Documents of Vatican II.* Vol. 1. Ed. Herbert Vorgrimler. New York: Herder, 1967.

_____. "Essays in the Structure of the Canonical Hours." *Pastoral Liturgy.* New York: Herder, 1962.

_____. "Why Was Cardinal Quinonez' Reformed Breviary a Failure?" *Pastoral Liturgy.* New York: Herder, 1962.

Keifer, Ralph. "Our Cluttered Vestibule: The Unreformed Entrance Rite." *Worship 48* (1974) 270–77.

Leclercq, Henri. "Liturgies neo-Gallicanes." *Dictionnaire d'archéologie chrétienne et de liturgie.* Ed. F. Cabrol and H. Leclercq. Vol. 9. Pt. 2. Paris, 1930.

Martimort, Aimé Georges. "The Liturgy of the Hours." *The Liturgy and Time.* The Church at Prayer, 4. Ed. A. G. Martimort and trans. from the French by Matthew J. O'Connell. Collegeville: The Liturgical Press, 1986.

_____. "Structure et lois de la célébration liturgique," *L'Église en Prière.* 3rd ed. Tournai: Desclée, 1965.

Mateos, Juan. "The Morning and Evening Office." *Worship 42* (1986) 31–47.

_____. "The Origins of the Divine Office." *Worship 41* (1967) 477–85.

_____. "La vigile cathédrale chez Egérie." *Orientalia Christiana Periodica 27* (1961) 281–312.

Mitchell, Nathan. "The Liturgical Code in the Rule of Benedict." *RB 1980: The Rule of St. Benedict in Latin and English with Notes.* Ed. Timothy Fry and others. Collegeville: The Liturgical Press, 1981.

Pascher, Joseph. "De psalmodia Vesperarum." *Ephemerides Liturgicae 79* (1965) 317–26.

_____. "Der Psalter für Laudes und Vesper im alten römischen Stundengebet." *Münchener theologische Zeitschrift* 8 (1957) 255-67.

_____. "The Divine Office." *The Commentary on the Constitution and on the Instruction on the Sacred Liturgy.* Ed. A. Bugnini and C. Braga and trans. V. P. Mallon. New York: Benziger, 1965.

_____. "Zur Frühgeschichte des römischen Wochenpsalteriums." *Ephemerides Liturgicae* 79 (1965) 55-58.

Rose, André. "La repartition des psaumes dans le cycle liturgique." *La Maison-Dieu* 105 (1971) 66-102.

Rotelle, John. "Patristic Readings in the Liturgy of the Hours: Genesis and Background." *Liturgia opera divina e umana: Studi sulla riforma liturgica offerti a S. E. Mons. Annibale Bugnini in occasione del suo 70⁰ compleanno.* Ed. P. Jounel, R. Kaczynski, and G. Pasqualetti. Bibliotheca "Ephemerides Liturgicae." "Subsidia" 26. Rome: CLV - Edizioni Liturgiche, 1982.

Salmon Pierre. "La prière des heures." *L'Église en prière.* Troislème éd. Ed. A. G. Martimort. Paris: Desclée, 1965.

Schnitker, Thaeddaeus, "Das offentliche Gebet der Kirche." *Liturgisches Jahrbuch* 32 (1982) 115-18. ("La prière publique de l'Église." *Questions liturgiques* 63 [1982] 41-44.)

Storey, William G. "The Liturgy of the Hours: Cathedral Versus Monastery." *Worship* 50 (1976) 50-70. Also appears in *Christians at Prayer.* Ed. John Gallen. Notre Dame: University of Notre Dame Press, 1977.

_____. "The Liturgy of the Hours: Principles and Practice." *Worship* 46 (1972) 194-203.

_____. "Parish Worship: The Liturgy of the Hours." *Worship* 49 (1975) 2-12.

Taft, Robert. "The Structural Analysis of Liturgical Units." *Worship* 52 (1978) 314-29. An adapted version appears in Robert Taft's *Beyond East and West: Problems in Liturgical Understanding.* Washington: Pastoral, 1984.

_____. "The Divine Office: Monastic Choir, Prayer Book, or Liturgy of the People of God? An Evaluation of the New Liturgy of the Hours in its Historical Context." *Vatican II: Assessment and Perspectives Twenty-five Years After (1962-1987).* Ed. Rene Latourelle. Vol. 2. New York: Paulist, 1989.

Winkler, Gabriele. "Über die Kathedralvesper in den verschiedenen Riten des Ostens und Westens." *Archiv für Liturgiewissenschaft* 16 (1974) 53-102.

Woofenden, Graham. "The Ancient Cathedral Office and Today's Needs." *Worship* 67 (1993) 388-407.

Index

Page numbers in italics refer to major consideration of a topic.

Group of Relators, 48, 61, 105–107, 115, 119, 172–173, 175, 180, 188, 191–192, 202, 211, 229
Guano, Emilio, 35, 183, 198, 202, 207, 226, 235
Gy, P. M., 20, 163, 175, 181, 188

Hours
   linked to other liturgical acts, 169–177, 271
   truth of *(veritas horarum* or *temporis)*, 35–36, 40, 78, 230, 270, 274
Hymns, 115, 177–182, 202, 213, 260

Incense, 187–188
Inculturation, 254, 259
Intercessions, 105, 128–131, 186–187, 191–192, 195–196, 198–205, 275–276
International Committee on English in the Liturgy (ICEL), xii
Invitatory, 107–110, 221, 280–281
Isnard, José, 100, 225, 235

Jounel, Pierre, xiv, 159, 180, 227, 235
Jungmann, Josef, 25, 43

Kervéadou, François, 230

Larraona, Arcadio, 32, 34, 44
Lauds, 2–3, 10, 80–83, 89, 91, 92, *93–107*, 148, 170–172, 179, *185–207*, 260–261, *266–267, 271–276*
Lengeling, Emil, xiv, 50, 76–77, 179, 181, 262
Lentini, Anselmo, 50, 147
Lercaro, Giacomo, 27–28, 44, 57, 61, 111–112, 180
Liturgia horarum, xiii, 75, 76–77, 122
Liturgy of the Hours, xi
Lord's Prayer, 132–135, 200–205, 274
Lucernarium, 103, 188

McManus, Frederick R., 95
Magnificat, 195, 197
Marian antiphon (at Compline), 235, 238
Martimort, Aimé Georges, xiv–xv, 43, 49, 52, 57, 61–63, 72, 76–77, 87–89, 93–94, 97–105, 107–108, 112–114, 118–119, 122, 126, 139, 151–153, 163, 168–170, 172, 174, 176, 180–182, 187–190, 203, 207, 210, 215–216, 218, 221–222, 225–227, 229, 232, 234, 237–238, 248–249, 252, 257–258, 262–263, 270, 276–277, 280
Martin, J. Albert, 90, 100–101, 116, 124, 213, 232

Psalter, 2, 4, 12, 17, 19, 20, 23–24, 56–59, 93–95, *137–169*, 193–194, 233–234, 266–267, 272–273, 281, 282

Questionnaires, 86–87
Quignonez, Francisco, 12–14

Raffa, Vincenzo, xv, 51, 147, 199–200, 227, 255
"Rapport général sur l'Office divin" (RG), 60, 99–104, 112–114, 151–153, 190
Readings, 223–224
    hagiographic, 214, 218, 220–222, 224
    patristic, 214, 217, 220, 224
    scriptural, 3, 18, 29, 75, 105, 187, 189–191, 194–195, 213, 225, 233, 268, 273–274, 282
Relators, 48–49. *See also* Group of Relators.
Rescript (1969) of SCRSI, 259
Responsories, 123–126, 195, 198–199, 218, 238, 269
de Reynal, Daniel, xvi
Righetti, Mario, 25
Roguet, A. M., 180, 189, 197
Roman Office
    early medieval, 5–9
    implementation of postconciliar reform of, 47
    medieval, 9–11
    modern, 11–15
    postconciliar experiments with, 64, 67, 73–74
    primitive, 1–5
    proposed reform of, 31–34
    Vatican II reform of, 35–41
Rose, André, 93, 137–138, 227
Rubrics, 25–26, 28–30
Rule of the Master, 2–3
Rule of St. Benedict, 2–3

Sacram Liturgiam, 45–46
Sacred Congregation of Rites, 18, 25, 43, 46, 52, 68, 247
Schema completum Divini Officii persolvendi (SCDO), 64, 108, 115, 119, 131, 134, 135, 155, 179, 194–201, 209–211, 216–219, 226, 234, 236
Schema for the Constitution on the Liturgy. *See De Sacra Liturgia*.
Schmidt, Herman, 43, 189
Schnitker, Thaddeus, xv–xvi
Schnitzler, Theodor, 181, 229–230
Sext. *See* Minor Hours.